Exemplary CEOs

Insights on Organisational Transformation

Exemplary CEOs

Insights on Organisational Transformation

Shrinivas Pandit
Leadership Counsellor

Tata McGraw-Hill Publishing Company Limited
NEW DELHI

McGraw-Hill Offices
New Delhi New York St Louis San Francisco Auckland
Bogotá Caracas Kuala Lumpur Lisbon London Madrid
Mexico City Milan Montreal San Juan Santiago
Singapore Sydney Tokyo Toronto

Information contained in this work has been obtained by Tata McGraw-Hill, from sources believed to be reliable. However, neither Tata McGraw-Hill nor its authors guarantee the accuracy or completeness of any information published herein, and neither Tata McGraw-Hill nor its authors shall be responsible for any errors, omissions, or damages arising out of use of this information. This work is published with the understanding that Tata McGraw-Hill and its authors are supplying information but are not attempting to render engineering or other professional services. If such services are required, the assistance of an appropriate professional should be sought.

 Tata McGraw-Hill

Copyright © 2005, by Tata McGraw-Hill Publishing Company Limited.

First reprint 2005
RZZCRRCBRQCDB

No part of this publication may be reproduced or distributed in any form or by any means, electronic, mechanical, photocopying, recording, or otherwise or stored in a database or retrieval system without the prior written permission of the publishers. The program listings (if any) may be entered, stored and executed in a computer system, but they may not be reproduced for publication.

This edition can be exported from India only by the publishers,
Tata McGraw-Hill Publishing Company Limited

ISBN 0-07-058812-0

Published by the Tata McGraw-Hill Publishing Company Limited,
7 West Patel Nagar, New Delhi 110 008, typeset in Times at
The Composers, 260, C.A. Apt., Paschim Vihar, New Delhi 110 063 and
printed at Sheel Print-N-Pack, D-132, Hosiery Complex,
Phase II Extension, Noida 201305

Cover: De-Unique

To
My inspiring grandchildren

Ulka, Manasi, Nupura, Kunal, Lori, Ved, Mihir, Ajinkya, Sahil, Aarya, and Saachi

Who find innovative ways to poke fun at my writing obsession

Preface

"Call the role in your memory of conspicuously successful business giants and...you will be struck by the fact that almost every one of them encountered inordinate difficulties sufficient to crush all but the gamest of spirits. Edison went hungry many times before he became famous".

—BC Forbes
How to Get the Most out of Business

This book is about seven exceptional business leaders, whose original thinking has created value and wealth. Their profiles have been penned by understanding first-hand, how they designed their thoughts and actions to overcome multifaceted difficulties posed by rapid technological changes and demands of globalisation.

My interest in interviewing leaders to record their lives as they narrate them, arises, I believe, from my prolonged search for human completeness and integration in leaders who created value, wealth, and made a difference to India through practical and ethical trials. I am not however, on an expedition to find perfect human beings. I avoid investigating deeper infirmities, if any, because even Gods (it is said) are not perfect. Throughout my interaction with them, their thoughts and their presence inspired me. I call these chiefs "Exemplary CEOs". In fact, they are ordinary men and women who have made a difference to India by becoming leaders through deep self-introspection, tremendous intelligent efforts, and discernment. Their success stories provide rich food for those who have the ambition to become leaders in their own right.

In Part One, *Seven Themes and the Stories of Exemplars*, I have debated seven topics: new paradigms, models of leading change, strategic insight, quality health service, business in aesthetics, effective way to show results, and qualitative transformation. Each theme is illustrated through an interview with a CEO. Seven CEOs have been profiled—four men and three women. Each sketch describes the leader's upbringing, mentor's influences, turning points, core values, difficulties encountered, and practices faithfully followed, that enabled their organisations to consistently demonstrate splendid performance. In brief, the essence of each personality has been portrayed with an understanding of the person, his thought world, and the significance of his distinctive contribution.

In Part Two, *The Alchemy of Changing Leadership*, I have collated the common features in the leaders' stories to discover seven valuable assets. How these assets were built and developed is shown in detail through a spiritual perspective on globalisation, organisational renewal, and a devotion to significant paths. Finally, the model has been validated by evaluating my personal assets.

The objective in writing this book on leadership was to study the alchemy that produces outstanding CEOs. It was important for me therefore, to make the selection process authentic. I wanted to take on board only the respected Number Ones of reputed organisations. India is fortunate in having many in this class. I did not want to go solely by the rankings of business or financial journals. I drew my shortlist of CEOs from those whom I had come to admire over last 15 years, and whose unique approaches in organisation development are repeatedly referred to with great appreciation by professionals whose opinions I value.

To make the selection reliable, I asked the thought leaders profiled in my earlier book as to whom they would like me to include in this new book. Their choice and my shortlist corroborated.

It gives me a deep sense of accomplishment in being able to present these respected CEOs: Amrita Patel—NDDB; Jamshed Irani—Tata Sons; Mallika Srinivasan—TAFE; Prathap Reddy—Apollo Hospitals; Simone Tata—Trent; Vaman Kamath—ICICI, and Venu Srinivasan—TVS Group.

The different industries they come from, their diverse backgrounds, rich experience, and especially their futuristic thinking, provides much food for thought. Their synergistic thinking and integral use of assets led them to success through trying periods and transformational processes. Their pattern of action-oriented, creative thinking is both instructive and appealing.

A structured questionnaire was sent to these leaders in late 2002. Interviews conducted over three or four sittings of two to three hours each, in 2003 and early 2004, were audiotaped. The interviews, though different for each CEO, had a number of common questions centred around certain prioritised themes. The intention was to acquire a holistic perspective. The purpose was served because these people are disarmingly simple. They expressed their views with humour, humility, and candour, in simple language.

The reason for incorporating a husband-wife pair of high professional standing—Venu and Mallika Srinivasan—was to understand the way they became successful independently and jointly. What supportive roles do they play? Venu and Mallika's explanation and acknowledgement of each other's inputs in business matters indicates how much they value interdependence.

Both are strong, independent personalities who get on well with their family and social commitments. Furthermore, they are sounding boards to each other, since their professional backgrounds and spiritual outlook provides complimentary matrices for holistic development. They appeared to me, a-made-for-each-other professional couple.

These CEOs sincerely walk their talk. They know their shortcomings. Like us, they have their distractions but they know how to get round them. They are quick in recognising global changes, and prompt in taking appropriate action at the organisational and individual level. What impressed me most was their insatiable desire to achieve breakthroughs and learn in every situation.

Their practices are easy to adopt, and their habits simple enough to internalise. All of us possess in some degree and quality the assets these leaders have. We only need to hone them to become uniquely productive.

Gender is no bar to becoming an effective CEO. More and more women are seen occupying the drivers' seats with aplomb. This is a welcome change. It emphasises that the creation of values and wealth is no longer a male monopoly. The fields are wide open and captured by ladies with great gusto. In that process they have proved that *success in any field is gender neutral*. So in this book 'he' fully includes 'she' and vice-versa. The CEOs are presented in first name alphabetical order.

From my interaction with and study of many leaders of this stature, I have chosen these seven CEOs so that despite the small sample size, they are a representative stereotype with which most eminent leaders will, I think, easily identify. This book is meant to serve as a reliable guide to managers who want to occupy leadership positions, and to those who aspire to become real inspiring CEOs, one day soon.

Shrinivas Pandit

Acknowledgements

Like my last book *Thought Leaders*, this one has been in preparation for three years.

It was difficult to get time from these extremely busy CEOs. Patience finally paid and they freely shared their world, helping me turn abstract concepts into drivers that make the difference. A billion thanks to all the CEOs.

Dr. Raghunath Mashelkar has been very supportive over my leadership studies. I appreciate his encouragement—many thanks.

Thanks are due to Valsaraj and Mazumdar, Tata Steel, Jinny, Trent, Balaji, TAFE, Malathi and Jayashri, Apollo Hospital, Girirajan, TVS Group, Elizabeth, ICICI, Balasubramaniam, and NDDB for fixing suitable appointments, providing information, and courtesies extended during my visits to their offices.

Special thanks to Madhav Das, Assistant General Manager, ICICI, and Sangita Reddy, Director, Apollo Hospitals for sharing their views on a number of important topics.

The young Chandani Palshetkar from our society, whom we have seen grow since her birth, volunteered to work on this project. She typed up the drafts on computer, compiled the bibliography and index, and took keen interest in the project process despite her job. Well done and thank you.

I am grateful to all my family members and close friends who wish to remain anonymous, for their thoughtful indifference to this sublime three-year voyage.

My apologies to those whose names may have been inadvertently left out; I thank them nonetheless.

Shrinivas Pandit

Contents

Preface	*vii*
Acknowledgements	*xi*

Part One
Seven Themes and Stories of Exemplars

1. **Leaders' New Paradigms**	3
♦ Exemplar *The Missionary—Amrita Patel*	17
2. **The Models for Leading Change**	55
♦ Exemplar *A Model Change Agent—Jamshed Irani*	67
3. **Strategic Insight Stimulates Drive for Achievement**	97
♦ Exemplar *A Strategic Thinker—Mallika Srinivasan*	115
4. **The Crux of Quality Health Service**	143
♦ Exemplar *The Dhanvantari in Global Health Space—Prathap Reddy*	159
5. **Business in Aesthetics**	197
♦ Exemplar *A Creative Businesswoman—Simone Tata*	211
6. **The Effective Way to Show Results**	233
♦ Exemplar *The 80/20 CEO—Vaman Kamath*	247

7. **The Nature of Qualitative Transformation**   291
   - Exemplar   *The Embodiment of Quality Performance—Venu Srinivasan*   315

Part Two
The Alchemy of Changing Leadership

8. **Adversity, The Father of Mindset Change**   351

9. **Spiritual Perspectives within the New Leadership**   373
   Globalisation, Organisational Renewal and Devotional Path of Significance

10. **Creating Value, Wealth, and a Better Future**   401

11. **Source Code Leads to Seven Assets**   419

12. **Valuation of Personal Assets to Validation of Model**   431

    Bibliography   451

    Index   *461*

PART ONE

Seven Themes and Stories of Exemplars

1

Leaders' New Paradigms

- ❖ Assumptions Make the Difference
- ❖ New Paradigms Lead to New Thinking
- ❖ The Hallmark of Thought Leaders is Giving
- ❖ Globalisation Leads to Co-creation
- ❖ Exemplar Shows the Way

- ♦ Exemplar—The Missionary, Amrita Patel

Probably the most visible and dramatic shift from old to new paradigm thinking for corporations today has been in the area of environmental protection. Public outrage and governmental regulation have accelerated an increasing sense of social responsibility in the business community. Most policy has now changed from reactive to preventive.

—Suzanne Gauntlett
The New Paradigm in Business

Introduction

This chapter is about thought leaders and how they question existing assumptions and lay down new paradigms, which power fundamental changes in the direction of their businesses. You will find that such leaders give more to the organisations than they take.

Assumptions Make the Difference

Although management is associated with business management, it is found all over the world in organs of governance and in societal institutions. Society is run on assumptions about life, living, aspiring, growing, its potentials and its limits. Basic assumptions about this multifaceted reality are called paradigms.

The practice of management is grounded in paradigms concerning aims, objectives, people, processes, businesses, and the results expected from the concerned institution. By definition, organisations are social systems with some shared norms, beliefs, and value systems, which determine the way things are done. The management conducts its business on what is right or wrong, and what is legitimate or not. The practice of benchmarking against the best practices of comparable companies has led to organisation behaviour becoming more normative; yet the individual personality of each organisation is scrupulously guarded.

Although management's scope is legally defined and circumscribed by national boundaries, technologies, markets, and end users, cataclysmic changes outside its scope have altered the reality. Management must now make meaning of mind-boggling global changes to identify the *paradigm shifts*—the basic assumptions on which its business edifice is built. If the assumptions are wrong, decisions based on them are bound to go wrong. The Jain Group of Jalgaon provides an illustration.

The Jain Group of Jalgaon, Maharashtra, has pledged itself to agriculture. The group has demonstrated that agriculture, the agro-processing industry, and related businesses, can be made profitable by educating farmers. Between 1991 and 1994 however, it diversified into unrelated areas like granite, computer hardware, software, and merchant banking. These projects were conceived based on instincts, and under the influence of the then euphoria of economy.

These businesses failed miserably. Known blunders were committed because Jains' did not assess its in-house core competencies. No in-depth studies were conducted. The selection of outside professionals was based on ideology rather than on competencies. Finally, there was no organisation in place to handle the complex tasks. The failure cost the group Rs 100 crore.

Bhavarlal Jain the Group's chairman said, "Most of them were not errors of judgement but the result of indomitable will and spirit which said, *we can do everything*". This assumption was flawed. It was not founded on facts. There was no reality check on whether or not we were competent and equipped to go into unrelated new areas. Instincts can go hopelessly wrong if not checked and rechecked against the ground level realities. This case illustrates that we need to constantly check assumptions about our organisations and ourselves.

There was also the other assumption that any business is doable if others can do it, provided we have the will and grit to do it. This pattern of thought is based on ideology and overconfidence rather than on objective considerations. Jain admitted it when he said, "Ideology got the better of me, so I don't call myself a successful businessman. I will do very well as an author, philosopher, and writer. I am going through terrible pain because of that".

Once they realised their blunders, Jain and his team spared no efforts to pull out of the quagmire. It took them four years but ultimately they did it. They quitted all those unrelated businesses, and concentrated on their domain—agriculture. They are now doing well.

The moral of the story: *do a reality check on your business paradigms and thought patterns before you venture into expansion, diversification, or new businesses.* In *Management Goals Through Poetry,* Satish Kakri says, "Your core objectives will give you a tough time, forcing you to review your own paradigm". How true!

Over the last decade (1994–2004), the world has become a smaller place. Speed has become of paramount importance. Processes matter as much as the quality of products and service. Economies are locked in do-or-die battles with ecology. Internet and markets are dictating the paradigm script.

In this catabolic process of change, people cannot be just managed anymore. They need to be led. Therefore, our inadequate knowledge about passion and humility, learning and listening, emotions and spirituality, connectivity and symbolic language, quarterly results and daily scorecard, individual and team scores, standards and models, needs to be refreshed and sharpened because it can profoundly change the postulates of management.

The science of management is embedded in its tools and techniques, the art in its human ensemble. In the knowledge management era, the emphasis has shifted fundamentally to the art of leading people because the people–knowledge asset has acquired a new meaning. From the 20th Century of Taylor's scientific management, the world has moved to the 21st Century of Six-Sigma team management of Wipro, and Mumbai's famous *Home Tiffin Box Carriers—Dabewallas*!

The 21st Century management is facing many challenges. It is not about information, technology, or productivity alone. The sum of all three leads us to think, that we have to manage institutions as "result producing" organs of the society. The investments are so high that no society in the world can afford to remain complacently by its old norms of work, attitude, and behaviour.

The context has changed the fulcrum of management. The character of its asset base has been unequivocally altered. It is no more *fixed*. It is a *flow*. If knowledge is the greatest asset, then one must remember that 'knowledge' is not static, it has a flow. Management must look after all its stakeholders, not only the shareholders, and provide equitable returns. The knowledge formulae have limited value and patent validity and are subject to brutal market forces operating on their true value and expiry dates.

Management has therefore to think anew, which means it must test its policies and measure results against the touchstone of a new paradigm:

> *Management must responsibly husband the resources within its domain control and also those beyond its legally defined boundaries, because both affect its performance and results.*

Such changes challenge management's competence in providing new direction. In *New Thinking for the New Millennium* Edward de Bono states that the analysis of the past will not help one design the future. Even if you have a roadmap you cannot construct new roads.

In sculpting the future, leaders must move from beyond traditional judgemental thinking, to the 'water logic' of patterning systems, where "movement" is of essence. It is only when one embraces the larger reality that affects one's resource inputs, that one begins to invest in husbanding them; and that is thoughtful management.

New Paradigms Lead to New Thinking

New paradigms tease management into imagining alternative scenarios. In the relatively stable socialist past, management occasionally checked its paradigms to see if they accurately reflected the reality. Today's digitised world coaxes management to do a reality check almost hourly because of its increased fluidity. How ICICI noticed the paradigm shift in customer expectations and reconfigured itself to meet the changed demand is a case in point. Said *Vaman Kamath, Chairman, ICICI*:

> *Before we came in, a Bank dealt with the customer on its own terms. We changed that paradigm. We said we deal with the customer the way he wants us to deal with him. To do that, we had to align ourselves with the entire paradigm shift in business caused by e-commerce. I would say electronic financial services are the key to the future. It is not as if no small foreign or Indian Bank may have tried it, but here I am talking on a scale of 5–10 million customers. Even banks in the public sector now want to emulate.*

Managers have to cultivate the habit of constantly doing reality checks to keep their ships on course. Such vigilance will allow the managers to make midterm corrections. It is said that desire always misreads fate. It follows: *if managers play up fate, and play down efforts, preparation, and planning, they are in fact abandoning all attempts to sculpt their future. They are becoming irresponsible.*

In my previous book *Design Your Career*, I have stated a new paradigm:

> *We have been rudely shaken out of the delusion that jobs are our ordained, eternal birthright. Our thinking needs to change radically to match the new paradigm. The Job is not a timeless fact of human existence. It is a social artifact...jobs die, work lives...The paradigm shift from "jobs" to "work" is asking you to Design Your Career for prosperity in the dejobbed economy.*

Governments are slowly removing the legal sheath around jobs, thereby considerably diluting unions' stranglehold, and freeing 'work' from their clutches. Now, management's responsibility does not end with declaring voluntary separation schemes and providing outplacement services to employees. It has to go out and persuasively communicate the paradigm shift in economy from "guaranteed employment" to available "remunerative work". Changing the mindset and creating the required ambience would, to some extent, reduce the pressure on management towards creating more jobs which it can ill afford.

If management contributes to managing the expectations upstream, it would be attuning the mindset of its employees and culture to new reality of the organisation. Thus, the purpose behind advance spotting of trends and patterns, and constructing new paradigms, would achieve its stated purpose—to show that the old set of assumptions no longer hold true, the new ones do. And the thought leaders provide us with the new insights.

The Hallmark of Thought Leaders is Giving

In the 21st Century, certain shifts in consciousness are symptomatic of the new paradigm:

- From "seeing is believing" to "believing is seeing". It has led to recognising that the inner experiences of the subconscious of an individual play a role in ushering new reality.

- The data based shared belief system anchored beyond speculation in the realm of centrality and causality of consciousness accepted among scientists, artists, environmentalists, and businessmen has increased our sensitivity about global connectedness, creativity and compassion for all living things and environment.

- There are some constants of the change process, like economy and community, visualisation and vision building, cooperation and co-creation, transformation and turnaround, alignment and empowerment, and learning potential connected to individual development, which need serious husbanding.

- The institutional context invariant like disappearance of hierarchy to team thinking, benefits to bonuses, seniority to performance and results indicate that there is no static template of criteria but an evolving process of TQM that matters in providing customer friendly products and services.

Even if one wants to follow the footsteps of Gandhi, Katherine Ingram asks, how should one lead his life in a world of seemingly intolerable suffering? In most societies the major influential community is that of business leaders. They are free to choose their lifestyles and the manner in which they put their enormous resources effectively in the service of the planet and its needy. Winston Churchill said, *"We make a living by what we get. We make a life by what we give"* (Ray, M., and A. Rinzler, 1993). Most unexpectedly, this truism walked up my way when I asked Venu Srinivasan, Chairman TVS Motors, "What makes the Chairman of Apollo Hospitals Dr. Prathap Reddy's leadership so special in the creation of health facilities on a grand institutional scale?" Said Venu, "Dr. Reddy gives more than he takes". This is a noticeable change in leaders' thinking, that the hallmark of thought leaders is 'giving'. It augurs well for the era of globalisation.

Globalisation Germinates Co-creation

The global concerns revolve about ecological insecurity, crisis of identity, values and meaning, and homogenisation of cultures. They have taken the old paradigm to a point of breakdown. The power of America and its advanced industrialised ability to alter the social and psychological environment of people is a cause of grave concern to many countries across the globe. It is a crisis about control.

The World Business Academy (WBA) considered the issue of control, competition, cooperation, and co-creation in the context of new business paradigms. Its objective was to enhance business leaders' awareness about situation specific choices they could make in operations both under their control and beyond. It became abundantly clear that unless there was appropriate resource allocation, commensurate to the ecological and psychological needs of the community, the desirable results could not be achieved. As Drucker says, "All results are on the outside. The inside is only about cost and effort".

The Latin roots indicate competition means *striving* together, cooperation is *working* together, and co-creation is *creating* together. The togetherness is unavoidable because ecology and economy are interdependent.

If one sees the process of globalisation in a limited context within the zero-sum game, then there will be winners and losers. Since competition is based on the assumption, "winner takes all", the CEOs' pay packages of bonuses, stock options, what have you, are sky high. In fact, the remuneration of those working in such affluent pastures becomes an eyesore when compared to that of employees labouring in unorganised sectors of the economy.

If the paradigm shift is towards team scores, then the rules of equitable sharing must apply because the process-oriented, cooperative mode provides more balance. It is not the same for all, but the differentiate must maintain a balance between providing scope for individual motivation and team synergy. Ideally, the same principle must guide corporations and nations towards sharing global wealth; at least the direction must be set for achieving some harmony.

In cooperation, different parallel forces operate, while in co-creation there is a fusion of forces. To face today's competitive world, management builds strong flexible working groups, like project teams to create the ambience required for cooperation. In this exercise, the TQM device has become a strong binding force for each company.

In many instances, organisations favour joint ventures where the balance of advantages gives an edge while competing against giant MNCs and other conglomerates. It is an arrangement of limited cooperation to fight the Godzillas of global market forces.

In this context, Drucker noted that political jurisdictions had ceased to be sovereign in controlling alliances, partnerships, joint ventures, and all kinds of multilateral relationships which cause business growth. Political and legal aspects are separated from economic reality in many such transactions; it is a question of interpreting law, bending it, seeking exemptions, or lobbying for change with the governments.

However, when a corporation aims at complete synergy, it must operate on the principle of total fusion, i.e. the whole is greater than the sum of its parts. It has to move beyond its boundaries to embrace the factors of ecology, which directly affect the roots of its business.

However, the total sell-out of production assets to exploitative market forces unleashed by globalisation has the potential to uproot earth's ecological infrastructure. The networks of small village cooperatives therefore, have to rise above the local political frays to protect their natural resources through co-creation.

In *Sur/Petition*, de Bono points out that those organisations that focused on value creation did well while those that concentrated on competition did badly. The business leaders have the competence to create value monopolies. They also have the clout and financial muscle to provide leadership. This is the clarion call of the 21st Century that they must take (de Bono, E., 1993).

Creation is envisioning a piece of art, a product, a service. It is bringing forth something that did not exist before. You produce something that gives you divine satisfaction. If working together is a difficult process, creating together is still harder. Says Robert Fritz in *Creating*, "*Most people have not been taught to create, consequently they do not do well when working in a group. Is it any wonder that many people end up loving humanity but hating people?*" (Fritz, R., 1991)

When you create together, you have to assign proper roles to group members by identifying their strengths. Some, as collaborators, are good at defining reality, forming a concept, and evolving a vision. Some are good as amplifiers—they add to the power of creation by making it louder and stronger. Technicians provide technical expertise, and supporters the necessary support. Different role players are required for different types of enterprises.

Furthermore, the role players need guidance, direction, and practice in the process of creation. They have to stretch beyond their current accomplishments into unfamiliar, new territories. It is an exploration where you focus on creation and not on your identity as creator.

Said Ricky Ponting, the Australian cricket captain, "We focus on making scores, which will raise the level of the game to new heights". This means the players, the artists, and the leaders, learn to expand their capacities. Such men and women question previously held assumptions. They set new goals for themselves and others in their teams, because they envision a better future. They immerse themselves in the act of creating. The exemplars of the new paradigm in games, art, philanthropy, social work, business are already functioning for the rest to emulate.

Exemplars Show the Way

Production and marketing of milk, and milk-based products, is a business on its threshold. Amrita Patel, and the National Dairy Development Board (NDDB), are now at that critical juncture where they have moved from competition to cooperation: they have made a joint venture with Mother Dairy. Amrita Patel's next move seems to be to align NDDB and milk cooperatives with the new paradigm of business—co-creation. It is to expand the scope of milk cooperatives: to look after water, forests and other elements of ecology. It means an upstream integration of resources.

In *The New Paradigm in Business* Michael Ray and Alan Rinzler (1993) note:

The business of business is no more only the business...it has to be responsible for the whole creation, for the well-being of the earth and all its creatures. The raw resources of the business await the hand of the sculptor to "chip away" excess materialistic practices.

Max de Pree's observation in *Leadership is an Art* (1987) is apt: *The first responsibility of a leader is to define reality. The last is to say thank you. In between, the leader is the servant.* The key seems to be the attitude that permeates the organisation.

Islands of relative opulence surround a large number of new organisations. We are witnesses to the peculiar problems leaders face in building new infratitude (infrastructure of attitudes) in such organisations. They require creative leadership to catalyse new thinking habits, and initiate actions that will percolate belief in the rediscovered value system.

Globalisation and technology are driving NDDB and milk cooperatives to the Gandhian model of authentic co-creation at the grassroots. To push them on, committed leaders, and exemplars, are needed who can read the paradigm correctly and move on. Amrita Patel is one such.

The Missionary— Amrita Patel

India's most successful cooperative venture, the giant National Dairy Development Board (NDDB) with assets worth Rs 2000 crore, is the Number One milk producer (84.6 million MT in 2001-02) in the world. It has 170 milk unions, and covers 1,01,000 village level societies, which are owned by nearly 11 million farmer members. Leading the mammoth operation of NDDB is its chairman, Dr. Amrita Patel.

*"If Cooperatives are not functioning,
my faith in God is driving me to do something about it."*

After the publication of my book *Thought Leaders* in January 2001, I met Dr. Kurien at Taj in Mumbai. He was in a relaxed mood. While discussing my new book on leadership, I asked him if he knew of any leader who might be included in it. Promptly he said, "Miss Patel", and proudly added, "I recruited her, groomed her, and installed her in my position. I know it is difficult to succeed me, but I think she is doing a good job". It is rare to hear such praise for one's successor from a boss. And here I was listening to it from none other than our idol of the *"milk revolution"*, Verghese Kurien who has any number of achievements to his name.

It took quite some time to get Amrita to meet me. Relentless persuasion worked. My admiration for Amrita grew as I heard the story of this ideological fighter. The master strategist Kurien and his protégé Amrita are currently at odds over issues of marketing policy and farmers' cooperatives. Their differences include strategies against MNCs like Nestle and Britannia. The MNCs' mighty distribution networks and capacity to engage in long drawn brand wars, are a threat of grave magnitude to NDDB and its network of cooperatives.

The farmers and their cooperatives are helplessly watching the sordid drama between National Dairy Development Board (NDDB) and Gujarat Cooperative Milk Marketing Federation (GCMMF). The town of Anand (joy) is grieving that a place of national pride might fall into the rut in which the rest of the cooperatives and government institutions have been languishing for decades.

Many people have asked me, "Why don't you write on why smart executives fail, or on those that have faced severe adversity?" However, I know many *successful* leaders who have faced obstacles, hazards, and inimical circumstances, and in this book I have decided to feature such leaders. Amrita is a person who fits this bill admirably. One who, at the time of writing this profile, is embroiled in a combat, where the end is nowhere in sight. Before we understand how Amrita is negotiating the perilous passage of her career and concomitantly that of the cooperatives and NDDB, let us look at her background to see how she grew.

The Making of a Tough Woman

Amrita is the youngest of ex-finance minister and ex-cabinet Secretary H. M. Patel's five daughters. From Delhi, she moved with him to Vidyanagar, Gujarat, where he relocated after retirement. There, he was Chairman of the Charutar Vidya Mandal, which runs a rural educational institution.

Said Amrita, "My father was my greatest mentor. He inculcated in me ethical values, like social service, integrity, intellectual honesty, hard work, and a free independent spirit. My mother developed my competence at housekeeping, as mothers do. My sisters brought me up; they nurtured in me a sense of aesthetics.

When the NDDB bill was being introduced in the parliament, Dr. Kurien was confined to bed with pneumonia, and so as Managing Director I had to take full responsibility. I had to meet a number of ministers and members of Parliament, to follow it through its passage. It was tedious. At one point I really gave up, but my father who was also a Member of Parliament said, 'No, you can't give up, you have to take it to its logical conclusion. Unless you get it passed, all your efforts will have been in vain'. This gave me the boost I needed to continue work on the unfinished task. Finally, the bill was passed. Even Dr. Kurien was surprised. I breathed a sigh of relief. That was practical training in how painful but meaningful work, ultimately leads to achieving historic milestones. To the oft repeated quote *No Pain No Gain*, I add a rider: *while traversing from one to another however, the only lasting gain you derive is the meaning.*

A trusted friend of mine shared his insights and perspectives on a number of issues: on the management of institutions, political interface, societal concerns; but most importantly, his concern for nature conservation and environmental protection. He helped shape my personality. Without his caring guidance I would perhaps have developed into a skewed person under a powerful boss—as an overbearing and domineering leader.

A vet used to visit the house to treat our three dogs. His job, he once told me, was to go out into the villages and treat the buffaloes of the cooperative members. I asked him to take me along one day, which he did, and that was when I saw how useful and satisfying it was to be a vet; because his patients—the buffaloes—were a source of livelihood for so many poor farmers. In fact, for most of them, their lives depended on their one buffalo. That is when I decided that I would study to be a vet, and come back to Anand and work for the cooperative, "Amul".

After graduating in veterinary science and animal husbandry from Bombay University, Amrita approached Kurien for a job. He told her bluntly that there were no jobs for women since the work was to be carried out in remote villages. Amrita was equally up front in telling him that she was not scared and was prepared to go to such places to gain experience, even if she was not paid a salary.

Coincidentally, a Scottish woman deputed to Anand by the Food and Agriculture Organisation (FAO) needed a woman at that time, and Amrita was hired on a temporary basis. Luck cleared the path. One after another, the male Nutrition Officers who were appointed left. Amrita was asked to stay on. She worked for six years as the Animal Nutrition Officer with the Kaira District Cooperative Milk Producers' Union's cattle feed factory at Kanjari, the largest in the country.

Her work there was very impressive. Said Kurien, "The FAO Assistant Director General, on a visit to Anand, asked me about this brilliant girl and offered her a scholarship for advanced training in animal nutrition at the Rowett Research Institute, Aberdeen, UK, under a FAO fellowship. I was pleased to send her immediately". Amrita had to sign a bond for Rs 30,000 for that training.

In 1967, Amrita returned from Scotland and was appointed Nutrition Officer at the cattle feed plant. Her mark showed in everything she did; but she did not like the working atmosphere of the place.

A: If papers were wanted from me, the concerned person would wait for me to leave the lab. The papers would then disappear from my desk. I felt they were spying on me. I conveyed my feelings to Dr. Kurien, and my desire to quit. He told me that if I quit, then I would have to pay the full bond money although I had finished two years and nine months. So I stayed on for the remaining period. In the meantime my mother died, and I wanted to shift to Delhi to be with my father there. He had just become a Member of Parliament. He was also recovering from a mild stroke, and I did not want him to be alone.

I quit Amul and accepted a job with the NDDB. Dr. Kurien gave me an assignment in Delhi. It was to organise the International Dairy Congress. It was the largest international conference held in India in 1974; when Vigyan Bhavan, the only venue available, was not all that well equipped to handle a gathering of over 2000 delegates.

S: *What do you mean?*

A: For example the garden was unkempt. I wanted the garden to be in full bloom. I called up the director of horticulture and told him that all the flowerbeds had to flower on December 4th, the first day of the Congress. When one flower was visible a week before the conference date, I called him up again and said, what is this? He said, "Madam what can be done, this is nature". I replied that I didn't care—every flowerbed had to be in bloom on the appointed day.

S: *Did he do it?*

A: He went round Delhi, got pots with plants which had flowers, and stuffed them up to the pot-rims in the ground. I watched him do that. It worked. We had a colourful garden. This is just one example. In fact I put into business many entrepreneurs who are now thriving in their businesses. I had to galvanise people into action. It was not easy by any means. I am a perfectionist, but I was not a very confident person then.

S: *And now?*

A: (*laughs*) I was not given any staff. People kept leaving, and finally I was made Secretary General for the event. Dr. Kurien said, "I am giving you nobody; you appoint your own staff on a temporary basis for this event". What was my experience? I had gone straight from cattle feed factory to Delhi, to manage this enormous event. A huge amount of work was involved.

S: *You demonstrated your organising skills.*

A: Obviously, I seem to have had some innate skills. The event is remembered for being the best organised Dairy Congress, which no one expected; as that was the first time the Dairy Congress had been organised outside a developed country. It was the last Congress to have its proceedings made available in English, French, and German. No Congress thereafter has done it.

S: *Could you reflect on what made those innate skills flower when the challenge was thrown at you?*

A: The most important factors were my determination and commitment: my desire for perfection, and care for every detail. There was also a looming threat. It was such an important event; we were putting India on the world dairy map. I couldn't afford to go wrong. I was therefore forced to think for all twenty four hours of the day and look into every little detail. I had to motivate everyone, and encourage them to make it the best event ever. It was motivating people, which enabled me to manage the event successfully.

S: *Do you think your caring personality and persuasive manners helped you do that? It was not the ordering, bossy style?*

A: Yes, I think so. It's not my nature to order. Even at the Dairy Board I am persuasive. It is an advantage. *It is not just working with people but caring for them.*

S: *Did you take any unusual steps?*

A: Yes, many. I had the audacity to put up a notice that nobody should get married for two years, i.e., until the event was over! Dr. Kurien said it was unconstitutional. I said, I couldn't help it, sorry. Everybody had to give me twenty four hours attention. Falling ill was not allowed either—a fellow went around every day giving malaria pills and vitamins to the employees.

S: *Sounds outrageous. In order to obtain that quality of commitment, I suppose you became quite demanding. One can appreciate that successful accomplishment of great tasks is not possible without uncommon measures. Motivation works wonders within the strictly implemented ground rules of any management activity. How many people had you to manage in your office?*

A: About twenty in the office, but a number of activities were outsourced. There were no computers in those days. I had a big board on my wall where we recorded each day's activities and progress. Even duties like changing the toilet rolls and soaps in the bathrooms were listed and specifically assigned! I was a vet but my housekeeping ability, picked up from my mother, came in very handy. Managing this major event was a turning point in my career.

An opportunity presented itself and Amrita grabbed it with both hands. Leaders are made of such quality determination. They are possessed by the objectives of their task, and obsessed with taking it to its logical conclusion with elan.

S: *Were there any other turning points, which made a deep impact in your career?*

A: The turning point was what I believe made a man, so to speak, out of me. It came about when we were setting up India's largest Foot and Mouth Disease Vaccine Plant at Hyderabad. We had to get the best know-how available in the world. After talking to the French and British, Dr. Kurien and I decided that we should obtain it from The Welcome Foundation of UK. We had to negotiate terms and enter into a Foreign Collaboration Agreement. Dr. Kurien said to me, "You have to negotiate with them". I said, "I have no experience". He added, "That is what I am offering you. *There is a first time for everything*. I will provide you with a lawyer".

S: *So, how did you fare?*

A: The negotiations were to be completed in four days in Delhi. Dr. Kurien stayed at a hotel. I had to shuttle between our office and the hotel at lunchtime and each evening, to keep Dr. Kurien informed of the progress. He would fire me—how did you agree to this, that, and the other. Everyday I would come close to tears while eating my lunch.

S: *This is rather unsavoury.*

A: On the third day it became unbearable. The British company was behaving as though India had no capabilities at all. At one point the discussion failed and there was a long silence when the Britisher said, "Well I don't have anything very pretty to look at, so then what do you want to do?" I said, "Mister, the best thing is for you to go home".

S: *And then?*

A: I told Dr. Kurien that there was no point in going ahead with such collaboration. After a few days Dr. Kurien said, "Look, the Prime Ministers of the two countries, Mr. James Callaghan and Mr. Morarji Desai, have agreed in principle to collaborate on this project. We can't just drop it. So let's go to London and meet the chairman of The Welcome Foundation".

S: *Who was the chairman, and how did the meeting go?*

A: Sir Alfred Shepherd was the chairman. We met, and I told him that his representatives were treating us like brown natives who knew nothing. It was humiliating, particularly the statements made by their representative. After hearing me out, he apologised and said, "I would never have let this happen to my daughter".

S: *What action did Sir Alfred take?*

A: He withdrew that person from our negotiations, and told me to choose from two other gentlemen to whom he introduced me. He said, "Decide whom you would like to work with. The choice is yours". I chose one to head the project. It was smooth sailing from then on.

S: *It was a toughening exercise!*

A: Yes, it made me realise that one couldn't just accept being bullied or allow others to make one feel inferior. I had to hold my ground and be more demanding. I learnt that I had to treat people differently, understand their background, objectives, intentions, ulterior motives, and why they interact the way they do. My antennae had to be up to make out what was being said, and why?

These two events toughened Amrita. The first one brought into play her organising skills; the second compelled her to take the bull by the horns. Brett Butler, American actress and author, said, "Most of the time, endurance is not an option. . . often we can look back at that space, that second, and know that living through it has made us stronger". Amrita drove out the unwanted partner and chose another partner for the project. With the support of the boss she fought the battle, and stayed on the project on her terms.

Kurien the Icon

Amrita's biodata is impressive, and Dr. Kurien's contribution in providing her with integrated experience from the grass roots—in working at a cattle feed factory, in village cooperatives, and in project management, staff and administration—to regional management, and then to general management is quite exemplary. He also exposed her to the international environment, where she was required to interact with the who's who of the international dairy world.

Kurien is a no-nonsense executive. He would not have taken such interest in Amrita were he not impressed with her outstanding performance in each assignment. As Amrita said, "He started relying on me heavily as he trusted my judgement". He sincerely believed that experience is the best guide. Said Albert Camus, "You cannot create experience, you undergo it". Sometimes, you pass through an experience involuntarily. Subsequently, how you process, derive meaning, and respond to that experience is important.

S: *Kurien played a role in toughening you, didn't he?*

A: Undoubtedly. He beat me into shape. Had he not given me that verbal thrashing, I might not have been sensitive enough to understand the nuances. That's why I said, this was an exercise that made a man out of me. There was a process of growing up professionally, in which he assisted me.

S: *Although initially he had reservations in hiring you because you were a woman, he did take interest in you.*

A: Yes, he did. The FAO expert found me the most competent amongst all the people she interacted with. Once I asked him, "Did you take me because I am my father's daughter?" He quickly responded, "Of course because you are H. M. Patel's daughter. But that wasn't the reason for your continued stay. You remained because of your own competence".

S: *He was honest enough to admit that you had gained his confidence because of your performance.*

A: Dr. Kurien rounded me off professionally. He provided me with all round experience. He had the vision to make a businesswoman out of me. From Delhi, he brought me to be Director, Administration and Commercial, NDDB, at Anand. Thereafter, he again transferred me to Delhi as Director, Northern Region. I was responsible for implementation of the 'Anand' pattern cooperatives in North India and other allied activities. In 1986, he made me Secretary, i.e. Chief Executive of the Dairy Board; in September 1988, Managing Director (Operations); and in 1990, Managing Director.

Amrita was ready to take charge as Managing Director of NDDB at the age of 47. As MD, she became responsible for planning and implementation of the third phase of Operation Flood, the world's largest developmental project with assistance from the World Bank and EEC. A total investment of approximately Rs 1000 crore was made during those eight years, 1990–98. Additionally about 20,000 village level societies were formed, bringing the total to 100,000 societies, and one crore members. The processing capacity increased from 158 litres per day (llpd) to 240 llpd. What a massive task! Amrita was appointed Chairman, NDDB, on November 27, 1998.

Kurien was adamant as far as the choice of his successor was concerned. The Government was ready to depute one of its IAS officers who had a veterinary degree, but Kurien was not ready to entertain any such nominee from outside. He fought with them over this issue, and finally got the nod for Amrita after the intervention of Prime Minister Atal Behari Vajpayee. How Kurien convinced the PM is worth recounting.

K: The PM happened to hold temporary charge of the Ministry of Agriculture at that time, i.e., in 1998. I told him apart from everything else, that this is also the decade of the Woman. You say you want one-third reservation for women. Here, a woman has been groomed, yet you are thinking of appointing a man. The PM felt I had a point, and she got it.

I remember the elan with which she organised the International Dairy Congress. I got all the credit for it but it was this girl who had done it. She blossomed under responsibility—it brought out her many wonderful qualities—and I selected her to be my successor.

Amrita worked independently and learned to manage on each job but credit went to Kurien for putting her in those independent positions. She admits, his style of developing was to put her into situations.

S: *How did you learn?*

A: By reading up on all the issues I was facing, studying in detail every thing that came to me, consulting friends inside and outside, and most importantly by focussing on the objectives, and being clear about the targets to be achieved. Dr. Kurien gave me the opportunities and the freedom to handle matters. The fact that he was ageing put greater responsibility on me.

S: *Did he play father to you?*

A: In a sense. It was father but only up to a point; most of the time it was boss. He had complete confidence in my decision-making capabilities. If I went in and said, please sign, he wouldn't even read, but he would sign. If somebody was sitting with him, he would tell the person, "I sign because *she* has put it before me".

S: *Will you please give an example?*

A: Promotions were earlier done only on the basis of seniority. When he put me in charge, I changed that, and recommended that some promotions be based on merit—in other words promotions were made out of turn in exceptional cases. He said, "You can do it, but are you sure it won't create unrest?" I said, "that's my problem". He signed the papers. That was the kind of trust he had in what I said and did.

S: Kurien managed to keep the Government at a distance. How is it now?

A: That was also one of his greatest contributions. He gave NDDB a distinctly independent character despite it being a government body. I have also succeeded in guarding our autonomy. In addition, I have developed public relations on a one-to-one basis with most of the government officials, right up to the top. I am perfectly comfortable contacting them and sharing our problems with them whenever there is a need.

Since time immemorial, the human race has needed gods and heroes, goddesses and heroines. Hero worship is a consequence. Our psychological need to see perfection is projected by us onto them. Through their courageous fights for a cause, and through successful achievement, they inspire us. Our need for an external model is met by their inspiring actions and examples.

The mammoth Operation Flood required a competent organiser, administrator, and a supreme tactician. We found it in Kurien. Said the scientist-entrepreneur, CSIR's Raghunath Mashelkar, "Amongst the management leaders in India, Kurien is not an icon, he is a miracle" (Pandit, S., 2001).

Amrita is sincere in telling the unvarnished truth that she and her colleagues worshipped Kurien. Under Kurien's leadership, Amrita, her colleagues, the farmers and their cooperatives grew. Most importantly, production of milk and milk products grew in quality, stature, and impact. The standard of living of farmers and staff improved. It is a heroic journey in the creation of recognisable wealth. It has been a win-win game throughout.

Cooperatives, Cooperation, and Competitiveness—3 Cs

Cooperatives came into existence on the fundamental assumption that cooperation amongst producers will lead to proper growth and an equitable distribution of income, which would then come together to protect community interests. The 3 Cs would work synchronously in a democratic set-up provided people are taught that it is in their best interests to work for the common weal. The 3 Cs communicate a relationship of profound significance, which has to be creatively managed. It cannot be done through egoistic posturing.

Webster's new collegiate dictionary (1973), defines cooperation as a dynamic social process in ecological aggregations (as communities or colonies) in which mutual benefits outweigh the disadvantages (as competition) of crowding. In Amrita's "back to nature" thinking there is a paradigm shift through a business model that shows keen awareness of marketing and socio-political realities.

S: *What is the status of the Government's interference in cooperatives?*

A: The same as it was before. Their interference is seen in transfers, promotions, deciding the price of milk—you name it. If a cooperative made a loss, they used to approach their government, to provide grants to meet the deficit. Now that has stopped.

S: *What about the Central Government?*

A: The Central Government has recently approved a rehabilitation package for cooperatives that have the potential to perform better, and where a projection can be made that their net worth will be positive in seven years. The Central Government contributes 50 per cent of the package, and the State Government the remaining 50 per cent. Our responsibility is to work with the cooperatives to make the plans and monitor their implementation. But the State Government's assurance is necessary in that they will allow the cooperatives the freedom to function; enable them to implement the plan; and most importantly, not change the Chief Executive without NDDB's consent. Regretfully, it is not working that way.

S: Why?

A: Because the minister and his department interfere. Officers are transferred without any regard to their competence, performance, or record of service. The governments continue to interfere in pricing, and in other areas of internal management. If a fellow has made a mess of one cooperative, he is transferred to another cooperative where he creates another mess. When the governments change, those who come into power do the exact opposite of what the former government has done. The cooperatives have become a political football. If the new Chief Minister wants to break the power base of the previous Chief Minister on the cooperatives, he may even go all out to supersede the Board and get his candidate elected as Chairman.

S: Did you not plead with them in the interests of poor farmers, to not indulge in such destructive, unproductive activity?

A: They agree when you meet them, but most often they have their own agenda. If the cooperative is a profit making one, it's good business. If it's a loss making unit, let it continue to make a loss—who cares? The bye-laws of the village cooperative state that a person can contest for the position of an office bearer in his society, only if he pours milk at his society for 300 days. The government that came into power in one state amended the bye-laws so anybody could stand for election irrespective of whether he is a milk producer or not. Imagine the havoc it has played. A cooperative is an institution of "users", i.e. its members should be the only producers.

S: What have you proposed to de-politicise the situation?

A: That's where we thought Marketing Joint Ventures could be one way of professionalising the key activity of marketing. Efficient marketing would in turn put pressure on the cooperatives to improve the efficiency of the plant, the transportation from the village, and the quality of raw milk and products.

The legislation on the formation of Producer Companies under the Companies Act, which was recently passed, is another path created to allow cooperatives to function on a level playing field with their private sector competitors. A cooperative can become a Producer Company if two-thirds of its General Body votes in favour of the conversion.

S: So you are partially privatising.

A: No—converting into a Producer Company is not privatising. All the essential principles of a cooperative are retained namely:

1. Only the shareholders can be producers,
2. One man, one vote,
3. Shares can be traded only amongst members,
4. A cap is set on dividend as stated under the Cooperative Societies Act, and
5. Investors cannot take over. There is discipline in complying with the requirements of the Companies Act. This provides for greater transparency; in the long run we hope such companies will provide an environment which will attract professionals who have greater freedom from government's red tapism in working.

Amrita is trying to strengthen the cooperation between cooperatives to improve their ability to compete against Britannia, Nestle, and other MNC giants. But she is facing opposition from the GCMMF. Their opposition is, she feels, against the interest of farmers, who unfortunately are at the mercy of power politics.

The PAN Brand and Local Brands

S: What should have happened?

A: Ideally cooperatives all over the country should have come together. Every state has its own brand. They are regional brands and need to be strengthened regionally. But there are too many brands to promote nationally. If the cooperatives had been mature enough, they would have selected two-thirds of the brands, say a northern brand, a southern brand, and so forth, to promote nationally. Then, for example, if Amul wanted to sell their products in Karnataka, the Karnataka Cooperative would have manufactured it over there and sold it, and vice versa. If Karnataka wanted to sell it's Nandini brand in Delhi, their product would have been made in the north and sold there. You save transport costs—everybody benefits.

S: Appears logical. What was the obstacle?

A: The cooperatives have not matured. They feel they can survive, and are still not concerned about the competition in the market place, particularly from private and multinational brands. The Gujarat Cooperative is the only one which has built a strong marketing infrastructure nationally. It is now capturing markets to which cooperatives in other states should in fact be marketing their milk and milk products.

S: But where is the need for all this? Why doesn't Amul fortify its hold over all of India, or spread wherever it has not reached, and compete like Britannia or Cadbury all over the world

A: Each cooperative is a political animal. They do not want to let go of their local brand. Nandini, for example, doesn't want to loose its identity. On the other hand it has ambitions to expand to other states. And why should they not, and how can you prevent them?

S: It becomes a competition between cooperatives on the one hand, and against Britannia and Nestle on the other. The MNCs will take advantage of this with their financial and marketing muscle power, won't they?

A: Amul now wants to expand its liquid milk market nationally because the market for products is getting saturated. This means they will be competing with cooperatives in each state; and most of the cooperatives are weak in marketing.

S: Since GCMMF does not accept this argument, you have had to take the joint venture route through Mother Dairy—is that what you are saying?

A: Yes, the joint ventures work at strengthening regional brands in each state, and thereby allow the growth of the markets and business of each cooperative. All this is essential because NDDB has invested over Rs 2000 crores in the cooperatives, and millions of rural producers depend upon milk for a livelihood. It is necessary for the NDDB to intervene.

Amrita is taking the holistic approach: a PAN brand is to coexist with a local or regional brand by uniting the cooperatives against the outside competition. Her thoughts on the subject of "Brands" are worth quoting from the talk she gave at a CII Conference on Corporate Image: Going Beyond Brands, on March 7, 2002, at New Delhi:

I believe our image should be the essence of the thoughts and feelings we want people to have about our corporation and to which we genuinely aspire as evidenced by our actions and the results we achieve. If our 'image' is truly based on integrity, quality, durability, value, innovation, and of genuine concern for our clients, then the customer may choose our brand—all of those positive images helping to convince her or him to buy our products or services.

There is another model, which I would like to place before you, a model, which integrates the best connotations of brand and corporate image—that is trust and dependability with production and supply. It is a model under which cooperative societies bond together to deliver produce to customers of quality and fair value, and the economic gains so derived are shared equitably over the entire length of the supply/value chain. Partnership is sustainable, exploitation is not.

My fundamental point is that it is values based on the true integrity of their performance that count, not the image. The crucial ingredient of success is the old fundamental concept "public service".

Amrita is saying that "images" must convey a true and justified "reputation", which is the only way to earn peoples' trust.

S: *Did you take advice from a marketing consultant?*

A: We did, from Rama Bijapurkar in the early stages. She agreed that the cooperatives had strong regional brands. Also, that these needed to be strengthened throughout the state with emphasis on the marketing of liquid milk, and other fresh products. However, products which need to be marketed nationally, should come under a single brand irrespective of the cooperative in which they are produced.

It appears Rama took the holistic approach. By keeping the interests of farmers' cooperatives intact, she addressed the reality of market forces and competition. Taking into account SWOTs of both national and regional bodies, she conceived the right mix of liquids and products with which consumers could easily identify. She has provided entry for strengths, and exit for weaknesses. The phased approach provides enough space for all parties to plan, and adjust to emerging realities.

When MNCs reach an understanding on segmented market monopolies to create cartels, it is imperative that cooperatives cooperate. The bargain Rama worked out carries inbuilt equity. It makes economic and logistic sense. In The 22 Immutable Laws of Branding, *the "positioning" guru Al Ries cautions against infringing two laws of branding: one is to put the name of the brand on everything and destroy it, and the other is to give it a generic name, which is the fastest route to failure (Ries, A., 2000).*

The route Rama and Amrita are taking, in accommodating the regional brands, might prove to be the saviour of the Amul brand. This is a strategic move to meet the forces of change. Variety in brands has appeal; a lack of it, is boring. Lack of variety indicates that the buyer has no choice. For a huge federal state like ours, this is Formula Number One!

From Project Management to Sector Management

NDDB's work profile has changed, and it requires a mindset change. It has moved from managing projects to managing a sector.

Amrita has had different challenges to face since she took over from her giant predecessor. As Kurien himself said, it is not easy to step into his shoes. Amrita knew this well as she explains: We hero-worshipped him. I wasn't sure how it would work without him in this seat. So I was careful about everything I did. I was conscious of the fact that I would be watched minutely by everyone, and therefore had to ensure that no one felt insecure in Kurien's absence.

When one takes over the number one position in any organisation, equations change. Each individual in the organisation watches how it is going to affect him. The power holders watch how the power equations change; how the policy changes. Loyalties are not transferred just because one is appointed to that position. The leader may have positional power, but he has to work hard to secure personal power. This is awfully difficult, when the earlier leader has achieved iconic status on the merits of a long innings of great achievements. It gets further complicated if the retired executive is active in the organisation, and is available in the vicinity. What skills did Amrita use to facilitate her acceptance?

A: Communication. I met people in different groups, and talked to them about what we were doing. I assessed their comfort levels. I tried to read the signals and to get them involved in course corrections if something was going wrong. That kept them occupied. I left them no time to while away in talking about the leader's departure and so on.

S: *It was a business-like approach, participative and transparent in character. A more caring effort from a woman must have appealed to different constituencies in the organisation.*

A: It was a shift, from a domineering boss whom nobody was allowed to question, to a more sharing and collaborative leader. When Dr. Kurien was here, we had a project with a framework. Afterwards, we moved on from managing projects to managing the dairy sector in a rapidly changing market environment.

S: *You are saying that the character of the organisation was changing from managing projects to managing a sector. The nature of the tasks was changing, requiring a shift in vision, perspective, objectives, and the use of different management skills.*

A: We looked at the whole sector. We scanned the performance and strategies of private and cooperative operations—their dairies, unions—and graded them. This helped decide where we should locate our state offices.

S: *But with Kurien, whom you respected throughout your career, what went wrong?*

A: It is a conflict of basic values. I would give you a few examples.

The Dairy Board had set up some commercial units, i.e. the Mother Dairy in Delhi, a vaccine and biological unit in Hyderabad, and a vegetable oil (Dhara) marketing venture. All these constituted the "empire" of NDDB, as Dr. Kurien often referred to them. We had always talked about the need to convert these units into companies once they were running at a profit. For example, the vaccine plant was set up, in a way, ahead of its time. The farmers were not willing to pay for the vaccine. The animal husbandry departments did not take control of the Foot and Mouth Disease (FMD) seriously, though it caused an annual loss of about Rs 4000 crore. It took us about 8–10 years to make a profit.

The Mother Dairy had a turnover of Rs 800 crore and was in fact a commercial unit that should have been paying tax. But he was extremely upset when he heard that it was being converted into a company. He asked, "Why are you destroying the empire?" I replied, "Because I don't want to be an emperor". We opened 18 state offices with multidisciplinary teams to get closer to where the cooperatives were situated, with the intention of working in partnership with them to strengthen them; this was not possible from Anand where we only complained that they were not functioning properly.

We started getting first hand information about operational issues like quality control, pricing, production processes, the quality of staff, their appropriate placements and management, the depth of political interference, etc. We could then hold dialogues with the cooperatives and the state governments on the interventions required. He referred to this as *"dismembering"* NDDB. Our studies revealed that most of the cooperatives were weak in marketing. He did not agree. We saw that the only state with a strong marketing infrastructure was Gujarat, but they were not willing to reach out to the other states to support them in marketing.

Further, with Dr. Kurien as Chairman, the NDDB had taken a World Bank loan from the Government of India, which in turn has been loaned, to the cooperatives. An amount of about Rs 1,200 crore has yet to be repaid to the Government over the next ten years, and we can do so only when the cooperatives pay us back, for which they need to make a profit. Quite a number of cooperatives are running at a loss but have the potential to do better, provided they can improve their marketing. Therefore, it was this area that NDDB was prepared to support; which Dr. Kurien considered unnecessary. He believed, to quote him, "All one needed was to have faith in cooperatives".

This conflict about values entails a commitment towards honouring the Government's loans, strengthening regional brands and cooperatives through marketing tie-ups, the restructuring of NDDB, and maintaining control over the management of a giant organisation.

Conflict of Values and Vision

It could be argued that this is also a conflict of vision. The values you add come from the personal values you hold, short-term Vs. long-term interests, commercial trade-off Vs. developmental solutions, confrontation Vs. cooperation. Differences between the values of leaders affect the organisation's mission and leadership styles for better or worse. The outcome of such conflicts depend upon the logic and validity of initial perceptions and changes in circumstances. If the input is rubbish, the product is trash. The means through which it is processed might also be faulty. To a great extent structure, systems, contexts, and circumstances, determine values.

To overcome these constraints, visions sometimes flash through the omniscient unknown inner self. Visions are like maps, which guide us through the complexities of life. Freedom from foreign rule was a vision. Establishing self-sufficient milk producers' cooperatives was a vision. Such visions outdate existing practices, and aim at touching Man's ultimate potential. You might term it as the gut feeling an individual has for what the future holds.

Amrita's and Kurien's stand on policies, strategies, and all the interrelated issues are therefore symptomatic of a conflict of vision.

Said Deepak Parekh, "A vision provides a sense of direction on the basis of an assessment of the present, the past, and the likely future. Visions can be wrong, hopelessly off the mark, if they are not born from strong values, strengthened and nurtured by an analytical ability to constantly assess emerging alternatives. This though is never enough. The objective part is normally enveloped with an uncanny intuitiveness for what lies ahead" (Pandit, S., 2001).

The clash is about the relative importance that needs to be given to developing competence in the NDDB's and cooperatives' mindset towards realising the cooperatives' potential. It also means enlarging your vision to secure the foundations of your present, and future related activities. Such expansion, to include water and ecology amounts to, a sort of annexation of territory. In A Conflict of Visions, *Dr. Thomas Sowell said, "Dedication to a cause may legitimately entail sacrifices of personal interests but not sacrifices of mind or conscience" (Sowell, T., 1987).*

The core issue is belief in the villagers' ability to share a vision in sculpting a distant future, and in their preparedness to sacrifice for it the present compelling existential demands. The job of catalyst Amrita, and NDDB, is not only in increasing awareness about the impending ecological disaster, it extends to translating that awareness into action that ensures sustainable development. These issues have not cropped up since Amrita took over—they were always there.

S: You thought that when you took over, you would shape the policy and direction of NDDB and the cooperatives, to the way you saw current reality—is that it? After you actually took over the chairmanship your perspective may have changed. Did you not discuss it with him?

A: I did. I tried to explain to him that for 35 years we have been blaming the Government and the cooperative Societies Act, which permit so much governmental and political interference, and the unbridled powers of the Registrar of cooperatives, for the sad state of the cooperatives. In Andhra Pradesh though, they now have a parallel Cooperative Societies Act, which gives cooperatives complete freedom to function if they do not have any Government equity; the cooperatives are diffident about letting go the Government's hand and standing on their own feet.

Dr. Kurien was not willing to accept that there was a problem with the working of the cooperatives, and that some restructuring was required. His response was *If democracy doesn't work, you need more democracy; you cannot give up democracy.*

S: But what about democracy within NDDB and GCMMF?

A: That is a good question. But that thought comes when one is being introspective. His remark makes a good newspaper headline. It became increasingly clear to me that unless we fought for democracy in producers' cooperatives, they would not survive. Dr. Kurien was not prepared to accept this view. He preferred to leave it to God, in whom I suspect he has no faith, whereas *my faith in God is driving me to do what I believe is right.*

The Fallen Icon

We see here a clear manifestation of conflict in values and belief systems. The strategies of NDDB, and GCMMF flow from this fundamental disagreement, and have been stoked to the current politicised atmosphere. The illiterate farmers, in whose wisdom Dr. Kurien and Amrita have immense faith, are probably upset by this sorry spectacle.

I did not approach Dr. Kurien to know his side of the story because I did not want to get into the controversy.

The public does not know that Amul is a cooperative venture. As Kurien said, "We sell a brand and not cooperatives". He may well be right. But it is not only a fight on brands and marketing. It is more a fight for control and management of cooperatives, GCMMF and NDDB. Now that Amrita has been given five year's extension as chairman of NDDB by the government she has the time to push through her agenda.

S: Will you please elucidate your vision of the future of the dairy industry?

A: While looking at the future of dairies, one needs to look at sustainable development in the broadest sense. One can't look at dairying as a business only, and ignore one's responsibilities towards the environment that sustains it. Dr. Kurien prefers to ignore these as he considers these inconsequential. This was the change I was trying to bring about in his thinking. I feel *the more technical you are the less you are able to concern yourself about the more fundamental ecological issues which makes your enterprise sustainable, particularly when it is so closely related to agriculture.*

S: I don't quite agree because I see many technical people are genuinely involved in ecological activities. But how are you taking care of these issues?

A: It is an important exercise but a difficult one. I am attempting to address it through The Foundation for Ecological Security (FES), an organisation that we initiated some years ago. If we do not care for our land and water resources we court ecological disaster. I do not subscribe to the proposition that limitless growth is possible. My officers do not share my view that there are limits to growth, but that does not mean the issue does not exist. The fact that it is there is more evident today than ever, and requires the most serious consideration by all of us who have a sense of responsibility for the future of our fellow citizens; and in any case for over 11 million farmers who are members of the cooperatives.

We know this is a wide subject. It is being deliberated all over the world. As executives, we need to define the time span and delineate the boundaries of our growth to ensure sustainable development. It is clear that we cannot continue to act in a thoughtless manner. This is the classical battle of trade off between narrow, short-term interests and broader, long-term interests. We know that the legacy we leave is based only on our current but rapidly growing knowledge of facts, and the limitations of our own thinking. All we can do is ensure that our current actions do the least possible harm to us in the future.

Being essentially the loyal person she is, Amrita's face does not hide her deep hurt and sorrow. To say she almost worshipped Kurien, and now on deep reflection communicate that he has fallen from grace is excruciating. It is only because she is gentle and caring that she is able to convey in the most decent language the pain she is undergoing for having to face her fallen hero.

Heroes have a thousand faces. Will Rogers said that being a hero is the shortest profession on earth. They are the glory of their times. They create efficiency-regimes. We need not feel guilty in making Kurien an icon. We are right in our assessment of his spectacular performance. There is real tension in Amrita's job, which is bound to cause deterioration in her health. This is the price achievers pay for the cause they espouse, when they are unable to relinquish the struggle.

Dwindling Tribe of Missionaries

The future can be built on the basis of our faith in the potential of our young generation.

S: What about the new generation of recruits?

A: There is much less idealism. I make it a point to meet the new entrants when they go through the induction programme. We tell them the history of NDDB, the spirit of the cooperative movement, the milk revolution, and what we have created. We present them our SWOT. It is extremely difficult to pass on the inspiration couched in an appropriate message, when they see so many cooperatives making a loss. They see that there is lack of professionalism, and to an extent they are right. But one has to breathe into them the ethos that goes with our responsibilities, and hold fast to our commitment to larger goals.

S: *Are you able to attract bright candidates?*

A: It is difficult. *The brighter you are the more likely it is that you have fewer ideals and that you are in life for yourself.* The Dairy Board's success so far has been that it has attracted people who believe they need a mission in life. They are missionaries, who are paid less and who do unconventional work when there was no glamour attached to it, e.g. working in a village. They accept and stay on because they derive satisfaction in seeing people better their lives. The tribe of such missionaries is rapidly dwindling.

S: *Will you please share a stirring experience from your missionary work?*

A: In my early years when I was in Ballia, a poor village in eastern UP, I saw women standing in a queue at the society, to deliver their vessels of milk. To one woman in a bright red sari, who had about 100 grams milk in a *lota* to sell, I said, "What a pretty saree you are wearing". She turned her face away. I realised I had said something wrong. Then I asked the society secretary why the woman was upset. He explained that there were six women in that family with just one sari between them, which they wore when they went out; at home, they dressed in newspapers. The money from the 100 grams of milk is required to feed six hungry bellies at home. If she can feed the cow and make her produce 200 grams instead of 100 grams it would improve her livelihood. Now tell me, how would you feel if you were faced with such stark poverty?

S: *Quite moving.*

A: I met a man at a chilling centre on the way to Pokhran before the second nuclear test. He takes out a twenty-rupee note from his pocket and tells me, "This is mine. I can now buy what I like. I don't have to go to the *baniya* (village moneylender) in the village and borrow money". What I saw was liberation. One doesn't realise what it means to live in a village and be bonded to a moneylender.

S: To make missionaries out of those working at NDDB in the midst of such blatant display of consumerism is damn difficult!

A: It is. The proportion of missionaries in society is generally dwindling in the face of growing materialism. However, in a group of thirty, we can still find two or three with a missionary zeal.

S: How is it in west?

A: They do not have poor farmers like we do. The disparity is not so great as it is over here. What is a Cooperative? It is a society formed to do business; where the producers are also the shareholders. The employees of the cooperatives are not paid as well as those of MNCs. They complain about it, but they also realise that they are paid to get maximum value for their employers—the members. Whether they get better prices by tying up with MNCs doesn't matter to producers. How the employees of the cooperatives do business is not the concern of the producers so long as they get them better prices for their produce. That is why the world over, cooperatives are merging and forming alliances, sometimes even with private companies.

S: If you have to compete with the MNCs and you need expertise, you cannot afford to stay hierarchical and pay according to seniority.

A: That is why at Mother Dairy we took a conscious decision about salaries. If the cooperatives pay less, we cannot do the same to the marketing employees or others whose expertise commands a much higher value. So we began paying a handful of people handsomely on the basis of their performance. When NDDB officers were deputed to the joint venture they were given 20% more to start with. Further increase depended on their performance.

S: Did this apply to people selected to head the state offices?

A: For the first time in NDDB the middle level officers were given recognition. Some of the youngest have become state directors. It brought in the realisation that if they go out and perform, they have prospects of better earning and recognition. You are given responsibility, position and authority, and with that comes accountability. They are proud of the positions they hold. In some cases they are not able to perform because the state governments are hopeless. What can one do if the Chief Minister is unhelpful, or his officers don't care about the developmental work that goes on under their jurisdiction?

S: Your decision making looks far more complex.

A: You are right. Decisions that affect the organisation are comparatively easy to take, whereas the ones that have political ramifications are difficult; and politics is in a state of constant flux. If the minister is interested in supporting particular district unions, we have to think of the political alignment and the worthiness of the proposal. Ministers change and with them, the ground reality.

S: It looks as if your decisions are based not so much on costs, risks, and commercial considerations as on goodwill and relationships.

A: You are right but one cannot lose the discipline necessary in the utilisation of money. Unless you earn, or save money somewhere, you cannot subsidise anything anywhere else. The moral responsibility to earn, remains. Interest rates matter and the value of money has to be recognised. It is not a free for all. There is a rigorous method in place of such decisions. Meanwhile, exceptional circumstances do arise and we do provide the fresh considerations they require.

S: You practise a caring and participatory leadership style; you take the stakeholders with you in fulfilling the mission you have set for yourselves. You must have seen such leaders elsewhere. What is distinctive about this style of leadership?

A: Humility, an absence of arrogance, the capacity to listen, share, and empathise, the desire to work in teams, for teams, and not for oneself. It all boils down to possessing a temperament, which is not dominating but caring.

S: *You were born in Gujarat, you speak Gujarati, and you became a vet. So you were able to mingle easily with the villagers, and understand their issues accurately—am I right? Acceptance was not an issue.*

A: Yes, that may have been an advantage in Gujarat, but we are a national body and need to converse with farmer elected representatives in their own regional languages. There were also many times when outside professionals (who seek fees we cannot afford), had to be inducted. I had to instil in them that feeling of being a missionary. Only then do they understand how much their expertise means to poor farmers and their starving institutions; ultimately, they enjoy working with them.

S: *To energise the cooperatives and the NDDB one needs such an infusion of enthusiasm.*

A missionary is a person devoted to the cause of the organisation. At NDDB or at the cooperatives, his mission does not involve working for charities—he has to achieve the commercial objectives of the organisation. But he has to remember that he is serving a cooperative organ of governance, formed to serve the cause of milk producers most of whom are landless, small and marginal farmers. His commitment to altruism must be firm. He must work with genuine fervour though he is neither with the best paid MNCs nor with the low paid most hazardous work of charities or the armed forces.

The stock of such a tribe of workers has steadily shrunk since independence. The chances of their growth and availability are high with ecological issues moving to the centre stage of the national agenda. Many professionals from different vocations have moved into neglected areas to work on issues of societal concerns, e.g. Dr. B. V. Parmeshwar Rao, Dimli, West Bengal, P. K. S. Madhavan of AWARE, Action for Welfare and Awakening for Rural Environmental and such others. Saving Nature from total debasement has acquired critical mass and more will join the battle.

Revitalising the Cooperatives

You can see that Kurien and Amrita have different perspectives on the future of NDDB and the cooperatives.

S: When did you start noticing the differences between Kurien's style of leadership and yours?

A: We began Phase III of Operation Flood in 1987. I was the secretary then. I noticed that he looked upon the exercise as managing a programme, organising people, and marketing a packaged product. It was almost a kind of military operation for him.

S: Times have changed since you took over, and you are required to think anew—is that it?

A: My fundamental approach is that although I get a salary, I must think as an employee of a cooperative—I need to act as a trustee. The villagers trust me to sell their produce at a profitable margin and to give them better returns. In 30 years' time I would like to see the villagers' educated sons run their businesses. I am not interested in keeping them illiterate so that their current despicable situation continues. Their elections will be more independent and free from rampant politicisation and corruption. Therefore I am banking on a more involved and participatory cooperative development (CD), where the genuine cooperative spirit can flower. In that development I can lay the seeds of mutual loyalty by putting together their innate skills and our professionalism. There will be a synergy of interests.

S: You are looking to the profit of the emerging farmer. You want to prepare both the present members and the new ones, so that they understand their roles and responsibilities towards themselves, their families, and genuine cooperative functioning. You also want to induct more women into the movement. As most studies and experiments have shown time and again, their influence in the families as economic partners will have a positive impact.

A: Yes. However when I approached Dr. Kurien, he instinctively said, "It's useless, but take the money because I don't know what CD means". In this characteristic way of teasing he dismissed CD as some music system, instead of acknowledging "cooperative development"! Whenever we spoke of it he would point a finger at me to indicate that it was my baby. He wanted nothing to do with it. He never accepted either the approach or the operation.

S: Your mission attempts to remake the person and his institution (the cooperative) at the grassroots level through process of education. You want to expose him to market realities and allow him to understand why it requires a different professional approach and working style, dress code, and demeanour. He should be educated to understand that some skills and competencies command higher rewards in the market place and that such realities cannot be wished away by false idealism.

A: Yes. It means making him understand that we don't want to exploit him but enable him to improve his awareness about the realities of doing business.

The Ecological Dimension

The world is witnessing the destruction of rain forests, droughts, famines, and the wayward floods of rivers, while they cause enormous damages year after year. The business charter for sustainable development has been signed by MNCs at the World Industry Conference on Environmental Management (WICEM). However, we have to resolve our own issues, whether they are about water, forests, or any other variable of our ecological system. Amrita, the evolved CEO, is struggling relentlessly to make the paradigm shift at NDDB and the cooperatives in the light of the changing global scenario and our stark realities.

S: You want to avoid all types of exploitation—both human and ecological?

A: Yes. My "limits to growth" theory incorporates both. Like agriculture, dairying in India depends very substantially on the productivity of living natural resources, and therefore the loss of biodiversity, particularly of plant life, is a cause of grave concern. If unsustainable exploitation continues unabated, it will undermine the very foundations of our ecological security irretrievably, with catastrophic consequences on our whole economy.

S: I feel you might have to go through the materialistic growth cycle before you talk of balanced growth in poor countries.

A: In northern Karnataka we have built dairies with huge capacities. Meanwhile, the water in the nearby wells has disappeared. The consequences can be imagined. Take another case—Rajasthan. Human and cattle migration used to occur because of scarcity of water. Over the last three years however, the farmers have been working to prevent human and animal encroachment into ecologically sensitive areas. This has improved the ecological foundations, and therefore the hydrology, of their locality. Former large scale migrations have reduced because the area has been able to recharge its water reservoirs. We have only to help nature to heal and renew herself to restore the most threatened resource in our lives today—water. FES is building models for sustainable development. I am exasperated because I am not able to convince the urban based decision makers about this obvious truth. Living as they do in an artificial environment, they are oblivious of natural phenomena. They jump to the wrong conclusion in believing that the application of short-term technological solutions is a permanent answer to our water problems.

S: Someone made the very telling observation: socialism collapsed because it did not allow prices to tell the economic truth; capitalism may collapse because it does not allow prices to tell the ecological truth. Socialism has allowed our human population to grow by 75 per cent, taking 1970 as the benchmark, from 548 to 960 million—whereas our breedable bovine population has grown by only 34 per cent. These figures are a damning epitaph to democracy. Does NDDB Managing Director Deepak Tikku agree with your view on applying the basics of ecological security?

A: No, not really. Technical people don't see it like that. I am coming to the conclusion that the more technical you are, the less environmentally sensitive you become, and therefore less understanding of nature and ecological processes.

S: That's a harsh condemnation, madam. India has millions of engineers. The entire Engineers' India Ltd., will bring a morcha (protest march) on you, costing the Government a few million rupees to halt it away from the precincts of Anand.

We both laugh.

A: In fact, through FES we are going to the basics of the survival and future of milk cooperatives. At milk cooperatives only those who have milk producing animals come together; who looks after the judicious use of land water resources? In my model therefore, the entire village community must come together to ensure its survival and development. So, we changed what was formerly the Tree Growers' Cooperative Federation (TGCF) to the Foundation for Ecological Security (FES). In other words we broadened and deepened the scope of FES to include all community concerns and interests.

S: How did the Rajasthan experiment begin?

A: Well, the proposal came from the State Director. He was closer to reality than most of us. He saw the problem between the relative haves and have-nots in the poor community. The water dimension had a far graver impact on their lives than milk. The protection and ecologically sensible use of land and in general, the protection and strengthening of all ecological processes became the central theme. The concerns of landless people were therefore addressed, and it will in time, strengthen in this model.

S: You should have a mechanism in place to show the correlation between water and the benefits obtained in the business of milk production.

A: You are absolutely right. To get our contemporary decision-makers to understand, we have to quantify the benefits. Our biggest problem in milk is that we have too many scrub (unproductive) cattle which cannot be improved or slaughtered. The breeding programmes are therefore totally compromised, levying a heavy burden on our overstretched national resources. *When you cannot eliminate the unproductive animals, you create a problem of potentially catastrophic implications.*

S: The problem is both political and religious. It is a very contentious issue. So we enter into the subject of the politics of water, the river linking project, etc.

A: Yes, that is correct. We cannot have milk without ensuring that adequate water is available. In Phase I of Operation Flood, we had people from NDDB work in villages. In the second phase, we allowed the cooperatives to do the groundwork. Now, at the Dairy Board, there are only a few with first hand experience of grassroot issues. They are too remote from the reality in the villages. The state offices we have opened are now providing us with some of these inputs. But it is FES that is emerging to build that vital strength. We need to constantly update our skills and levels of awareness about the changing realities at ground level.

S: It might be construed as a conflict of ideologies as far as Kurien is concerned. I suppose you must also be facing opposition from the Board in the financing of such schemes that go far beyond immediate milk business concerns. Also, you will be seen as superimposing your personal agenda on the business model and the basic objectives of NDDB.

A: Yes. I want a march on "back to basics". I am very clear that I have to suffer opposition to reach that.

There is an emerging awareness in the corporate world of the vital importance of environmental protection. Tragically, it is not widespread. The awareness grew from an increasing demand from consumers for green organic products and from global concerns about community interests. This is slowly influencing organisational values. The enormous task of protecting ourselves from ecological disaster, needs an equally enormous effort at changing the mindset of the class of people who own mammoth enterprises and believe that they are creating wealth through the conversion of natural resources into cash. They have not been attuned to caring for resources beyond their own network of supply and distribution. Undoubtedly, their response to the critical need for change is slow.

Visuals are Persuasive

To transform an organisation from within, to change its goals and constitution, to give it a broader vision however genuine, is a daunting task if it does not meet the immediate needs of the organisation. It requires tremendous stamina, and creative sellable breakthroughs.

S: What practical steps are you taking to pursue your goals?

A: We made power point presentations on the Annual Report of FES to governors, chief ministers, and secretaries. The response has been encouraging. We made a visual of the need for a land use policy, and the impact of 'development' on the poorest. We have figures to prove all the points we are making.

S: It is necessary. As a banker I don't fund you however idealistic the proposal maybe, unless it makes business sense. You know money doesn't come easily.

A: It has happened through communities doing *Shramadan* (donating their labour). We have played a catalytic role. In the milk business, we set up a cooperative, buy their milk, process it, and market it. In this experiment, however, we have built their thought processes—we have showed them how to operate a bank account in their village, how to use funds carefully, how to pay for a watchman, etc.

S: So it's an NGO.

A: Yes, supported by NDDB, and by the Canadians and the Swiss so far.

The impact of visuals is there to be seen. Next to the demonstration effects of prototypes, visuals play the most important role in the sale of a product. In selling concepts however, it is the other way around. You are able to effectively communicate the correlations between interventions and results—the ROI—and how missions once considered idealistic or impossible, have been fulfilled. These modern tools play a dramatic role. Even missionary work needs to be packaged attractively for buyers, sponsers, philanthropists, donors, and new recruits.

The Missionary

Now I am able to see Amrita in a different light. She is decidedly on a mission encompassing not only milk production, cooperatives, and marketing, but the fundamentals that sustain these and much else. Her vision is local with ecological and global dimensions.

S: What was your mission at the start of your career and what is it today?

A: My exposure to villages at a very young age made me feel that I would like to improve the quality of life of people in the villages. At that age I could see that this would be possible through animal husbandry. As a consequence, I was drawn to the veterinary profession. I could see myself making a contribution by qualifying in that field. As a vet, one didn't just treat animals but became an important link between villages and Anand. I sat and had tea with them. I saw through the same window they used, to look at world around them.

S: Gradually your mission underwent a change.

A: I thought if milk can do so much, water will do so much more. The underlying desire to serve the poor remained unaltered but I felt I needed to move on to broader dimensions to include many more who required help.

S: So the medium changed from milk to water while the basic mission to serve the poor remained intact.

A: Yes, but not just water. It goes beyond—to secure and strengthen the life support systems that sustain us all and the economy on which our livelihoods depend. The land is being rapidly degraded—through villagers gathering firewood, through overgrazing, etc. The rejuvenation of the land can be brought about through the participation of the local villagers, who can prevent degradation of the natural vegetation of the uplands. Equally important is that the state must:

(a) Reinforce protection of uplands to restore forests through natural regeneration, and where necessary through seeding of endemic species of vegetation, and

(b) Introduce legislation declaring such state forests as "National" not just "Forests" since the ecological benefits derived from providing full protection goes well beyond state boundaries.

S: You have done so much over here that you understand the role finance plays in this resurrection process. What role has your entrepreneurial competence played in this success?

A: I have the passion and commitment, which is most important, and believe that I have the capacity to make a persuasive case. I think people see that I have no selfish motives. I say this on the basis of my experience in raising money for the hospital for which I am responsible. People say that they give me money because they know it is safe in my hands.

S: What you have become today is due to a combination of luck, chance, and real effort. What would you ascribe your success to?

A: Mainly to these elements combined, but also to sustained intellectual effort. To the vision, the mission, the absence of self-centred motives, preparedness to fight for what I believe in, and suffer the consequences as I do, to be of service to others.

Amrita's indomitable spirit is felt in her presence. I have experienced it. In one person you meet a missionary and an exemplary CEO. She symbolises that remarkable courage which fights for others and not for oneself. She has put her whole being into a vital holistic cause.

We have ample professional protestors garbed as social activists, NGOs, and what have you. At the same time we also have genuine rebels bringing about change at the grassroots with quiet, missionary zeal. But rarely do we come across a rebel CEO working for poor, I mean an authentic missionary! And Amrita is one such. For those who want to do something creative and meaningful for others she is an inspiring role model! We need more Amritas, don't we!

★ ★ ★

2

The Models for Leading Change

- ❖ The Story of Change
- ❖ Building Coalitions
- ❖ Sharing Experiences
- ❖ Change Agents
- ❖ Powerful Women Alchemists
- ❖ Tracklayers of the Change Trajectory

- ♦ Exemplar—A Model Change Agent, Jamshed Irani

"The individuals who will succeed and flourish will also be masters of change: adept at re-orienting their own and others' activities in untried directions to bring about higher levels of achievement. They will be able to acquire and use power to produce innovation."

—Rosabeth Moss Kanter
The Change Masters

Introduction

This story is about change—about the coalition between knowledge, biology, information technology, and markets. It is familiar to us through stories of the past. The significant difference in the current version is that its velocity and ferocity are greater, having multiplied over the last 15 years.

This increased turbulence calls for more innovation, entrepreneurship, and integrative action, based on a holistic vision for survival and growth. How the track-layers change trajectories and lead their organisations through apparent chaos, is narrated here with their experiences.

The Story of Change

Models emerge against backdrop of incidents that bear messages. The models however, may not reveal their true worth at once because we weave stories around them as they unfold. Over our long history, we have developed the skills required to construct realistic stories. Let us glance through the story of change as it is germane to our study.

Technology changes with a pace that leaves organisations with no alternative than to gain the competitive advantage of speed. For instance, General Electric now makes customised industrial circuits in three days instead of three weeks.

Progressive organisations have moved from management control to become leaders of accelerated change. Change outmanoeuvres unprepared institutions, and with it, the nations. This includes organs of governance, universities, B-schools, hospitals, religious bodies, employer confederations, unions, industry associations, research and development outfits, NGOs, press, and media. Organisations are caught unawares by such change, when their sensors for trends in technology and market are outdated. In such cases, management's assumptions about business growth, and strategies for turnarounds, are equally outmoded.

Those who did not manage change were perhaps under the impression that there was something mystical about it, or that it was the familiar occurrence of recession. They may have been labouring under misconceptions such as:

- sunset industries like textiles, and jute, are bound to suffer anyway

- sunrise industries like IT, and biotech will be on top

- no crisis in sight, so why bother now—let us cross the bridge when it comes

- it won't hurt the giants

In the nineties, businessmen had yet to move beyond the trading mentality. The protective environment, ethos of corruption, and short-sightedness had lulled many into complacency. The root cause seems to be the underlying assumption that *change is partial*, which it is not. It led leaders to misread the change phenomenon, which is impartial and neutral. Leaders who correctly grasped the import of impending vicissitudes were ready for the change. If 60 per cent of the enterprises folded up, it is to an extent, an indication of the fact that we suffer from a paucity of leaders.

The efforts made by leaders to accommodate change, have been paraded under many banners like total quality management, re-engineering, re-structuring, mergers and acquisitions, turnarounds, etc. In *Making Change Happen,* John P. Kotter (1999) notes that the process of change in successful transformations, involves establishing coalitions and a sense of urgency, creating, communicating, institutionalising new approaches, and empowering others to act on the vision. Change leaders make their organisations grow tall through this radical mutation.

Building Coalitions

To help them face the waves of change, leaders of modern complex organisations must build strong alliances with stakeholders, employees, unions, suppliers, distributors, regulatory authorities, ecologists, and other societal institutions in the circle of their business interests. They cannot know where the resistance will spring from. More importantly, an institution's objectives cannot be achieved without it developing a network of supportive relationships in the technological age.

Coalition involves gathering together a mutually exclusive and collectively exhaustive set of skills, and experience in working together, in flexible project teams formed from people inside and outside the organisation. Inside the organisation, competencies and experiences from different disciplines and divisions need to morph to address the needs of particular tasks. Coalitions bring in a diversity of views. The challenge is to expand the scope of such coalitions because they are capable of achieving federal goals beyond the confines of each constituency.

In such ambience, team members learn to care for each other's interests, give credit where it is due, and accept shortcomings voluntarily. Managers learn to be hard on results but considerate about people. Over a period of time, personnel problems surface. Issues concerning an appropriate mix of skill, energy levels, and trust, require adroit handling. Developing the right chemistry becomes all important.

Coalitions work through persuasion and inspiration. A leader inspires when he has a vision. Without one, the leader is blind. But with vision, he is not necessarily effective unless he manages multiple time lines synergistically. He has to communicate the vision to obtain the commitment of employees. The vision has to be translated into their language—the one that inspires them, the one they understand and use.

"Understanding the change process", said Kotter, "is essential to many aspects of a leader's job". Two skills in particular—building coalitions and creating a vision—are especially relevant to our times. This is because change cannot be managed by one person. It requires strong partners who can bring in different viewpoints. The strength of such coalitions is better equipped to deal with change.

We know that this is correct because over the last twenty years ITC, Reliance Petrochemicals, Hero Honda, Hindustan Lever (HLL), etc., have grown in volumes and profits. The management of such successful organisations built durable institutions not just by managing change, but by leading change. ITC through its *eChaupal* scheme and HLL through strengthening its rural distribution network, have made considerable impact in the remotest villages of the country.

These were not ad hoc decisions or chance occurrences. These coalitions were well thought out, and strategically built by engaging the right talent, which worked in teams specially formed for the purpose. They used scenario-building tools for sharing vision, and drawing a roadmap for action. They have followed Kotter's guidelines in building guiding coalitions.

Sharing Experiences

The change process requires skilled leaders to integrate effective coalitions. Grooming such leaders is the most challenging task of top management, especially the CEO. And CEOs' experiences in transformating organisations are readily the most effective way of influencing potential leaders. It helps in inculcating a sense of values and meaning, heightening the consciousness, and providing powerful role models.

In *Corporate Success and Transformational Leadership,* Pritam Singh and Asha Bhandarkar (1992) present their studies on six CEOs. These are: Mr R. H. Mody, Chairman, TISCO; S. V. S. Raghavan, Chairman, MMTC; S. N. Jain, Managing Director, NFL; Pankaj Sinha, Chief General Manager, WCL Pench Area; and S. P. Sharma, General Manager, IFFCO.

Singh and Bhandarkar state:

> *All our transformational leaders are capable of successfully articulating their inspiration, vision, and goals. All of them have played an active role at various levels of the government, society, and community...leaders operated not through authority and power of the organisation, but through their personal power and influence.*

Chairman and Managing Director of SAIL, M. R. R. Nair had mentioned that after noticing the changed market needs, they had to produce steel, which was different from what they had earlier produced and sold. They had to improve on operational efficiency, customer satisfaction, and competitiveness. It required a fundamental change in the behaviour of employees. This was the problem many organisations had to face—to move from a regulated environment and sellers' market, to a buyers' market. SAIL improved in its performance through a radical programme of revitalising people.

In *Managing Radical Change,* Ghosal, Piramal, and Bartlett (2000) state:

> *In incremental change companies need to realign some aspects of their strategy, organisation, or culture, while retaining others. Some companies in India are healthy and need gradual evolution. Infosys, HDFC, Wipro have grown steadily without the cleansing need of tidal waves.*

While playing a catalytic role, CEOs also share the vision, and create a compelling need for change. It is the people processes and the CEO's role that are paramount in such transformations.

Change Agents

Management requires change agents—leaders who can initiate and lead the change phase to its successful completion. Deveshwar (ITC), Dhirubhai, Mukesh and Anil (Reliance), Munjals (Hero Honda), Datta and Dadiseth (HLL), Murthy (Infosys), Parekh (HDFC), Premji (Wipro), Kurien (NDDB), and Mashelkar (CSIR), led the change processes in their organisations. Azim Premji, Chairman, Wipro, says that *successful leadership is the same across all fields... but leadership has become more demanding over the years. The pace of change has accelerated, and the ability to lead change has become even more important.* The change experts, and organisations adept at anticipating the need for, and of leading productive change, are the ones who will be in great demand.

The above change masters have certain characteristics. They:

- question assumptions and construct new paradigms
- see change as an opportunity
- change willingly what is already there, take the lead in innovation, and create something new and sellable
- hold a vision of the future, and are prepared to weed out what is unproductive—products, services, processes, employees, divisions, depots, whatever—what Drucker calls 'Organised Abandonment'
- bring in systematic improvements through use of processes like TQM
- exploit one's strengths and successes
- audit themselves and the organisation on two counts, viz. the time and budget spent on the present—maintenance—and the future
- reorient their own and their teams' activities in untried directions to reach a higher level of achievement
- maintain a balance between change and continuity

Powerful Women Alchemists

There is another noticeable theme in the story of change. Increasingly, women have started occupying strategic posts in politics, business, civil services, research, development, social work, and education. *Business Today (BT)*, in its issue of November 23, 2003, featured the 25 most powerful women from diverse businesses. These cover energy, environment, biotechnology, media, newspapers, dairy development and cooperatives, autos, two-wheelers, beauty care, cosmetics, pharmaceuticals, banking, insurance, retailing, tractor manufacturing, civil service...you name it.

I became aware of woman-power in the early sixties, while working at Bank of India. I remember the conversations I had as a young officer, with senior mangers who had all kinds of objections (silly, I dare say now) for recruiting women. The three principle reasons were (i) will they be able to lift those huge, bulky, current accounts ledger books; (ii) will they be able to sit late and finish work; and (iii) how can they be transferred to locations inconveniently far from residence, or outside the city of appointment?

However, we persisted in appointing women, and after a while, those very managers were honest enough to admit that the young girls were meticulous in work, able to balance books faster, had a keen sense of duty, and were willing to take on additional responsibilities. They were ready to be transferred and had no difficulty in lifting those heavy ledgers.

Later in the eighties, at Siemens, I was amazed to find that some of my colleagues were still rather unwilling to recruit women because of a general belief that they couldn't go to remote places to install, say X-ray machines, in hospitals. However, when we went ahead with the recruitment of women, reports came in on how they travelled to such places and did a "manly" job. The objectors had to swallow some pride. Not that they were convinced, or that they welcomed the ladies to their divisions. I have heard similar stories from other engineering giants. Such were the managers: completely frozen in their attitudes and unprepared to see emerging realities. But they formed the matrix of organisation culture!

In the industrial revolution, male prototypical worker came to the forefront. Now in the information age it is the woman worker leading the revolution in all its facets of living and working. The 25 most powerful women in business featured by *BT*, bear eloquent testimony to this major change. World wide, 84 per cent of working women are a part of the information/service sector. Forty-four per cent (ages 25–64) are college educated, compared with 20 per cent in 1965. More ladies opt to major in IT today.

In the last two decades we have shifted from the models and metaphors of physics to those of biology to help understand the changing world. In Megatrends 2000, *John Naisbitt and Patricia Aburdene (2000) note that:*

> Physics as metaphor suggests: energy intensive, linear, mechanistic, deterministic, outer-directed. Whereas biology suggests: information-intensive, inner-directed, holistic. It draws on the words, like virus, and vaccines instead of caterpillar, etc.

These trends, and my belief that women entrepreneurship is coming up in businesses and professions, led me to profile Kiran Mazumdar-Shaw and Anu Aga in my previous book, Thought Leaders. *Kiran is India's biotech icon, and Anu is the conscience keeper of corporate India. Here, I have included the paradigm shifter Amrita Patel, the creative businesswoman Simone Tata, and the strategic thinker Mallika Srinivasan.*

There are many whose achievements deserve to be studied to understand this profound shift in human consciousness. The facts certify the arrival of the Woman's era.

For the 21st Century symphony of IT, biotechnology, service, travel, tourism, media, entertainment, and sports, ladies in leadership seem a more synergistic fit. Their track record promises the emergence of more ethical role models to enhance India Inc.'s corporate image. It does not mean male leaders will be consigned to history, or that women leaders do not have any weaknesses, but their SWOT currently looks a better fit. We cannot ignore the fact that many male leaders are also welcoming this shift.

The important point to note is that we have to move from management to leadership, to sculpt a positive future through the bewildering phenomenon of change. Leaders and managers differ in assumptions, orientation, behaviour, strategies, energy use, foresight, ambition, creativity, and ultimately results.

Tracklayers of the Change Trajectory

In his book *The Second Coming*, Pradip Chanda, while discussing creativity in corporate turnarounds, notes that, "A new change agent is required at the top. Shareholders have to force the issue especially in the owner managed corporations. The CEO's selection is critical" (Chanda, P., 2000). This is equally applicable to public limited companies. The issue is not only about ownership but also about the fact that existing management is bogged down by traditional styles of working. It has no clue as to what *out-of-box thinking* means, and how to revive the company from the current morass.

In *Control Your Destiny or Someone Else Will*, Noel M. Tichy and Stratford Sherman (1994) comment on Jack Welch's selection to the top post of GE stating that the most important characteristic, the one that got him the top job, was his ability to change. Don Kane, a senior member of the EMS staff at GE, explains why:

> *The company had a tremendous need for change, so a different kind of person was needed—a change agent had to come in. But if that change agent had not the ability to change himself, how could he be trusted to change the company?*

This is a profound observation. This is the single most important criterion that members of a board must look to, while choosing a person for CEO's position in this era of rapid change that has dawned on us. I am aware of Manoj Tirodkar, Global Tele-Systems (Pandit, S., 2001), and Venu Srinivasan, TVS Group, undergoing a conscious self-change process, which has helped them lead change in their organisations.

In *The New Leaders*, Daniel Goleman (2002) says that the leader pays attention to the hidden dimensions and undercurrents of the emotional reality in the organisation, and to the culture that holds it together. Goleman has cited an Indian example: that of Keki Dadiseth of Hindustan Lever. Dadiseth followed certain basic rules that trigger change:

- bought to people's notice, the underlying blockages and solutions that could create common ground, and understood what needed change and why

- got people to talk about their hopes for the future—it helped the leader find out what held their dedication

- modeled new behaviour which helped the leader move from talk to action—that is the leader's function

If business leaders are called upon to sensitively husband ecology, then it is incumbent on them to husband far more attentively, the emotional resources of employees and stakeholders. Such leaders are track-layers of the unfolding change trajectory. They thrive by helping people find meaning in the face of seemingly senseless change. They have to make it look sensible. They have to be genuine and convinced of the cause. *If the messenger is trusted, the message is accepted.*

Jamshed Irani is one such leader. He has consciously and convincingly played the role of a *Model Change Agent* in bringing about significant change at TISCO. In the process he has provided a model for leading change in organisations.

A Model Change Agent—Jamshed Irani

World Steel Dynamics ranked India's best known symbol of industrial growth, Tata Steel, formerly TISCO. Its gross revenue in 2001 figured at Rs 7,814.58 crore and Profit After Tax (PAT) at Rs 533.44 crore. With 46,000 employees (2001), it ranks number one amongst the world's top twelve best steel producers. The single largest, integrated steel works in the private sector, it is the biggest exporter of high quality, value-added steel products. Dr. Jamshed Irani, who retired in July 2001 as Managing Director, was the change agent who led his teams to achieve this unique status.

"Say what you think, do what you say: let everyone experience that it is so"

Tall, happy looking Dr. Jamshed Irani occupies a stately office on the fourth floor of Bombay House, headquarters of Tata Group. As I was passing through the security check on that floor, I intuitively knew that I would meet a relaxed and noble Parsi. During my days at Bank of India, I came in close contact with Parsis, and I associate them with nobility, kindness, and compassion. That strong association probably permeated me at that moment. His secretary Valsaraj made me comfortable. After successfully turning round Tata Steel as CEO, Jamshed moved over from Jamshedpur to Mumbai. Ratan Tata the Chairman of the group has entrusted him with numerous non-executive responsibilities. In addition to being the Chairman of Tata Teleservices, Tata Refractories, Tata Ryerson, etc, Jamshed is Director on the board of several companies like Tata Sons, Telco, Mico. He is also involved with NGOs in social development. After battling at the front, and leading Tata Steel through a historic turnaround Jamshed now mentors and guides senior executives of the companies he is connected with, to sculpt a better future.

Jamshed's Solid Foundation

Jamshed's father Jiji Irani, was employed with Tatas. His mother Khorshed was a housewife. Jamshed grew up in Nagpur. In addition to normal family values like honesty, integrity, etc., Jamshed recalls that particular efforts were made to teach him right from wrong, and the importance of being independent. He describes Jiji as his best friend and mentor. In Jiji's often quoted phrase—*out of every ten men, who are born in this world, nine have to work for the tenth; prepare yourself to be the tenth*—lies the foundation of Jamshed's ascendance to the top leadership position.

Jamshed holds a brilliant academic record. He was awarded a gold medal for his B.Sc. and M.Sc. in Geology at Nagpur University. He did his Master's and Ph.D. in Metallurgy at Sheffield University, U.K. He was also awarded a gold medal for his Ph. D. thesis. Professional career guidance as it is practised today was unknown then. Jamshed studied subjects he was best at, and laid a solid foundation. This piling of academic knowledge helped him immensely in TISCO's grand renewal.

He chose his career when, as a student, he visited Jamshedpur. While observing supervisors and managers, he resolved to become a leader there one day. What brought him to Tata Steel? J. R. D. Tata (JRD), the Chairman of Tata Group! While Jamshed was at Sheffield, he received a letter from JRD—Come to India and join TISCO (Tata Steel). He joined the R&D department as his inclination was to make a career in research. But after he saw how the organisation worked, he changed over to Operations and Management, realising that they provided a better scope for his goals.

These incidents influenced Jamshed's thinking. He understood that *luck is when preparation meets opportunity. Focus on what you want to be.* In *Thought Leaders*, I wrote that critical events often become turning points in life as a result of a shift in awareness. The trigger, the event, leads one to look to the deeper currents of one's life. We all face turning points in life. But we do not try to understand their true significance as leaders like Jamshed do. At times unconsciously, but most often consciously, these leaders identify their paths, select the correct route, and reach their goals with a disciplined resolve.

In Jamshed's case, the observation of actual working of TISCO led to his first resolve, to become a leader in TISCO one day. Secondly, JRD's letter lured him more than the available opportunities at UK. He did not change his original resolve. The glamour of UK did not estrange him from his original thought. And thirdly, the experience and observations through actual work, and the focus on his goal to become a leader, caused his move to Operations. It was decidedly a better route to the top of the ladder.

> Jamshed's icon JRD, taught him the virtues of fairness, humility, and thrift. In his wife Daisy, he met an ideal companion. Her companionship provided him the true meaning of sharing, learning, and realism. His father, Jiji was a good friend.

Jamshed's office has a British ambience. I said, "You have filled out the questionnaire so well that little remains to be asked". His equally appreciative response, "It took considerable time—thinking before answering each question—since it's quite a comprehensive questionnaire", fortified my feelings. Since management of teams at various levels holds the key to successful organisation-change programmes, I started interview on that topic.

Team Working at the Top

S: How did you develop teams at board, committee, and executive levels?

J: Through openness, discussions, voicing my concerns, making my demands, reaching consensus, and taking logical, clear cut decisions, followed by immediate action. At the executive level I was very careful in ensuring that no favouritism takes place, and that we do not shy away from difficult situations.

S: Give me an example please.

J: You saw these ten people leave my room just now. They are from our Telecom side. Mr. Tata has given me the responsibility of doing to Telecom what he thinks I have been able to do in steel—bring co-ordination between managing directors of three different companies. Each one wants to protect his company. They have an interface but not a seamless one. It is my job to blend them as a team, and I told them that we have to achieve a synergy rather than engage in a combat.

S: Are the issues functional, or territorial, or what?

J: Functionally territorial but not geographically so. Who takes the lead when they are looking at the customer, is the question. All three should not approach. The one who is most appropriate should approach, make the deal, and share the spoils. This attitude has to be inculcated. This is similar to the situation steel or any other industry. It is a natural instinct for everyone to fend for themselves, forgetting that this doesn't result in synergy.

S: It seems to me that the reward system is strongly linked to bottom line results, which drive them to be functionally sectarian.

J: More than sectarian, it is working in a silo mentality, not giving due attention to the group loosing a customer. Maybe the other company in the group can provide better service. They must take a group view, a global view. Today I spent two hours with them in this room. I did not find any animosity. Finally, they all agreed to the proposal on the table. We cannot entertain hidden agendas. We have to learn to take totality into account. And people do learn through such forums that I create, where free debate and group view is encouraged.

What this case illustrates is that servicing customers by group companies, is a task that requires a truly collaborative "work product". Rotating the leadership role amongst three constituent companies, depended upon who could provide optimum service advantage to the customer. And executives of the three companies will hold each other mutually accountable, depending upon how the service product is to be delivered.

Co-author Jon R. Katzenbach of The Wisdom of Teams *(1999), recommends six elements of team discipline—small size, common purpose, clear performance goals, explicit work approach, and mutual accountability. I saw most of these elements at work, though not in full measure, in Jamshed's approach to building teams at top. In effect he was playing the role of the eleventh leader—the ten were waiting to be led. While doing so he was enacting his father's wish.*

S: What values guided you in team building?

J: The Tata values, credibility, learning, and sharing. Information is no longer power. One must be ready to lead a team, a company, and a nation.

S: But why do you think information is no longer power?

J: In the past it may have been so because it proved one's indispensability, but not any more, since collaboration and team work are critical to success.

Jamshed gave an example of how an electrical engineer responsible for running the blast furnace was fired, because he was absent from the work knowing full well that the furnace had stopped working and that his colleagues did not possess the know-how to start it. This caused financial loss to the company. The moral of the story: **critical knowledge has to be shared.**

Values are important for building excellence in teams and organisations. Levi–Strauss famous for its jeans, is also known for its visionary approach to culture. In 1964, its CEO Robert D. Haas said, "We base our approach to ethics on a value orientation, that includes six principles: honesty, keeping promises, fairness, respect for others, compassion, and integrity". They practised this approach in all business decisions. They have been practised by TISCO since 1904 when the late Jamshetji Tata founded it.

Way back in 1895, Jamshetji said:

> We do not claim to be more unselfish, more generous, or more philanthropic than others, but we think, we started on sound and straightforward business principles considering the interests of the shareholders, our own, and the health and welfare of our employees...the sure foundation of our prosperity.

In that era such values were in fact, taken for granted. Visions were articulated through various talks that they gave. However, as companies grew in size, complexity, and sheer number of employees they began to have efficient communication systems, with an articulated vision document.

J: We meandered, tasted, tested, and finally, we chose a proven world class approach. We needed radical changes. Breakthrough improvements. A major mind shift was essential. *Mindsets are not permanent; they can be changed with determined action.* I convinced the board to invest in technology and modernise the company to become best, most efficient in the world.

This articulation was germane to the business and times (1992–2001, the first decade of liberalisation) in which Jamshed was in the driver's seat. It was Jamshed's Techno Vision. Jamshed realised the vision through sustained execution of details. He knew that *an ounce of application is worth a ton of abstraction.*

Transformation of Tata Steel

Tata Steel led the pack of success stories, which proved that liberalisation frees business to expand, compete, grow, and make profits. The world steel industries' holy book World Steel Dynamics, *stated in its 2001 report, "Tata Steel is India's only world class steel maker and one of the few steel companies in the world with such a standing". It became the lowest cost steel maker in the world. It was so ranked against other leaders like Nucor of US, Nippon of Japan, Posco of South Korea, and Usinor of France.*

The story is worth recapitulating. In the socialist manufactured era of shortages, steel was being distributed, rather rationed, like cement and rock oil. Tata Steel, like many other companies, was in a cost-plus position. There was no need seen for modernisation and "no money" excuses shot down many proposals in every company.

J: Once I jokingly told JRD that unless we modernise our plant, both you and I will stand at the gates of the company selling tickets and saying, "Come and see the steel museum". JRD said, "Don't accept what the finance people keep telling you. Ask them why they cannot become more modern?" That gave us the inspiration, the rest is history.

In the early nineties Ratan Tata and Jamshed had gone abroad to collect $100 million for their convertible stock issue. The defining moment came when investors asked, "why do you need 78,000 people?" As good employers, many companies went on adding people, since labour costs were cheap. That was the day of reckoning for Tatas. The investors' criteria for the measurement of efficiency demanded a much reduced manpower. Jamshed and his team started acting in right earnest, taking unions into confidence, sending union leaders to Japan, and South-East Asia to see how they functioned, introducing voluntary separation schemes, launching major communications drives; and in phases reduced the manpower to approximately 46,000 in 8 years. Quite an achievement!

That wake up call led to further refining of the strategic objectives for creating wealth. The management decided to:

- create a culture of continuous learning and change
- achieve world class status in services and products
- become the most cost competitive steel producer
- establish industry leadership

The cost competitiveness could be achieved only if the cost of raw material was brought down substantially. Joda mines, which had unutilised deposits, were developed into the main supplier of iron ore.

J: We started using Blue dust, which we avoided at one time. This was a major change. But in my opinion, the biggest change that made us a low-cost producer, was the introduction of a new coke-making technology. India has medium cooking coal only. SAIL imports such coal from outside. We must use our own resources—this was a campaign I led myself. We had to make good quality coke from our poor quality coal. Such technology didn't exist in the world in the 80's, because nobody had this kind of problem. We had to solve it ourselves. So over a period of ten years, we developed what is known as stamp charging technology, through painstaking laboratory tests and pilot plants.

S: *How did they actually put it to use?*

J: First we converted one of our coke oven batteries. After some tweaking, it gave us the confidence to change our batteries also. Now the entire plant have changed over to the new technology. India has very low-cost medium coal, which we are converting to low-cost coke, a low-cost fuel. I would say that, that is the number one reason behind our becoming a low-cost producer. It is far more important than reducing manpower.

The Balanced Scorecard methodology was used to implement the cost reduction strategy and performance improvement. TISCO, like many other companies, was in the practice of employing a son or daughter of the existing employee at the company. In a communication meeting once, an employee complained that, that right was being taken away by the company. The MD shot back, "Forget your son's employment. Unless we both do what is required in the new situation, I am worried about your job and mine".

I have always found that the unions adapt to new ideas faster than the lower levels of management. Once, when we closed down one of our units, workers realised we meant business and allowed us to dispense with 400 workers on Voluntary Separation Scheme. We had to turn the union from an adversary to a partner.

This gigantic and risky exercise of rewriting the "social contract" was carried out in the 80s and 90s in politically sensitive, socialist Bihar.

Simultaneously, TISCO undertook quality improvement in hand. They employed four techniques to get to the top of the quality wagon:

1. value engineering
2. adoption of ISO 9000
3. JRD Quality Value (JRDQV) process, which led to JRD Tata Quality Value Award (equivalent to US Malcolm Baldridge Award)

4. six sigma process—each was taken in hand, one at a time

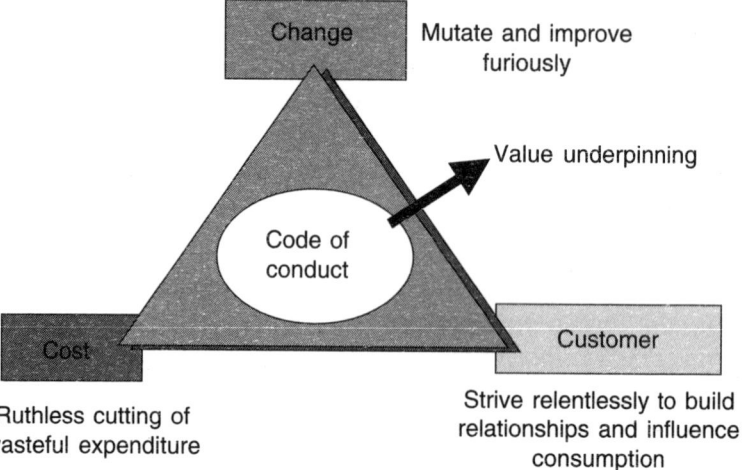

Fig. 2.1 TISCO's Communication Thrust to Masses

This is called a staircase approach. At the heart of it are capabilities. With every step, the organisation gains additional capabilities through experience. The head of Hero Honda, Brijmohan Lall Munjal said, "I never try to jump from the ground floor to the second floor, but to grow step by step". You can call it experiential learning if you like. Jamshed added, "We used the downcycles to invest in the building of cold and hot rolling mills (CRM and HRM) during these times".

The transformation of Tata Steel is visible to the naked eye at Jamshedpur, and the bottom line results show in the balance sheets. Transformation here, means changing the configuration of operations. In this metamorphosis there were five basic elements:

- the decision of the board to invest in the process of upgradation
- technological breakthrough in developing low-cost fuel
- step by step upgradation of quality
- reduction of manpower, with union involvement through the partnership route

- sustained effort to change the mindset through value based actions, model leadership, and communications

Professors Richard Whittington, Andrew Pettigrew, and Winifred Ruigrok, in *New Notions of Organisational "Fit"*, confirm that innovative organisations like ABB, BP Amoco, and Unilever studied the whole system change approach, for organisational transformation. They say it delivers significant pay-off, and that such change is rare. That is why we also get few examples like TISCO, ICICI, and Sundaram Clayton, of successful transformations.

Jamshed believes that CEO's must:

- lead the change process through its phases—awareness, promotion, interpretation and excellence—and take personal ownership; the responsibility cannot be delegated

- play the role model, and be the first to change; personal involvement with time commitment is key to success

- create frequent opportunities for two-way communication

- create a sense of urgency (not panic); embrace change even when it doesn't appear necessary

- set up a small handpicked group, to drive change in the organisation; train and empower them

- set key result areas (KRAs) carefully, and include them in the MD's scorecard

TISCO became a world class organisation. I wanted to know if there were any universally applicable principles, and Jamshed elaborated the dos and don'ts

This is a turnaround story of mammoth proportions and profound impact. Most ideally, it fits in Prof. Pradip Khandwalla's Pioneering-Innovative (PI) *style of management (2003). Jamshed employed what Khandwalla describes as the* humane *rather than the* surgical *turnaround strategy, which works in the developmental context. I would add, it is the only one that works in the* ayurvedic *mindset of India. For personal transformation, ayurveda is useful.*

Table 2.1 Dos and don'ts of a World Class Organisation

Dos Install and encourage	Don'ts Avoid or Discourage
Listening posts; plain talk	Rumours, Sycophancy
Task forces	Extra constitutional bodies
Fair and efficient systems	Deal makers, Wheeler—dealers, King makers
Promptness	Discount on delays
Decision making at appropriate levels	Procrastination; passing the buck
Risk taking	Cynicism
Inspire an individual/team to perform beyond its capabilities	Talking down

I agree when Jamshed emphasizes that CEOs must play role model because the right role model can be very inspirational. Said Paul D. Shafer, "the most important single influence in the life of a person is another person.... who is worthy of emulation."

Evaluation of Experience

In the questionnaire sent to the participants of this study, I had requested them to evaluate their experience gained at junior, middle, and senior levels in terms of quality, value, and learning. Jamshed responded:

Junior—New ideas cannot be imposed from outside. Win over your colleagues, share credit, praise, and responsibilities with them.

Middle—Do not be afraid of being outspoken. Try to help peers.

Senior—Try for consensus. If it is not achieved, explain the reasons for your decision(s) and go ahead. Be firm; show no hesitancy. But be prepared to learn from mistakes.

J: Being CEO of Tata Steel was very action oriented. Decision making was fast—it is not so in the present environment at Bombay House. In ambiguous situations, one got as much information as possible, and acted. Delaying matters did not always lead to a better decision. While obtaining commitment from others and retaining a certain amount of flexibility, one had to be fair and make a judgement call. As long as those affected had the confidence that I was acting in the interests of the company/group, my actions were accepted. Also, they knew that I would follow up on actions—understanding the SWOT of people, placing them in jobs, explaining our expectations, and demanding that results should be obtained objectively. The teams responded. Success was rewarded, failure counselled up to a point and lack of attention reprimanded.

S: *Would you please spell out the details of this follow up mechanism?*

J: If I had given instructions, a week or ten days later they would get a reminder, "what have you done?" My office would follow. I maintained a diary for important things and reviewed its notes every ten days or so. This is how I inculcated discipline. I was known to be a maniac of follow up.

What struck me was the emphasis Jamshed put on the rigorous system of follow up that helped in the implementation and execution of decisions, plans, policies, recommendations, and commitments made. I recall a similar story told to me in 1975 by the Works Manager of Thane-Belapur plant of Herdillia Chemical. He said, "We had organised a farewell function for my predecessor, a British expatriate, after I took charge. In my speech I asked him, 'Tell me in one word what helped you to show such extraordinary results here in India'. He went to the blackboard and wrote in bold capitals **FOLLOW UP.** *He didn't elaborate his crisp one word message. It was self-evident".*

The failure to follow through is widespread in business, and a major cause of poor execution. Larry Bossidy and Ram Charan (2002) have stated in their book Execution, *that by creating a follow through mechanism, CEOs ensure that everyone does what they are supposed to.*

J: There were two significant challenges. One was to change the old outdated plant, which needed modernisation for survival, and the second, to remove the problems created for the Board and me, by my predecessor.

S: *What did you do? What role had you to play?*

J: I did what was right according to our value system. In the process I put my job on the block. But the board knew what was right and the story had a happy end.

In facing adverse situations with management, unions, and peers, sincerity and credibility were my strengths; and in each case a different solution and technique was used. The large majority of issues were settled satisfactorily. I learnt to live by the oft quoted dictum—change what you can, accept what you cannot, and have the judgement/wisdom to differentiate between the two. *Bad judgement is usually placing a person in the wrong position. An expedient solution usually revisits you later.*

S: *Where did you acquire your robust concepts and models?*

J: Largely from discussions and experience, not through management books!

S: *How did you shape your identity?*

J: I was committed to credibility. I built up trust. People realised I was an honest change agent. I say what I think, and will do what I say. No double talk.

S: *Handling a large mass of employees—anywhere above say 3,000, and here it was 78,000 to begin with—requires mobilising collective action regardless of circumstances. A leader is required to tell stories, and use allegories, to make an impact. What did you do?*

J: Addressed large gatherings under urgent situations. Explained the circumstances clearly, and also outlined the course of action, and why that course was taken. I was prepared to change that course if the right feedback was given.

Many times I had to tell them, we are in the ICU (Intensive Care Unit) act, or we would be carried out horizontally (i.e.

dead). I also provided similes to one's way of life. At times I told stories, which the simple folk would understand and appreciate. Always explain why a certain course of action was needed.

The telecom expert Sam Pitroda said, "Leadership is the capacity to move and inspire a large number of people to act together in the pursuit of an end".

I have addressed large worker meetings. I know how one has to give examples that fit into their context and concerns. The purpose is to help them make significant meaning out of the dilemmas of their daily existence. They have to be shown how collaboration and changing perceptions, help find solutions, and not confrontation through adversarial relationship. Success blessed me in my humble efforts.

J: The principle *you must do, what you say you will do* is cardinal for establishing credibility. You must be well read on a wide variety of topics, be skilled at communication, and be as transparent a personality as courage for self-disclosure permits.

In *The Transparent Self*, Prof. Sidney M. Gourard (1971) notes, that self-disclosure is the act of making yourself manifest...so others can perceive you.

Innovative Jamshed

What comes out of Jamshed's self-evaluation? He is a helper, team and consensus builder, but more, a learner! In this frank analysis, there is a lesson for executives working at all levels. It does not mean that it has to be adapted ditto. It provides clues to the kind of make-up of a career executive.

S: How did you sense the growth opportunities?

J: Through comparisons with what happened in other economies. Reading about other countries, studying their advances, visiting them, comparing where we stand and where we should be heading provides insight in the alchemy of growth. In India, 'flat products' were required—steel for cars, white goods, etc. So we made TISCO strong in that area. TISCO's strength is in raw material base. Technologies were evolved to make the best use of that strength, and we succeeded.

To improve performance and spread the innovative climate, TISCO did what all organisations do, viz. institute job rotations, suggestion schemes, recognition and rewards, training courses, and challenging opportunities for deserving candidates. The distinguishing factors however, were leading by example, and liberally establishing libraries of books and videos all over the organisation. In modernising the plant— introducing the new coke making technology—TISCO benchmarked itself against the best in the world, and secured the number one rank amongst world steel producers. TISCO is today's modern steel giant, successful and strong.

Jamshed's innovation was based on the need to use TISCO's raw material to the best advantage. The urgent need to gatecrash was economic and technical, both. These were long standing problems. Solutions had to be found as soon as possible.

J: I felt I must do this because it will change the face of the company. We had tried several alternatives, even foreign technology, but without success. We had to solve it ourselves. There were the usual emotional upheavals—cannot be done, we have tried this before syndrome.

S: *What helped?*

J: Patience and persistence paid off. I provided them a picture of what would be at the end of the road, and that helped a great deal. In a picture you can capture the ingredients of a completed job. The visuals produce the necessary impacts.

Jamshed followed Louis Pasteur, who said, "Let me tell you the secret that has led me to my goal: my strength lies solely in my tenacity."

Metallurgy of Leadership

TISCO is a beehive of metallurgists. A metallurgist is not a metal worker. He is a scientist, and metallurgy is the science and technology of metals. Innovators lay down the ground rules for running industry. It was the clarion call of Jamshed's profession, and he honoured it with significant innovation.

This was a decade long voyage for TISCO and Jamshed. The voyage sailed through four phases—awareness, promotion, integration, and excellence.

J: In this journey to excellence, we meandered, tested, and finally we chose a proven world class approach.

S: In this voyage, what challenges did you love to face?

J: Getting people to work with me, accept me as a leader.

S: What was the problem? You were already appointed a CEO.

J: You may be appointed, but you still have to win over your colleagues. You cannot exercise your positional authority from day one, and in any case, you lose it fast if you do that. You have to earn respect for yourself as a person, for the quality of leadership you provide. Acceptance comes from the heart and you have to work for it. That was the challenge I enjoyed.

Jamshed enjoyed this challenge because he was confident about himself. Self-acceptance is important. How you feel about yourself is more important than how others feel about you.

S: That was when you were appointed CEO of Tata Steel. But today, you are asked by the chairman to look into a specific issue, or to co-ordinate some activities. You are not the CEO. How do you exercise your leadership? Managers are required to play both the leadership roles, executive and advisory.

J: You must put on the other guy's shoes. This morning, I had a meeting with the managing directors of Tata

Teleservices, VSNL, erstwhile Hughes Teleservices, and representatives from Chairman's office. I was thinking, how do I bring these gentlemen together, what could be the synergy? None of the guys are going to like being pulled up, in front of others. In a way I am an extra constitutional authority. I knew that some of these people needed corrective action, a course correction. I was thinking from each one's angle—their individual apprehensions about authority erosion or whatever. As the leader of the meeting, I want X to agree, but how would he take it—loss of face, loss of power, or what? And if the answer is 'yes', then how do I effect it without his feeling that way. For some, it is water off the duck's back, while some may be very sensitive, so one has to be careful about that. The leader is a person who extracts the best out of subordinates and colleagues.

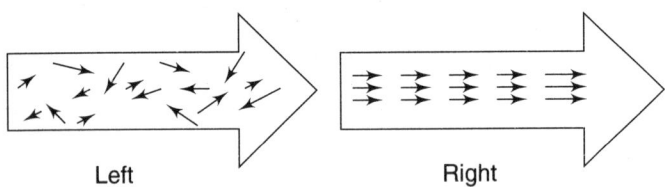

Fig. 2.2 Working in an Organisation

Look at Fig. 2.2. In the arrow on left hand side, you see everyone working at cross-purposes, some times intentionally, sometimes unintentionally. The strategic objectives cannot be achieved unless you align all initiatives, as in the right-hand arrow. This way, you reach the objective faster.

S: Easier said than done!

J: Yes, you are right. Obviously, overall objective is also not straight. The point is to get people moving in the same direction.

S: Is there any metallurgical principle in that?

J: Yes, there is. If you take a bar of iron and put it in a magnetic coil, then all units which contribute to magnetism get aligned in the same direction. This is how I explain it as a physicist. This is the principle of the dynamo of an ordinary motor, where you put a bar and a coil, and pass the current through the coil. Magnetism gets it aligned in the same direction. So I say the leader is the coil. Once he is lit up, he gets everybody else aligned in the same direction.

S: In human dynamics, the leader is that energy, vision, direction—all that encompasses leadership in his person, am I right?

J: It is the influence that person has in that organisation, in that situation. I am of the firm belief that everyone cannot possess it. Firstly, one requires mastery in his domain science.

S: Of what are you the master?

J: Seeing through a problem, visualising the end result, removing filters and lenses, which mask or distort true picture and objective.

S: Where does your drive come from?

J: Self-satisfaction largely, and marginally, from the appreciation shown by peers.

S: A touch of philosophy brings contentment in our reciprocal gestures. Of all the obstacles you had to face, the hardest to overcome was…?

J: Ability in myself. But this reduced with time, as I went from strength to strength. I overcame it through increasing self-confidence, and through the realisation that *I have to continue learning all the time. I am never shy of the phrase, "I do not know"*. I have not learnt to use computers though: not interested because there are others to do the job for me.

Twenty-five years back one of my assistants took out his pocket calculator, put it in front of me and said, "Sir if you feel my figures are incorrect, would you like to check them yourself?" I pushed the calculator back to him and quipped, "I do not know how to operate that. And in any case, you young folks are there to do it for me". With a mischievous smile he put the calculator back in his pocket and said, "Sir you told us that executives should be constant learners!" We both lustily cheered that piece of conversation and called for coffee.

Jamshed is a metallurgist who has demonstrated through his performance, the effective qualities of leadership in communication, innovation, credibility, change management, and turnaround strategy, to name a significant few. Together, they mean transforming the ingredients of leadership to a higher grade, like lower grade coal to higher grade coke. He appears to have applied the same thinking process to his leadership upgradation.

Therefore the metallurgy of leadership here, means the methods and techniques a leader uses in leading people to achieve the desired organisational goals. Such a leader uses technical language, and provides a technical method for achieving a practical purpose. This is very true when one is dealing with IIT, REC, IIM graduates, or for that matter, the entire mass of graduates coming out from our educational system. One has to speak the lingo they are accustomed to hearing, and comfortable in dealing. The users and listeners share a meaning. In addition, there is a pure technical jargon in each discipline, and it varies from marketing to production, and so forth.

Also, each industry and company has it's own flavour. A shared vocabulary comes into existence within, and among industries. And in multilingual India, one also encounters a local hybrid lexicon. A leader cannot afford to be naïve to these changes, which have become major requirements in making communication effective. Several managers do not expand their lexicon beyond their functional expertise, and thus unknowingly, raise a bar to their promotion to general management.

In Beyond the Hype, Robert G. Eccles and Nitin Nohria (1992) have noted, that real change depends upon new use of language of persuasion. Words matter. Words hurt; words heal. By using correct words and phrases, one frames situations in a way that can influence others to take certain actions. The eminent scholar of organisations, Karl Weick, said that we need to translate organisational action into the language of individuals.

When Jamshed illustrated the deep thought he was giving that morning to the handling of a particular meeting, he was in fact considering what not to say, and how to say what was essential. It was important to choose the right words, in order to address properly the sensitivities of the players in the drama. And all this was necessary to achieve a certain result from those discussions. It shows the time a thoughtful leader devotes to developing that competency to handle delicate issues deftly.

One has to admit that sometimes situations throws up a leader in the right position at the right time. Jamshed has put in a lot of emphasis on the need for a leader to earn respect, and on building credibility.

S: How did you build credibility?

J: If you ask me, the one significant factor of my success as a leader, or what the leader must have, is, in one word, *credibility*—not knowledge, not strength, not discipline—I mean all those one must have, but without credibility they carry little meaning and weight.

S: What are the ingredients of credibility?

J: Consistency in thought, process, and action. He will do what he says he will—walk his talk—call it what you like. When a person writes to you, you must promptly send a reply even if it is an interim one, or close the loop by giving a touch of finality to whatever you want to convey.

The Managing Director of Kodak, Humayun Dhanrajgir, told me that he had to find a way to work in the vast wired network of Kodak, which was very different from Glaxo, where he spent the bulk of his career. His mailbox would be full every morning and he was expected to respond promptly. That was Kodak culture.

Kodak is an American corporation, and Glaxo, British. The speed tracks are different. The economy, competition, composition of the work force, their age groups, and the cultures are different. How did Humayun cope up? In his words, "I discovered the art of giving an interim response, a technique to create space". (Pandit, S., 2001)

Humayun's credibility amongst employees and in management circles has always been high. The technique used by two eminent CEOs Jamshed and Humayun, is here for us to see. One who wants to become an effective leader, needs to master it, period.

Correlates of Performance

There are many competencies embedded in a successful CEO, which we must decipher for our benefit. Entrepreneurial competence is one such. It is first and foremost, a search for opportunity—where is the business, the chance to earn money. Often Jamshed spotted opportunities through a study of other economies. In that study, he used techniques of forecasting what India would need in it move forward. He is a keen observer of local markets, and felt they lacked both, content and systems. It is the strength of the entrepreneurs, that they first locate gaps in existing markets, in products and services, and look out to make an entry into the future on the basis of scenarios and forecasts. Initially for Jamshed, the framework was India; later it became global.

It was difficult for Jamshed to pinpoint where this entrepreneurial competency originated in him. He gained a little in his early life abroad, and a little through translating observations into 'present day' situations. He took enormous risks in some cases, as in converting low quality coal to high quality coke, where the total investment was to the tune of Rs 1,500–1,800 crore. Failure would have meant severe hardship on TISCO operations. So chances of failure had to be reduced to the bare minimum during the 'preparation' stage, and commercial viability had to be determined through analyses and discussions. It is understood: this is organisational entrepreneurship, but a credible leader at the front, undoubtedly puts his head on the block.

J: It took some six years for pilot plant experimentation, and another eight years for final and full implementation, after they changed the parameters. Simultaneously, the organisation slimmed from 72,000 to 45,000. The sheer size and complexity of these operations are mind boggling.

In the hey days of union supremacy, when the unions dictated the terms on how organisation operations would be run, it was well nigh impossible to make any paradigm shift in the adversarial relationship between union and management. There are few exceptions and TISCO was one such. In this respect Jamshed provided an example of his out of box thinking and out of mould actions in Jamshedpur.

J: We never sprang any surprises on union leaders. In fact we informed them in advance of any severe actions to be taken. We made a fundamental shift in treating them as partners and not combatants. When we launched our quality movement, I coined a slogan, *Cost of Quality is immaterial, Cost of Poor Quality is much higher.*

In the performance–success–achievement matrix, we find there is a contribution of factors like luck, chance, competencies—skill set and attitudes, and teams of colleagues, bosses, and subordinates. In his case Jamshed believes, the composition looks like, luck—2%, Competencies—49%, and Teams—49%. His definition of luck—where preparation meets with opportunity. You will observe the negligible weight given to luck.

This pattern of thought is seen in most of the successful business leaders I have met. Percentages given to different elements differ. They do not disregard luck, as it plays a part. However, they feel no control over it. These leaders prefer to talk about that which can be practised, controlled, and which will lead to better results. More specifically, they engage in discussions about competencies, teams, their contribution, and performance. They believe in Drucker's dictum: what get measured, gets managed. *This is how it should be.*

How to Develop Leaders

The need to develop outstanding leaders, like Jamshed, is unquestionably high. Many well run organisations have systematic training and development programmes. Quite a few are well structured and methodically conducted. Leadership is learned through experience on the job. Training helps develop new skills. Genetics and nurturance also play a part in leadership development. The first advantage definitely goes to positive genetic predisposition. However, there is agreement among researchers and practitioners, that these deficiencies can be corrected with intensive formal training, and by providing challenging assignments, especially those that involve hardship and conflicts.

There is abundant evidence that the transformational–situational–nurturant style of leadership, proves effective in the Indian milieu. Challenging assignments build self-confidence, toughness, and ability to manage interpersonal relations more adroitly. Hardships reveal personal limits. Ambitious managers crave to learn more about creativity, to make breakthroughs. Their preparedness is an omen of maturing leadership competencies. This occurs through sustained exposure to international and industry forums, and personal mentoring.

However there is a gap in our knowledge about the insights Indian leaders have on leadership development. We need to fill it through leaders like Jamshed who are prepared to share their insights.

S: *What insight can you share about developing people, into leaders like you?*

J: I think, if the person is disciplined and analytical enough to find out where he is going, he will find the path. I have done that throughout my career—a systematic study of my progress. After you have developed a long term perspective, you get down to managing the micro level. I am disciplined in preparing for a meeting. I decide every morning what is it I want to achieve that day. One should be able to programme oneself and think about one's idea and activities wherever one is.

S: *In India, the house of Tata is the oldest conglomerate of industrial organisations. Its durability is priceless, brand immutable. You can bet on Tata shares. This sustainability for over hundred years, came from leaders with vision, commit-*

ment, entrepreneurship, and skills in building institution. The difference now and in the bygone era, is global scale, competitive markets, technological advances, and the speed trajectory; internet revolution has changed it. In this changed scenario, what would you like to include in the syllabus of leader development as the subject of top priority to sustain Tata durability?

J: It is a matter of values, isn't it Shrinivas? We do not go against, even a grain, of our value system. We talked about the problems we faced. There are certain things that cannot be written in black and white. There are shades of grey. We must imbibe as a religious diktat that we shall not cross the line. Come what may, we shall stick to our values.

S: There is no question that every organisation should make the inculcation of values, top priority. In any case, it has become a globally important topic, in view of brazen looting of public money, frauds, and what have you. It has shaken the confidence of the public and corporate world. Let's say there is a professional manager who doesn't have your kind of background, nurturance, mentors, and an organisation like TISCO. What should he do?

J: The first thing he should do is find an icon. I had JRD and my father in my personal life, and professionally, JRD was my father. So find an icon and follow him.

S: Ok, understood. We also know we should develop two things. One, attitude, and two, competency.

J: And the third is discipline.

S: A certain drill is prescribed for inculcating discipline. What is the drill for the development of attitudes and competencies?

J: The discipline of what is right and wrong. Practice with right attitudes when the chips are down. If on a lunch table, somebody is having chicken, you need not have it if it does not suit you. Competencies are a certain set of skills, and some discipline will be prescribed which must be adhered to.

S: Discipline involves giving up something, and strict monitoring of whatever you undertake to do or not do.

J: To understand the concept, let me give you a simple example, which I followed for a while. I am very fond of food, and I like non-vegetarian dishes. For personal reasons I decided to give up non-vegetarian food for a year and I announced it to the family. Believe me, my willpower was stretched to the limit. During the last month particularly, I would constantly go to the fridge, open it, and see if I could eat this or that, and then with great restraint close it without touching any of the stuff. My children would joke, "What is going to happen to the world if you eat, come on dad".

S: *So you went on a kind of a fast.*

J: No.

S: *You practised a kind of self-denial advocated in every religion and all philosophies.*

J: No. I did not deny myself anything.

S: *You did. For example, if I want to concentrate on improving my value system I must deny myself two hours I spend on what I like, say music. The principle emerges that to the exclusion of everything else, I will concentrate on what I have decided to devote time.*

J: Yes, that I think is a very strong point.

S: *And that is discipline.*

J: Something that has got to be done. Right from my research days in UK to tackling a particular problem in TISCO, I have burnt the midnight oil. After resolving the situational problems, I slept well.

S: *These ingredients—self-discipline, attitude development, and competency building—lead to a change in mindset. You must have encountered obstacles at the middle level, and I suppose elsewhere also. How did you manage the frustration, to control your emotions?*

J: Often in the beginning, I used to blow my fuse. This is one way of releasing frustration. People would know I was not doing it for personal reasons, it was situational. However offensive the behaviour was, they would still think they deserved it.

S: You bet they did.

In Learning to Lead, Jay A. Cogner (1992) comes to a very useful conclusion from his survey of training practices, about transforming managers into leaders. He notes, "It should be clear that to be effective, leadership training must incorporate all four approaches: personal growth experiences, conceptual development, feedback, and skill building. Each integrates and builds upon the other".

Jamshed's contribution to these process issues is immense. His emphasis on self-discipline, inculcation of values, and last but not the least, in spotting an icon and following him, is very strong. The latter requires one to launch an intensive and creative search. It is difficult to spot an icon, and like millions one may only succeed in not finding one. But the search itself is a great learning experience.

The Model Change Agent

Jamshed's style of leadership was pioneering. He believes, "I look upon myself as The Change Agent for TISCO". He is approachable but does not consider himself a mild father figure. In the change management also, one encounters the dilemma of the Bell Curve. Those who actively seek change

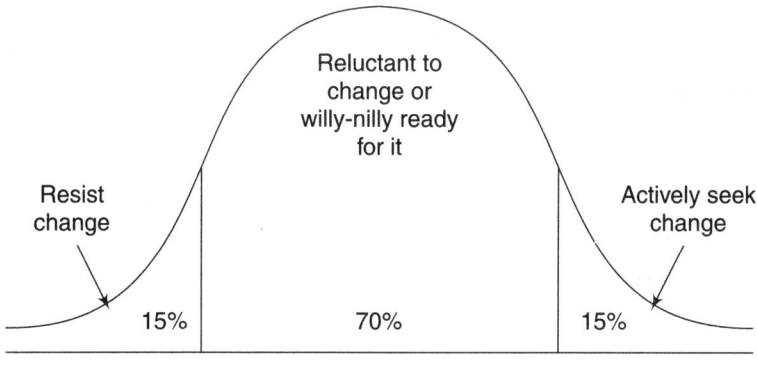

Bell curve

Fig. 2.3 Organisation Population Distribution Indicating Preparedness for Change

and resist change, each form 15 per cent of the population. Those reluctant to change or willy-nilly ready for it, form the middle bulk of 70 per cent. That is what Jamshed faced. He experienced difficulty in getting commitment from the middle management. He reduced their cycle time of response through quality improvement movement.

Strategically, Jamshed first attacked the resistance stronghold of unions and workers. The middle groups saw that grip loosened, and then that unions and workers were beginning to cooperate. That brought incremental changes in the workers' output. Consequently, the reluctance of junior and middle management started waning. The key point is that Jamshed understood it was reluctance not resistance.

Political, social, and religious leaders or saints, get many followers, but business leaders do not. They, like civil servants, and men from armed forces, have many admirers but few followers. Jamshed is no exception. This is a general phenomenon worth investigation. Suffice to note here, that the first category acquires followers because they represent ideals, concerns, and the aspirations of the public. There is an element of shared belief system and feeling of oneness, which provides satisfaction to one's alter ego. They acquire power, which in the beginning at least, is not positional. Whereas the latter category appears distant, and power comes from position. In such long established perceptions however, a select few do reach iconic status—like the legendary JRD Tata. Jamshed prefers to remain in the 'change agent' category with few followers. That in itself is a great achievement.

The change, Jamshed introduced in TISCO, is of monumental proportions. The transformation that he personally underwent in the process, made him a master craftsman of change management. He was trying to pull his inner depths from the old "command and control" style to a new culture of "commitment to partnership". This was as tough as all such transitions are. Such actions embolden the visionary, courageous, and humble leader, to act. And Jamshed did act, didn't he?

The chief learning officer of GE's Crotonville leadership education centre, Steven Kerr notes, *"To be an effective leader, one must be an effective change agent*. That means, giving people a sense of inclusion, helping them understand why change is necessary, and helping them shape the direction of change in their own businesses or departments". The apt saying comes to mind: *people don't resist change, they resist being changed.*

Managers therefore, who choose a systematic approach suitable to their individual company contexts, and combine processes and incentives, can hope to become successful change agents. Jamshed repeated the famous dictum:

Ultimately every CEO must abide by the mantra that God gives me:

- the strength to change what I can
- the humility to accept what I cannot
- the wisdom to know the difference

What impressed me most, was Jamshed's dictum to himself. It is hand written and encased in a thick square acrylic slab, which is put on the bookcase. It enhances the beauty of his office. You would love to read the same:

What I (as CEO) must do:

- *Develop a personal vision—what do I want to accomplish in my life?*
- *Tell the truth about current reality.*
- *Do the tough things no one else wants to do.*
- *Restructure the Top Team, if necessary.*
- *Build a powerful guiding coalition—management and board.*
- *Guide the creation of a shared VISION.*
- *Take the responsibility of being the main change agent.*
- *Create endless opportunities for two-way communications.*
- *Create opportunities for Innovations in the rank and file.*
- *Maintain focus.*
- *Realign HR systems; overcome obstacles.*
- *Model the desired managerial behaviour—above all maintain CREDIBILITY.*
- *Preserve the core values of TATAs (and my own).*

—JJI.

Many organisations want change. Thousands of investors, venture capitalists, and shareholders, wait helplessly for their investments to yield respectable returns. The only hope they might like to explore, is to look for a leader of Jamshed's quality in the company in which they have stakes. If they as alert stakeholders, do not initiate change, who will? They would get an added bonus in such a leader, **a model change agent** who would transform their Non-Performing Assets (NPAs) into Performing Assets (PAs).

★ ★ ★

3

Strategic Insight Stimulates Drive for Achievement

- ❖ The Strategic Grit
- ❖ Design a Comprehensive Strategy
- ❖ Listening Leads to Insight
- ❖ Intuition Nurtures Strategic Insight

- ◆ Exemplar—A Strategic Thinker, Mallika Srinivasan

"Insight and a consequent drive for achievement, often amounting to a sense of mission, fuel a thought process which is basically creative and intuitive rather than rational... Great strategies, like great works of art or great scientific discoveries, call for technical mastery in the working out, but originate in insights that are beyond the reach of conscious analysis."

—Kenechi Ohmae
The Mind of the Strategist

Introduction

This chapter explains how thought leaders develop strategic grit through bewildering issues, and direct their organisations to achieve healthy growth. The design and listening skills lead them to heart of the matter—the coolant that nurtures strategic insight.

The Strategic Grit

Grit means, unyielding courage in the face of hardship when the organisation is threatened by danger. It could be internal, as in a labour revolt, or in-fighting at the top; an external threat, like severe competition, or a natural calamity; or a combination of the two. If the leader has grit, then the firmness of mind and spirit will be seen in action, in the face of adverse factors.

At such junctures, a leader has to unravel the scheme beneath the forces at play, that might be challenging the vision and shaking the foundation of the institution. The undercurrents may point to tectonic shifts in markets, technology, or geopolitical ground realities. In such situations, a leader is required to question assumptions on which the business may have been carried on until then. Such a search might lead to the identification of a paradigm shift—a call that the leader has to take.

What is the guiding mechanism that a leader can depend on? Forecasting, trend analysis, opinion polls, or any system of assessment of what future holds, has no dependable, predictive value. Quantitative methods and mechanistic approaches alone, are proving inadequate for management to design growth strategies. They are as good or bad as the weather forecasts. The leader might study them but cannot depend upon them. He has to access alternatives to obtain a glimpse of what the future holds.

It has also become imperative for the leader to integrate the visions of all stakeholders, not those of shareholders alone. These stakeholders have become significant in the knowledge driven economy. The young knowledge workers have value-adding visions to share, which must be considered with the seriousness they deserve. Ideas, aspirations, skills, and motivation of employees, gird the direction an organisation takes. Their involvement also ensures implementation and accountability.

A leader is required to conceive a strategy for the future. In *Competing for the Future,* Prof. C. K. Prahalad writes:

> *Competing for the future means maintaining continuity by ensuring that the company is constantly creating new sources of profit. It is about competing for opportunity share rather than market share. You have to look at the company as a portfolio of competencies.*
>
> (Hamel, G. and C. K. Prahalad, 1996)

Strategic architecture is a broad agenda for acquiring and leveraging new competencies, deploying new functionality, and reconfiguring the customer interface.

In selecting strategy, the leader uses the broad agenda, data, and views of relevant others. The tool he uses is scenario planning, because it ensures people involvement, pooling in of ideas, and a chance to share visions. The leader provides direction with a position paper, and participants have the freedom to debate by giving shape to their aspirations and beliefs. Management creates the forum where coherent exploration of possibilities and building alternative scenarios, can take place based on new assumptions.

According to *James A Ogilvy*, co-founder of Global Business Network, scenario planning is not a tool for making predictions (Ogilvy, 2002). Rather, it is a tool for better decision making, a qualitative new way of thinking. It does not contain a mass of statistical data or formulae to predict the future. The future remains as unpredictable as ever. This practice of building scenarios, enables management to move away from dependence on the judgement of a single person, a hero, to a 'leader and his team'—*more than one, less than all*.

In *Creating Better Futures*, Ogilvy (2002) uses his rich experience of scenario planning techniques in observing:

> *I have become convinced that positive scenarios, normative scenarios, and scenarios that lift our sights and inspire our hopes, are far more effective than pessimistic morality plays, at moving people towards a voluntary history. Negative scenarios are psychologically difficult to entertain, but intellectually easy to create.*

The difference a positive scenario builder can make, like Mashelkar did at the Council for Scientific and Industrial Research (CSIR) when he took over as its Director General in 1995, is worth narrating. CSIR is a lumbering scientific giant, with 40-odd laboratories and 80 field centres engaged in fundamental and applied research in the whole gamut of science and technology.

Mashelkar put in place the architecture of "Vision 2001 and Strategy". The white paper, prepared in full consultation with the CSIR family, set the organisation's goals, measurable targets, and a road map to reach the vision. He involved directors of all 40 labs in preparing the vision document. He said, "I want them to feel that Vision 2001 is not my brain-child—it's theirs, and they must own it".

If the source of technology is in science, then that source is rooted in knowledge. Mashelkar, a scientist, became the visionary CEO of a network of research establishments in the knowledge era. He galvanised the 10,000-odd scientific community to think anew. "Team CSIR" spirit made research, business oriented. The lab directors were made the change agents of their individual fields. Ratan Tata, in a private meeting, said, "It is a unique corporate-like document from a public funded organisation, which is both bold and visionary" (Pandit, S., 2001).

In restructuring CSIR, attempting the mindset change was not easy. It was a relatively easy task to move the scientific community out of torpor, but not so the unions. Mashelkar had to face a situation where the government worked according to union dictates. He developed the strategic grit by bringing the lab directors and scientific community on his side first. They were committed to the new direction that they were setting for themselves. Mashelkar functioned like the CEO of a commercial organisation, and succeeded in moving the government monolith forward, in a professional manner.

Another example is that of Ratan Tata who, in 1991, took over the reins of Tata Group from his uncle, the legendary JRD Tata. The group is a confederation of different companies, which are run independently by powerful managing directors (MDs). The MDs were heavyweights in there own right. They are accountable to the board and not to the holding company, Tata Sons. Knowledge of the impending change at Bombay House (Headquarters of Tata Group), since JRD had aged, had the CEOs jockeying for power. It was the topic of business circle conversations.

Ratan Tata came from Nelco—which was not the star of the group. Senior chiefs were not obliged to report to him. He was faced with:

(a) establishing his authority,

(b) restoring the health of many companies,

(c) maintaining the cohesion of the group, and

(d) pushing the group forward to reach its potential in the post liberalised era.

The strength of the group lies in its shared vision and values. Though initially it had a dominance of Parsi ownership, it is the most cosmopolitan and professionally managed business group in India. Neither could it derive any benefits of a family run organisation (JRD was not in that sense the *karta* of the family) nor advantages if any, of regional or language dominance. The source of executive authority lay more in the persona of JRD, which Ratan Tata had to acquire. He had barely time to settle in the chair before he was required to face the storm. Globalisation, technological advances, and internet do not offer solutions to problems of cooperation and collaboration. Traditional boundaries were blurred. New processes had taken over and functioned across boundaries.

In such a transitional situation, leaders were expected to acquire new styles of managing overlaps and resources that are not under their direct control. They had to set direction despite several unprecedented changes, reconcile interests of different stakeholders, and coordinate the network of organisations outside their authority. Such leaders were not sufficiently available within the Tata group. Therefore, management hired people from outside, and acculturated them to Tata values. This put into place cross-functional teams which moved on different agendas.

Ratan Tata had to address the deeper issues of leaders' motivation embedded in conflicts of personality, and in power equations. He had to put it all together. It was the toughest challenge he had to face. Writing about leaders in his excellent book *Shaping the Future*, Arun Maira (2002), observed that:

> *They have to get people to collaborate: people divided by organisational boundaries, by differences in beliefs... expertise...perspectives. They have to lead many people to learn together. And they themselves need to learn to lead in such complex situations...Their twin challenge is "leading to learn" and "learning to lead".*

While 'learning to lead', Ratan Tata developed strategic grit. He:

- was at the front, to lead the group
- used consulting firms to get fresh ideas

- had teams brainstorm to present alternative scenarios for the future
- had the gut feel about what was 'wanted'
- rekindled the spirit through Tata's durable alchemy—its shared vision and values
- sought value addition from young and new entrants by sharing their visions and ideas
- kept a check on obstructionists and nay-sayers

The Tata shine is back on cars, trucks, steel, and other businesses. After weathering the internal storm and external turbulence for 13 years, the future Ratan Tata shaped for his group has arrived and looks more promising.

Similarly Jamshed Irani, TISCO, Venu Srinivasan, TVS, and his wife Mallika, TAFE, played pivotal roles in transforming their organisations. They used methods and tools like:

- consulting organisations, building scenarios, and reengineering business for clarifying and resetting vision, values, goals, and strategy
- employee involvement in the rejuvenation process, by forming multidisciplinary task forces and opening up new communication channels
- change process, facilitated by removing hurdles

These leaders were able to develop strategic grit because of:

- a deep understanding of macro level shifts in alliances between technology, markets, shrewd business minds, and geo-political realities
- their ability to gauge its impact on their business, and to share it with colleagues
- their readiness to form cross-functional teams, and assign specific tasks in preparing position papers on how to move forward by removing bottlenecks
- focus on implementation

- a large network of contacts and easy access to information
- their minds, which were constantly engaged in listening, scanning data, processing information, and looking for opportunities to forge fruitful alliances for the growth of their organisation
- an uncanny ability in influencing people, decisions, events, and direction
- an immense patience to fight drawn out battles and adverse circumstances.

To make the strategy work one requires a well thought out plan, a document, in place. Courage alone, will not help achieve the objectives.

Design a Comprehensive Strategy

Strategy requires considerable out of box thinking. It requires dismantling boxes, and removing, to a large extent, departmental boundaries and interpersonal barriers. Organisational boundaries (and also those within an organisation), have become porous and permeable, allowing an exchange of ideas and actions. Organisations now function through interlocking circles (task forces, etc), rather than through hierarchical organisation trees.

Strategy is designed by integrating inputs from a variety of sources, including the views of a large sample of employees from across the organisation. It is not only collation of data but alignment of vision, values, and goals. It is a fusion of aspirations, ideas, and the human striving to realise them, with different scenarios and projections of quantified data. Management decides to invest its resources in such collectively crafted strategy.

Maira found that leaders really needed a strategy formulation process, designed to scan, sense, fire, observe, adjust, and fire again. It is a process of rapid and effective learning, requiring quick reflexes, and the flexibility to meet, if not accurately anticipate, change in all its various forms.

This of course applies when you are acting from a 'reactive mode'. In a 'proactive mode', *producing change is about 80 percent leadership—establishing direction, aligning, motivating, and inspiring people; about 20 percent is management—planning, budgeting, organising, and problem solving.*(Kotter, Joh, P., 1999).

Successful leaders (like Azim Premji, Kumar Managalam Birla, Mukesh and Anil Ambani, Anji Reddy, and similar others) exhibit a grasp over a wide range of issues that occupy the global space at the macro level, and organisations at the micro level. They create space for their teams to craft comprehensive and competitive strategies.

While creating such a strategy, the teams take into account the following factors:

- vision, mission, and goals
- emerging global standards
- regional shifts, similar to those happening in Asia at present
- international and domestic markets with shifting boundaries as a paradigm change
- homogenised and/or niche consumer cultures
- impact of IT, media, brands, patents, WTO, deregulation, privatisation, and environmental concerns
- corporate and SBU growth
- SWOTs of finance, production, marketing, technological advances, people talent, and learnability
- competitors' SWOTs of investments, products, services, and marketing
- opportunity analysis of contacts, alliances, and geopolitical movements

- internal tightening—cost saving, general economy drives, destruction and introduction of products, trimming organisational limbs
- benchmarking innovation in quality of products and services with focus on customers

These factors can be grouped and named differently in each organisation. The purpose is to prepare a comprehensive strategy for execution. If one already has a strategy one needs to review it to face emerging realities, and tighten the processes where execution may have failed. If all this still does not work one needs to get in fresh inputs from consultants.

Rosabeth Moss Kanter advises leaders who hope to guide their companies toward world-class standards, to rethink their strategies (1983). They must accumulate the three assets of world-class: concepts, competence, and connections. People don't become assets until what they know is deployed on behalf of the customer. They must perform professionally, collaborate openly, and be innovative.

Unless mental models of the leaders and senior managers, are defined on what new values to introduce, plans for strategic innovation will not produce a sustainable advantage. Safe quotes of precedent and linear extrapolation do not rescue leaders, uncommon wisdom does.

While taking all these factors into account what one imagines one can contribute in one's specialty becomes important. The whole is larger than the sum of its parts. The design skills come from one's creative self. The skill lies in conceiving and making new patterns in machines, workflow, logistics, distribution reach, supply chains, finish, colour scheme, shape, etc. The new method, device, arrangement, product, or service must stand tests in efficiency, cost saving, user friendliness, flow, aesthetics, and all put together, value addition.

As a designer, the leader:

- does the conceptual mapping of strategy in creating space for expansion, penetration, deconstruction, and reconstruction

- periodically recharges the batteries of the human side of enterprise by sharing vision and aligning their interests
- envisions products, services, and strategic timing, to lift up the spirit of the organisation

Listening Leads to Insight

An interesting find from the interviews for my previous book *Thought Leaders*, was that the leaders were not very good listeners in the beginning. They gradually overcame this weakness to an extent but felt the need to improve further. Said Lao-tzu, *"Knowing the constant gives an impartial perspective"*. If leaders believe that people constantly make a significant difference in the knowledge driven economy, then it is incumbent on them to cultivate the art of listening because listening is a gateway to heart.

In the last two decades, there has been a marked shift towards emphasising the need to listen. This change has come about because the command and control style of leadership has become unworkable (except in emergency or severe crisis). It has been replaced by a nurturing style of leadership, which is democratic, team dependent, and relationship centric.

To a question, "What one thing have you learnt?" Gary Hamel replied, "It's to talk less and listen more." In listening, you acknowledge the other person, and his point of view. You enhance his self-worth. It is the listening manager who stands better prospects of filling the top leadership slot.

Manoj Tirodkar, Managing Director, Global Tele-Systems says, "If change is the only constant, then learning and listening are it's other constants" (Pandit, S., 2001). It means 'learning' and 'listening' are context invariant attributes. If leaders do not have time for conversation, they lose touch. There is no opportunity for dialogue.

In communication, the correct practice is to periodically confirm whether what you have heard and understood is correct or not. It gives the speaker the confidence that he is being listened to with respect, and that efforts to understand him are genuine. Intent listening conveys empathy, which is the foundation for establishing a trustworthy relationship.

I remember that from the 70s to the 90s programmes on the art of communication were much in demand. Speakers used to emphasise the importance of listening in communications, but more focus was given to: establishing understanding and trust, conveying the message briefly and accurately, using correct words and body language, and developing meaningful relationships.

I have found that people come for consultation and counselling because they are satisfied after I listen to them. In fact, the problems for which they come are often sidelined; they are content to have found a willing listener. Since the purpose of the visit must not be lost sight of, I continue the dialogue and make some tentative, alternative suggestions: in other words, I make an effort to bring back the focus. But it proves to be in vain in several cases. The reason is simple, the persons have already moved into a non-listening mode.

Intent listening means hearing with thoughtful attention, which evokes the heart centre. You move between the facts and feelings of an other person. Where attention goes, energy flows. In your gestures and body language, you convey that your energy is directed towards knowing what the other has to say; that you value his observations, opinions, knowledge, and experience. It is a dialogue. This process builds the self-esteem of both parties.

You may have attended meetings dominated by active talkers. It should not worry you so long as you have meaningfully communicated, absorbed, and implemented what was essential. Good listening opens options and increases negotiating power because it provides more information about another's interests. As an intent listener, I have been able to identify more clearly, areas of agreement and disagreement in contentious union negotiations. Many sales colleagues have vouched that, that this is also their experience.

Listening enables leaders to connect emotionally, establish rapport, and create resonance. The following examples come to mind where such abilities created the bond to get results:

- **Listening Organisation**—Mallika Srinivsan made listening, a part of organisation culture

- **Organisation Change**—Jamshed Irani evoked a response from people while shaking the giant TISCO. He became a model change agent by changing himself first

- **Talent Management**—I have seen how Kiran Mazumdar-Shaw connects emotionally with her staff. It cued me to the glue in Biocon: it was Kiran, who built interpersonal relationships from scratch

- **Leadership through Personal Hardship**—After the sudden demise of her husband Rohinton, Anu Aga had to take over the reins of the engineering and environment major, Thermax.

Intent listening brings about an emotional impact. Goleman describes that the new leader is likely to be a limbic 'attractor', exerting a palpable force on the emotional brains of the people around her.

In *A Vedic Consecration to the Spiritual Heart,* Vamadeva Shastri explains the significance of link between listening and heart:

> *What is important is to learn to merge our speech, breath, mind, eye, ear, and other faculties into the heart. Whatever we trace to its origins takes us back to heart, whether it is the thought-current, the breath-current, the current of attention through listening, or the place of focus of perception (the eye).*

This return to the heart, many prophets have stated, is the return to our true origin and to the Self.

Whether the leader believes it or not, listening leads to heart, and heart leads to insight.

Intuition Nurtures Strategic Insight

Each person has intellect, intuition, and insight—the content and quality however differs. Only the person can rate himself on this score. When Venu Srinivasan carefully listened to the advice he was getting from old hands at TVS, he realised that he could not dictate others on mere intuition. He needed a rational process to realise what he intuitively knew was realisable.

In psychology and metaphysics, intuition is treated as a verifiable phenomenon. It is known that intuition arrives spontaneously but rather slowly. It provides direction. Even scientists like Einstein have acknowledged the role intuition plays in the discovery of new phenomena. In the information age when you are inundated with a welter of facts and opinions, leaders know that they need developed intuition to guide them. Many leaders have shared with me their experiences of intuition in their lives.

R. Gopalkrishnan, President, All India Management Association, puts it beautifully in *The Changing Fabric*:

> *Businessmen, like chess players, find that problems can, in theory, have many solutions, but there is only so much time available to find solutions. This is where intuition comes into play. It gives the benefit of the holistic approach to problem solving and reflects the value of cumulative experience.*
>
> (*Business Standard*, 2004)

Time and again, leaders have emphasised that the use of intuition is the differentiator. No matter how advanced and powerful the technology becomes, it can never be a substitute for intuition.

Both intuition and insight, emanate from the heart centre (*hridaya—anahata chakra*). It is the faculty of attaining direct knowledge without rational inference, a mode of understanding without conscious thought or judgement. Both provide responses to subtle cues in complex situations. Both are interchangeably used, and commonly understood as carrying the same meaning. This is not incorrect. There is however, a slight difference, which should not be ignored. Intuition is more holistic, and connotes expanse. Insight, on the other hand, is more penetrating, shows depth, apprehends inner nature of things, restructures patterns, and envisages new relationships relevant to the solution.

To gain insight, is to become aware of some fact about ourselves that we have not been conscious before, or to look at some aspect of external reality in a different way. It entails change in perspective, replacing an old way of viewing something with a new standpoint. The change in perception leads to a fundamentally different state of mind and manner in which we experience ourselves.

Such a change may come about after a period of severe stress, depression, or an unbearable loss whether in business or personal life. In *Choices,* Frederic F Flach says, "It is no coincidence that the development of insight is triggered by a shift in one's equilibrium—a stress—significant enough to induce pain".

We must understand that it is the job of pain to awaken our insight. In *The Brilliant Function of Pain,* Milton Ward (1977) writes, "Pain is a warning system. It is also an efficient guiding system. More often than not, the cure for problem is indicated by pain. We search for cures everywhere while our brilliant inner nature is pointing to specific action". Pain and problem perform the same function, to point towards a malfunctioning in the system, of which one must take note, and act.

Mallika Srinivasan's insightful look into the agony caused by demand in market, led her to find a solution within the organisation. She reconfigured internal processes, enforced thrift, and reoriented the mindset of people. The external danger led her to deep introspection, which eventually spurred insight. If a leader ignores warnings, the organisation is doomed to failure. Mallika heeded the warnings and therefore TAFE sailed safely.

As noted earlier the centre of origin is heart. And the heart of matter is *love*. Saints and gurus appeal to our hearts and we are inspired to undertake causes dear to us. This is not what is expected of business leaders. They operate in the transactional culture of the commercial world, where people assets cannot be mobilised by homilies on asceticism.

Within the framework of business game rules, without infringing on the code of conduct, a leader can express affection to build rapport, motivate, and get results. The earlier leadership styles were somewhat dry and spiritless. People were looking for inspiring styles. Daniel Goleman's findings, based on brain research, shows that new leaders require emotional intelligence to inspire. One doesn't get that intelligence unless one has a silent stream of knowledge about spiritualism flowing through him.

Although sermons are ridiculed, simplicity, and private asceticism (culturally owned and adored leadership style in Asia) is very much revered. It appeals to hearts and helps build public assets. Insightful leaders communicate from the bottom of heart. That insight, which is nurtured by heart, makes impact.

However, in bringing insight to fruition you require analysis. The ability to synthesise unrelated phenomena is far more important. Plain hard work, method, and discipline are required for the process to ripen. The USP of insight is *timing*. When to share the idea, when to get people committed to it, and when to stretch schedules for achieving results, have all to be timed perfectly. Each move is strategic.

No one can claim that he has reduced strategic success to a formula. It is not possible. You cannot become a strategic thinker by reading a book on strategy or attending a seminar on it. These are habits of the mind, and modes of thought, that can be acquired only through practice of the creative power of the subconscious. This enables one to improve one's competence in designing winning strategic concepts.

Ratan Tata and Kumar Manglam Birla, have shown true grit in strategically spearheading their organisations, through an admixture of different problems, to a new stature. Simone Tata showed great insight in moving from cosmetics to retailing at the most appropriate time. Prathap Reddy similarly, gave a glimpse of his strategic insight when he left his lucrative medical practice to venture as an entrepreneur in hospital business. Vaman Kamath displayed great strategic insight in moving ICICI out of project finance business to a financial supermarket with global ambitions.

Mallika Srinivasan was at her best when she tactically abstained from pushing tractors in the market, and used that time instead to revamp the organisation and re-enter with new models. With great insight she designed a comprehensive strategy for TAFE's rejuvenation.

A Strategic Thinker—Mallika Srinivasan

Tractors and Farm Equipment Limited (TAFE)—TO: Rs 970 crore, Assets: Rs 547 crore—has listened to the heartbeats of a farmer and turned them to the heartbeats of a tractor's engine. A hugely successful tractor organisation TAFE has at its helm, Director Mallika Srinivasan, known as the Tractor Queen of India.

"The more competent teams you build, the more you realise how much competence you need."

The Tractor Queen

Business India described Mallika Srinivasan, Director, TAFE as *'Tractor Queen'*. I had read about TAFE's progressive strides in the field of tractors. Mallika's leadership in revamping TAFE has been recognised by industry leaders and journalists. I was therefore looking forward to meeting this short, petite, Wharton graduate who made a name in the male bastion, and in the business of making and selling tractors at that!

My gender-biased association instantly unrolled Finance, Banking, Advertising, HR, Marketing, IT, Pharmaceuticals, and Beauty Care as vocationally and temperamentally compatible fields for ladies, despite the fact that ladies have left hardly any field as exclusive preserve for men. That said, I could not resist thinking of what Mallika was doing in this emotionally dry and unattractive masculine field.

Mallika's secretary, the cordial and helpful Balaji took me to her office. The first thing I noticed was the delicate looking furniture, which made the atmosphere light. As she moved forward to shake hands, her beaming smile brightened the room. In her gold embroidered, black *salwar kameez*, Mallika looked smart. Petite as she is, she fitted my mental gallery of beautiful princesses from Thailand and Malaysia. While exchanging pleasantries she made me feel that we knew each other.

Nurturing the Winners

Mallika grew up in a traditional business family, where grandfather Anantharamkrishnan, founder of Amalgamation Group (29 companies with a turnover of Rs 3,000 crore), and its current Chairman, her father Sivasailam, had a 24-hour menu for business discussions! Not surprising then that Mallika's daughter Laxmi, raises her eyebrows, drops her shoulders, and mischievously mutters, "Mom, has everything got to lead to tractors and TAFE?"

Mallika was nurtured in the value set of love, honesty, integrity, learning, discipline, commitment, piety, and faith in god and gurus. Her teachers and professors reinforced these values with rigour. Mallika's mother encouraged her, and Jayashri Venkatraman her sister, to take an interest in what the patriarchs of the family were doing. The family was not very academically oriented. Her father is a perfectionist and her mother wanted Mallika to graduate in music. She used to tell her, "You have the talent. You must study. If you need help I will give it to you". Mallika read a lot, and was not spoon fed. She joined the President's scout's guide. It was intellectually stimulating, and she became self-reliant.

Her upbringing also shows how a caring and silently ambitious mother, skilfully projects a role for her daughter to adopt. This is a case where a woman wanted to realise through her daughter, her dream of getting education and becoming an achiever like her husband. You see the mother planting the seeds in her daughter through her *wishcraft*. It is the transference of the unfulfilled agenda of desires that takes place in such intimate parent-child dyads in the traditional model.

Parents today are required to give tremendous inputs to their children; nothing of this kind existed in those days. The responsibility falls mostly on mothers, and most noticeably on working mothers these days! They have to train their children to enjoy what they are doing, provide encouragement, and teach that they have to struggle to earn their laurels.

S: What did you specifically do for your children?

M: If you have an issue, guide them; make them more inquisitive, and encourage searching. I tell them, if you have a doubt, proceed to find out, ask other people, don't gloss over, don't give up, struggle. I have seen to it that they don't just mug and scrape through. If they say, "sort of looked into it",

I know they have not. There is only one rule in the house: your work must be diligently done. I can't do your studies, you have to do them neatly, intelligently. Once you understand the subject properly your fundamentals become strong. The habit of thorough preparation has to be firmly inculcated in school and college days. When I find mangers haven't prepared well, I pass the subject back to them.

It is noticeable that an educated mother's emphasis has shifted to instilling habits of curiosity, search, struggle, and most importantly thorough preparation. These are seeds of creativity vital for germinating a career of achievements. This process of mindful development has the potential to produce even a genius.

In *Wishcraft*, Barbara Sher (1983) says, "The environment that creates winners is almost always made up of winners". Mallika's mother asked her to follow the winners—grandfather and father. Mallika guided her own children by emphasising the value of the process that produces winners. It is not suggested that they must have consciously done either to the exclusion of the other. The point to note is that the environment was vibrating with winner streaks.

Learning from the Father

When Mallika's grandfather S. Anantharamakrishnan died in 1964, the mantle fell on her father Sivasailam, who had returned after a few years in the accounting profession in UK. Finance Minister, T. T. Krishnamachari, had then enhanced the estate duty to an astounding 85 per cent, leaving the family with a serious crisis to face.

Mallika's father sought the guidance of the eminent lawyer N. A. Palkhivala; a strong friendship developed between the two men. Though six years later an equitable judgement from the tax authorities was received, Sivasailam was faced with the problem of meeting the huge liability. The challenge successfully met ahead of time and without the disposal of any assets.

At the same time, the judgement was contested by a member of the family who probably sought to use this litigation as a Damocles' sword in order to further his own ambition. Mallika's father, his brother, and Palkhivala, continued to battle until, in 1991, the Supreme Court upheld the original judgement.

During the early 1970s, Amalgamation Group also witnessed a series of industrial disputes—which were on occasion quite violent—adding to the stress of growth; until a cordial atmosphere with a strong accent on productivity was established.

Some characteristics of Sivasailam's leadership that stood out are that he:

(a) was very wise, patient yet very firm, and used a fair approach

(b) had the ability to stay calm during crisis—excellent at handling crises

(c) had total trust in colleagues who were designated to handle and negotiate issues

(d) had the ability to get involvement from all his colleagues

(e) and above all, acquired a very high degree of trust and loyalty from employees, bankers and partners

This was very valuable learning for Mallika.

That was the period in which she grew. As a child, even if one only witnesses the ongoing drama, one picks up values, the right and wrong of issues, and the vagaries of human nature. Mallika understood the undercurrents. The home was secure but the girls had to handle the tension in the family. Everybody was reticent but knew exactly what was happening.

If one is perceptive one develops patience, becomes cool, and learns to deal with stress with one's feet on the ground. One doesn't consciously think about it but one realises.

A lot of energy was spent on this feud. Mallika's father had to go through stretch and stress, run the business, pay taxes, repay loans, what have you. It gave him sensitivity, empathy and compassion on one side, and toughness on the other. In such a tense atmosphere, the lessons are there for those who want to learn. You live the life and learn by it. Hostilities of long duration toughen you.

S: *So you grew up in the shadow of an authority figure.*

M: Whatever you wanted to say, you were required to say it politely. There was a line you could not cross. There was certainly a strong authority and you could not disrespect that authority. They did not enforce discipline but it was understood. The behaviour of the elders, the way they showed commitment to values and took care of you, made you absorb those values. Therefore, we did not resent. If you enforce discipline rather rigidly, children don't accept it. You have to earn the respect. With my mother we would take a bit of liberty.

S: *How did you go to US?*

M: It was my mother who encouraged me. A few favourite professors also supported my going. I got married, had a daughter, and then went to Wharton.

It is interesting to note that Mallika did not loose focus on her interest in higher studies while going through those traumatic years. More interesting is the fact that it is her mother who encouraged that pursuit. Two years of serious studies in a high standard school like Wharton, with a baby to look after, is no easy task. Although she had a nanny, and other support services to take care of her and the house, handling stressful demands on the family front while pursuing her ambition toughened her.

Grit Enables the Realisation of Vision

I wanted to see whether this toughening was evident in Mallika when she was faced with an adverse situation on the job, especially because Amalgamations is a family group and she was working under her father.

Adversity has a binding power. It tests the tensile strength of a leader. *In an interview with Kumar Mangalam Birla in Mumbai, Bill Gates said, "When we interview top level executives, we concentrate on seeing what adverse situation the candidate had faced in his career".*

In the stable era that Indian organisations passed through before liberalisation, I came across very few executives who had faced real tough situations either in the market or within organisations. Inside organisations, the most critical situations were in industrial relations and production. Outside, it was a seller's market. Now that the economy has been opened up, executives with experience in handling situations of fierce competition, and the challenge of globalisation, are becoming available. Such examples are valuable.

S: *In fifteen years you must have faced many ups and downs. Did you face any extraordinary adverse situation?*

M: Oh yes! The last three years have been the most challenging, and at the same time very satisfying. We operate in a very cyclical market. For the first ten years we just grew. The challenges of growth were exhilarating. We expanded the capacity. We developed a completely different set of skills. Then, the tractor market collapsed by a 40–50 per cent drop; the fundamentals were changing. We had huge over capacities. It's what happened to the truck market five years back, but they had only two players. Here, we had many players, and many more are coming in. It was a situation of continuous draught, compounded by the fact that we had surplus food grains. The bottom just fell out of the market. We managed with phenomenal patience.

S: *Was it an agricultural cycle, or a geographical spread, or what?*

M: Most of it was because of fluctuations in agriculture produce, problems of plenty somewhere, or scarcity elsewhere, earthquake, and a combination of things.

S: *Do you do forecasting? Did anybody forecast earthquake in Saurashtra?*

M: Not really. Someone said, forecasting is dead. It is as good or as bad as the weather forecast. We require a very flexible and adaptable approach. We incur maximum expenditure on R&D; so we need to keep other costs down, ourselves trim, and profitable. We keep our vision statement in mind and do not divert resources from long-term goals. We have a system of early sensors to pick up signals of change. Our consultation process at the middle and top level is quite well knit. We keep our system flexible. *Our response time is little because the mindset is responsive.*

S: *What did you learn from adverse situations?*

M: You get more grit. We did not sacrifice our long-term vision, which was documented with the involvement of some seventy managers. It was a thorough exercise. People recommitted to realising it with total dedication. Although the market is known to be cyclical, nobody expected it to take such a sharp turn. Nevertheless we stuck to our vision of the future. In effect, we continued to invest in production engineering, technology, IT, and R&D.

At the AdAsia conference held in Jaipur in November 2003, author of Positioning, *Jack Trout said, "Do not ignore competition. Focus and differentiation are critical in a competitive world and CEOs must be willing to sacrifice something instead of growth". Mallika and her TAFE sacrificed short-term bottomline results but not long-term growth.*

S: *I understand grit gives firmness of mind and spirit—it enabled you to realise your long-term vision. But where did you get the money?*

M: That's the beauty. There was no question of borrowing, not even from the central kitty of Amalgamations. In fact, we gave the kitty its dividends. We had so much extra capacity. We generated the resources internally. It was the fundamental basis on which we faced the crisis. In hindsight, one is amazed to find how much potential there is for internal mopping up. We brought down the breakeven, cut down on all expenses, really tightened our belts.

S: *When an adverse situation develops, it may be necessary to give up things that are expendable. However, it should be a tactical and fighting withdrawal, not a cowardly retreat. Thrift makes economic sense I know, but the competitors must have done the same thing. What was so special about it?*

M: We understood that this was a genuine demand drop, whereas the competitors continued to fill in the pipeline. They pushed tractors into the market, right to the house, even on "pay when able basis". We knew the limits of this phenomenon called "advancing". We took a cut in market share because it was a genuine demand drop. Our ability to say "no" came in handy.

It is always a good idea to pull back temporarily. Such withdrawal, enables one to evaluate the situation calmly and objectively. A leader's foresight unfolds in respecting the authentic drop in customer requirement caused by calamities, and moving backwards until that have passed. It is a mark of strategic sagacity.

S: *You took a reality bite.*

M: Yes. We reduced working capital, dues, and borrowing. We changed our focus completely. We started going to the market place, to the villages. We stepped up our sales teams. From sixty people, we increased the strength to two hundred people, in six months. We changed roles. We walked through India with our dealers. We worked out systems that made dealers go out. We kept our focus on retail marketing, so as not to lose sight of changing ground realities. We turned the crisis into an opportunity for serious learning. We took a holistic view, did not lose sight of our vision, and developed grit and patience in the process.

S: *To make a deal with the reality is to master it in the long term. Did you then intuitively judge the situation?*

M: Of course I had the data, but I also had a macro view. *I had a feel of the pulse, no churning of data.* We went to the market to test whether our perceptions were correct by talking to farmers, dealers, and common people. There is a big picture, a shifting macro level reality, and one has to take the call.

S: *How did you make people think on these new lines?*

M: That was not very difficult because they accepted our diagnosis. We considered "best case–worst case" scenarios. We called our process "Vision to Reality", where we—the top twenty five people—discussed our progress against our vision and values. Necessary changes were incorporated in the light of our collective experience. The problem was to change over to a new way of working, to fit in the new paradigm, removing the distribution approach, and developing the retail focus. So there was no more sitting in the office. It meant going to the dealers, and with them to the fields, to close the deals. It's to re-train, to reset the mindset, and that had been done in sixty days.

About dealing with adversity, J. Paul Getty says:

> True business leaders often give their most important demonstrations of leadership and brilliance, at the very times when they are temporarily forced to go over to the defensive, when they are at bay. And this is precisely what sets them apart, and raises them above the level of other, less successful businessmen.

Draught Ends, Eagles Fly

At appropriate time, TAFE brought in consultants to play a catalytic role. They helped handhold the implementation. They used aggressive project slogans like PACE (Power to Achieve Corporate Excellence), to mobilise internal action. Products like EAGLE were launched with slogans like *"Eagles will fly"*. The whole atmosphere was humming Eagle, Eagle, Eagle!

Another step Mallika took, was to bring in executives from other companies to share their experiences on how they effected, say, cost cutting. It helped because it gave TAFE employees the confidence to do it too. Mallika was always present when wanted—her availability was never an issue.

M: Although, those were the toughest years, they were the best because they taught us so many things.

The issue of 'unknown unknowns' is serious and the leader has to provide an early sensing system for managing the operations. TAFE was sandwiched between technological change and zigzag market. The matrix of constants and variables therefore, called for the formation of flexible multi-skilled teams for all platforms, and also for a variety of projects that needed to be done simultaneously. Flexible teams are so vital for success that one needs to probe deeper to get an insight into its morphing process.

S: *What kind of teams did you build to make the organisation flexible?*

M: *The more competent teams you build, the more you realise how much competence you need.* It is a constantly moving target and the job is never complete. We started breaking down silos and get coordination teams in place—like quality circles, assessment workshops, etc.

S: *Would you please give me an example?*

M: Okay, let's take a recent example of forming a team for the development of a new product. You need the marketing guy to provide the customer perspective, the web designer, the commercial chap, the application fellow, and all of them together, to work seamlessly. All team members needed open minds and the ability to think laterally. To make low cost tractors, or to redefine the market, one requires breakthrough thinking because one is changing the very paradigm on which the market is structured. One must not shoot down an idea just because it does not fit in with one's experience. One has to change mode and show that one is prepared to go into great detail.

S: *It is most difficult to find suitable project leaders for such tasks.*

M: You are right. We recently selected a lady, a senior professional who majored in psychology, to be project leader of a technical project—a product introduction effort. While the team consisted of top quality, highly experienced engineers, the skill we were looking for to augment the design and manufacturing skills was project management expertise and an ability to pull people together and make the team work truly effective, demonstrating the large benefits that can be thus accrued.

S: *Quite a bold decision, to ask a non-technical person to head a technical task force!*

A: The important thing is that the mind should be open and willing to learn new things. Of course, a focused approach, and detailing an honest assessment of where the project stands, are important too. Passion, commitment, and an ability to inspire all team members, are the keys to success. These qualities prompted me to put her in charge. She has to learn a lot, and I am sure she will. To that end, I have made myself a strong technical person, a mentor of the group; and it is working out well.

S: *What kind of skills were you personally required to use, to build such teams?*

M: The key point is that one has to gain credibility. Though my father was there when I joined, I had to gain credibility with my peers through value addition, whether it was in productivity improvement or market penetration. I had to understand the subject thoroughly. People around one teach, but the insights and ideas one develops, must add value. One must inspire them, make them think differently. That's the way to get accepted by very senior people. It was a must.

S: *They must have observed the difference in style, and the fresh views.*

M: Of course, I was required to exercise a high level of social skills. I began to understand that I was there as a part of the team. I learnt their points of views. It meant, leading them to think in terms of solutions, not offer solutions on a platter. One has to first get into a learning mode with them so as to get the grip. Then the teams start functioning on their own. Thereafter, review only the progress.

S: *So your role over the years has, it appears, changed from COO to CEO.*

M: Well, it is transiting from COO to more of CEO responsibilities, like vision, technology, and HR building. I do get involved at times in brainstorming sessions on some particular issues, but then again, it is to ensure that they remain focussed, and do not lose sight of the vision. It ends up driving the implementation process, and seeing to it that the systems are in place. The execution responsibilities are delegated and there is a co-ordination group in place. When the time comes, I will have to formally appoint a COO, which I will do. Today the greatest challenge is HR: get good people, develop them and their internal talent, retain them, build performing teams, and lead from up front. If you have all this under control, you can handle technology.

Over the past three years, TAFE has become flexible. Once it had numerous cross-functional teams on different assignments, roles changed, and confidence and credibility got boosted. Rosabeth Moss Kanter says that the organisations now emerging as successful, will need to be flexible in the face of changing environment. They must put into practice a whole host of sensing mechanisms for recognising emerging changes and their implications. As we know, adversity always binds together the members collectively, as they struggle for joint survival in times of natural calamities or war.

Build Robust Systems and Processes

While passing through tumultuomus periods, an organisation requires anchors. Strong systems and processes provide them. I know Wharton gives good grounding in systems and process management to its graduates. It helps them make significant changes in strategic review, organisation design, and operation management. It disciplines the mind and performance. Systems, together with Strategy and Structure, are referred to as the three hard "Ss"; and Skills, Shared values, Staff and Style as four soft "Ss" by McKinsey in the "The Seven Ss" framework developed by them in the late 1970s (Hindle, T., 2000). They used this for analysing organisations all over the world, and contended that where organisations work successfully, all seven elements function synergistically.

Process improvement requires re-configuring groups of inter-related activities that together create value for the customer. The two together, systems and processes, are what I believe James Champy and Michel Hammer called "business process re-engineering" (BPR). It helps slice the functional silos, which are overprotective of the information they possess, and whatever is under their command and control.

BT's A. T. Kearney, recently conducted study on India's best managed companies 2003. They found that best managed companies clearly laid out system and process in areas of strategic review, operations, and people management, to sustain superior performance and growth. Western companies were found better at hard Ss, while the astounding progress in manufacturing by Japanese companies, was due to the judicious use of all seven Ss.

Siemens, where I once worked, is known the world over for its perfection in system management. However, I found that the mindset was so highly system oriented that it had become rigid. It suited the engineering temperament. System perfection lead to rigid structures and boundary conflicts. It reduced the creativity of brilliant managers as all excesses do. The law of diminishing returns was operating. It left little space for individual creativity.

I wanted to find out how Mallika made use of the knowledge gained from her alma mater. My focus in eliciting response for this query was not so much on strategy as it was on operations and people management.

S: *Wharton graduates develop a strong systems and processes approach to organisation development. How useful was it for you at TAFE?*

M: We built a system. Formats which spell out what, who, when, and how—it showed the kind of channelling and detailing is required for the flow of work. The approach helped build competence, as well as the process, by puncturing the silo mentality. Detailing is a habit, which you acquire if you build that rigor of implementation. You have to be creative in problem solving. For effective implementation, the involvement of all concerned, their consensus, and rigorous follow up, are three key requirements.

When I asked her for an exhibit of detailing, she showed me a pocket size laminated card which had vision, and values on one side, and the 7 QC tools on the other. What remains etched in my memory are tools with diagrams (see next page).

S: Which of these is more difficult?

M: Implementation and competence building. Competencies will have to be continuously updated. Building competency may today be in execution, and tomorrow, in advance technical skills. I had to personally spend a lot of time in building competence and ushering in a culture of implementation.

A. T. Kearney's study found that the best-managed companies make use of systems and processes, to streamline routine and workflow, to increase internal efficiency. They put in place robust review processes. Apart from investing money in building systems and processes, it is important to note that the top management spends time in getting the internal organisation in shape. This is precisely what the Wharton graduate did. Using consultants wherever necessary, Mallika provided leadership, and spent an enormous amount personal time in getting systems and processes in place.

In three adverse years TAFE's fundamentally different approach led to:

- *Maximum number of new products with advanced deliveries*
- *Breakthrough technologies*
- *Complete redefining of markets and approach to market penetration*

TAFE

The 7 QC TOOLS

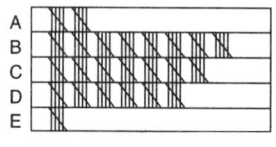

1. **Check Sheet**
   A simple form used to enable data to be collected and interpreted by making check marks.

2. **Pareto Diagram**
   A diagram which identifies 'Vital Few'–'Trivial Many' problems, the 80-20 rule.

3. **Histogram**
   A graphic summary of variation in a set of data (also known as Frequency Distribution Diagram).

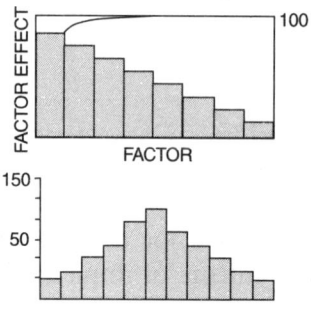

4. **Cause and Effect Diagram**
   A useful method for identifying potential root causes of a problem (effect). Used in conjunction with 'Brainstorming Technique'.

5. **Graphs and Control Chart**
   Graph: A diagram for plotting data and showing temporal changes to easily understand the overall situation.

   Control Chart: A line graph used to assess and maintain the stability of a process for reducing process variability.

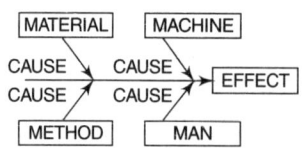

6. **Scatter Diagram**
   A diagram that expresses the correlation between two sets of data.

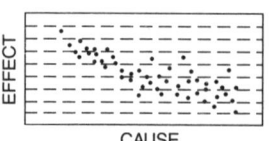

7. **Stratification**
   A method of grouping data by common points to understand similarities and characteristics of data.

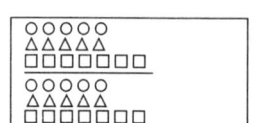

Fig. 3.1 Achieving "World Class Quality" through "World Class Standards"

Many things happened during this period:

1. *Productivity improved—it got built in as a feature of the systems innovation*
2. *Resources were used creatively, with complete attention to cost cutting*
3. *Grit developed*
4. *Transparency in the making of decisions regarding technology, people, and all other issues improved. Technology upgradation was a major driver*
5. *Re-engineered the supply chain process*
6. *New people came up; those that could not build up their competencies had to go*
7. *Functional silos were broken and employees felt more stable*
8. *Open, vocal debates took place on organisation health and future potential*

For Mallika, the biggest challenge was to develop grit in all the layers of the organisation, usher in an open climate, and restore TAFE to the number two position after it had slipped to number four during the storm. She had to take some gutsy calls on borrowing, accurate understanding of customer behaviour, and focus on retailing.

M: To achieve my global ambition I have to concentrate more on technology and people development. I believe in skewed development. Up to a point one has to have TQM, which will propel one to a higher level in everything one does, but an organisation should not be perfect in everything.

What Mallika means is that an organisation has to be better with a select set of competencies that are critical to its business, but it doesn't have to be so superior in every other facet.

Certain Things Just Happen

S: *You are neither a technologist nor an engineer. Are you able to understand nuances in these areas?*

M: I am a student of science with a strong dose of common sense. Sometimes I understand, sometimes I don't. It's a good thing because you can then ask questions like, what is the problem? Why can't it be done? What is the benchmark? How are others doing it? Why are all these excuses being given to me? Can anybody else do it over here?

S: *You take a perspective and leave the detailing to them.*

M: Yes, otherwise what dimension would I be adding?

S: *What was the source of your inspiration?*

M: I cannot attribute it to one thing and correlate. At various times I spoke with various people: Prof. Bhattacharya of Warwick University, who works closely with technology and manufacturing groups; with my father, on net worth in the market or cost cuts; Venu might say something, which would be significant; and so forth. All that adds up. You get an insight through these discussions.

S: *You kind of get stuck—something gets on your mind, and you seek input from knowledgeable others.*

M: Yes. Sometimes one hears an innocuous comment from a stranger, like, "It's okay, one or two bad years after ten good years; not such a bad thing". It puts things in perspective. Finally, one has to work on oneself. It has to come from within. You might have a guru, an experienced leader, a colleague, or a friend who might call up and say, "Hey, a couple of bad years is no great shakes—it will come back". It clicks. There is a philosophical truth. One has to pick up messages from all sources, absorb them, and go ahead.

S: *One has to be alert, and receptive to messages emanating from myriad origins, including symbols and signs. What is important though, is to interpret them correctly and examine their applicability to one's situation. The test one could apply is, "Does the use of that information improve synchronicity and utility?" However, will you not say that at the foundation it's your searching mechanism.*

M: Yes, that is very true. One is searching for answers. Sometimes one recognises them and gets them vetted. One is prepared to take them on board wherever they come from. The search leads through its own route, to a source one may not have thought of. My daughter would say, "Mom, all those lead to tractors or what?" It would make me think. She is connecting my conversation to a totally unconnected area. It might be a social or contextual example. The fundamental principle is to look to the theme and connection.

It may not be a conscious search because one internalises so much. One cannot show an exact connection because one soaks it in—somebody saying something, you reading something, seeing patterns, parallels, drawing your own inferences, and allowing them to stay, to produce their own action. It means creativity, doesn't it?

S: In the marathon battle over the last three years, did you enhance your capacity to be more open, more receptive?

M: Of course, but you cannot fit it into a theory.

S: I am not talking of any theory. I am trying to find out if there is any underlying system at work. Did you meditate to develop your intuition?

M: No, certain things just happen. You really don't know why they happen, or how they happen—they just happen. The quality of your thinking is important. You can't develop everything. Some people are born with it, and some don't have it, period.

S: Your grandpa was an entrepreneur, your father an executive and an entrepreneur. You have more executive competence than entrepreneurial, am I right?

M: If one has only executive competence, and one is the leader, business will die. You have to have entrepreneurial competence as well. It is essential.

S: *But you inherited certain things. You had to work with certain givens. Your contribution is that you made them stable. You built on competency. It was not entrepreneurship from the word go. Entrepreneurship means taking risks.*

M: Not only that. Based on analysis of core competencies, we now have a reasonable size of top quality people. One of our core competencies is in franchising. We can go into allied areas, drop some of our existing activities, add some, etc. It's not only these two competencies but also a fusion of both with higher value addition. Entrepreneurship is in genes only. I strongly feel you can train a manager but not an entrepreneur.

S: *Then how is it entrepreneurship schools have sprung up all over. What do they do?*

M: Well, you can give some structure to the thinking, hone their skills on implementation, etc. I don't believe you can make entrepreneurs. They are just born. First, you must have conviction in your idea, a rational framework for others to buy, e.g. Kiran Mazumdar-Shaw of Biocon, or Narayana Murthy of Infosys, are first generation entrepreneurs. See how they have built organisations. The entrepreneurial role is probably a bit more difficult. One can't be a rule bound manager. One has to be a bit of an entrepreneur to move forward. The two roles, entrepreneurial and executive, are now inseparable.

Let's take another example. When you are recasting your old business, your old competencies are not enough. Today I say that global sourcing is possible. We are trying to move manufacturing contracts from America to India. It is beginning to work. We will have lots of alliances, with our partners and others, that will take us forward. Purely executive competence will not work. One needs elements of creativity to think beyond; proactive leadership, that others don't have.

S: *Will you please give an example?*

M: Yes. I know of a top ranking manager who is frustrated because he is not getting the number one position. The problem is, he does not inspire confidence in others that he is the man they can look to for leadership. Not showing any entrepreneurial ability, no new ways of working, and not recognising the diverse talents of people that work with him, are probably the reasons he is not getting the top job. It looks like he doesn't have it in his blood in the first place.

S: *You belong to the school of thought that believes genetic coding is important.*

M: Yes, partly there is stock in trade. Open environment, honing in skills, consciously improving communications and networking, training and development—all that helps. It is situational, and differs from person to person. If you take me, and put me in a different environment, married differently, I would have been a different person. The environment, the exposure, the network, the training, help, if the basic instincts for a particular vocation are there. The raw material has to be of a certain quality.

The Listening Leadership

What basically nourishes or inhibits the development of subordinates into better managers or leaders, is the leadership style of their superior—like the growth of children is vitally dependant on their parents. However, whether it is authoritative, participative, situational, nurturing, pioneering or transformational style, one factor is common among all styles, and that is, listening. Even an authoritative leader listens though he listens selectively, and that weakness often turns out to be his undoing. Mallika feels that her leadership style is situational, and that one can play around with all styles.

Unless the leader is a fairly good listener, nobody will admire him, let alone follow him. Saints, gurus, teachers, politicians, sportsmen, artists, and entertainers, have large followings. Followers imitate their leaders; admirers have only regard. Few organisational leaders influence people working with them beyond the call of duty. Most organisational leaders therefore have more admirers than followers.

S: *You seem to influence greatly with your nurturing style. Is it because of your position, out of box thinking, or the personal push that you give to issues?*

M: No, it's a part of my job, what's so fancy about it? It means understanding life and people, very simple! You have to be genuine. Yesterday, our people spoke to me about the huge controversy, on which Product Life Management (PLM) system to purchase. All the data was there. The rationale was argued. It is about a computer software system, which enables you to capture the data, from design to the end life of that product, through its entire life history. This will help us change customer expectations by offering new products and services. All logic pointed in one direction.

S: *What role were you playing?*

M: Listener! Everybody must feel that he is being listened to, and that his point of view is being given due consideration. They must essentially trust you one-on-one, and as a group.

Mallika has made listening a part of organisation culture, which is borne out by TAFE's quote:

> I have listened to the heartbeats of a farmer, and
>
> tuned them to the heartbeats of a tractor's engine.
>
> I am TAFE

Mallika learnt to assess the reality of undercurrents in the business environment of the challenging times that she grew in—labour militancy being one component of it. Unconsciously she learnt the art of listening, which comes handy in her leadership role.

Lead by Example

M: Business leadership is not a jackpot or a lottery. Fortune favours the bold. You do your bit and God will do his. *Individual competency, which includes building and managing* teams, is fundamental and constant. And remember, positive attitude is also a competency. One has to be passionate about whatever one is trying to create, believe in what one is doing and in the expected outcome. One must have an open mind to learn with. One must also have implementation capability.

S: *How do you activate this competency?*

M: By encouraging those with a positive attitude to take on newer challenges. And secondly, by focusing on the details. Detailing is a habit. Let's take positive attitude. If you really are a person with a positive attitude, optimistic about the future, with no cynicism, then it will manifest in your interactions with other people. They will observe this attitude in your conversation and actions. Similarly, detailed analysis of issues is a habit. It is seen in the work one does all the time. Intellectual honesty and consistency in behaviour, help build trust. People develop confidence in one because of the predictability in one's behaviour. *God is in details, observed in behaviour, work, and results.*

S: *Will you please give an example?*

M: Let us say we are running a programme, implementing a project, rolling out an innovative scheme, or entering a new international market—its success lies in perfect execution. Detailed planning and monitoring hold the key. If such a project appears too simplistic, then my antennae are certainly up to check if adequate preparation has been made or not. This is a problem with many but more so with IIM graduates who are not good at detailing and follow-up. When detailed project planning, going through the last detail, rechecking, fixing responsibilities for execution within stipulated deadlines, follow-up, and weekly progress monitoring is slipshod, execution is weak.

S: *You seem to have executive competency of a high order.*

M: I definitely have to possess that. In an organisation we don't need many entrepreneurs, we need a lot of people to execute. At senior levels of course, we need entrepreneurship. The main tasks are improvisation in execution, building on it, and continuous improvement. *Immaculate execution is the key to prompt deliverables.*

S: If you are leading by example, you must have noticed gaps in your execution capabilities early on and consciously bridged them.

M: Absolutely correct, I had to—oh lord, how do I do that? Let's go back and see where I missed out. Then I began to understand how detailed it had to be to get it properly implemented, correctly followed.

S: *In that process, does your credibility get established, especially with the old timers?*

M: With the elders it was a bit of that, but more of participating and developing solutions—implementation comes later. It's a stage earlier, and only they are willing to take on implementation. If you are sincere in what you say, and you are prepared, then the credibility is higher. It's not one thing today and another tomorrow. If you keep changing directions it takes you nowhere.

S: *You may have conceptual competency, but translating it into results is what really matters. In execution-implementation, there is skill development.*

M: Yes there is, which in India is a major problem. One seems to come across it more often in the western world than in India. If they take up the job, one can be pretty sure they have looked into all its details and depths. We are pretty intellectually sharp. Once we have intellectually grasped the situation, we go to the next step before confirming that the first step has been accurately completed. This is quite common.

S: *In your style of leading by example, are you required to instil this execution skill to start with?*

M: We are working at it. It is hard but through robust systems and process detailing, we ensure that they are inculcated.

In Execution, *Larry Bossidy and Ram Charan (2002) put it succinctly, "The biggest single difference between businesses that execute and those that don't, is the rigour and intensity with which the leader prosecutes these processes". So although the manager is supposed to implement the nitty-gritty, the leader has to lead from up front.*

A Strategic Thinker

Although Mallika had the protection of her illustrious father at TAFE, she grew on her own merits. To lead an organisation through a disastrous drought situation, where the fulcrum of business is good monsoon, agriculture, and farmers' capacity to buy tractors, is not an easy task even for the most seasoned professional.

Her competency is demonstrated in her steadfast long-term view of the market, introduction of robust systems and processes, and leadership by example. Fathers can protect their siblings but not promote them beyond the level of their competence. If they do, they ossify the organisation. The Peter Principle *becomes functional in the organisation, corresponding to the level of the leader's incompetence. Her vision of the TAFE strategy needs reproduction.*

M: Our strategy is based on a clear definition of our long-term vision, and this sharp focus has been the driving force of our strategy. We did not lose focus during times of crisis, and this has been a key factor behind the pattern of resource allocation over the years. Our entire plan is derived not just from this vision—it has a well-defined, clearly articulated, and well-understood link to it.

Good segmentation of the market has resulted from the clear focus and strategy aims, in offering a customer 'The Product' that meets his requirements—orchard farmers, paddy farmers, mining contractors and fleet owners alike. As a result, we have successfully introduced a large number of products over the last three years, with many more to follow. The definition of 'The Product' has changed to include the entire package, viz. financing, lifetime warranty, and an online value added farm advisory services.

Systematic deepening of our reach, and understanding of our customer base through 'walking the villages' and through innovative approaches like the 'Krishi Ratna' nation-wide competitions, have identified for us new market opportunities. These opportunities, while being large in terms of untapped potential, require a paradigm shift in the approach to providing a product that will dramatically change the current value proposition. This will be our focus over the next 2–3 years and it offers exciting challenges.

In building a strong and international brand we have built an approach that is based on:

(a) An understanding of our strengths relative to the tractor majors of the world, be it in cost, horse power segment, or innovative niche application products, and

(b) Building and strengthening alliances with international players that cover tractors, components and kits.

We strongly believe that India can earn for itself a pre-eminent position in the field of farm mechanisation, and that we will play a leading part in this.

TAFE has also acted as a 'venture capitalist' for opportunities that the Group has identified as potential growth avenues, incubating and nurturing projects until a critical stage is reached when they can be spun off as independent companies.

Mallika's clear understanding of each element of an adverse situation is seen in the way she has detailed and tackled them:

- *Drought*
- *Demand drop in market*
- *Focus on long-term vision*
- *Accepting short-term dip in revenues*
- *Building robust systems and processes*
- *Mopping up internal resources through cost cuts, and eliminating wasteful practices*
- *Leading by listening, and a combination of rational analysis and imagination*
- *Restructuring the organisation in the most advantageous way*

In facing this challenge TAFE has acquired resilience. Managers and sales teams made a habit of visiting villages and farms, where change happens first. The managers and sales teams themselves collected first hand information from the field. With such information, Mallika took a new strategic direction, knowing well that strategies decay over time.

Ohmae says that successful business strategies result not from rigorous strategies but from a particular state of mind of the strategist, from insight and the consequent drive for achievement, often amounting to a sense of mission. It fuels thought processes, which are basically creative and intuitive rather than rational. This process is similar to that of a chess player anticipating the moves of the opponent; or the foresight developed through enormous hard work by a business leader in the face of stiff competition.

Mallika ferreted out the key perceptions and paradigms on which the competitor strategies were based. Her troops walked the villages to get first hand inputs. In The Power of Simplicity, *marketing guru Jack Trout says:*

To become a great strategist, you have to put your mind in the mud of the market place. Running a company in this competitive world is like running a war. It has to run with what the military call the KISS principle (keep it simple, stupid).

(Trout, J., 1999)

Mallika came up with winning strategic concepts through applied creativity, which qualifies her as a strategist.

S: *Your strategic thinking has made the organisation grow systematically. For every successful organisation, there is a leader who becomes the brand, like Narayana Murthy or Kiran Mazumdar-Shaw. Have you become like that in the tractor industry? In any case you have been described as the Tractor Queen!*

M: An organisation may get associated with a person for a certain time. But if you are building an organisation it has to go beyond the person. I am concerned with building a brand for the company, for the products, and for the services it provides to the customers. I am not thinking about personal image. It's all right to build a reputation with the Government, the financial institutions, the dealers and suppliers, but the sustainable entity is the organisation brand. That is the truth.

S: However, you will be recognised for your contribution. Managers, and society, are looking for role models and therefore you cannot underplay it.

M: Let it be, but I work for my mission. If it comes as a by-product, it's okay.

S: In this communications era of Internet, media, and press, it cannot be relegated to the by-product status. Managers, students, and society are looking for business role models, especially because creation of wealth is the single most fundamental need of our country.

M: There are a number of people in every walk of life, who are doing exceptionally well and can truly be role models to aspiring young people. If I can play a role in this process, I will be happy to do so, particularly if it will help aspiring women.

S: You accept your contributory role.

M: Correct, because you will be recognised, as a role model for what you are doing. If you don't do it correctly, you will cease to be a role model.

Mallika beautifully brings out the missionary role a leader plays in building the brand. It demonstrates her rationale to issues of substance. It is my submission that behind a successful multidimensional role player, there is an integral personality.

★ ★ ★

4

The Crux of Quality Health Service

- ❖ Globalisation Opens World Health Space
- ❖ The Outline of Healthcare Market
- ❖ Capture the Health Space
- ❖ The Credo for Patient Care
- ❖ The Calling

- ♦ Exemplar—The Dhanvantari in Global Health Space, Prathap Reddy

"Among the oldest discoveries in the practice of medicine is the fact that human beings come equipped with resources for healing that are best mobilised not by detached scientific efficiency but by communication and supportive human outreach."

—Norman Cousins
The Healing Heart

Introduction

This chapter documents how globalisation has opened up world health space to creative businessmen for providing extraordinary health care and superior products to patients. It is a call to businessmen and medical professionals to provide service standards of the highest order. We get a glimpse here of what is attempted to meet this tall order.

Globalisation Opens World Health Space

The concept of globalisation has unleashed creative forces in every sphere of business and life. It has demolished boundaries in thought and created a vast space for human creativity to flourish. Internet, the main product of this cataclysmic change process, has revolutionised mindsets.

Globalisation has enabled free flow of people, information, ideas, knowledge, and products. It has catalysed people into thinking the unthinkable. In health care, it had lead hospitals to become health clinics, illness to health, surgery to healing, and patient treatment to patient care. It is a path many businessmen, entrepreneurs, doctors, and professionals have chosen to tread. It shows a paradigm shift in service industry, which has far reaching implications on individual and global well-being.

The fulcrum of business is now in IT, biotechnology, telecom, and service industry. The most difficult of these is the service sector, whose success depends on infrastructure, regulatory policies, labour laws, and most importantly on people, group ethos, and team work of a very high order. Therefore, service organisations require leaders. The key differentiating element, is a service mindset imbued with genuine love and care for people, demonstrated by a "give more than take" attitude.

In travel, tourism, back office work, financial and consulting practice, and hospitality, it is the commercialisation of service products that has become important. There, one can reimburse the loss to customers, or pay damages for faulty services. In health care however, one is responsible for the health of a patient, and negligence can costs lives. Therefore, the focus is shifting from medical and surgical treatment to patient services.

Globalisation has opened up the global health space. Advanced medical technology and posh hospitals are available but the cry for better service is still heard all over the world. The USP for capturing a significant portion of that space would therefore be a system of hospital administration, services, and treatment processes in which tender loving care for patients lies embedded.

Entrepreneurs have started attracting patients with additional products, like convalescence facilities at tourist spots, some sightseeing, etc. When you mix patients' needs and tourists' needs, you open up a phenomenal space for business in medical tourism.

The Outline of Healthcare Market

Database

National Council for Applied Economic Research (NCAER) conducted a study in 1993–94. This countrywide survey estimates the size of the Indian health market at 248 million people: average hospitalisation expenses work out to Rs 2098 per person, and the market size to Rs 5429 crore. At an inflation rate of seven percent, this figure changed to Rs 7,116 crore in 1997–98. For 2004–05 a safe guess would be Rs 9000 crore.

In *Health Care Expenditure in India*, Berman (Srinivasan, A. V., 2000) noted that non-government sources of health expenditure far exceeded that of government sources. The out of pocket expenditure of individuals and households was 45 per cent compared to 21 per cent in the states and 10 per cent in central government. Local bodies contributed three per cent and private sector 21 per cent. It worked out to approximately Rs 1339 per employee.

If one looks at the structure of the service provided, two-thirds of hospital beds in public sector facilities stands in contrast with two-thirds of qualified allopathic care providers available on mobile care units, practice privately along with an unknown number of other systems of medicine.

In some countries, medical care supply can create its own demand. This indicates that the multiple recognised systems of medicine in eastern countries, will substantially increase the amount of private care provided, and consequently private health expenditures.

To support his argument Berman compared his data with Duggal and Amin's study of Jalgaon, Maharashtra and West Java, Indonesia. He found that the out of pocket spending in India was significantly higher despite lower rates of illnesses reported. It showed a higher propensity to use alternative treatments.

This is not simply a function of greater health needs but of greater availability and access to private health care. This includes a number of 'eclectic' treatments—a combination of therapies from more than one medicine, including some elements of allopathy. India, it appears, spends a higher proportion of its income on health care when compared with other countries in Asia. This means Indians are either more health conscious or subject to more sicknesses or both.

The Technology Information Forecasting Assessment Council (TIFAC) of the Government of India, constituted panels in 1994 to make long-term predictions. The documents released in the series VISION 2020 predicted the following with regard to health care sector:

- **Infectious Diseases**—AIDS, Tuberculosis, Diarrhoea, and vector-borne diseases will receive highest priority, though their incidence level will decline perceptibly

- **Non-communicable Diseases**—Cancer in women, Ischaemic heart diseases, and strokes will attract high priority

- **Increased Disease Burden**—caused by accidents, suicides and homicides, emotional and psychiatric problems

- **Indigenous Systems**—will be used to identify and synthesise new drugs for the treatment of chronic diseases

- **Clinical Trials**—undertaken in India for medicines and technologies developed overseas

- **Imaging Equipment**—its production, Hepatitis, Anti-rabies vaccine, and diagnostic kits will receive added attention

- **Technology Status**—Technologies to prevent, diagnose, and treat diseases of high priority are far from satisfactory

- **Alternative Systems**—will thrive and have the potential to displace allopathy and modern medicine

- **Pattern of Growth**

    1. There will be more growth in nursing homes than in large multi-disciplinary hospitals

    2. Two fast growing areas: one, health care set up by medical professionals and entrepreneurs, and two, industrial houses participating in setting up hospitals as joint ventures, e.g. Wockhardt Heart Hospital

    3. Hospitals will be run more as commercial organisations on professional lines, with careful planning, cost control, quality service, efficient management, and patient satisfaction

4. Integrated health care networks will function widely to bring facilities to the population at affordable prices.

Future Scenario

In *Envisioning an Empowered Nation*, A. P. J. Abdul Kalam and A. Sivathanu Pillai (2004) state:

> *The healthcare industry is on the threshold of a major growth spiral, which shall assimilate all new technologies to provide cost-effective healthcare. It is poised to become the biggest employer in all countries ... also a large proportion of the skilled workforce.*

This is a business opportunity of great potential. Hospitals can now import technology and connectivity to grow into healthcare institutions. In alternative medicine, this might lead to a logical strategy for managing IPR regulations. Healthcare and research institutions, pharmaceutical R&D units, and interested organisations from abroad can use a consortium approach to import technology.

Value Addition through Connectivity

Healthcare organisations will work closely with educational and social institutions towards prevention and diagnosis of infectious diseases. Their collaboration with drug research institutes has the potential to develop backward integration. Their institution based services will help form a new relationship with nursing homes and Cooperatives. Information technology applications, particularly networked communication will be exploited effectively, e.g. Apollo's tele-medicine enterprise, to reach out to villages. Such multilayered connectivity will add value to the service provided to the patient.

Upsurge in Entrepreneurship

Medical professionals will get together and start cooperative clinics, nursing homes, with public participation, e.g. Dr. Hegdewar Hospital in Aurangabad. Hospital administrators, trained management, turnkey project consultants, and non-banking institutions specialised in raising finance for hospitals will spring up. By opening a state of art hospital in Colombo, Apollo has also shown that India can export its expertise in top class healthcare facility. This speaks volumes for overseas market development strategy.

Mindset Change

Dr. A. V. Srinivasan in his book, *Managing a Modern Hospital* (2000) says:

- *The social mores of medical professionals and patients will change to a positive attitude. This will open up new avenues of employment and secured employment.*
- *Healthcare institutions and NGOs will provide education and training on a large scale, particularly in rural areas and urban slums on preventive measures.*

Employment has picked up in this sector. We already see a change in the mindset of medical professionals, and such inputs being provided to the under-privileged.

Capture the Health Space

Courtesy globalisation, a vast health space currently valued at US$ 21 billion, and with an estimated growth of 17 per cent per annum, projected at US$ 39 billion by 2006, has been created. Our insurance companies' involvement in healthcare is pretty poor compared with those in the west. Private hospitals are mainly driving this boom with 70 per cent market share. It is growing at 2.5 per cent annually.

The scope for capture of the global space is immense; we do not see much competition. The market has no global business brands like GE, J&J, or Sony. Filling the global health space gainfully is a call on our creativity, and we must take it.

The global health space can be captured: technology is importable, capital is available, infrastructure can be built, and management is do-able. We have key players in the private sector like Apollo, Wockhardt, Escorts, and Max India. Apollo is investing Rs 2000 crore in setting up super specialty hospitals in Mumbai, Nepal, and Malaysia. As in all areas of human endeavour, here also, we need creative leadership and we claim we have it. That said, it might sound a wee bit incongruous to think that what is still in scarce supply are seer skills.

In *The Five Faces of Genius,* Annette Moser-Wellman (2001) says that the key business principles of the seer are to visualise new opportunities and potential outcomes, be a mission maker, visualise unmet needs, and set steps to accomplish the vision.

Seers use the power of image, which leads to the breakthrough. Look at Ray Kroc's McDonald. The quick service, quality food, and low price formula engaged Kroc's mind, and he created a fast food empire.

Seers move beyond their mental contours to see space differently. They visualise a great deal, in great detail, and are obsessed with their images, as they firmly believe them to contain ideas worthy of pursuit. They go to ground zero to analyse the landscape and its limitations. This is known as the 'helicopter jump'. With your idea you take off and soar in the sky. After a while, you drop down to the ground to check the reality. Creative leaders use this method to manipulate their ideas. In other words, they play ceaselessly with their ideas. Breakthrough solutions come from thinking big and mentally shifting the boundaries of ground realities.

Prathap Reddy is doing the same. He has a picture in mind of Apollo health clinics spread across the global health space. Globalisation triggered him to think big. There are no MNCs operating in healthcare industry. People have started thinking positively about health. They have moved conceptually from sickness to health, from operations to holistic living and healing. The old adage, *prevention is better than cure* has returned to occupy people's minds. Prathap put it together in thinking of hospitals that will grow into healing clinics to meet the new demand.

The creative foray however, is not only in thinking big, or putting bricks, mortars, and hospital staff together and leveraging the posh product. It is more in providing quality service of immeasurable dimensions, which captures the hearts of patients. It means making available a continuous attention process built on **Tender Loving Care**, TLC as he calls it. Whether receptionists, ward boys, nurses, or doctors, they will be treating the patients, poor and rich, with these cardinal values. This is a difficult call but the staff at Apollo have taken it. This is the need of the global patient, and Prathap is trying hard to meet it.

The seer in Prathap saw the missing link needed to capture global health space. In product-service supply chains, missing links provide invaluable clues to improvisation. There is money in the gaps where handicaps are marginalised. As in any game, one has to find the space—it requires different seeing.

In business, the search for uncaptured space leads to spotting unmet needs, which stimulate dreams and opportunities. The leader goes through a malleable frame of thinking as he resolves the phenomenon to get a clear picture. To this end, he assembles people with appropriate attitudes and skills, and shares the dream. He gives shape to its realisation step by step.

The Credo for Patient Care

In the "sickness to health", and "curing to healing" processes, Prathap caught hold of the correct pulse of global patient—compassion and affection. He rightly thought that affectionate care will endear the hospital staff to its patients, which in turn will transform the hospital to a health clinic. In the process, they become missionaries. Seers are missionaries, aren't they? *"Tender Loving Care"* is not a product. Prathap has made it a credo—serve the patients on their terms.

The health space cannot be captured with five star facilities, sophisticated equipment, or tautological service brands. It has to be genuine, continuous care, from the heart. As Prathap says, "Care for everyone with the same genuine affection, evident in your gaze, body language, and actions, as you will care for your dearest one".

The American consumer giant Johnson & Johnson (J&J, founded in 1886), is known all over the world for commitment to its credo: the company exists "to alleviate pain and disease". The core ideology, i.e. the credo, spells its hierarchy of responsibilities as customers first, employees second, society third, and shareholders fourth.

Jim Burke, Chairman and CEO of J&J, spent 40 per cent of his time communicating this philosophy in a passionate manner, as if J&J were his private company. That is how great CEOs go about their beliefs and jobs. Jim (James) Collins studied 15 companies for his well known book *Build to Last* (1996). In it, only three figure as visionary companies: GE, Ford, and J&J.

Prathap and his Apollo—established in 1983—have a long way to go. Prathap is laying down the correct foundation. The positivist in us remembers that well begun is half done. However, continuous caring service is dicey business because it is totally dependent on missionary zeal. That kind of a passion is easily seen in the natural habitat of charities. In a business setting, it is a rare sapling to nurture; one is not working only for the poor or handicapped. It has no religious or ideological billing. It has almost no content of sacrifice.

In commercial ventures, maintaining the tempo of commitment to credo is a gigantic task. It calls for sustained efforts at keeping leaders with the same pedigree of commitment, enthusiasm, and creativity. And the calling is sacred because it is concerned with the lives of people.

The Calling

Visionary leaders like Jamshetji Tata, T. V. Sundaram Iyengar, Ghanashyamdas Birla, Henry Ford, Merck&Co's George Merck II, GE's Thomas Edison, J&J's Robert W. Johnson, and Sony's Masaru Ibuka, are inspired by three main callings—to do one's best, to help people, and to build a better world.

Way back in 1886, pioneering industrialist Jamshetji Tata had two successful mills under his belt, the Empress Mills at Nagpur, and Swadeshi Mills in Bombay. He and his colleagues had the wherewithal, drive, and imagination, to multiply their wealth by expanding the textile business. He then decided to venture into something totally unknown to him—steel, hydroelectric power, and technical education. Tata Steel, Tata Hydroelectric Company, and Indian Institute of Science in Bangalore, were thus born.

While writing about this impulse for diversification in *The Creation of Wealth*, R. M. Lala said, "Something had happened to Jasmshetji. The nation had become his business (Lala, R. M., 1991)." His vision lay beyond his self, family, and community. This is borne out by his following observation in making advanced technical education available to Indians:

> *What advances a nation or community is not so much to prop up its weakest and most helpless members, as to lift up the best and most gifted so as to make them of the greatest service to the country.*

> —Jamshetji

JRD who later led the Tata group for over 50 years articulated their calling:

> *The wealth gathered by Jamshetji Tata and his sons in half a century of industrial pioneering formed but a minute fraction of the amount by which they enriched the nation. The whole of that wealth is held in trust for the people and used exclusively for their benefit. The cycle is thus complete; what comes from the people has gone back to the people many times over.*

In 1916, Henry Ford enunciated the philosophy of his business calling:

> *I don't believe we should make such an awful profit on our cars. A reasonable profit is right, but not too much...it is better to sell a large number of cars at a reasonably small profit...because it enables a large number of people to buy and enjoy the use of a car and it gives a large number of men employment at good wages. Those are the two aims I have in life.*

The pragmatic idealism of George Merck II is displayed when he explains the core ideology of the company:

> *We try never to forget that medicine is for the people. It is not for the profits. The profits follow, and if we have remembered it, the larger they have been...We are in the business of preserving and improving human life. All our action must be measured by our success in achieving this goal.*

Thomas Edison's vision was a company that would light a nation, producing all the elements of electrical components, electrical power stations, and electric lamps to accomplish this feat. He believed that politics should not constrain business, that business should receive the rewards derived from patents, and that management not unions, should make business decisions.

Robert W. Johnson, who founded Johnson & Johnson in 1886 on the idealistic mission, "to alleviate pain and disease", placed customer service and concern for employees ahead of return to shareholders. Credo meetings were held at regular intervals in J&J offices throughout the world. Since I headed the personnel division in 1980–82, I am fully acquainted with the commitment with which the credo meetings were conducted. The wording of the credo may have been revised slightly when necessary but the essential ideology remains unchanged.

As the saying goes, *the test of the pudding lies in eating.* J&J had to face the Tylenol crisis in 1982. Seven deaths were reported in Chicago where someone had tampered with Tylenol by lacing it with cyanide. The management removed all Tylenol capsules from the market at a cost of $100 million. It earned them a reputation: *this company does what is right regardless of the cost.* The company remained true to its calling, by rushing to recall the bottles so no further harm was caused to their customers.

In 1945, Japan was defeated in World War II. In the midst of that devastation Masaru Ibuka started Sony. While facing day to day survival issues, Ibuka articulated the core ideology of the company, which its famous chief executive Akio Morita described:

> *Sony is a pioneer and intends never to follow others. Sony wants to serve the whole world. It shall always be a seeker of the unknown. It has a principle of respecting and encouraging one's ability ... and always tries to bring out the best in a person. This is the vital force of the society.*

The vision for building a business organisation was explicit from the start, despite the problems of survival in a devastated economy. The architectural approach helped the Sony founder and his dedicated employees realise his dream. Sony's footprints are there to be seen in Japan's growth through its galaxy of branded products.

In their book on visionary companies *Build To Last*, Jim (James) Collins and Jerry Porras say:

> *As we look back on our findings, one giant realisation towers above all the others: just anyone can be a protagonist in building an extraordinary business institution. The lessons of these companies can be learned and applied by the vast majority of managers at all levels.*

All these visionaries have answered their calling by doing their best, by helping people and by building a better world. They were integrated professionals without business school education or management degrees. In fact, the emergence of separate business schools was the product of their unique thinking, achievements, and devotion to societal and national causes.

Visionary leaders engage in philanthropic activities of different types, and donate large sums to a variety of social causes. They work for the needy sections of the society. They build institutions of art, culture, music, dance, drama, education, science, craft, you name it. Concern for the unfortunates of the society, wider environment and excellence is so ingrained in their character that the business is used as a tool for making profits and ploughing them into creative venture of improving life for all.

Mihaly Csikzentmihalyi, in his latest book *Good Business* (2003) says of vision and calling that:

> *The word vision is not adequate, for it connotes a visual or mental image of what leaders intend to achieve. What drives them is more a visceral image than a mental one. Instead of being transient visitors to this planet, they feel they have a permanent place in the cosmos ... a calling.*

With the same ingredients of calling, viz. do one's best, help others, and build a better world, Prathap wants to capture the newly created global health space. He is a *dhanvantari*—a doctor with a healing touch. He has seen the space and brought entrepreneurship into it, to fulfil his calling.

The Dhanvantari in Global Health Space— Prathap Reddy

Established in 1986, Apollo Hospitals Enterprises Ltd. (AHEL) had a turnover of Rs 438.20 crore, and a profit of Rs 27.50 crore, as of March 2003. It has a network of 27 hospitals, including one in Colombo, Sri Lanka; 10 clinics; over 4800 licensed beds; 10,000 employees; and a network of 72 retail pharmacies across the country. The energetic Dr. Prathap Reddy is the Chairman.

"A commitment not to accept even 1 per cent failure is the key to progress".

Apollo is a prestigious brand in healthcare. I met the architect of that creation—the tall, well-built Prathap—on the ground floor office of his hospital at Chennai. We began talking as if we were picking up the threads of a conversation from the day before. It felt great to start the interview in that tenor.

This was my second meeting that day, the first being Venu Srinivasan of TVS Group. I narrated to Prathap what Venu said about his leadership. In response to my question, "What makes Dr. Reddy's leadership so special in the creation of healthcare facilities on a grand institutional scale?" he replied, "Dr. Reddy gives more than he takes, a hallmark of thought leadership!"

The Art of Recognising Gratitude

P: I would put it the other way—*what I receive is many times more than what I give.* The only thing is that one can't quantify it. When patients leave with their relatives, they only know the precious thing they got back: life, health, or whatever. They know they have to pay the bill. They only look at you. Probably they cannot express their feelings. But if one looks in their faces, one will see abundant satisfaction and gratitude. That is what I experience in that gaze. A silent meeting of hearts makes me speechless and grateful to God. What more can one want?

S: *Where does this sense of deep gratitude to God comes from?*

P: My mother shaped and brought out the softer side in me. I believe her special love propelled me ceaselessly during my growth years. My wife's strong spiritual influence has made the single largest impact on all of us. She is my greatest asset. My father was an agriculturist, and a pillar of peace in the village. These influences helped me realise that we are but instruments in the Master's hand.

While Prathap lays the credit at the Master's feet, I believe it is his capacity to empathise and unite with the intimate feelings of his patients that deepened his sense of gratitude towards both patients and God. The art of recognising gratitude lies in being in a state of acceptance, in a receptive mood, when someone is offering something. One must develop the ability to perceive clearly that which is being communicated through silence, word, gesture, whatever. That competency is a sure index of one's humility and spiritual health.

S: Feeling at one with the patient is one thing and feeling for the patient is another. Giving more and taking less is a difficult philosophy to adapt in the growing commercial culture and the transactional upbringing that all of us go through. With such pervasive corrosion of human values how did you build the sensitivity of your staff?

P: You are right—people don't know how to receive a patient properly, treat him lovingly, or feel the gratitude in his eyes and body language. They want to hear it in words, or see it in writing. On the other hand, most patients and their relatives don't have the words to express themselves, or they don't know how. I tell my boys in uniform, or the nurses, or the house keeping boys who clean toilets, "Watch the gratefulness in his eyes. Don't wait for his words. Remain humble inside. Imagine what you and your ailing mother would have felt while leaving the hospital; and you will be able to understand the meaning of his expressions and the million thanks conveyed in his profoundly potent silence. This is a competency you will develop with application". It took time, but they saw me do it; and I was not tired of telling them again and again.

The Death of a Patient and the Birth of a Hospital

S: You are a cardiologist. Where did you pick up this entrepreneurial bug?

P: I am not a entrepreneur. I was not looking for a business opportunity. I was comfortable in America. I returned in 1971 because my father said, "of what use is your expertise if the country does not from it benefit?" On my return, I got established in Chennai. I found, I could do everything here that I was doing over there. In 1979, a young man who could not go to the US for heart surgery, because he could not afford the cost, died on Deepavali day. His young wife had then to look after two children. I had never lost a patient in that way. I could not bear the pain, and that was the turning point in my life.

Death is a critical event and a turning point. In Thought Leaders, *I have observed:*

> *They (leaders) made the difference with their unique perceptive thinking. They did not take the event lightly. They treated it seriously, to change their careers. Depending upon the depth of one's sensitivity at the moment of watching the death, it can bring about a critical shift in awareness. (Pandit, S., 2001)*

Such events trigger one to look at deeper meaning of life and its connection to one's calling.

S: How was it a turning point?"

P: I felt it should not happen to anybody. If Indians abroad can show excellence there, what prevents them from showing it over here? I am equal or better over there, then why not here? I couldn't get an ordinary telephone; and other such well-known hassles were bugging me. The outside infrastructure, inside equipment, and the infrattitude (infrastructure of attitudes), are the bottlenecks to decent healthcare. I went back to States in 1981 to share my feelings with my friends on what could be done.

S: *What did they say?*

P: All my doctor colleagues had grown in specialisation, stature, and assets. All of them were sceptical, wondering how I would get anything done in India without the political and bureaucratic interference? I said, I could your support. They replied, of course it is there, so that was it. I think all of us have intelligence. *How much you can bring out depends upon your belief in yourself, and belief is power.* If you know in your heart that you can do it, you surely can.

S: *You are a skilled doctor but building an infrastructure is a tedious job, with all the known red-tapism. It is a big challenge. How did you handle it?*

P: Urban land ceiling problems consumed one and a half years. Import of medical equipment, number of applications to be made, visits to Delhi, you name it; and guess the time spent on it.

S: *You had to wade through the mud of delays and agonising follow-ups. The little things are a great hassle. What about the secretarial help?*

P: At the HM hospital where I was working, I requested the owner to construct two rooms over the car shed. Whenever I had the time, I went upstairs and dictated to my daughters. The greatest secretarial help came from my four daughters. They have the fire. They prepared the hospital brochure so well, that when I took it abroad they were surprised to see such good quality material from India. They were school and college girls. They have been involved in this venture since that time. They are a great source of strength to me. The team is not just Apollo, it extends to the family as well. Today every Apollo member is a family member.

S: *Most of the doctors are interested only in their knitting, i.e. actual surgery or whatever their expertise. The hassle of building an infrastructure facility is not their cup of tea. It is boring, and a colossal waste of energy to say the least.*

P: Apollo's success is depended exactly on that point. We completely took away the doctor from all these hassles. I brought up that extra in me to do that, i.e. build a hospital. I bought the plot for Rs 22 lakhs and I was getting Rs 3 crore.

A friend said, "sell the plot, make money and do something else". I didn't take it for the money. That was not my purpose. I did it to fill in the void, the gap.

S: Gap finding shows an entrepreneurial spirit. Entrepreneurs are good at building infrastructures. So you spotted the gap and jumped in to make some profit from it. Isn't it?

P: Any protein you give should have a price tag on it. In this venture, the price tag is cost effective good health. I didn't want to be known as the guy who came from abroad and made money on sicknesses. Profit is not a bad word, e.g. pharmaceuticals make money in the medical field—you do not call them bad. The media lambasted us initially. In the last five or six years they have stopped. In the first three years, whenever we published results, they criticised us, "What are you bloating on, you are making profits on a sick man's money, etc". The press used to eat me up. Profit was one aspect but my drive was to fill in the gap, the void in the deficient healthcare area.

Thus a hospital was born. See the sequence of events. Prathap loses a heart patient because he could not afford to go to US for surgery. Not so much the shock of death but that his life could not be saved in India for want of adequate facilities, sent shivers down Prathap's spine. That turmoil within, led to his thinking afresh on life's purpose, goals— and on what could be done to save the next life from such a disaster. This friction within gave birth to the idea of building a healthcare facility—and the hospital was born.

Claudia Setzer says, "The body dies, but the spirit is not entombed". We see here the death of a patient leading to a fresh embodiment of the spirit in the form of a hospital. Joseph Brown believes, "There is no death. Only a change of worlds". Here we see it: a change from the personal world to the institutional world, and hopefully a more lasting world. In death, some serve a better cause. The patient who died wanted to remain anonymous.

Here, we are able to establish a clear nexus between cause and effect, trigger and event, reason and result. Between the death of a person and the birth of a healthcare institution was a cardiologist called Prathap Reddy, who had the heart to play the role of midwife in the creation of something unique!

A Professional Model

Prathap then met a man who made the difference in the western world, Thomas First Jr. He was the cardiologist at Nashville, Tennessee who created the Hospital Corporation of America (HCA). It is almost identical to what Apollo is doing here. The concept came from him.

When Prathap went a second time to US, in 1981, he felt he should do something on the lines of Thomas First Jr's HCA, in India. Thomas Jr had also felt that his patients were getting a raw deal. Their treatment was not good enough and the cost was high, all because of a lack of professional management. The hospitals were not run on any system. Thomas Jr told Prathap, "If you could introduce proper systems you would make a big difference. You could provide quality service and reduce costs". Today, HCA has 200 hospitals.

P: I should not get the credit, he should. He created the first professional corporate hospital in the world. Thomas Jr spent a lot of time in building departments, corporate planning, HR, etc. He took away the power from the doctors, the power of running the hospitals, because he did everything. However, he gave doctors the bigger power of concentrating on treating patients. It was a pleasure meeting him and learning from him first-hand, to think more clearly on planning various activities.

My friends said, "Come on, you won't get an appointment like that." Undeterred, I went to Thomas Jr's office and met his secretary. I had not carried a visiting card, and so wrote on a piece of paper, my name, and that I wanted to start a hospital in India for which I needed his guidance. Promptly came the reply, "I will join in an hour's time for lunch". He asked someone to walk me around the office in the mean time. Thomas Jr turned up for lunch on time, and took to an Indian restaurant for a vegetarian lunch.

In Thomas First Jr and HCA, Prathap found his role model. We need a role model to follow because imitation is a necessity of human nature. Said William James, "Each of us is in fact what he is, almost exclusively by virtue of his imitativeness". The right role models are always inspirational, and lucky are those who stumble upon an admirably perfect one. Paul D. Shafer quotes "The most important single influence in the life of a person is another person who is worthy of emulation".

P: I don't know if I learnt any specific systems from him, but listening to him was good enough. Thomas Jr had the same thought as to why should anyone do surgery less efficiently? Hospitals and doctors have to work at zero defect efficiency, and there cannot be any compromise in the promptness and quality of service.

Apollo is a multidisciplinary healthcare facility but Prathap always quotes heart first—a sign of his first love. In the first year, they did 270 surgeries with a 97 per cent success rate compared to 87 per cent elsewhere. The skills have not changed. All Prathap did was to build support systems at all levels, to relieve doctors of the problems emanating from them.

P: We brought in professionalism at the pre-operative, operative, and post-operative phases of patient care. Like that, we brought in effective controls in every discipline in the hospital. The entire facility is run by professionals, which brought accountability at all levels.

S: Was it not first difficult to attract professionals, doctors, nurses to a new place like this, since they are known to prefer established hospitals? Your salaries could not have been comparably attractive, were they?

P: Yes, we faced those teething problems but my reputation helped at the start, and we offered comparable pay packages. Retention of nurses is a big headache all over the world. They have a great demand in domestic market, as also overseas. We have started a nursing college to fulfil our needs, and tide over the constant turnover of this category. Our nurses are in great demand because of the training they receive, and the discipline they show in work. They are instantly recruited and absorbed.

S: Was it not difficult to provide at the start, the disciplined approach and excellence you had dreamt of?

P: It was not easy. To work according to systems requires re-conditioning of mind. I had to constantly tell them, "I don't need extra physical labour from you. All I need is you to work our way, so that you will produce better results, and more, you will enjoy it". We had trainers but I personally gave my inputs and inspected whether they were following the systems or not. Also, I used to solve their problems on the spot. Adoption of professional systems and decentralisation worked. Our commitment to it was total and visible. The CEOs of all units take daytoday decisions. The daughters carry the owner's responsibility but their approach is professional.

S: What are your plans for the future?

P: My vision is to make Apollo a healthcare destination of the world, and India the global health capital. The mission is to explore the entire health space development of our country, not just illness but wellness. We have done enough for Apollo and ourselves; our vision now must expand to embrace national healthcare. The road ahead is to associate with the national health scenario and see how the gaps can be bridged.

Prathap's global thinking is not restricted only to Apollo's growth—it envisions securing a place for India on the global map. There are numerous family owned organisations in India from the Daburs in Delhi, to Amalgamations in Chennai, which have patriarchs at the top but are managed by professionals, and run on professional lines.

The interface between the family members, whose second and third generation members are also professionally qualified, and outside professionals, is handled sensitively. Priority is given to establishing role clarity and trust. It did not therefore surprise me to find Apollo in that category, doing as well as any MNC or Indian professional joint stock company, if not better.

The model is professional, showing excellent performance, and that's what matters. Entrepreneurs begin with family members and known friends because the trust level is high. It is presumptuous to think that they do not take their competencies into account. Some accommodation on considerations other than capabilities cannot be ruled out. However, they are shrewd enough to weigh the final composition, which must give them a cutting edge over competitors, and good returns. What needs to be understood is that the mere presence of owners does not make an outfit any less professional.

Demolition of Myths

Two months later, I met Prathap at his Hyderabad hospital. On my way, I read some of the literature on Apollo, and came across an item titled *Sleep Laboratories*. For me, honestly, it was a bit intriguing, since I had not heard about them before.

S: *What is a sleep laboratory?*

P: We all think if a person snores, he sleeps well. Very few people know that this is a dangerous symptom. Snoring is an obstruction to the air passage. It means that while you sleep, you are not able to inhale sufficient oxygen. Your whole system is under-saturated, and the organ worst affected by this is your brain. Next morning, when such a person gets up, he is not fresh. Everyone thinks, he has slept a lot because he snored and now he must keep awake.

S: *Will you please give an example?*

P: Our company secretary Subrahmanyam had this experience. We diagnosed him, performed a small surgery, and watched him recover after resting in the sleep lab. He now tells me, "Sir, I used to drink 20 cups of coffee because I had to come to the office in the morning. It would be 11 o'clock by the time I could reach the office, and get back my normal thinking process. Today at six in the morning I am fine".

S: *How is Subrahmanyam now; and what are the worst dangers?*

P: Now he sleeps without snoring, he sleeps comfortably, and his oxygen saturation is good. Whenever your oxygen saturation is low, and you have a borderline heart problem, it can lead to death. For this purpose, we have developed world class sleep labs in Chennai, Hyderabad, and Delhi.

S: *How do they function?*

P: Each lab can simultaneously observe and treat four patients at night. It can study their patterns, measure the activity to see if it is moderate, and give mild treatments wherever necessary. We advise breathing exercises. In three-fourths of a month the problem gets resolved. In serious cases, like Subrahmanyam's, we do surgery.

S: *Where did you get the idea?*

P: Well I saw it abroad, and brought the technology over. We bring whatever is helpful, from wherever it is available, to break some of our myths. *We demolish such myths, that a person who snores, sleeps well.*

S: *Large chunks of our society still live on mythical tenets, and will continue to do so. However, it is essential to demolish such ill-founded beliefs in order to induce a scientific temper.*

The Faith in *Gurus*

P: We believe in gurus. They prayed for years together and survived because they were able to take ordinary air in and convert it into energy. I don't think it is mystical. I met Sri Sri Ravi Shankar of the *Art of Living* fame. I was amazed with the influence he had on people. He transmits pure joy, and asks for nothing. Whether in private audiences, or in a gathering of 10,000, or while talking to prisoners, he oozes pure energy. I believe it is conversion of air to energy through his silent system.

S: *Any personal experience?*

P: My grandson Aditya was not in tune with himself. He used to go out with friends, smoke, drink, and had become considerably irritable. Suddenly one day I saw him totally different. He was telling his sister, "Vidya, you should be more balanced". I asked him what happened? He said, "I attended a seminar on the 'Art of Living'". His mother intervened to say that the Art of Living seminar has done wonders to him.

S: *It is the access to a smooth supply of air and the capacity to convert it to energy that matters.*

P: Yes, the access is important. We have camouflaged ourselves—built walls between our inner strengths and outer performances. I feel we have so much potential that we are not able to use what God has given to us, because we don't know how to get it. Sri Sri Ravi Shankar has explored this concept. I believe the age has come for India to regain its glory. It has been there for ten thousand years. Such persona must emerge, and through them, experiences of this kind must come. This is going to happen, and it is not dependent on your bank balance but on your brains.

S: *What else did he say?*

P: In fact, he said very little. He did not make a vigorous speech. He encouraged people to ask questions, and while giving answers he expounded his thoughts, theories, and practices. He was laughing continuously, to his heart's content. He was pouring out energy.

Sri Sri Ravi Shankar follows a system of dialogue propounded by Plato and practised by many a philosophers, the latest being J. Krishnamurthy. Many of us attended his meetings and participated silently in his dialogues with the audience. Sometimes I felt I was the questioner, and quite a few times sensed that he was giving my answers.

S: *Personally, you cannot employ Ravi Shankar's questions–answer system of establishing communication with your doctors, nurses, ward boys, managers, office staff— none.*

P: I feel for my patients. I do what I genuinely feel I should do. And I tell all those people you mentioned, exactly that—do whatever you are doing as if you are doing it to yourself. At the end of the day you feel happy. When I pray, I thank the patients and God for giving me the opportunity to serve. I could not sleep for the first two years of running the hospital because there were innumerable problems like a basement full of water, electrical short circuits, patients in serious conditions, shortage of nurses, politicians calling, you name it. I don't know how or when it happened but now, as soon as I enter the car, I take off my shoes, begin meditation, and the mind turns off. When the car reaches the portico I am back in the world.

S: *That's great. Has a guru ever put his hand on your head, or have you had Tirupati darshan, or some such event of spiritual significance?*

P: Tirupati always played a very significant role in my life. I attribute everything that has happened in my life to Lord Venkateswara. The story about the certificate of registration for Apollo is important and interesting. Would you like to hear it?

S: *Yes.*

P: The late Charan Singh threw our application for registration in the waste paper basket. It took great efforts to convince Mr Venkataraman of the sincerity of my cause. He was the first to put his signature on Apollo approval, confirming that it could attract NRI funds. After we received the certificate I told my secretary Malathi that I wanted to go to Tirupathi. She said, "No sir, you cannot, you have so many appointments". I said, "Forget it, I will work till whatever time you want but I must leave by 2.30 p.m. and reach Tirupati with the certificate tonight". She arranged things and we reached at 6.30 p.m.

The staff at the temple told me, "Dr. Reddy, we waited for you, but it's now 6.45 p.m. and this is one day in the year when the temple closes at 6.30 p.m". I said, "Don't bother. I have come to stay for night". However, I went to the temple and saw the gate open, so I entered. I saw the *pujari* (priest) placing the curtain on the God. The *pujari* saw us and repeated exactly what the staff had said. I told him that I had come to put this certificate at the God's feet—would please put it there, do the *arti* (song of prayer) in the morning, and give us the certificate thereafter. In three minutes the *pujari* came back, raised the curtain, did the arti, and gave us the certificate then and there. We were so happy we had no words to express our gratitude. I believe this story was narrated to the head priest, who said next day, "I don't know how this happened". I said, "It's a process I understand".

S: There is some unseen force, call it God, who has been helping you probably from your childhood!

P: I think slightly differently. I think he is continuously laying down the path for me. And it is my business to walk on it without questioning. I always remember Jagadguru Kanchi Shankaracharya's words.

S: What were those words?

P: Shankaracharya was about to start his all-India *padayatra*. I was the last person to see him. I explained to him my concept of Apollo hospital and how I was going to realise it. I asked him, "Will I be able to do it? Should I do it?" He said, "Who am I to tell you, should or should not. You have already given it a name. God has given it to you. So God has left it in your hands. All that you can now ask is, how well will I be able to bring it up? Let me now tell you, you will do it. You will do a beautiful thing, like a rose. But you won't be able to beautify your house with it, like people buy roses for beautifying their homes. Also the rose has many thorns. You are going to be daunted by the task before you get that beautiful rose. It will be so beautiful and so fragrant, it will be the best in the world". I was thrilled.

S: You are saying that despite facing millions of obstacles, there is some parallel force which takes you through them. It shows you the path bit by bit and helps you navigate safely.

P: That's correct. We almost bought Adyar Gate hotel for Rs 25 lakh. I paid an advance of Rs 1.25 lakh, and signed the papers. We took the map and started discussing with architects how to convert the hotel into a hospital. With all that I went to see Shankaracharya. He was then camping at Belgaum. I was told he was in *maunam*—silence. I was slightly dejected. Later on, when I was about to go for a bath, I was told that he had broken *maunam*. I thought then, that I would now get a chance to meet him before he retreated again in *maunam*.

S: *Did you get to meet him?*

P: Yes, I did. He saw our plans, listened to us, and said our place was not for hospital. I was so disappointed that I told him, "Do you know there is an urban land ceiling act, and I am getting this property for nothing. The balance payment of Rs 24 lakh was to be made at my convenience. The banks are also accommodative". He heard me out and replied, "That *vastu* is not for a hospital. If you want to do any other business that's different". I told him, I would put up a temple there. But he would not say anything more, so that was it.

S: *What did you do next?*

P: I told to myself that it didn't matter. Let's go and meet the present *Peethadhipati* in Hyderabad, Swami Jayendra Saraswati. When I reached the *peetham* he had finished the *pooja*. As he was coming down, he saw us and asked us to wait in the adjoining room. The first thing he said was, "You want to know if the hotel site you have chosen is appropriate for building the hospital?" I said, "How did you know?" He smiled, and said, "When a patient goes to a doctor, he must tell him his true complaint. So you have come only for this, am I right?" I said, "yes".

S: *What did he say?*

P: He started saying, "When Perival says that...", and I interrupted, "How do you know what he said in Belgaum yesterday?" There were no cell phones in those days. He said, "If we do not have that much of connectivity, what am I here for? What has he done to bring me to this position?" I asked him a few more questions. He finally said, "Don't even think of it. Why are you bothered? He has already blessed you, and told you that you will build the hospital, period." I said to myself that there was no point in pushing this matter further.

S: *You had to walk out of the deal!*

P: Everyone, including my brother, told me to keep the property as I had obtained it for peanuts. I told them, "No, I did not buy it to make money. It will defeat the very purpose of my cause". I sent an emissary to the seller, who interestingly, had received another proposal in the meantime, but did not know how to tell me and withdraw. He was thinking of offering me Rs 25 lakh to buy back the property. Mind you, I had only paid him an advance of Rs 1.5 lakh. The emissary, who knew what *swamiji* had told me, returned with this new proposal. He said, "I know what *swamiji* has told you. How about making some money?" He told me of the seller's proposal. I replied, "I did not make the deal to make money—just get my cheque of the advanced amount back, period."

As I returned to my office, my secretary brought in a cover which contained the auction notice of a good property. I saw the property, liked it, felt its aura was good, and bought it. Again, a relative came forward after some days and said, "We have an offer of Rs 4 crore", and I gave him the familiar reply, "I am not here to make money in land deals". The hospital is standing on that site today.

Two important points emerge from this narration:

1. *Prathap's faith in gurus, and*

2. *His commitment to build the hospital only on the site of his choice, and not make any money in property deals for which he had many attractive offers.*

In the sixties and seventies, few discussions used to take place amongst the corporate on personal belief systems, and spiritual practices, like meditation, regular visits to religious places, dhyan, dharana, satsang, or on consulting gurus, astrologers, counsellors, etc. From the mid-eighties, it became an accepted part of substantive discussions, and the lingo that went with it. It could be construed that for producing still better results, leaders were trying to access spiritual power after having reached the limits of intellectual and emotional power.

I found Prathap did not deviate from the rational frame of thinking. In life, we require doctors, advisers, consultants, counsellors, teachers, guides, astrologers, and gurus for different purposes and paths. Whom and what to believe depends upon the mix of traditional doctrines, upbringing, and experience. Whom to consult is an individual's choice, and one has to respect its sanctity. Said G. K. Chesterton, "Reason is itself a matter of faith. It is an act of faith to assert that our thoughts have any relation to reality at all".

The second point is that Prathap did not fall prey to monetary allurements in property transactions. Ethically, this is highly significant. His crystal clear thinking on the purpose of why he wanted a property, comes through with amazing consistency, i.e. build a hospital. He did not deviate from that original objective.

This illustrates that a great institution, devoted to a noble cause, gets built on a value-based foundation. Unless we get a glimpse of the inner world of a creative mind like Prathap's, our understanding of what led to what, will remain incomplete, and therefore unusable. If you want to connect his belief system to action, then the outcome is what we crave for public life. The faith in gurus in selecting the right property for a hospital, and not making money in land deals but religiously sticking to his mission of building a hospital on whichever property he finally buys, looks sanguine enough for adoption. Ultimately our faith and belief create our reality.

Nurse Centered Brand

From a single hospital in Chennai, the Apollo Group has shot to centre stage of India's health space. By striving to remain on the cutting edge of technology, the group is trying to bring healthcare of international standards within the reach of every individual. The group's product band-width of clinics, tele-medicine, local community involvement, integrated delivery network, and specialty hospitals has enhanced its reach factor many times over.

Prathap's farsighted leadership has given Apollo stature. Behind recognised brands, there are always tall personalities. They are brands in themselves. Yet while institutionalising their creation, they put up a logo which reflects their philosophy. Apollo's brand has a Red Cross, and a nurse carrying a torch. I was impressed. I asked Prathap to explain the thought behind it.

P: *Caring for human beings is the motto*, not looking at watches, as factory workers or clerks in other organisations do. *Sickness has no holiday. Every person working in the hospital must leave the continuity of process intact.* That's why logo selection was a thoughtful game. It is understood that we were supposed to bring in the latest technology to make the big difference, but to the patient, it is the human face. We debated many proposals. I gave it long thought. The only person who gives *continuity to patient care* is the nurse. She takes orders from doctors, gives orders to housekeepers, F&B staff, and she is responsible for process continuity.

S: *She is the pivot around which things move to reach the patient.*

P: Correct. Even today, patients have the greatest pride in the individual, i.e. the nurse. So we put her at the centre of our logo. Despite turnover, our nurses have been able to maintain the quality and continuity of service to patients. The reason is the culture we have built in the hospital. It is based on the principle that we are born into this profession to provide continuous care to the patients.

S: *The feedback from patients...*

P: It corroborates with what I am saying. If you go through the letters received, none of them have referred to the doctor. He was forgotten. The excellent equipment is not remembered. But they always mention that the nurse was very good, and the F&B guy, for the way he served food, or the politeness of the housekeeping boys, etc. It does not mean that they are not grateful to the doctor for having saved their lives, or giving effective treatment. But their satisfaction depends heavily upon these other services, which elsewhere are woefully inadequate, if not altogether callous and careless. We realise that when we make the difference in these areas, it means a lot to the patients, it really does.

S: *How is the demand in the west for your nurses?*

P: Fantastic. They are rated as the finest nurses. They are selected automatically, as soon as they state they are from Apollo. I tell them, "If you put in that extra bit, you will be super girls. You must always think, how can I do better? I don't think you believe that there is some energy that you are not unlocking. We have this Global Nursing Programme, which is a golden opportunity, don't miss it.

S: *How do they present themselves?*

P: That's the problem. We have now started a "Finishing School" for our nurses, where we have a free three week course for nurses going abroad. The idea is that they learn to speak well, dress well, and present themselves. Anybody going from India must be instantly accepted. The nurses there do not have any better knowledge, but they impress because they present themselves well. I want our nurses to be their first choices.

S: *You mean they lack the selling skills.*

P: Very much. When HCA officers came, they found our girls far superior to those they saw from other hospitals in India. They said there was no match. We trained them. It is not that they were not capable. They had no opportunity and training. And we provided it. We took a holistic look at the nurse's job and devised methods to arrest the turnover.

What Prathap did was to accept the reality:

(a) *lucrative jobs abroad will lure anybody to apply and emigrate*

(b) *in the societal order, the job of a nurse is considered of a lower status*

(c) *there was no pride left in the job, though the responsibility was enormous*

(d) *the credit always went to the doctors, adversely affecting the nurse's self-esteem*

He took the following steps to alter it:

(a) gave more responsibility, rewards, and recognition, which enriched the nurse's job

(b) pushed the job to the centre stage of the entire hospital operating system

(c) started a nursing college to keep the pipeline full

(d) evinced keen interest in bettering their prospects in the overseas market by providing all round training on personality development

(e) encouraged going abroad if better opportunities came up, and in fact, prepared them for such emigration

This proactive approach endeared Apollo to the migratory tribe of nurses, and to an extent, helped keep the turnover down to manageable proportions. It was a good policy decision, reflecting great foresight and mature thought. If one doesn't create a niche in the customers' mind, one's future options become limited. Prathap positioned the nurse in the minds of patients by creating a nurse centred brand.

Management guru Peter Drucker once said: you have to decide what business your are in, by looking from "outside in", from the point of customer and market. This is exactly what Prathap gave a deep thought to. What is it that the patient wants and remembers? It is consistent care. Brand expert Jack Trout says, "More than anything else, successful positioning requires consistency". In making nurses the pivot of the entire operative system, he ensured delivery of consistent care to the patients.

Experience the Apollo

P: What we did, was make the Nurse, the brand ambassador. The service staff must empathise with patients, and provide continuous care: this is the focus of our philosophy. Whether it means food and beverages, or housekeeping, all functions are important but contact with the patient happens through the nurse. She coordinates and ensures that the patient is looked after with care.

S: *What about the quality of the food?*

P: When we opened the hospital, people said things like, that the goddamn *idli* doesn't break. I spoke to the F&B staff, and today they make the finest *idli* in the world. My philosophy is very simple. I say to the doctors, nurses, technologists, and receptionists, "Don't do any more than you would have done if that patient was your friend, father, mother, sister, or cousin. Don't do anything special. Just imagine that the other person is close to you. That philosophy grew in time. Now of course, we have more systematic induction and training programmes.

S: *You wanted your staff to meet patient requirements on the patients' terms. In other industries they call it customer satisfaction.*

P: Yes. They have expectations, and we must fulfil them. In the initial years, we used to say, we must have satisfied patients, excellent service, etc. We then began saying, the patient must go back with a passion for life. Now we say, since we have achieved a certain level in fulfilling patient expectations, we must go beyond those expectations.

S: *And what would that be?*

P: *The patient must experience Apollo*. This thought is evolving out of the patients' articulation of their genuine needs. I need to fine-tune it. We tell the staff, whatever you do, please add TLC to it, i.e. *Tender Loving Care*. You will see the big difference it makes to the patient. You are the real heroes because you maintain the momentum and the quality of services we provide. When you retire, you must have the satisfaction of the job well done and the blessings of needy patients.

Said Oscar Wilde, "Experience is the name everyone gives to their mistakes". It is not uncommon for most people to narrate experiences, which have negative and pessimistic, even cynical connotations. It is not a reflection of reality but of a mindset that tends to ignore the hopeful, positive, optimistic, creative parts of experiencing. It is selective experiencing: as you think, so you see! Such seeing and storing as experience is safe because it fits into the vault of similar collections. Most of us are not brought up to experience life positively.

S: In resetting the mindset of your staff, you are trying for a major breakthrough in providing patient care, by redefining the purpose of a hospital. There is big money in this perceptual jump. It will be easier for staff to make meaning of the concept if it is backed by examples. Are you giving such examples?

P: Yes. If the boiler or sterilisation unit did not work, patients would say the hospital has come to a standstill. So one must ensure that the boiler works round the clock, 365 days of the year. That is the kind of individual commitment we want, and so far we have been able to get it.

Prathap has passionately tried to inculcate pride in his staff over what they do. He has appealed to their emotions, emphasised that the patients are like their near and dear relatives; he has thus influenced them to empathise. We know people dread going to a hospital. Norman Cousins in his classic, The Healing Heart *says, "Nothing is more essential in the treatment of a serious disease than liberating the patient from panic and foreboding". In sculpting a reassuring future such as this, a new idea like "Experience the Apollo" is a step in the right direction. I wondered where Prathap got such novel concepts? He said, "I love what I do".*

The influential anthropologist Abraham Maslow, says that people become more authentic, more self-disciplined by honouring the commitments they value most. They just do what they say they will do. Marsha Sinetar's best seller, Do What You Love The Money Will Follow *(1987), narrates how work, love, play, and even devotion, are unified into a cohesive activity for the fully developed, self-actualising personality. Prathap loves what he is doing. His results would not surprise Marsha, because he fits her bill of a self-actualising personality!*

S: *You have done everything so thoughtfully—there must be story and a thought behind christening the hospital 'Apollo'.*

P: There was a long discussion over it. It was my daughter Suneeta who suggested it. Apollo landed on the moon in 1970, while we were staying three miles away from the launch pad, and we saw it from very close quarters. Suneeta comes out with ideas, which we laugh at many times. I thought she was joking, so I said, "Don't be foolish". She replied, "Daddy, I am not kidding. You want name that depicts both science and medicine. Apollo is a Greek god. The God of healing!"

S: *Jack Trout in his latest book,* The 22 Immutable Laws of Branding *says, "The most important branding decision you will ever make is what to name your product or service because in the long run a brand is nothing more than a name". That's how you came to give it the name, Apollo, the God of healing.*

P: This was in 1979. My wife consulted a numerology astrologer, who said that only "Apollo Hospital" didn't add to a propitious number. He suggested Apollo Hospitals Enterprise Ltd. (AHEL). He also added 's' to make it "Hospitals". It was a resounding name because it gave me a new concept—to build not one hospital but many hospitals. He had predicted Apollo would take us places, and that the whole country would be talking about our giant strides in healthcare space. To our pleasant surprise his prediction came true.

S: *Was this the only rationale behind opening so many multidisciplinary hospitals?*

P: No. Earlier, on a visit to Boston, a colleague of mine, said, "Prathap, why are you building only a heart hospital? You know heart problems are the result of many other problems. You can't treat the heart in isolation. You are trying to treat one organ where you need to tackle the totality, the whole human system. Look at Mass General—it is famous because it has facilities for every discipline". I was glad to have this 'whole system perspective' brought to my attention. And we decided that the hospital should be multidisciplinary.

This *"whole system" approach incubated in Prathap for a decade to produce the idea of making hospital an experience to cherish.* Experiencing the hospital *is undoubtedly a creative breakthrough! Hospital and best service, healthcare, and health space are compatible partners but "experiencing" and a hospital at that, is beyond the ken of billions of people like me. This is a conceptual jump to provide service at six-sigma level! Now the challenge faced by Prathap and his team lies in elevating the quality of service mindset to its highest potential. That, I am sure they know, is a tall order indeed!*

So one thing led to another—not in any particular sequence though. In the birth and growth of a chain of multipurpose hospitals we see circumstantial, rational, and belief system inputs crystallising Prathap's thought process.

- *Circumstantial: The death of a patient leading to fundamental thinking on the unavailability of hospital equipment and the need to build a well-equipped facility. The death of a patient led to the birth of an institution. The availability of a role model in Thomas First Jr and his Hospital Corporation of America (HCA) provided a moral boost.*

- *Rational: Keith's advice on "whole system approach" led to the building of multipurpose hospitals rather than heart hospitals. There was no desire to make money in property deals because the purpose was to build a hospital, and hospital only.*

- *Belief System: His religious wife Sucharitha's belief in God, rishis, and astrologers has played a significant role. Prathap and Sucharitha consulted them with faith. Their advice given according to the* shastras *(sciences), strengthened the couple's faith in the implicate order.*

An Overview of Contributions

Prathap had to leave for an unscheduled urgent meeting. Although, I had not interviewed for this book any person apart from the list of people profiled, I thought of using the time available to meet his daughter Sangita, who looks after HR. In retrospect, it was a useful intermission. Her observations provided a better understanding of her father, Apollo organisation, and the daughters' contribution. From the very beginning, Sangita (San) and her three sisters participated in the unfolding of this reality. I decided to probe the professional aspect of organisation behaviour.

S: *Apollo's SWOT looks good. What are the threats that concern you?*

San: Competition from the evolution of large groups could be a threat. We have yet to see a healthcare organisation of our scale and depth, but every geography has its local threats, e.g. a local hospital in cardiology at Hyderabad, L V hospital in eye programmes, and some paediatric hospitals. At Delhi, there is Escorts for cardiac treatment, at Chennai or Banglore there are others. It's a very regional kind of competition, or in niche areas. Sizing the potential of the huge Indian market, international players entering two years down the line cannot be overlooked. Yet, daddy believes competition is good. It keeps everyone on their toes, provides great impetus for improvement, and results in better facilities for the patients.

S: *What is Apollo's USP?*

San: It is of course daddy, our institutionalised personal touch, and technology. In that personal touch, the skills and commitment of our doctors, nurses, and other staff is a vital ingredient. Daddy still holds that very special place in peoples' minds. If he were to retire, there would certainly be a gap. It would be difficult to fill that gap. But as he says, the teams will carry on effectively and a leader will emerge.

S: *Will you please give an example of commitment in action?*

San: If a similar 1,200-bed hospital was being commissioned in one year by an organisation, without a completely structured central office, or HR function, you would have been surprised to see it done so well. It was possible because of peoples' commitment. This is what management wants, what is good to do, what I am supposed to do, and it shall be done, was the attitude that translated commitment into action. The doubters and the questioners were few. Our ability to move fast was the key.

S: *How did you get this kind of commitment?*

San: It is a part of daddy's psyche. He doesn't leave things for tomorrow if they can be done today, this hour, this minute. His bias is towards action and movement. That action focus is again related to the basic philosophy that directly or indirectly "what I do" goes on to contribute to patient care and building the country's infrastructure. This unwavering commitment has now become a part of the organisation psyche.

S: *Do doctors and others own the ideas and Apollo culture?*

San: Yes, by drawing inspiration from him, we have inculcated his way of thinking in every member of the organisation. To energise the doctors and others with his ideals is the task of the foundation. At present, they defend those ideals more strongly than the promoter himself. I believe that it is something that comes from within, and if you ignite that in people, they do it with added vigour. If you take a round here, you will come across many doctors, ward boys, nurses, etc, with their individual stories about their commitment to Apollo.

S: *Can you provide an example?*

San: One of India's leading cardiologist, who works with us, was invited by a private hospital to join them. The chief of that hospital told him, "You are not number one at Apollo. We will offer you anything you want, join us". The doctor asked for Rs 4 crore. I said, "How could you ask for such a figure?" He said he knew they would never be able to give him that kind of an amount.

S: *What happened then?*

San: He told them, twelve years back, "immediately after I joined Apollo, I obtained a fellowship from France. I felt embarrassed to ask Apollo to let me go, because less than two months had elapsed since my six months of training in France, on their behalf". However, he garnered the courage to mention it to daddy casually. Daddy immediately told him to go since that opportunity was a good.

S: Good thinking.

San: The next day I remember our CEO met us in the corridor. He handed over a cover to the doctor saying, "Dr.Reddy wondered how you would fund the tickets, and manage other expenses. So he asked me to hand this over to you". The doctor said, "That Rs 20,000 is worth 5 crore today. I know people with such large heart are not available elsewhere. I will never leave Apollo". Such stories come in legions at Apollo.

This is not compassion—it's a replicable example of foresight and strategic investment in a rare asset—in a good cardiologist! While building specialty institutions one has difficulty in gathering the best brains in the country. Only a leader of tremendous foresight knows how to attract them, invest in them, and retain them.

When the atomic research centre was being set up at Bombay, I remember having read about JRD telling Homi Bhabha to tour the world and find the best scientists at whatever the cost. His dictum was that such institutions are built around people: you cannot fit them in boxes shown on an organisation chart and build an institution of scientific excellence. *And what an astounding institution Bhabha built!*

S: *Clearly, the whole business of healthcare is built on people strengths because ultimately healthcare means people looking after other people.*

San: You may have beautiful buildings, the best technology, but ultimately its doctors, nurses, and others serving the patients. It's the feeling, caring, and commitment, which matter. It's the institution with a sense of belonging, which functions on that deep note. One of our weaknesses could be the rate at which we are growing, the momentum, the spread, and whether we will be able to maintain the quality and depth of our commitment. The organisation is in place, and the products are there. The mind, the heart, and the hands are also there, which make an institution.

S: *And you are trying to systematise Prathap's philosophy?*

San: Well, where does it come from? It comes from daddy because he feels that *the vision is beyond individual self.* He feels the Indian healthcare scenario needs a lot. Every effort goes towards building his kind of affectionate relationship towards every patient who comes to us. This is an ideology and not a system. System means how you admit, register, move the patient, provide service and treatment, keep records, and the rest. He laid that down clearly right at the beginning when there were just three people. Later Eichers, Eupen, and Mani came in and strengthened the systems in different areas.

S: *Keeping the focus on diversification and growth with the same value system is your concern.*

San: Exactly. That's why our geography-wise SWOT is different. We try to integrate the strengths, to minimise the weaknesses. Daddy saw it happening probably two or three years ago, and that's why his emphasis on IT, connectivity, and communications.

S: *It is the same issue. Those who have not gone deep into the core competencies and spread beyond it, are suffering from competition.*

San: Correct. We have all the building blocks necessary for the most powerful healthcare structure—what is known as Integrated Delivery Network (IDN). For its effective functioning though, one requires the tertiary care, IT connectivity, clinics, and in-depth knowledge.

S: *You can outsource some things but not TLC,* Tender Loving Care!

San: We should grow inside. In terms of opportunities, there are plenty within the country as well as internationally. Colombo reached cash break even point within eight months, which, none of our hospitals in India have been able to achieve. We are looking at markets in the Middle East, UK, and even US.

S: *How are you organised at the top?*

San: There is an executive council of CEOs and directors. All functions are represented. CFO is the secretary. Daddy doesn't sit on the council, which enables a frank discussion on all major subjects. In his presence the members are hesitant in bringing up the bad points, even though we need to know them. One doesn't have to be physically present for council meetings, we do it over the telecom.

S: *Is the council a policy making body?*

San: In many cases, yes. Directors have veto power on some issues, which we are delimiting as the council matures. It will take some time. We have a bottom–up approach, which gels well, with daddy giving broad direction.

S: *It is a delicate subject of how one integrates stakeholder and family interests, with professionals and operational decision-making issues. The way you present your organisation, the language you use, and the problems you tackle give me the impression that you are a professional.*

San: Exactly. If anybody is doing a better job, I am prepared to learn from them. I do not disqualify from becoming a professional simply because I am a family member, do I? If someone can do a better job with the same commitment, drive, and dedication to the objectives, we can absorb or even step down when the time comes. We believe we have contributed substantially to this venture from the start. Venture capitalists understand the entrepreneurial contribution but do not fully appreciate the tremendous value-addition made by the family in building a professional hospital. You may say we were fortuitously placed to do so, but that was an unalterable given, which daddy exploited to the hilt.

S: *Prathap's thought processes, ideals, and vision might come naturally to either or all of you, being his daughters; but are any of you doctors?*

San: None.

S: *Your motto is to provide TLC. Mothers provide it instinctively. If you are a mother, you are a mother. A child needs a mother's touch, and it is irreplaceable. It cannot be formally provided for while planning succession. TLC is personal. It is a kind of sharing, difficult to institutionalise. Have you given a thought to how you daughters are going to carry forward the ideology after Prathap?*

San: In terms of business development we definitely plan how we work now, and how we could work later on. In terms of the special role that he plays, it is not what we can plan now. Our focus and thrust for inculcating the spirit of TLC is on a nurse, who is a surrogate mother. She comes in everybody's life at some point or the other. For want of a better word, TLC is a difficult "product" to produce and deliver. This is a product, which comes through the amalgam of the mind, hand, and heart. It is not an easy alchemy to understand, and much more difficult to adopt. Its origins are beyond even these three elements.

S: TLC is a product of the heart, which heals patients. The patient has a healing system too, which needs to be freed to do the job. It is the responsibility of the physician and the nurse to provide the TLC, to free it. You have a unique and complex need to handle!

San: We are providing the congenial environment and framework for such innovative work. In this ambience one works beyond self-interests, or that of one's family, and the call of duty. Here, one identifies with the patient. To the extent possible, we give systematic inputs but what is of a metaphysical nature cannot be fully put into a training module beyond exposure to the application of Emotional Intelligence. Each one of us, the sisters, doctors, administrators, and others, spreads the message as best we can. It's a process of ongoing nurturance and we are at it, ceaselessly.

S: Prathap told me that he made you work as a secretary when he was operating from the garage. You were probably sitting on the bonnet of your car while he told you to do some thing.

San: Yes, if I had a microbiology paper, and he had a press conference, he would say, "That is not important. This is more important, write this out first". So there I would be, typing a note instead of studying. This is something we have grown up with. He has an ability to nurture talent. But my sister actually did a lot more than I did in the early days.

S: It is the same competency he has extended in assembling the Apollo family and nurturing it—with a passion for getting things done.

San: You see how the housekeeping boys perform. They do not think of themselves as just broom pushers. They know they are important to the organisation. They have gone through basic life support courses. Let's take the office boys. Each one of them is in charge of a position, e.g. the one who is in charge of gas utilities, has machinery worth Rs 50 lakh under him. He is made aware of it. We make them responsible, and entrust duties with faith.

S: *You mean it is doable.*

San: 100 per cent. We have to keep on building these elements of excellence, which will matter in peoples' minds as the key differentiates from our competition.

S: *What does the HR SWOT look like, and what are the current concerns?*

San: It is a mix old and new blood. Each hospital has different issues. It is our ability to handle the migration from slightly older to a new culture. The old have loyalty but their capacity to keep pace with new systems poses problems. They are a part of the family and to tell them that they are redundant is heart breaking. Assimilating new professionals in the new culture is another issue.

S: *How is the interface between doctors and management?*

San: Very often, the perceptions of interests are at loggerheads. We are not fighting but working towards creation of more health space. We have tapped our doctors' medical capabilities, which are most important, but we haven't tapped their community leadership potential. When daddy goes into the community, he commands 100 per cent respect. We have to build that degree of acceptance in other doctors. *We are a portal through which we are all aligned together.* I meet all 40 doctors in Hyderabad on a regular basis, and our CEOs at each location meet similarly to get their feedback and look after their needs.

S: *Have you benchmarked against best hospitals here and abroad?*

San: We are comparable, and in some cases even better. There is a lot to do in areas like performance appraisals. The work for a hospital is divided on the basis of geography. If you see the organisation chart, there is a fairly clear demarcation of responsibilities. As far as doctors' recruitment is concerned, daddy is still involved in a big way. He plays a central role because it's a specialist recruitment, which affects the patients crucially. The roles of his daughters are also clearly defined.

I returned to Prathap's room. I have not asked the leaders I interviewed for this book, their opinion on each colleague's contribution because they have all recognised the contribution made by their teams through the most glorious terms, and that was sufficient for my purpose. However, I asked Prathap for his opinion about his daughters' contribution because in the public perception one comes across an occasional comment that the entire show is run by his daughters.

He had no hesitation in saying that all his four daughters are very talented. They have different strengths in organisation functions like, finance, projects, general management, HR, etc. On their own merits, they have earned the respect of their colleagues and staff; for their knowledge, leadership, and interpersonal relations. They have contributed substantially to building Apollo to what it is today.

With four daughters entrenched in top decision making positions, the family hold over the organisation cannot be denied, but they are not there without significant contribution. How the organisation manages the transition to the post patriarch period is to be seen. There are many signposts, like the TVS group, plenty of research, and expert counsel, to guide them. For the present however, when Prathap says, "Each of them has individually and severally contributed to the phenomenal growth of Apollo", we can take it as a sufficient testimony of the ground reality.

This overview from Prathap about contributions made by doctors, nurses, staff, and his daughters, helps us to formulate a new law—the law of Contributory Care. It demonstrates that individually and collectively, excellent customer care can be provided on a continuous basis. Each one not only does his job but volunteers to do a bit of others' as well. Consequently, there are no omissions in service in overlapping functions, or during shift change. Building a culture of care is a gigantic but achievable task.

Process the Efforts Continuously

Prathap's entrepreneurship has won him many accolades. His creation, Apollo, bears testimony to his passionate commitment to build a world class healthcare facility.

His pioneering leadership has laid the foundation for making India a global healthcare destination. In all such success stories, there are elements of luck, effort, competencies (and positive attitude is also a competency), which conspire to produce outstanding results.

S: What do you think are the correlates of your performance.

P: I think fate probably puts one into a certain mode; it has definitely a role to play. But to march ahead one needs to put in relentless efforts. A patient has to survive. It is not the hospital efforts alone that can do that—he must reach the hospital on time. All of us have both fate and effort. Fate puts us in right place at right time. Through our efforts, we do our best to grow.

S: It is difficult to establish the exact correlation between the various factors that contributed to your success. Nonetheless, what would you mainly ascribe it to?

P: It is my continuous effort—100 per cent—to do more. The luck aspect is not in our hands, so what can be rationally connected are our efforts. I could have kept quiet after returning to India. Within three years, I was a leading cardiologist at Chennai. I was earning so well, the income tax folks called me a fool because I didn't know the number one and number two business, i.e. how to hide my income from the IT department by accepting payments in cash and not disclosing it. My secretaries collected the fees and I paid some 68 per cent tax. They used to say that they had no option but to be honest. See where fate leads you. Because I had white money, I could build the hospital.

S: In America also, you could have earned much more and led a comfortable life. That apart, did you make any special effort to remove the deficiencies in your work, so that the improvements are measurable in direct proportion to improved method of working? You have to make intelligent efforts, isn't it? You have to do a scientific analysis of your efforts and their linkage to results—some kind of process mapping.

P: Right. I was at the Mass General hospital when they did one of their first coronary angiographies. Unfortunately we lost the patient. MIT advisors were present inside the operation theatre. Exactly a week later, they brought another catheter for another angiogram. They said, "Would you now do it?" I picked up that experimental approach to efforts, i.e. to try out new things.

S: How did you use that in Apollo?

P: We have trained 270 doctors in the country in angioplasty. The lesson is, don't lose heart in the procedure. One is not inventing it. One is only bettering one's own technology skills. Do it again and see what happens. We are genuinely proud of what we have given to others.

S: In medical science, there is diagnosis, testing, and treatment, by trial and error and application, to proceed further. Over a period of time, that becomes scientific knowledge. These are the symptoms and this is the line of treatment. Similarly, did you apply the same method to improve the content and quality of your efforts?

P: You are asking a difficult question. My practice was different. At Apollo, the experience is different because everything has been done for the first time. Our intention was clear, it must be right every time. It cannot be like a factory—that you do 99 per cent right and 1 per cent is treated as rejection. In a hospital 99 per cent is not good enough. Here, rejection means death. Even then, we sometimes fail. So, *continuous improvement is the only answer, and a commitment not to accept even 1 per cent failure is the key to progress.*

S: How is the progress graph on surgeries?

P: Take a surgeon. His results elsewhere are usually 85 per cent success. When he is taken into Apollo, his first year the result is 97 per cent. Nobody in the country believes we did 270 surgeries at 97 per cent success rate. Next year, we did

600 surgeries at 97.8 per cent success rate. The whole country woke up. I told people that there is no secret in this.

S: *How come?*

P: I did not improve the skills of the surgeons. I analysed the whole problem. What are the steps necessary in the pre-operative stage, starting from admission, blood test, grouping, pre-operative preparations, getting the operation room ready, 100 per cent back up, then operation, and 100 per cent post-operation back up. That's all we perfected by making the necessary changes. The success rate improved dramatically. Analysis this year shows 99.3 per cent success.

S: *This is a system improvement carried out very professionally. In India, where is the major problem encountered?*

P: 7 per cent of the complications occur through blood transfusion. That's why we do our own blood tests, whether it is from the patients' relatives or whoever. It is as safe as in Seattle or Washington. We have enough emergency stock for three months.

S: *Would you please give an example?*

P: Dr. Soonawala from Bombay came to me in Delhi and said, "You have the greatest hospital in the whole world. Nowhere else in the world could a patient have survived with the kind of problem I faced in a delivery today". I said, "Coming from you doctor, I would like to say it compliments every one here. Tell me the story".

The minister for commerce, Rudy Pratap Singh's wife wanted to come to Bombay for delivery. Finally Mr Singh convinced Dr. Soonawala to fly to Delhi to do the delivery at Apollo. Dr. Soonawala said, "I finished the delivery and was about to remove the placenta. It had grown into the blood vessels, and as I removed it, the vessels broke. Blood was gushing out. For a minute I did not know what to do. Believe me, I never called, but in one minute flat there were three supporting doctors to help me out. 42 bottles of blood was given in the first hour. Nowhere else could it have been done with that kind of a dispatch. The Apollo doctors asked me to step back. They took over. This morning, after three days, they opened and stitched all the wounds, and the lady is back home, alive.

S: Amazing team work, passion to save the patient, extra alert support service, speedy application, and whatever else management pundits want to encapsulate and eulogise.

P: This is all possible. One must plan the whole process, to be ready to get into that gear in a matter of few minutes. You need an institution of that size...

S: ... peopled with a proactive mindset. What happens if a doctor doesn't perform properly?

P: Merciless—we send out those who do not perform to our standards. I tell the doctors, "I will give you all you want but I am going to ask for results, i.e. patient satisfaction". Once a doctor at our Delhi hospital was removed for dereliction of duty. Twenty members from Bihar came to see me. I told them, "I don't interfere in the decisions of the committee. If he has been found performing below our standards and the committee has recommended his removal, that's it". They approached the health minister, then the finance minister, and finally the Prime Minister, who called me up. I was surprised. I told him, "If you are not satisfied with the recommendation of that committee, I can appoint another one. But I have no reason to reverse their decision. They have not taken the decision for my sake, but for the sake of other patients".

This kind of bold and principled stand, against the Prime Minister, requires guts and belief in the logic of what one has done. One can be certain that the morale of the committee and staff soared high, and needless to add, respect for Prathap. This is high quality leadership rarely seen these days.

The Dhanvantari in Global Health Space

Prathap is ceaseless in his efforts to improve his practice and better his performance. His rational thinking in solving problems, and craze for doing things 100 per cent right, makes him improve processes and systems. People observe his actions to find that he is the same person who does what he says must be done. No empty talk!

Prathap is inviting the doctors' attention to their noble calling, "Heal the Patient". Only Prathap can take such a holistic approach. If Apollo is the God of healing, Prathap is a doctor with the healing touch, a *dhanvantari*, and he is guiding them towards *a path of healing*. Our tradition of *dhanvantaries* is age old and rich. Modern *dhanvantaries* use alternative medicines in addition to allopathy to cure patients. Their faith in supernatural powers is well known.

Prathap has immense faith in God and the role supernatural powers play in shaping our destiny. It was not known then, but becomes clear now, what God's intention was in naming the hospital Apollo. Only the God of healing, Apollo, can create global health space. God's intentions are always unknown. We are only instruments in his hands. With that faith, it looks like Pratap has been ordained to make India the world's destination for quality healthcare.

The space is vast, the health poor, and opportunities therefore innumerable. Health is wealth and India needs both, so does Asia, and the whole world. With the opening of a facility in Colombo, Prathap has taken the first step towards capturing the global health space. What A. V. Srinivasan says in *Managing a Modern Hospital* is pertinent: a quiet revolution is taking place ... the private sector participation in healthcare is on the increase because entrepreneurs and technocrats see immense opportunity for earning in this sector.

Not that there are none like Prathap amongst us. But we need a few hundred like him: entrepreneurial *dhanvantaries*. We also need such healthcare hospitals, where the word hospital becomes a misnomer, and *Healing Clinic* becomes an unbelievable reality. Names, like words and phrases, make a difference. They hurt or heal: Apollo heals. We have the market and people potential. We require inspiring examples to follow, and you just read one—Prathap and his Apollo.

★ ★ ★

5

Business in Aesthetics

- ❖ Aestheticisation of Everyday Life
- ❖ Creative Business Designing
- ❖ Assimilation of Cultures
- ❖ Evolutions and Transitions

- ♦ Exemplar—A Creative Businesswoman, Simone Tata

We can choose to live, on a daily basis, out of the highest standard of ethics, aesthetics, or health. Holistic choices express and let us better understand our own personal aesthetic: how we like to do things, what we stand for, what we find pleasing, necessary, and life enhancing.

—Marsha Sinetar
Elegant Choices, Healing Choices

Introduction

This chapter is about how business in aesthetics is fertilised through the inducement of art-conscious life styles and creative business designs. It's an evolutionary process, which leads the businessman to learn customer cultures and manage transitions smoothly.

Aestheticisation of Everyday Life

We see massive changes in life styles, in the way people have begun to live their daily lives. They appear to be making their lives into projects of beauty. They see themselves and their environments as objects of art. Therefore, the desire to see a coherent style in clothes, household furnishings, decor, and colour schemes is evident in the designer living!

When post-modernist writers describe this phenomenon as *aestheticisation of everyday life*, it sounds unfamiliar. Well it is. But the meaning is simple. It is their claim that the division between art and everyday life is being eroded. Artists and laymen, unknowingly and subconsciously, are collaborating to turn everyday life into aesthetic projects filled with art objects.

The noted Marathi humourist and playwright P. L. Deshpande, in his play *Asa Me Asamee* said, "From footwear, clothes, to hairstyles, you see everything matches, except the two in them". His mischievous face and body language poke fun at the numerous mismatched couples. The packed theatre giggles and laughs.

Increasingly, people are realising that life is to be lived beautifully every minute. It means looks, dresses, interiors—all have become important in the unending search for a perfect match of complementarity and contrasts. Marketing creatively evokes the right emotions to sell its products. Logic does not change emotions, perception does. The perceptual change is brought about by the use of mass media, models, and stories, which provoke the search for identity, and influence choices. In this transformation, retailing got the impetus—it has acquired a new dimension.

In effect, one sees that our dream towards designer lives is conspiring with forces of globalisation to mass customise our life styles and homogenise our cultures. This provides a staple diet for social forum activists, who claim to fight for the poor and the have-nots of the world. These protagonists conveniently ignore that the size and composition of today's middle and rich classes have considerably changed. Many amongst them belonged to the poor class not too long ago.

The other fundamental, albeit forgotten truth is that neither the capitalists nor the developed countries ever advocated mass production of human beings. Excess population can be a menace. At the same time, it provides a challenge to society, to meet the needs of a growing population. Market forces sense the demand and step in to fulfil it. New ventures are born.

Former US ambassador to India, Prof. Galbraith, said "The business of business is to make man a more wanting animal" and to make him so is precisely the function of marketing. Marketing impregnates dreams, titillates desires, and produces artefacts for fulfilling the stoked longings. In upwardly mobile societies, it is more the feel of the product than the utility that matters—the look, the designer status, that become the USP.

These new sections of society are prepared to pay for products that feed their fantasies. It prompts innovative businessmen and women to invest in newer creations, evocative advertising, creative branding, and aggressive marketing drives. Says Ernest Sternberg, "This has led to a new stage in the development of an economy of icons. In this wondrous marketplace we find displayed not only designer clothes, but designer environments, and people with designer personalities!"

Designer living has opened up a whole new business in aesthetics. Whether it is property supplements in the newspapers, new shopping plazas, the flood of ads, or the settings in soap operas and movies, they are all in designer language, icons, quotations, and statements, that enhance one's self-esteem. It eventually tempts one to go in for the buy.

It is not a "need-based" basic business, but a "want-created" business. Look at any product, whether Pond's lotions, Hindustan Lever's shampoos, or the attractive dress lines at Shopper's Stop—they all are attempting to etch messages on one's subconscious mind. That is the rationale for post-modern business. The "need to want" business journey is through the portals of brand and ad management; call it the "art of inducement [or] seduction", whatever you like!

Creative Business Designing

The battle for inducement is fought on the mental turf. Occupation of mental space becomes crucial, and is done through creative advertising and various marketing techniques. Through colourful visuals and punch lines identifying with models, symbols, and feel-good anchors, the products are positioned in one's mind. Images are created in defining an event, a person, or an era, through electronic media and other communication devices. With repeated messages, the desire gets converted into active buying.

Whether it is the latest Sony sound system, or Madhuri Dixit certified herbal creams, or Sachin Tendulkar signature Palio car, it is the creative faculty of business people and their expert teams that design our wants, and fulfil them. They faithfully honour Prof. Galbraith's truism. It is the simultaneous designing of want and product, that creates new business.

If we were to stick to the basic, bare minimum needs of *roti, kapda, makan*, we would be glued to poverty as we have been. The hierarchy of needs shift constantly. Once the physiological safety and social needs are met, people move to the needs of esteem and self-actualisation. Large sections of our society are still at the basic physiological and safety needs level. These are being met through low priced affordable goods that we manufacture and sell through bazaars. It is the esteem needs—status, recognition, and sense of achievement—that the upwardly mobile class seeks, to which business houses pander.

To what extent we should go on this wanton creation is a debatable issue of societal balance. But one thing is certain— the route to alleviation of poverty and equitable distribution is through want creation; "growth first" is the underlying principle. *Our potential for creating prosperity is high but our propensity for living in poverty has been much higher.* However, the demographics are slowly changing. People are in an upbeat mood to experience prosperity, and that augurs well.

Unless the creative amongst us design prosperity, we cannot be ejected out of this all-pervasive ethos of poverty. One cannot design the future by analysing the past. Non-conventional thinking is required to move forward. Says Edward de Bono "Design thinking is very different from traditional judgement thinking. For judgement thinking, the desired output is truth, or apparent truth. For design thinking, the output is value".

An atmosphere of free enterprise releases creative forces, which we are seeing in India. Creativity is seen in any act, idea, or product, that transforms an existing domain—the sphere of activity. Look at the way the business of banking or retailing is now conducted. Although the results are achieved through teams, at the heart of such creation is an individual, a creative person.

The creative individual is someone whose thoughts or actions changes a domain or establishes a new one. He regularly solves problems, fashions products, and raises questions challenging existing assumptions that lead to new insights and novel solutions. Jamshetji Tata and Ghanshyam Das Birla were creative businessmen.

These people use creativity as an instrument, not only for personal and social gain, but more for a deep philosophical search for meaning. The quest for meaning is an ongoing activity, which these people conduct in the terrain of their expertise, whether it is biotechnology, steel, milk, housing, banking, pharmaceuticals, petrochemicals, or IT.

Some of those whom I interviewed had made conscious or unconscious attempts at penetrating the deeper layers of the mystery of the self, and perhaps even the greater mystery of being. The central theme appears to be *can we change the story of life, by design?* The medium is business, and for the expression of creative impulses one needs to be situated in one's domain. These knowledge workers are, I guess, determinedly focused on changing the course of their lives. It positively influences others who work with them.

In this book you will see this theme running through the stories of Vaman Kamath, Venu Srinivasan, Amrita Patel, Prathap Reddy, Jamshed Irani, Mallika Srinivasan and Simone Tata. Look at the way Simone made Lakme a brand. The mission was to make Indian women look more beautiful with her products, whether lipstick, eyeliners, or whatever, which were then not available in India.

Simone's transition from cosmetics to successfully establishing the retail chain Westside was also creative. In fact, many times the correct solution to a problem is an aesthetic one, and she found it grounded in her domain strength. It is not only creative product designing—Simone excelled in creatively designing the business as well. This will have a lasting impact in the field of retailing.

The global corporate leaders recently attended a workshop on *creativity* at Davos, where they had gathered for the World Economic Forum meeting. Quincy Jones said, "Walk in the shoes of the greatest people you know. Everyone can be artistic. One doesn't have to be a painter or musician to be artistic. It is being an artist in whatever you do". This book persuades you to put on the shoes of seven esteemed leaders, walk through their life stories, and experience the difference it makes to your thinking.

At the same workshop, a learning expert from Denmark, Lotte Dorsoe quoted Plato's well-known view that there are three ways of knowing the world—the good, the true, and the beautiful. In the specialised industrial age the world concentrated on what was "true", now it is focusing on ethics, i.e. what is "good"—good governance, etc—and gradually moving into the arts, i.e. what is "beautiful". We are developing an integrated way of thinking and working.

Dr. Swati Piramal Head, Strategic Alliances and Communications, Nicholas Piramal, sent dispatches on this conference titled *Davos Diary* to Times of India. She penned a piece *Thought Leaders Go on a Flight of Fancy*. Says Piramal, "Now, creativity is an admired and sought after trait in business. But despite, or perhaps because of, the premium that creativity commands, there is no easy way of cultivating it".

Piramal is right, it is not easy to cultivate creativity. That does not mean it is only inborn and cannot be developed at all. What is inborn could be considered a "gift". Training modules are available. Prof. Pradip Khandwalla has done some commendable work in this field. His two volumes, *Corporate Creativity*, and *Life Long Creativity* bear testimony to it.

In the creative process, the driving force is the desire to produce a specific time bound result. With the solid experience of Lakme under her belt, Simone cautiously but confidently moved into retailing, using her aesthetic sense. She loved her creation enough to bring it into being. Her learning curve has been high. Learners do not assume a fixed level of capacities and expand beyond them. Creative persons practice objectively observing current reality. Their search for quality improvement in service and products is unending. In long-term projects, they are able to hold on to structural tension for years between their vision and the relevant current reality. This trait is found in creative scientists, artists, and performers. Robert Fritz says that structural tension is an incredibly powerful force in creation but it is impossible to develop if one does not know what one wants. Picture the result you want, i.e. visualise the outcome.

That's why one sees creative people:

- choose certain domains, because of a powerful calling to do so, an inner urge to dedicate life to that field
- set deadlines for organising actions, to enable people to build energy and momentum
- think to design new possibilities
- focus on creation rather than on them

While talking about their achievements I could see in their eyes glints of joy about the creation, their piece of art so to speak. The "ME" in it was hardly visible.

Through stories scripted here, or known otherwise, we know that people are born with some inherent talents. Together with that asset, factors of luck and grace of God are at work in bestowing recognition on them. Whether an artist or a businessman, without access to domain and the support of his field, he has no chance of getting recognition. However, through personal creativity a person can still make his day-to-day experiences more rewarding. With innovative thinking and new ideas one is able to substantially reduce boredom. It works as a tonic against passages of "low" feeling. I have experienced it and so have you. Haven't you?

Creative people:

- have huge stocks of energy
- rarely get exhausted or distracted
- know how to gainfully use that flow of energy because they are less lazy

- are more disciplined in controlling their time, i.e. energy, space, and activity

- are curious about everything and cultivate interest in many things

- have the capacity to get surprised and surprise others in newer dimensions of everyday experiences

The cerebral hardware is the same but these business leaders and managers have special thinking skills. The way they think about what they think is significantly different.

Assimilation of Cultures

The world has always been multicultural. The understanding of other cultures however, has been limited. It has improved considerably with the current information age, and feelings of racial superiority have subsided to a great extent. Whether or not assimilation of societal cultures beyond a point is desirable, is contentious. Many consider it not so healthy because it gives rise to the feeling of loss of identity.

The stakeholders largely shape the culture of the organisation although business operates on economic parameters and measure it by financial results. Many organisations have absorbed the quality culture, just-in-time (JIT) approach and manufacturing process from Japan. Most of the management concepts from "Management by Objectives" (MBO) to "Branding" have come from America. The management of corporate culture became a hot issue in the late 20th Century. Now mergers, acquisitions, and globalisation, have again brought it to the fore. The organisational lingo which shapes the culture is western in any case.

Further, a company's culture is determined by a set of priorities over a long period of history. It is made public in its mission and vision statements. It is seen in its structure and distribution of power between different functions and departments. In India, from 1950 to 1975, power was with production and manufacturing. Between 1975 and 2000, it gradually passed on to marketing. Currently, human resources (HR) is acquiring some power, which basically means, the CEOs have begun to handle it themselves. Many CEOs spend considerable time in establishing synergy between HR and other divisional heads rather than in playing divisive games. That malady infested a large number of organisations in the past. The reasons for this change are:

- people assets have become strategically crucial—there is shortage of talent
- HR is recognised as an integral function
- young knowledge workers demand transparency in HR policies, practices, and performance
- internet and restructuring of organisations have lead to more open communications

The style change at the top had a major positive impact on organisation cultures. There are many assumptions and beliefs which managers carry, which are debated openly. The leader's style is an important ingredient in that basket of suppositions. They stand to gain from allowing employees to air their views freely.

An expatriate businessman has a choice in the adoption of cultures. He may decide to absorb the host country's culture for the purpose of business but not in private life, or get wholly soaked in it because he takes a liking to it.

For creative leaders though, such reasons based on business considerations and material advantages, may not be enough for the absorption of cultures. Operating within one's domain is more rewarding and appealing even if one's business is in a foreign country. To become successful in the host country one must understand the nuances of different cultures.

It is this passion that makes a leader an eternal learner and assimilator of different cultures. Simone did not jump from cosmetics to retailing just because huge opportunities were opening up. They may have provided the trigger but what essentially led her to decide was the great urge to express her love for aesthetics.

To find the right mix of colours for fabric and design layout is the secret of brain cell's behaviour or to make the shopping ambience an experience for the customers to cherish, is in itself energising, irrespective of the rewards in it. None might know about it; yet the designer or artist in a businessman likes to engage in that self-satisfying activity. This emotion is not found in large number of managers.

In Creativity, Mihaly Csikszentmihalyi says, *"Consuming culture is never as rewarding as producing it"*. Simone and her team produced Lakme. Now her Westside stores, with their collection of beautiful products and friendly ambience, offer an experience in elegant shopping. It appears that her tremendous capacity for cultural assimilation has made her aesthetic sense increasingly fertile. A Swiss by birth, her global mind has taken firm roots in local ethos. A unique cultivation indeed! I see her moves synchronised with world events.

Evolutions and Transitions

The dissolution of the socialist empire of USSR, along with advent of globalisation and Internet gave a jerky and bewildering start in 1990 to the whole process of global restructuring. It is now becoming clear that it was the start of an evolutionary process. It has forced world power blocks, especially America, to move from parochial divisive thinking to unitary all-inclusive global thinking. 9/11 has given it a further boost.

Evolution often moves forward by leaps of trans-causal events. Swiss psychologist Carl Jung said, "Synchronicity suggests that there is an interconnection or unity of causally unrelated events". The conjunction of these events gives credence to Jung's postulation.

People however, find it scary to make this transition from a world of secure lifetime employment, to an insecure world dictated by the behaviour of markets, where jobs are available but not protected employment of the kind we were accustomed to. However, the fact remains that markets will continue to rule for the time being, and the new order will unfold within a decade from the present turbulence.

We are witnesses to a marathon between developing countries to capture a fair share of the global market for goods and services. It is to the credit of our entrepreneurs that they took the initiative when the government relaxed its hold on economy (around the period 1990–1992). Their drive to coax the middle class to buy more is a major lever in the growth of economy. Businessmen the world over have recognised this opportunity and are using all manner of marketing gimmicks to allure that class to newer products and services. Daniel Griswold, Associate Director, Centre for Trade Policy Studies, Cato Institute said, "We need to look at a different set of criteria for what it takes to create a truly global middle class, in the next 50 years" (*Business Today*, February 29, 2004). You can see the importance being attached to this creation. This is where creative work is involved—in changing the mindset of the middle class from saving to spending. It's a major transition.

In this structural change, retailing presents a great global opportunity. And it was this emerging trend, of the bulging middle class's potential to buy, that businesswomen like Simone saw in the late eighties and early nineties. It was also an evolutionary process for all business-minds. What we are currently witnessing is its unfathomable speed.

However, at the individual level, one needs to reflect on the passages of one's life. It is not that one needs to think about major transitions only at the intersection of the tryout twenties, turbulent thirties, flourishing forties, flaming fifties, serene sixties, and sage seventies that Gail Sheehy talked about in her best seller *Passages* (1995). With the flow of time one must constantly think ahead about changes in career, business, vocation, hobbies, or style. There is a wide overlap between any two "passages".

Such reflection leads one to think how to identify periods of transitions—between the end and the beginning—and learn to manage them. I found in my discussions with various business leaders that when confronted with a problematic situation they take the following steps:

- think why they are uncomfortable in a particular situation
- explore all sides of change: see it through a prism
- talk to someone knowledgeable and trustworthy
- take a stock of the unfinished agenda of life—what is waiting to happen
- don't take strong action—prefer not to make abrupt ends
- arrange temporary structures in phasing out operations in business
- recognise that transitions have a characteristic shape

There is an emptiness and germination between the end of one business and the beginning of another, or while changing vocations, roles, relocations etc. Said Ralph Waldo Emerson, "Not in his goals but in his transitions, Man is great".

A Creative Businesswoman— Simone Tata

India's best known cosmetic company Lakme (brand value Rs 200 crore) belonged to the House of Tatas. Westside, the retailing venture of Tatas (turnover Rs 112 crore; profit after tax Rs 17 crore as of March 2003) operates a chain of twelve stores in major metros across the country. The retail stores have become the darling of India's burgeoning middle and elite class. Both are creations of the connoisseur of aesthetics, its chairperson, the stately Simone Tata.

"Change the furniture in mind to develop curiosity."

Simone Tata occupies a small office in the grand Bombay House on Sir Homi Mody Street in Fort, Mumbai. Bombay House occupies a place of pride in every Indian's heart. From there beams India's most endearing, durable and dignified corporate brand—*Tata*. The Tata empire is run from this august small edifice.

Whenever I had the occasion to visit Bombay House I smelled and stored the ambience reverentially. It was because JRD Tata was, and still is, an idol for true professionals in India. His presence in that house, as in our minds, gave us the ensemble of hope, humility, the joy in doing good work, the desire to search for knowledge and strive for a successful professional career. I saw JRD's bust as I got into the elevator. His saying, *Nothing worthwhile is ever achieved without deep thought and hardwork* rang in my mind as I reached Simone's office on the second floor. Jinny, her secretary, extended the usual courtesies.

Swiss by birth, Simone Naval Tata at 73, is a graceful lady, always immaculately dressed. Simone is an honours graduate in Arts from Geneva University. Over the years, she accompanied her husband, the successful industrialist Naval Tata, to many meetings and functions. She carries herself impressively in her European attire. Walking behind Naval, taking her seat in the front row as he walked to the dais, she always looked to me the model of a traditional Indian lady accompanying her husband.

Naval was a noble soul with a charming personality. He represented India with distinction in a number of tripartite meetings on labour–management issues. His passion for bringing labour and management together is unequalled. The more I saw them, the more my admiration for this made-for-each-other couple grew. Simone's creation Lakme had always attracted me. I was curious to hear its story from the creator.

Lakme with its range of cosmetic products like powders, moisturisers, toners, cleansers, foundation creams, nail enamel, eye-liners, compacts, and many more, became a hot favourite with Indian ladies across the length and breadth of the country. My knowledge of it though was understandably limited.

With the advent of liberalisation, Lakme anticipated the entry of a number of foreign companies into India, a direct threat to Lakme's market share and leading position. To keep up with such competitors would have been an uphill task with heavy marketing investment. Instead, they turned to retailing, a green field project in an industry still underdeveloped in the country, and closer to the aesthetic proclivities of Simone.

When I walk through Westside at Hughes Road in Mumbai, I experience the atmosphere of my favourite Marks & Spencer at Oxford Street, London. These two successful brand launches, Lakme and Westside, incensed my desire to include Simone in this study of outstanding leaders.

Interviewing Simone was facilitated because she had diligently filled in the 22-page questionnaire sent to her earlier. Interestingly, Jamshed Irani has similarly applied himself fully while filling in the questionnaire. I do not know whether this commitment to fill in the necessary forms is a discipline of the house of Tatas. But it came handy for me. A completed questionnaire provides a framework to the interviewer to prepare well, focus on important issues, and gainfully use my time—the scarce resource of such top executives.

Simone (Sim) grew up in a family of traditional Swiss values. In the value map provided in the questionnaire she had shown how her parents and her husband shaped her personality during the growth phases. While her father engraved discipline, family values and respect for others, her mother taught her care and affection.

S: And Naval?

Sim: Dedication, hardwork, analysis, and reading. I grew up in a post world war environment, where values were very high, economy weak, and display of wealth or power unknown. This background, coupled with my husband's personality made me what I am—a rather private person.

Naval Encourages Simone

Simone had no business education and no need to earn a living. In those days, a lady-married-to-a-rich-person stereotype was supposed to play the role of a good housewife and enjoy the party circle of the rich and famous. Simone, you will see, stood out as exceptional.

S: How did you come into business?

Sim: I never had to earn a living, and never had a feeling of insecurity. I started work because of the interest in business, infused by Naval. Through his wide international exposure, Naval raised my understanding of the world's problems. His dedication to the Tata group, family, and country, was quite inspiring. That remained foremost in his mind and action. His understanding of the economic, political and social systems of India and the world, their historical evolution, and business in its broad outlook, influenced my thinking. He developed in me, a keen interest in India, and always encouraged me to fly with my own wings by taking on responsibilities.

Because of favourable circumstances, I never felt threatened. I was not dependent on anybody. Yet, everybody doesn't necessarily feel comfortable in a new situation. Many people do not have the urge to do anything at all. Not everybody is ready for a life like that. There are sacrifices like no free time, not even for friends. Essentially, it gave me a certain freedom to experiment and act.

Naval never questioned me about my business. I was self-made. Whether it was work preparation, organisation, performance, commercial acumen, or taking challenges, I learnt it all by myself. In financial and legal matters, however, I always took advice from a senior Tata director on my Board. In finance I felt for a long time like Alice in Wonderland.

A Technocrat in Lipstick

The entire business world, in my opinion, was a wonderland for Simone. She came into a business environment, listening to business talks. She developed the interest. Her contacts with women who knew business were helpful. She was a happy-go-lucky person with no great ambition in her school days.

S: In Bombay, you could have become a party going, bridge-playing lady, but you chose a different path. What was the trigger?

Sim: I came to join Lakme by accident. A director from Tata Sons once asked me, "Why don't you join the Lakme board?" My first question was how much time will it take. He said two hours every 3 months, and I agreed. Not knowing how a company works I was told why don't you do this or that, or look into development. Slowly it became half-a-day job. I began typing my mail at home on an old typewriter.

At some stage Tata Oil Mills (of which Lakme was a subsidiary) decided they needed a Managing Director for Lakme. One Board member sounded me out, but my husband's reaction was a "no, no, no". I asked Naval how he could make such a decision on my behalf? In retrospect, I think they offered me this job because I was the only *technocrat in lipstick* they could lay their hands on. Besides, Lakme was so broke, it could not pay the salary of an MD.

S: How did I not see this unpaid director on the footpaths here at flora fountain in 1964.

Sim: Whatever we were manufacturing, inside the Sewree factory of Tata Oil Mills, was distributed by them. We had a chemist and a few people working there. We learnt the basics. We produced samples. It was on-the-job learning, reading material, and application.

The Evolution of Lakme

Sim: In my visits abroad I used to collect samples and give them to a chemist to benchmark. I had a very fashionable cousin in Paris. When I went to Paris and my father gave me money for dresses I did not buy them. Instead, I went to beauty parlours with my cousin to learn to do a professional make-up: how to take care of skins, textures, etc. In other words, I studied cosmetics. One thing led to another. It was all an evolution.

S: *Evolution in any case is not a force. It is a process, slow in nature. What kind of structure and strategy did you have in Lakme at the start?*

Sim: Up to the 70s, our structure just evolved with the needs of the organisation, starting with basic infrastructure: recruiting a small sales force, creating a one man sales and marketing department, followed by a regional office. Structures became much more defined in the 80s. Strategies in those days were more evolutionary. An export strategy, however, was developed since the Indian market became non-profitable due to the yearly hike in excise duty, which reduced margins to almost zero.

S: *Building a team at Lakme must have been difficult?*

Sim: Some people came from Tata Oil Mills, some from IIM, Ahmedabad. The glamour attracted people. But retention was a problem. Frequent interaction, an open door atmosphere, and sharing the values of the house of Tatas gave us a feeling of camaraderie.

S: *The aura and glamour of working in Tatas must have been an advantage.*

Sim: The name Tata would also convey a certain awe which kept people at a distance. It was somewhat counter productive. Being a woman, a Tata, and a foreigner is quite intimidating.

S: *How did you overcome the counter productive factors?*

Sim: Knowledge of products, and a feel for the product and the category gives you that authority. My strength was my knowledge.

Simone is right. As a leader you may have a charming personality but if you don't have the in-depth knowledge of your products, processes, and markets, you lose the respect of people working for you. The business of cosmetics was not known then in India. A lot therefore, depended on the understanding of the issues involved in that emerging business.

Sim: My reading, free access to markets abroad, some aesthetic sense, and the insight I developed helped me contribute. These strengths motivated people.

At the beginning, people were perhaps hesitant to approach Simone because of her reserved nature and the weight of the negative baggage that she carried, namely, that she is a foreigner and a Tata. But her open door policy led to more interactions with people. Simultaneously her knowledge of all facets of business deepened, and the dialogues became more meaningful.

It is difficult to dissect and say what the leader did and team did. However, in the nascent cosmetic industry of India, her expertise in shaping the identity of Lakme, the excellence of its products, labelling, packaging, and positioning, established her authority. That I think led to the acceptance of her leadership in its own right. She undoubtedly played a potter's role.

S: *How did your people describe you then?*

Sim: I never bothered to find out.

S: *Where did you catch the germ of turning Lakme into the Revlon of India?*

Sim: In the 60s Revlon was the leading cosmetic company in the world. And Revlon had a number of brands (Revlon, Moon Drops, Intimate, etc) positioned at various price level, each price level consistent with the brands. E.g. Revlon was a mass brand, Moon Drops was for the women between 25 to 40 years, Intimate, a very expensive range, for very sophisticated older women. And each brand had a full cosmetic range and a perfect identity. It was excellent marketing.

S: So you adopted it for Lakme?

Sim: While developing Lakme, I knew that without an array of products to answer the needs of all women, we would remain marginal. Of course, some products sold very little and did not pay their way. Others became good cash cows. It is known in this industry that out of ten products, only three make money. But there is this necessity of a full offering, to retain your customer and not to let them go to other brands. What worked for Revlon, with each brand, became a model for Lakme. We introduced a number of products, well ahead of their time. Some became a big success, others hardly covered their cost, but it enabled Lakme to answer any woman's needs.

S: And what about the quality?

Sim: Of course, there was the quality angle, which we did not compromise on, and which put a lot of stress on our R&D department. For several years, raw materials and packing materials could not be imported and had to be substituted.

So the brand was not only the driver but also Simone's vision. From her early days in Lakme, her vision was to make available to Indian women, products that were not available here, even if the market was insignificant. Said Simone, "This has been, in retrospect, one of our best brand building tool over many decades".

Lakme means *Lakshmi*, Unbelievable!

The story about how the Tatas came into cosmetic business is worth narrating. In 1948–49, Pandit Nehru decided to stop import of what he called "perfumes and powders". When people like Vijayalaxmi Pandit, Padmaja Naidu, and others asked him what they would do without perfumes and powders, Nehru asked the Tatas to get into this business. Since the Tatas did not know anything about this business, they dragged their feet for quite a while. There were several reminders from the Prime Minister's office before the beginning was made.

S: *Where did you get the name Lakme from? What does it mean?*

Sim: My husband was looking for a name for a cosmetic company. One day, while in Paris, he went to the Opera, which was playing "Lakme", written at the turn of the century, by a French composer called Leo Delipe. The story of Lakme is a story of two French soldiers lost in the Sunderbans, in Bengal. It was a kind of a desert of land-forest-swamp. These lost soldiers saw a light in the distance. They walked towards that light and found a temple. The temple keeper had a beautiful daughter called *Lakshmi*. One of the soldiers fell in love with her. The composer knew the story, changed *Lakshmi* to Lakme.

S: *Unbelievable!*

Many people always ask, "What's in a name?" A name symbolises some meaning. A brand is a name, a special kind of a name. Most loyal users of Lakme's various products probably don't know this story but what a profound significance it has. Lakshmi means Goddess of Wealth. *With the use of Lakme products the beautiful women of India look more beautiful. They put on a modern look.* Literally, the "Goddess of wealth" fetched Tatas Rs 200 crore when they sold their cash cow Lakme to Hindustan Lever. *What a coincidence that Naval should visit that opera and come across a name that gelled in with our culture!*

From Lakme to Westside

What prompted the selling of Lakme and the opening of a chain of retail stores? Several factors—competition from multinationals, liberalisation, the Tata group's decision to exit from non-core areas, need for huge investment in building marketing muscle and compulsions of the domestic scenario. Simone started thinking of options in 1992.

Sim: We didn't want to see our brand face competition both from brands in the unorganised sector as well as from premium international labels. We did not want to see our brand devalued over time.

Post 1992, several multinationals, Americans, French, Japanese, approached Lakme with projects for joint ventures or complete buy-out. Almost all the large international brands came knocking at my door. It was a rather fascinating experience. Finally, the best terms were obtained from Hindustan Lever Ltd. In early 1996 a 50–50 marketing joint venture was formed with Lakme retaining the manufacturing side. Some 200 employees from the marketing and sales departments were transferred to the joint venture. The six member Board had equal representation. I remained as the Chairman.

However, in 1998, HLL made an offer for the total Company, which was irresistible, and Lakme was eventually hived off to HLL.

S: *Of all the obstacles you have encountered in life, which was the hardest to overcome?*

Sim: The sale of the cosmetics business.

S: *How did you overcome it?*

Sim: I grieved silently, put up a brave front, and convinced myself that the interests of the shareholders had been protected.

Simone was, carefully assessing various options. Retailing was closest to her heart. It was very underdeveloped in India. As a first move in December 1997, Lakme Exports, a wholly owned subsidiary of Lakme, decided to take over Littlewoods stores in Bangalore. The latter was a 100 per cent subsidiary of Littlewood PLC, UK. The final merger was effected in March 1998, and the new company was named Trent—Tata Retail Enterprise.

S: *What made Tatas decide to go into retailing?*

Sim: I thought then that retailing was an industry of the future. At that stage, it was still very underdeveloped, an unexplored territory. Retail chains did not exist. We undertook many studies, which I presented to the group Chairman, who gave me a go-ahead.

Westside is a success story. The chain of twelve stores in Mumbai (2), Delhi (2), Bangalore, Kolkata, Chennai, Hyderabad, Pune, Nagpur, Ahmedabad, and Noida, is a shopper's paradise. Ninety per cent of what it sells whether linen, pottery, or apparel, are Indian in origin.

Westside sources its merchandise from all over India. They work in-house on their designs, colour, and quality. Besides, they are trendy and affordable.

Sim: We are definitely modern in our presentation. Our products are in line with world trends. Besides, the "value for money" equation is paramount. It is to give to the greatest number of people, fashionable products in line with western fashion but adapted to Indian conditions.

We keep giving a new look to our stores, all the while changing collections according to the seasons. Buying trendy stuff in a beautiful setting of spacious layouts, cute coffee corners, children enclosures, and light music, provides a memorable ambience.

Transitions of a Craftsman

The seven year (1995–2002) period transformed Simone's identity from a pioneer in cosmetic business to a grand dame of retailing. However, the underlying vocation remained unaffected—*a craftswoman in aesthetics.* In her passage from 65 to 72, this charming lady allowed the grown-up child Lakme to fly away. She further took a creative leap by giving birth to a brand that addresses the needs not only of ladies but also of children and men. In the process, Simone's personal bandwidth expanded—she grew.

There is an important lesson in the transitions Simone made in her eventful journey. There is an end (Lakme), a period of distress probably in the fog of confusion (the joint venture with HLL), and a new beginning (Westside). It is seldom realised, that it is difficult to disengage from the earlier identity, the unique circumstances of our individual lives, the safe cocoons of defined roles, the responsibilities and predictable returns. In an organisation, as also in individual life, if one reflects carefully, one realises that every transition had an "end", a "neutral zone-confusion/distress" and a "new beginning" cycle.

There are ways to facilitate such transitions. Simone went through the known process of scrutinising options, visiting various facilities abroad, talking to many people, etc. She did not abandon the earlier baby nor adopt a new one in haste. She developed new skills in negotiating the perilous passages.

More importantly, Simone arranged temporary (50:50 venture) structure, and used transitions as the impetus for a new kind of learning and discovering. She found something (perhaps unconsciously) that fitted into the texture of her fundamental know-how and liking—aesthetics, a sense of beauty! She made correct sense of life's changes. While making her choices she must have thought to herself: to what degree will the work I do reflect my basic interests? Does it allow me and the company to use our abilities fully? Lakme did, and retailing required the same chemistry. Aesthetics was the ballast of Simone's right choice.

Lessons from Difficult Times

S: *What challenges did you face?*

Sim: In 38 years of management, there has been many challenges, internal and external, each one of a different magnitude, some threatening the life of an organisation, like Tata

Pharma or labour problems at our Deonar factory. Tata Pharma was a bad decision. There were no compelling circumstances to jump into it, and yet we made a wrong judgement. Other pharmaceutical companies like Wockhardt, Ranbaxy, Cadilla, were far more entrepreneurial. We did not have the wherewithal or the people. However, it did not disturb my sleep. The lesson in Pharma's failure was that one should not get into a completely different product line without the know-how.

The name Tata could not salvage the pharma venture. Throughout Asia Al Ries saw the same pattern, viz. rampant line extensions destroyed brands. He said, "When you expand, you reduce the power of the brand. When you contract, you increase its power". After Ratan Tata became Chairman, Tatas exited from its non-core areas. The focus was regained. The confidence of investors was boosted. The glory of Tata, the immutable brand, was restored.

Sim: My other challenge was expanding business overseas. Visiting Moscow was a nightmare. For networking, I had to get contacts from embassies (how frustrating it was!). I know one contact leads to another. However, with meagre foreign exchange, not too many good hotels to choose from, and at first, to move alone in a foreign land in those difficult times, were quite threatening experiences. Often, there was eighteen months' time lag between efforts and results.

We must guess how Simone coped with the situation to produce results. In establishing contacts and a network, the ability to communicate is critical. Simone is a person of few words. It is the body language that must have enabled her to network effectively. And who will deny that Simone is graceful. She appears to have utilised her strength productively.

In Power Networking *Donna Fisher and Sandy Vilas (1991) have noted, "Communication consists of 7 per cent verbal information and 93 per cent body language, tone of voice, speed of delivery, and facial expressions. The lone ranger mentality is a major stumbling block for potential networkers". Books take us back to basics, don't they?*

It was a very difficult union situation in Lakme's Deonar factory. There was gross indiscipline, and the company was loosing its right to manage.

Sim: Ratan recommended a consultant. I took the decision that the consultant will not only advise but also implement his recommendations. Straightway, he started taking actions in the factory. Since nothing was working I did not consult anybody. It was a decision imposed from the top. It worked well in the end. *When nothing is working and the situation is speedily going out of hand act, act, and act.*

S: What strategies did you employ in meeting the challenges, and what did you learn?

Sim: Patience, objective thinking, and looking for new opportunities. At some intervals consultants were called, to get an objective view, to confirm one's views, scan and advise on strategic proposals. The sense of timing is often instinctive—the sum of many experiences, reading, and listening. There is always a ray of sunshine at the end of the tunnel. Therefore, it is essential to remain optimistic.

S: Judging a situation in hand is extremely difficult. How does one decide whether it is an opportunity or threat, strength or weakness, crisis or hope, and if there is the chance of success?

Sim: One knows, often by instinct, almost immediately where the land lies. Sometimes the strengths and weaknesses, hope and crisis, or chances of success and failure go together. I always draw a list of pros and cons and attempt to be totally honest with myself.

Instinct is a natural aptitude, a spontaneous specific response to environmental stimuli. It is animated by an inner agency operating below the conscious level. Simone draws a list of favourable and unfavourable factors to reason out, and take a truthful call on the uprightness of her action. The rationale is to test the validity of impulse against certain values that form the fabric of a personality. The methodical approach of Simone works. This manner of thinking falls in the stereotype of great thought leaders. Said philosopher George Santayana, "Well-bred instinct meets reason half way".

Creativity Leads to Competence

Simone sensed growth opportunities basically through situational analysis of national and international scenarios. Watching carefully their evolution and trying to balance the needs against world developments, she even took the risk of being too far ahead of times.

Sim: For me, innovation is based upon study of projections, economic trends, common sense, and most importantly, identifying the gaps in the market. If we were not pioneering a concept or product, we came out with a competitive product of a better quality, or refined an existing concept and brought it to the market with better delivery.

The competence to identify gaps, is the foundation for the creative upsurge, coupled with a competitive urge to stay ahead of the competition by catching the trends upstream. Simone did exactly that. I was delighted to attend the function on June 21, 2003, when Bombay Management Association conferred on Simone a special award for innovation.

Sim: I have always believed that one should never be satisfied, even with success in hand. One has to constantly question, re-work, improve and re-invent. Innovative thinking is often the result of feedback received, or thoughts gathered from reading, but especially of teamwork and brain storming sessions which stimulate everyone present.

The Lakme team functioned that way, by creating a beauty culture that did not exist or was frowned upon by society at large. Hence, market expansion became a focus point for 25 years, till a certain threshold was achieved. This characteristic is seen in the new Trent team, which has launched the first "own brand" chain of department stores in India.

Simone and team took advantage of demographic and life style changes that emerged in the evolution of the society. Barring the growth of the middle and upper class, the rise in their income, and the emergence of youth as a new class of customers, were a big change in the consumer goods sector.

Sim: The drive comes to me from colleagues working under me, my team. I deal with them with affinity. I can feel their vibes, feel their personalities. My team inspires me.

Creative people possess a high degree of self-sufficiency. They have need of others but they do not allow them to short-circuit the free flow of creative energy; they select them who are aware and responsible enough not to become blockages in their creative space. Simone has come to know this, the poise says so.

If you are like Simone, you can create products and markets, build effective teams and organisations. In India, seniority used to signify status. The concept has been on the stretcher for a decade now. In the knowledge driven economy, creativity will determine status. It is creativity and competence that matters, as Simone's example shows.

Simone's creativity is not abstract—it is concrete and result driven. Her initiative falls into what Jack Welch "A" class (GE's 1998 annual report) applies admirably to Simone:

> *These initiatives are being driven across the businesses and across the globe by a unique brand of 21st Century business leaders—the "A" player, the leader who embodies what we call the four "Es": high Energy; the ability to Energise others; "Edge" the ability to make the tough calls; and finally, Execute, the consistent ability to turn vision into result.*

Competence Opens up Opportunities

If one develops the skills to identify gaps, analyse trends, build scenarios, and stretch one's intellect to improve perception, one will be able to envision opportunities where none exist. Competence opens up opportunities. Simone did with beauty care.

S: How did you spot opportunities?

Sim: Scanning the world through reading and travelling. Backing market research, which often threw clues and going rather deep into the details of the products, and the ability of the company to execute and deliver. Opportunities knock at the doors of those who are prepared to take them.

Opportunity brings along with it an element of risk. One has to weigh the risk. The whole subject of risk analysis has become important in modern day business venture. Venture capital is available. One can take money from private investors. But there are no free lunches. Each one must assess the element of risk involved.

Lakme took a risk in venturing into pharmaceutical business, which was a failure. We launched Tata Pharma without expertise or adequate professional team. The division lost money every year and finally had to be sold; all its fundamentals were beyond repair and a restructure would have needed large investments.

S: *Entrepreneurs take risks. Can you comment on entrepreneurial and executive competence.*

Sim: Entrepreneurs do take more risks because they run their own business. You require entrepreneurial competence in the beginning. In a public limited company, shareholders' interests prevail. You become structured, more organisational. Your authority is embedded in the team, its consensus. It is issue and interest based.

In a limited liability company, the risks directors and employees take are also limited. They assess the worth of their individual competencies and capacities. However, you must have the entrepreneurial streak. The sum of individual competencies must add up to more than the tally of individual competencies. The whole is greater than sum of the parts. In the summation, there are the seeds of growth and discernible value addition of the team.

S: *How do you compare the beginning of Lakme with the beginning of Trent?*

Sim: When I joined Lakme it was still a 100 per cent subsidiary of Tata Oil Mills, a little subsidiary which did not attract any attention from stakeholders. Hence those years were comparatively easy, away from the spotlight of the stock market. But when Trent was launched, we were a public company and cash rich too. The spotlight was very much on us and the jump into a hitherto unknown industry created some anxiety as much in the Tata Group as with our shareholders. "What is retailing?" was the question asked to us.

However, between the two start-ups, the world has changed. Management has evolved rapidly with each passing year. Information technology, which did not exist in 1962, has been the backbone of Trent. People with more relevant skills were available and putting together a team made the start quicker and easier.

Change the Furniture in Mind

S: Where did you get entrepreneurial competency from?

Sim: Through an inborn curiosity, which is still insatiable today.

S: I appreciate curiosity may be largely inborn. But what can be done to develop it?

Sim: Hardwork, a tendency to reach to solutions quickly, discussing problems with seniors and experts, and working on systems. I admire the works of Homi Bhabha, Vikram Sarabhai, Raja Ramanna, JRD, Kumarmangalam Birla, F. C. Kohli, and Jamshed Irani. Kohli is no more in the limelight but what a pioneer he has been for the IT industry!

The influence of scientific minds seems to have refined Simone's creative faculties. The basic commodity is of course a seamless attribute, curiosity–creativity. *I probe for her insight in this value creating alchemy.*

Sim: I follow my instinct and intuition. There are so many things amalgamated in the storehouse of your brain (pointing her finger at her head), philosophy, religion, art, and science, all put together.

S: Any effort at self-improvement activates that faculty.

Sim: You should read literature, get out of the routine, go to concerts, to exhibitions, to conferences, and you will learn a lot. Observe how other people live, travel, eat, behave, generally study their habits. *Take more interest in others than you do.* Don't remain in your shell: look out; and that will show you how to look within. You should always be searching for fresh inputs for yourself. *Change the furniture in mind to develop curiosity*, it depends upon how passionate you are.

British actor Peter Ustinov said: "Once we are destined to live out our lives in the prison of our mind, our duty is to furnish it well". Simone goes a step further when she says change the very furniture in mind because change itself is permanent. Author of the best seller Notes to Myself *Hugh Prather (1970) said, "Just when I think I have learnt the way to live, life changes". By cultivating a niche, an edge, a talent, creative artists make a difference. Cultivation means, the use of intellectual labour to change and improve the yield, product, service, performance, or whatever.*

S: *If we feel that westerners put on an air of superiority in their demeanour towards us, then this statement from a Swiss of singular achievements on Indian soil should change that opinion.*

Sim: *God has not made me a genius, I need others.* Not having been brought up in India, has deprived me of the finer points and particularities of Indian society.

S: *How did you develop the art of intrepid "Out of Box" thinking and unique doing?*

Sim: The thinking was not so intrepid and the doing not unique. No kidding, please.

S: *What enabled you to show sustained performance?*

Sim: Luck only knocks at one's door 4.5 times in one's life— I think that is rather correct. Respect and learning from my teams, trust in delegating, and then often passing to someone the ownership of ideas.

I learned to learn constantly and update myself to understand what motivated people to build teams and to forecast markets. I learned to listen more and talk less, especially to learn from middle aged and young people, and to absorb the movements which take place with each new generation, new management theories, the evolution of societies leading to better forecasting and efficiencies.

A Creative Businesswoman

I did not discuss with Simone if she, Naval, or the house of Tatas believed in the significance of coincidences, as some corporates do. The Swiss psychologist Carl Jung has seriously studied "meaningful coincidences". He called this phenomenon *synchronicity*, a term currently in circulation in the management fraternity. It suggests that there is an interconnection or unity of causally unrelated events, and postulates a unitary aspect of being. Managers have realised synchronicity fetches better results than silo mentality.

Simone constantly mentioned how one thing led to another in evolution of Lakme. That led me to remember James Redfield's best seller, *The Celestine Prophecy*. Redfield states that, "evolution often moves forward by leaps of transcausal events. Coincidence is the mechanism of growth, the how of evolution. Life has a purpose ... events happen for a reason!" I believe coincidences play a major role in the evolution of our thought. Coincidences are watermarks in evolution. Both develop intuition; provide direction.

Graduating from a carefree student life, marrying a foreigner, settling in a different civilisation, and stepping into an unknown business world are all significant transitions. At once they prove one thing, Simone has in her that streak of adventure and confidence to take on challenges. Negotiating these transitions must have been tough. No pain, no gain!

In the process, however, she became a successful businesswoman, a role model for ladies whether foreigners or Indians. Simone set an example and *examples have more followers than reason*. In *Transitions*, William Bridges (1996) says, "Genuine beginnings depend upon this kind of inner re-alignment rather than on external shifts, for when we are aligned with deep longings we become powerfully motivated". And Simone at 73 is highly motivated, isn't she?

Simone, the mother figure, leads in her characteristic nurturant style. She believes that Indian people are far more receptive to a nurturant CEO than the citizens of many other countries. To suppress their voice and prevent them from expressing their views, would be as damaging to the individual as to the organisation. They also have much talent.

This observation corroborates the conclusions reached by Prof. Jai B P Sinha in his study *The Cultural Context of Leadership and Power* (1995). Sinha notes that the nurturant style of leadership is more appropriate in our context. Employees feel comfortable when someone takes care of them, guides them, tells them what to do and what not, and they are happy to build one-to-one relationships with emotional linkages.

A foreigner, married to an Indian, came to an entirely different cultural continent. To adjust to a culture entirely different from her's must have been difficult. In India, she discovered a different world entirely different from Europe. She learnt to grow in it and own it. She did not tread the beaten path. She chose to be different and scooped profound meaning out of her life.

Simone made elegant choices in marrying Naval, joining Tatas, leading Lakme, and creating Westside. These show beauty, courage, and quality. Simone's career shows her search for the creative evolution of beauty. Leveraged through her domain, *aesthetics,* and with significant value addition, she built two classy brands. It is not the form or polished appearance of her craft that is mesmerising, although the pull is not denied. It is not even the sense of propriety and aesthetics in her choices. It is the quality of her discretionary faculty in selecting fertile fields for giving expression to her personality, which is most appealing. We have plenty of scope in refining our choice-making abilities by applying Simone's touchstone.

Although Lakme had made a formal beginning before Simone joined, she nurtured its healthy growth, gave it an identity, and made it a popular brand. Westside is outright her conception. These are no mean achievements in a foreign land. These are an artist's creation in aesthetics. On the merits of performance, and the bottom line figures, she has proven her credentials as an executive of exceptional talent, in a business world dominated by men. In this colourful and sublime journey, Simone reflectively scripted her story and deservedly secured a place as a creative businesswoman in the *enclosure of exceptional* Indian businessmen. We admire Simone!

★ ★ ★

6

The Effective Way to Show Results

- ❖ The Habits of Effectivity
- ❖ Flair for Observation
- ❖ Speed, the Seed Capital
- ❖ Balanced Scorecard

- ♦ Exemplar—The 80/20 CEO, Vaman Kamath

"The power to make and keep commitments to ourselves is the essence of developing the basic habits of effectiveness. Synergy is effectiveness in an interdependent reality—it is teamwork, team building, the development of unity and creativity with other human beings."

—Stephen R Covey
The 7 Habits of Effective People

Introduction

This chapter focuses on how dynamic CEOs show results by cultivating habits of 80/20 thinking, and keen observation. The CEOs' use creative processes for changing the symbolic domain in the culture of their organisations. Treating speed as the seed capital, they leverage the deliverables to remain ahead of competition. The progress is monitored through use of a Balanced Scorecard.

The Habits of Effectivity

Habits are what we repeatedly do, consciously or compulsively. When it recurs with increased frequency, it shows a behaviour pattern. Habits are stronger than reason and reconcile to everything with the exception of change. They are deeply embedded in our psyche. We hardly realise that they possess us in all our choices: eating, drinking, gambling, playing, dressing, touching, cuddling, working, performing, and most importantly thinking.

Strong habits lead to obsessive-compulsive behaviours which degenerate into disorders, e.g. not honouring commitments made about returning phone calls, submitting home grocery bills in reimbursements claimed from company for actual expenses incurred for entertaining clients at home, using company stationery for personal use, procrastination, and what have you. Excesses deteriorate into addiction, like drinking, and gambling.

Habits die hard is a known proverb. We take refuge under it for not changing. What is true at the individual level is equally applicable at the group level. And society consists of groups where the herd mentality holds sway. Said William Wordsworth, "Habits rule the unreflecting herd". This explains why changing the mindset of a society is so difficult.

For example, in India "no-work, full pay", "promotion by seniority, not merit", protests, strikes, *bandhs*, and *rasta rokos* form the ethos to which people got habituated in the socialist era. In such an atmosphere, getting performance and result orientation were uphill tasks. They still are, in the monstrous government sector. In 1890, psychologist William James said that habit is, "The enormous flywheel of the society, its most precious conservative agent". It became most destructive to productivity, progress, and growth after independence in India.

One of the reasons for higher result orientation in the private sector, is because of its habits of efficient work, discipline, and accountability. Enlightened management provides an environment conducive to higher productivity and facilities for continuous learning. The aim of training and development activity, is to influence employees to become self-introspective, independent, resourceful thinkers, responsible enough to undertake a conscious programme of self-change. This basically involves showing methods and providing tools for changing unproductive and unhealthy habits into proactive and positive thinking habits that change action orientation.

The whole atmosphere echoes the culture of measured performance, and commitment to better results, year after year. Effective leaders seriously apply the 80/20 principle. It has become their second nature.

The Italian economist Vilfredo Pareto originally enunciated the 80/20 principle in 1897. He found a pattern in the distribution of wealth and income, i.e. a small minority earned disproportionately higher than the large majority of the total. This principle became applicable to other activities of the society as well.

Later, Joseph Moses Juran christened it the Rule of the Vital Few in his famous *The Quality Control Handbook (1988)*. He successfully applied the concept to eliminate quality faults by focussing on the vital few causes, which raised the quality consciousness of Japanese managers and workers. His unique contribution led to the faster growth of Japan during 1957–1989 period.

It became self-evident that 80 per cent of the results come from 20 per cent of the causes. The distinction between the Vital Few and the Trivial Many became abundantly clear. I was pleased to see Pareto's diagram being used for drawing this distinction between different problems by Mallika Srinivasan in TAFE, in her drive for world class quality.

Richard Koch, former consultant with The Boston Consulting Group, wrote in *The 80/20 Principle* (2002), "To become effective or happy, realise the importance of just a few people or things. If you concentrate on the few things that work best for you, you can get what you want".

Japan, one time known for shoddy goods has become world renowned for quality goods. What a transformation! National pride, extraordinary teamwork, and discipline drove it. Like Japan, we also had lifetime secured employment, but lost the advantage because of the absence of these three factors. As if that was not sufficient, we cultivated an adversarial relationship through anti-work and anti-productivity labour laws in the muddled socialist ethos. It is a shame that the roots of our national sclerosis should lie in our attitude to work, despite having drunk for centuries, the "work is worship" nectar from *Bhagawad Gita*!

This has been changing for the better since 1990, with the realisation that value comes from growth. In addition, economic liberalisation has unleashed the market forces of global competition, and young knowledge workers have moved to the centre of sunrise industries. About the new employees, Sumantra Ghoshal and Christopher Bartlett note in

The Individualized Corporation (1997) that they have the courage and confidence to abandon the stability of lifetime employment and embrace the invigorating force of continuous learning and personal development.

Growth means that something monetarily worthy is created, which gives a fair return on investments like new ideas, discoveries, products, and services. Individuals drive such growth through small teams, whether in big corporations or new start-ups. A few critical contributions by members of different teams lead to major chunks of result.

This is seen in publicity shy Tilloo's DGP Hinoday Industries and Chaudhari's Praj Industries. The former made great strides in ceramic magnets, ferrite cores, and automatic castings, and the latter supplies alcohol and brewery plants (S Pandit, 2001). The team members there, do not consider themselves as employees but commit wholeheartedly to the progress of the institution, as if they own it. It is indicative of the new awareness about the stakes involved.

Intel's Andy Grove said, "No matter where you work, you are not an employee. You are in business with one employer—yourself—and in competition with millions of similar businesses world-wide. Nobody owes you a career, you own it as sole proprietor. And the key to survival is to learn to add more value every day". This means, one must apply the 80/20 principle, as the effective sole proprietor does, to the chain of activities from resources to results. There are no short cuts to value creation, except artful husbanding of one's personal resources, i.e. You & Co, your skills and attitudes, your intelligence, emotional, and spiritual quotients—IQ, EQ, and SQ. Together they make one resourceful.

Ideas and individuals matter. Long back, Winston Churchill, said "The emperor of the future will be the emperor of ideas". That future is here, *now*. We have to apply the 80/20 rule to ideas and individuals, to power the "now", to shape the future. Bill Gates made a profound observation, "Take away our twenty most important people, and I tell you we will become an unimportant company".

The Chicago Philharmonic went from a mediocre orchestra to world class one, when a new conductor took over. Peter

Drucker found out the secret. The conductor had noticed the gap between excellent people and others whose average was constant. He concentrated on the top performers to raise their standard, which automatically led to overall improvement.

The principle is the same: concentrate on the vital few to make a significant difference. The focus and efforts have to shift to opportunities. A creative leader spots opportunities when he finds gaps in asset utilisation. The leader moves forward to provide the missing link, uplifting the skill levels and group synergy, spiced with his presence and motivating communication.

The 80/20 rule is being gradually applied to all other industries. The asset utilisation is being fine-tuned to the principle, "Less is More". As much as excess body flab has to be trimmed down through workouts and a healthy diet, organisations have to maintain their fitness by applying the principles of effectivity.

Flair for Observation

The other important attribute in improving effectiveness, is a keen sense of observation. One does not learn everything in one's academic career. In fact, all management education is driven by volume consideration, not value. Our science and engineering graduates do not have much liking for arts and literature, which results in their stunted growth. And the demand for thought leaders with integral knowledge is on the increase; supply woefully short.

This reality forces management to undertake intensive in-company training in different aspects of art, like listening, learning, living, thinking, time management, observation, you name it. One has to develop a flair for as many attributes in this basket as possible. These are the scaffoldings on which one's leadership competencies like self-awareness, confidence, empathy, social awareness, relationship management, etc, are built. Emotional intelligence is measured against this set of competencies, which primes good feeling in those one leads, and frees the best in people to flower.

The thought leaders I studied know that God and the devil are both hidden in detail. They greet God or beat the devil by refining their observational skills. This is because observers not only notice but also cherish details, while they inspire awe in the world around them. Their constant curiosity and eye for beauty provides ideas. While observing how tiles are laid in hotels, or fixed to walls, Kamath imagined how he would make a beautiful quilt of titles in his ICICI Towers at the Bandra-Kurla complex, in Mumbai.

Walt Disney had the idea of family theme parks from observing his daughter on the rides, while he was just stood by twiddling his thumbs. He saw a reflection of his boredom in the eyes of other parents. He also noticed the badly maintained parks and the squalor all over. That keen observation led him to build a well laid-out and beautifully maintained theme park for family entertainment.

The adept observer's curiosity constantly scans the environment for details that lead to big ideas. If it does not, then the potential to turn that ability into something much more meaningful remains unutilised. Details inspire them to be creative. Curiosity undergirds observation.

What others find ordinary is extraordinary to skilled observers, because it leads them to produce something new that suits their purpose. It is the art of mixing, and churning new value-added concepts, products and services, that gives them the artist's satisfaction.

The advertising icon Leo Brunnet said, *"Curiosity is the secret of great creative people"*. In creative observers one finds constant reference to the question "Why?" After his discussion with Hitachi of Japan, Sudheer Tilloo, Managing Director Hinoday, Pune, said, "We had to use Hitachi Metals' 'know-why' and our 'know-how' to optimise the Indian resource mix. We need technology knowledge, 'know-why'... let them pass it on to my executives. The 'know-how' has to suit local conditions" (Pandit, S., 2001).

Observers learn to love their questions, which helps them to discover what truly interests them. They begin to understand the connection between their responsibilities and passions. I am curious and a fairly good observer of aesthetic details but I am not consistent in connecting them to my vocation, my passion. The connector is the catalyst, who in me, proved to be not developed enough to convert latent assets into habitual advantage.

Occasional flights of fancy however provided some satisfying experiences. In 1976, we mounted a unique employee development programme at Herdillia Chemicals, which transformed the hostile culture of that organisation. The entire (450 plus) workforce was put through three day modules. The training room was specially prepared for the purpose.

We had designed a special wall-to-wall unit for employees, to show them that we were producing a very valuable intermediate product, like phenol, which is finally used in products that reach consumers. On the shelf, we had kept bottles of the actual raw material, which were used for making our products. These products were artistically connected throughout the entire product process. How other companies, which finally produced the consumer goods, used our products was also displayed. The value connection was prominently shown.

The objective was to emphasise that if we go on increasing our prices to meet high wage expectations, we as consumers, ultimately get hurt. It had the desired impact. Despite the fact that companies in Thane-Belapur belt were on a wage spree stoked by firebrand union leaders, we were able to keep the worker demands without giving exorbitant raises, because we had made a breakthrough in "managing expectations". Through visual display at the colourful wall unit, we positioned the price spiralling process in their minds, and in my talks I brought to their attention the role they play in causing it.

The idea of designing the unit came to me, when in my factory round, workers had proudly shown me how our products went into making footwear and in the same breath complained about it becoming expensive in the market. I imagined the entire process that converted the basic ingredients of raw material, say naphtha, through a chain of conversion joints (different companies) to finished products. Minute observation of the process flow dotted my mental screen, with a chain of intermediate products that finally blended into consumer goods.

The "alchemist" in me took the "observer" to make the contribution, the wall unit. A very small creation but self-motivating nonetheless! It added value by keeping the wage costs to a reasonable level.

When one sees the ICICI Towers at Mumbai, or the Infosys campus at Bangalore one is awestruck by the sheer beauty of the layout, the decor, and interior design. It creates a soothing ambience for productive work. The architects, the designers and many craftsmen must have contributed, but Kamath and Murthy's observer skills played a significant part in these prestigious creations. Attention to minute details or important whispers around, is important for modern business development. This skill helps them analyse people, events, and problems.

Problems invite attention, which snaps energy because where attention goes, energy flows. In practice it means listing things that need to be done but more importantly noting what discomforts them. It leads them to think anew of alternatives and what they can offer to resolve the dilemma, whether it is a customer complaint or rearrangement of space in the store. Their combinatorial thinking skills provide unique clues.

Annette Moser-Wellman states that a 'seer', an 'observer', an 'alchemist', a 'fool' and a 'sage' are the five faces of a genius, whose creative thinking styles succeed at work. She says, "The observer brings you closer to your creative genius. By selectively slowing down, you encounter the mystery that brings meaning to work. Honour your curiosity and your questions. Theses are the gateways to the creative the life of a business artist".

Said William James, "Genius, in truth, means a little more than the faculty of perceiving in an unhabitual way". This positive interpretation of genius tells us that we all carry some genius genes in us. Everybody is a genius at least once a year; a real genius has his original ideas closer together. The leaders I have studied, appear to be generating more ideas with shorter breaks and dependable frequency, otherwise the results would not have been as impressive as they are, almost every year.

Once the vicious grip of socialism was loosened India set out on a renaissance. Otherwise, *in the Indian republic of socialist mediocrity, talent and genius have been treated with contempt.* Oscar Wilde, who said, "The public is wonderfully tolerant. It forgives everything except genius", supports this.

Napoleon Bonaparte said, "Men of genius are meteors destined to burn themselves out in lighting up their age". Jamshetji Tata, one such, who laid the foundation of enlightened management in a hostile, colonial atmosphere, said *adversity I believe conspires to turn ordinary men into talented performers. But genius is that in whose power, Man acts as a tool.*

Whether the contemporary business leaders I am studying, will go down in business history books as geniuses is to be seen, but some of them show promise.

Speed, the Seed Capital

The demands on such business artists are too stressful. Deliverables and deadlines have become the life saving jackets of all businesses. The key assets in the marathon for timely deliverables, whether to an internal customer or external client are "speed and creativity". For achieving mastery in both, one requires a different set of skills.

One cannot deliver just by executing the functions expected of one. It is much more. It is going beyond what is expected, setting one's own standards that surpass others' expectations. In sports, success and failure are clearly defined. It has a short time-span. Mental and physical discomfort maturing into exhaustive stress is taken for granted. The stakes are high. The one-dayers in cricket truly illustrate how speed determines the outcome minute by minute. That's why the speedsters of today are in a race to make tachometers obsolete. Only a Tendulkar or a Schumacher blaze in this competition.

Such is not the case in business. Success there, is a slow walker. It is not glamorous. It is an act, which has no public acclaim, ear deafening applause, or repetitive TV commercials. The underlying principles in improving speed skills are the same. It is mind and muscle training for both. Since one works on computers in offices, one requires dexterity and a quick movement of the fingers. In sports, it may be the flexibility and dexterity of the wrist elbow and other joints that matter.

In business, one requires innovative thinking, search skills, cognitive and conversational skills, relationship skills, and more importantly mathematical skills. The mental calculus is always at work. The speed with which one's computational skill function gives one tremendous advantage in executing deliverables within stipulated deadlines.

Practice is certainly paramount in the development of any skill, whether in sports, business, or creativity. The world has moved into the fifth gear, where time zone differences do not matter any more. In fact, leaders who aspire to make a difference in whatever they do, exploit such differences to the hilt.

When Kamath proclaims, *"Speed is the seed capital"*, he points to a paradigm shift in business, and knows that sports are also a business. It is the competition, Internet revolution, and technological advances, that are challenging people to move faster and faster. In this daily marathon for survival and growth, the crucial differentiating factor is the speed of thought and action. Said Aldous Huxley, "Speed is the one genuinely modern pleasure". Is it? I doubt it. It depends upon what your definition of pleasure is.

At the same time, it is interesting to note that in this perpetual race one is required to keep one's cool, especially in times of crisis. Says Martina Navratilova, "I just try to concentrate on concentrating". One cannot get that concentration if one is agitated inside. Therefore, remaining cool becomes a condition precedent not only for concentration but also for giving creative responses to an evolving situation. Creativity flowers when one is relaxed, and even more so in stressful situations.

One must be "free to create" says Frank Barron in *Creators on Creating*. It suggests a balance between inner constraint and abandon, openness to movement and the action of mind, spirit, and emotion. Creativity is a process in which a symbolic domain is changed.

Several artists, dancers, cartoonists believe that what keeps them motivated is the quality of experience they feel in their chosen activity. Says Mihlay Csikszentmihalyi in *Creativity* (1996), "This feeling did not come when they were taking alcohol or consuming the expensive privileges of wealth. Rather, it often involved painful, risky, difficult activities that stretched the person's capacity and involved an element of novelty and discovery. This optimal experience is what I called *flow*".

I believe business artists also experience "flow" while working in their domain, and in no small measure due to their creative leaps. India is now witnessing renaissance.

To get into the top gear in business one requires creativity. To develop creativity one needs to practice inner calm through meditation or whatever, and for action *at the speed of thought* one is required to take lessons in arithmetic and sprinting. "Speed the seed capital" cannot otherwise be effectively used. A balance between calmness and acceleration is the key.

Balanced Scorecard

Whether or not a CEO is balanced can be measured on the modern device, a Balanced Scorecard. Robert Kaplan, a professor of accounting at Harvard Business School, with David Norton, President of Renaissance Strategy Group, developed *The Balanced Scorecard—Measures that Drive Performance* (1992). In the nineties, it replaced activity-based costing. It was an extension of Peter Drucker's theme, "What gets measured, gets done". If one measures only the financial performance, then one will get only that.

However one will be able to achieve other goals if one measures performance from different angles. For example, if one takes customer expectations, internal processes, innovation, etc, into account one will improve the overall performance of the company. This helps the company move from worrying about shareholders interests alone, to the broader concerns of different stakeholders. It provides a more holistic and futuristic approach to evaluate company performance.

The current issues that are on the top of any management's agenda are:

- leadership development
- mindset change
- retention of talent
- change management
- governance
- building brand identity
- learning culture
- result producing teams
- quality improvement
- innovation

If one starts evaluating performance against this criterion on an integral device, like the balanced scorecard, one will get to know a company's:

- real SWOT
- focus on creating breakthrough performance
- comprehensive view of interdependent activities
- harmonic or inharmonic progress with its superordinate goals

A CEO is the measure of all things that the organisation stands for, and does; his balanced scorecard speaks for his achievements. He epitomises the effective way to results. One such CEO is Vaman Kamath. He has creatively piloted ICICI to the global orbit with a balanced approach.

The 80/20 CEO— Vaman Kamath

India's second largest bank, ICICI, is the most admired bank in the country. It has total assets of over Rs One Trillion, a network of over 450 branches, 1,750 ATMs, India's largest call centre, and is among the world's largest in Internet banking. It has an incredible base of 7 million banking customers, 1.5 m credit card holders, 4 m debit card holders, 3 million net banking accounts, 11,000 employees and a profit after tax of $260 million. Heading it is its dynamic leader, Vaman Kamath (56), Chairman and Managing Director, who in 7 years transformed this project finance institution into a global bank.

"Speed is the Seed Capital."

Six feet three inches tall, suave Vaman Kamath sits in an elegant roomy office on the 10th floor of ICICI Towers, in the swanky Bandra Kurla complex, Mumbai. The steel building, with eco-friendly tinted glass, looks imposing from a distance.

I am struck by the huge space, the transparent tall, wide glass walls at the entrance, and the wide water curtain on the smooth blue tiled wall on the left. As I stand near the receptionist, at the centre of the spacious ground floor, I feel the polished ambience. I remember the plush Oracle headquarters at Redwood Shores in the Bay area. My eyes glisten with national pride. They faithfully do, when anything Indian that aesthetically matches international class attracts attention. Where attention goes, energy flows.

The receptionist's manners demonstrate the vitality of that organisation's culture. She looks smart in her silk saree as she hands over the visitors' pass. The guide then accompanies me to the 10th floor in a special elevator. On his walkie-talkie, he instructs the supervisor in the parking lot to get my car parked. He also informs the 10th floor receptionist and Vaman's secretary of my arrival.

As the elevator opens, a smiling lady welcomes me with "Good morning Mr Pandit", and takes me to the sitting room. The studious Madhav Das, Assistant General Manager of corporate communications, who had organised the meeting, joins me. We start chatting. In fact, Madhav sat through all the interviews. He made a couple of useful comments. Every time I went to see Vaman, this drill was carried out to professional perfection.

Father Shapes Character

In the literature I had collected from Madhav, I had read a little about Vaman's father Vishwanath Kamath. He was an influential social worker and political leader in South Kanara. He contested elections in his student days and took part in freedom struggle. He joined the Congress party and held leadership positions at municipal, *taluka,* and district levels in Mangalore. Whether it was the Venkatramanna Development Educational Trust, or the temple, or the *Sriniwas pathshala* (school for *vedic* learning), Vishwanath helped build institutions of repute.

As if to replicate the father's script, Vaman became president of the students' union at the Karnataka Regional Engineering College, from which he graduated in 1969, in mechanical engineering. This first brush with leadership provided him with experience in coordinating the needs and aspirations of a diverse group of students, drawn from across the country.

As Vaman walks towards us, I get up to shake hands. We sit. We exchange visiting cards. Coffee is served. We begin talking about his upbringing.

S: Has leadership come naturally to you from your father?

V: My father laid strong emphasis on education, ethics, and leadership. He used to say, "Education is the only legacy a father can leave his child. Whatever you want to do, do it in educating yourself; and you should lead from the front" I took that advice when I was ready for it.

S: How did you decide you were ready?

V: I felt ready in my final year of engineering. I took stock, i.e. made sure I had it in me to do it. Then I spoke with my friends. I made a fair assessment of the nature of competition, my pluses and minuses, who were behind me and who ahead. This analysis indicated the strengths and shortcomings.

S: What ethical values did your father imbibe?

V: Most of his time was spent in public service. He brought to bear very high standards of ethics on issues and events. He would go that extra mile to articulate it, stand and fight for it. He made it his business to make his displeasure known, when he was uncomfortable, or when other people were unethical. That I think was a great influence. In his case, it was political life; in my case, it is business life.

S: *And what about your mother Uma?*

S: I guess, the way she could think through things influenced me. During a phase in my college days, I used to smoke cigarettes—a few every day. I remember once she casually asked, "How much do you spend on cigarettes?" I gave her some figure, which she asked me to calculate on an annual basis. She said, "Money in the bank earns you 10 per cent interest. What's the capital amount you would require to meet this habit on an ongoing basis?" That was a sizeable amount. This happened some thirty five years back. Her unique way of thinking and presenting things stuck in my mind.

My Mother had only passed her SSC—Secondary School Certificate Examination. She was fluent in English, being convent educated. She was a linguist; she knew Hindi, Konkani, Kannada, and Tulu. She was articulate and could travel anywhere in the world, alone. She was strong willed and independent in her thinking, and it has left a lasting impression on me.

Vaman's grasp of the import of my questions and observations was in nanoseconds. His eagerness to respond with speed and precision vectored the dialogue to a higher plane. It required me to catch his speed of thought, a tall order for me! His accurate use of words and flow of sentences were pleasing to the ears. The seeds of achievement motivation were planted in Vaman by his parents in the kind of value-set they nurtured in their family. This practice fits into the pattern established by different studies on this subject. Additionally, in his father, he had a leadership model to emulate.

Kamath took over the reins at ICICI in May 1996, and since then has directed the transformation of ICICI from a single-product, developmental financial institution, to a vibrant multi-product, multi-channel universal bank, which is today the second largest bank in India, and among the most admired. Kamath himself figures in the top 10 most powerful CEOs in the country in a recent survey commissioned by the Economic Times, and one among only two bankers in the list, the other being Deepak Parekh—Chairman of India's largest housing finance company and one of the premier financial services groups.

According to the Economic Times, of May 2, 2004 "The reason why Kamath is seen as more powerful than many others in corporate India, is because his years at ICICI have been the most action-packed, as compared to any other CEO. The shy, soft-spoken and somewhat reticent Kamath has made ICICI Bank one of the fastest growing banks in the financial world. He has carved a new ICICI, India's first universal bank, with a strong retail franchise".

And all this he achieved in just seven years at the helm!

S: To what do you attribute the success of this transformation?

V: The transformation was possible because of the way Team ICICI responded to the strategic vision of the organisation, and set about achieving it on the ground. The empowerment given to the young managers was one of the keys to the effecting rapid change. They came in with a different mindset, which helped them become change managers.

Further, an early call to make technology the backbone of this change, made all the difference and enabled the speedy transformation of the bank into a low cost, high reach vehicle, with a significant qualitative advantage when compared with its peers. The fast growth through technology, has brought in a customer base of about 7 million, that is only growing.

So a clear vision, a strong team, and early call on technology, were probably the cornerstones to the transformational success of ICICI Bank. But how did it happen? These things are available to other CEOs too, then why did Kamath succeed much more than others? I probe further, and find that it was really a process of change, a process which involved the break down of many things along the way—mindsets, business paradigms, etc.—and a process which transformed Kamath too. And during that probe I realised the truly transformational disposition of this man.

When Kamath came in 1996, he had a vision for ICICI, on a different plane. Along the way, his leadership style evolved to play a truly transformational role. The process was a learning experience that transformed him.

Atrophy of Mind

One of the most important roles of business leaders is to bring the organisation in-sync with the CEO, to be able to execute his vision. Kamath realised that it needed a mindset change. We start discussing managers' mindsets and their development.

V: Despite having computers, the usage was low and there was no consistency—we used different fonts and formats in 1996. For some reason it was not standardised. The youngsters were not conscious enough to see it right.

A senior colleague once asked one of his youngsters to prepare a few standardised letters to be sent to our corporate clients. All it required was to merge the letters and the addresses, and shoot them out. However, it took the officer more than a day. When Nachiket enquired, the youngster said, "My secretary is preparing it". Nachiket did it himself in less than an hour.

Why were these youngsters who were so smart in school behaving like this? What had happened to their minds? Why were we losing this ability to think, the ability to innovate? I was struggling with this central theme. I knew this atrophy would impact something far more critical—*change management*. We want people to change but their arrested development—atrophy—comes in the way.

Development is arrested because of the degeneration of an organ incidental to normal development, a wasting away of tissue caused by disease. I submit, the disease is caused by non-use of the tissues. This is the result of our faulty educational system and far more importantly, flippant parenting.

Michael Schulman studied infants and Nobel laureates for his excellent book The Passionate Mind *(1991). Both, says Schulman, seek to discover the same four things: what is out there, what leads to what, what makes things happen, and* what is controllable. He argues that the same four concerns underlie the scientist's search for knowledge, the artist's search for truth, and indeed all our attempts in work and daily activities to learn more and perform better.

In his latest book Managers Not MBAs, Henry Mintzberg says, "The traditional MBA qualification, is wrong because it prepares people for nothing. Their concentration is on dry analysis. Synthesis, not analysis is the very essence of management".

Meritocracy leads to Mindset Change

Vaman got the answer to his central question about the atrophy of mind, from J Kumar, a brilliant engineer who was teaching economics at Harvard. This was their dialogue:

Kumar: On what scale do you assess a group of people?

Vaman: Six-point scale

Kumar: How many are there at the top end?

Vaman: 90 per cent

Kumar: You are an engineer. You know there is something called a normal distribution in curve whatever you do. This doesn't fit there. You are not doing it properly. You guys are not running a meritocracy.

Vaman: We always believed we ran a meritocracy.

Kumar: You are not. Its going to be hard but you will have to force people to do it. First year, very tough; second, less tough; third, easy. You will see the benefits as you go along. The mindset will change.

V: We had to run a meritocracy. We decided that we need to fit our employee's performance into a normal distribution bell curve. You won't believe the trouble I had putting it in place. Our heads of businesses were rating their people. Somebody was saying X is good, and the other was saying, no he is not, and so on. But now they needed to be fitted into the organisational bell curve. There were emotional outbursts ready to escalate into fist fights. The atmosphere in the room was tense. Over a period of time, the process toughened us. Disciplined thinking made us fair assessors.

We decided not to have more than X number as high performers, the bulk in the middle, and some at the lower end. I learnt there are classical solutions; one has to modify them. After the exercise, I looked at the exceptional cases and sorted them out. Some criteria emerged for treatment of exceptions as well. I raised the bonus of star performers to 200 per cent. I raised the bar very high so that people had to strive to get there, and those already there had to struggle to stay there. To me, it was plotting on the Bell Curve.

Interesting things happened. In the first year itself, those who thought they were high performers did not find themselves in that bracket, and left the organisation. The parting was swift. They were competent but did not fit in. If they had stayed, they would have perhaps made lives mutually miserable. Within a year my colleagues said, "We made the wrong call. These people whom we made stars, were not really stars. Now that we have clear benchmarks on what and how to evaluate, we will be more objective next year". Some stars fell out. New people got in. ICICI became a functioning meritocracy.

This is a significant achievement. Establishing measurable criteria for the assessment of performance is always a difficult ball game, e.g. quantifiable performance measurement of staff jobs poses enormous problems. Therefore, understanding the limitations of quantification and the structural issues in deciding the criteria, is the crux of the matter. The success of performance appraisal systems, depends primarily on the leader building a consensus, on the philosophy of a normal distribution curve, some norms, and following the discipline of the process. The leader must ensure that by and large the outcome reflects that the meritorious have been rewarded.

In the 60s, an incident occurred at Bank of India, while I was working there. Recruitment of staff and promotion to officers' cadre were always contentious issues then. In a heated dialogue between management and union, the management representative argued that both the systems were objective. The union representatives punched holes in his arguement, with derisive laughs.

At one point, the no-nonsense, diminutive union leader, the late Mr. Chitnis, got very upset and said, "We will not accept your version of objective criteria as we do not see the outcomes reflect that. We will have only one measurable objective criteria, i.e. service seniority for 90 per cent posts and you can keep 10 per cent for your vashilebaji (corrupting influence) under the title "merit" if you feel virtuous in calling it that way". Abruptly, he got up and left the room puffing his cigarette!

Meritocracy, bureaucracy, autocracy, theocracy, democracy, mobocracy–each one is a "cracy". And "cracy" means a form of government, or a social or political class of powerful people.

Autocracy: *a government in which one person has unlimited power.*

Bureaucracy: *a body of non-elective government officials who are notorious for indulging in red tapism.*

Theocracy: *a government of the state run by immediate divine guidance.*

Democracy: *a rule of the elected majority government.*

Mobocracy: *the rule by mob.*

Meritocracy: *leadership by the talented.*

The accepted system of governance in civilised societies, is through democracy and bureaucracy. Both need meritocracy for efficient functioning. If the industrial and commercial organisations function somewhat better, it is because they are governed by systems of meritocracy, however imperfect they may be. The scope for refining models and methods exist, but the principle of normal distribution curve is not completely violated. It is the sacred thread of professional efficiency. Vaman and his team have woven that thread into *the mental fabric of ICICI and the results speak for themselves.*

S: *What impact it had on structure?*

V: *We literally pulled apart the organisation and put it together again. First time,* chaos. *Second time,* turbulence, but not chaos. *Third time,* understanding, *that it was worthwhile. Fourth time, when the merger of ICICI with ICICI Bank took place, we effected another organisational change, and not an eyebrow was raised.*

Vaman seems to have thrived on chaos. A la Tom Peters! Said Peters, "If you are not reconfiguring your organisation to become fast changing, high-value-adding creator of niche markets you are simply out of step".

The process of restructuring and its outcome got internalised. The whole thing started ticking. The organisation learned to live with meritocracy, live with change. It understood structures were not permanent, they needed change. Vaman instilled the entrepreneurial spirit and organisational capability of the new economy within the disciplined architecture of the financial institution. He was able to transform the organisational mindset—ICICI could now foresee, manage, and ride change, with him enabling its successful transformation.

With introduction of the system of meritocracy that is based on the application of the principle of normal distribution curve the issue of atrophy got addressed. Vaman was quick to revert to the mindset issue. We spoke about engineers, their lack of liberal arts training and quality consciousness. The reason for CEOs' success is principally the ability to change. The organisation can spin on its toes. This ability is what distinguishes them from other players, domestic or global. They are not afraid. They can run at their speed. However, this did not happen suddenly. In Vaman's case, it took seven years. Releasing energy from blocked mindsets is a slow process.

Developing Communication Skills

Besides the mindset issue, Kamath encountered another peculiar problem when he assessed the preparedness of the organisation to embark on the transformational journey with him. This was, a problem with written and oral communications skills, which he feels are essential for the success of the modern manager or leader.

Kamath found that the oral and written communications of managers and staff were weak, if not poor, when he took over at ICICI. They were some of the brightest managers and executives, but they lacked this critical skill. Probably because most of them were either engineers or commerce graduates, who are not trained in liberal arts.

Interestingly, Kamath, an engineer himself, confesses these skills were missing in him too. A training in liberal arts is required to make these unschooled minds, well-rounded personalities. Kamath pushes them to do courses in communications and writing skills. As long as one gets these kind of people, one has to encourage them to undertake such training.

Initially, Vaman did not believe that liberal arts added value. However, the more he saw this deficiency, the more he came to believe that the qualitative aspects of liberal arts enable a person to look from a much wider platform. This is a shortcoming that hinders the process of mindset change. It's an issue of poor quality, and more seriously, it is *atrophy of mind*. The growth of a holistic mind is arrested in colleges and engineering institutes. Their skewed mentality does not prepare them for leadership roles.

The **core mastery skills** Schulman notes, are **reading, writing, and arithmetic.** Those who acquire these skills early in childhood will evince high intellectual achievement later, exceptions apart. These core skills lay down the foundation for gaining mastery in problem solving skills and crafting strategies. These findings tell, how lack of reading and writing habits lead to the degeneration of concerned tissues.

The loss of communication skills and curiosity is wholly due to parental neglect. Generally parents, but more so I dare say fathers, are perfect non-communicating role models. They exemplify callous disregard for reading and writing habits. One can see why we are able to produce millions of software engineers but very few managers, and still fewer leaders. The reason is we are very good at numerical, computational, and mathematical skills, but not at the core mastery skills, reading and writing. Unless these fundamental core competencies are acquired, one cannot turn out competent leaders The leaders I studied, have excellent reading habits and they write well. Their communication competency is way above others.

The Mentor's Spirit

S: Who mentored you?

V: Nadkarni and Vaghul (former CEOs of ICICI). What Nadkarni showcased was passion for excellence. Nadkarni used to say, "you don't mind doing the appraisal again, as long as it takes to be perfect". As his executive assistant, I could observe his style of functioning. When he appointed me chief of leasing function, he allowed me to experiment in technology.

When Vaghul took over, it became a much wider platform with critical dimensions. He gave me the degree of freedom Nadkarni could not because I was too junior. That freedom allowed me to step out, experiment, make mistakes, go back to him and learn. Two outstanding minds! I can't underplay the influence they had on me.

When one is in the company of such excellent minds, one imbibes what they have, tries to understand their processes, and chooses one's path. Very few people have the ability to mentor but these two certainly had that charisma and skill. That's why so many of our clients swear by them. Both mentored in different styles.

Like accomplished sportsmen need a coach, proven leaders need mentors. Leaders need someone to turn to, who has a superior perception of reality. An authentic mentor helps to solve routine problems with a certain detachment. He can guide a leader to "see" the situation differently, provide a prism view. He is innovative and solution minded.

A mentor of leaders establishes a climate of trust where a dialogue can take place. Vaman was fortunate in meeting such mentors. That there is a clear link between mentoring and unleashing of leadership power is eloquent in this case. Sinetar affirms that we need *the mentor's spirit:* an unseen, affirming influence and positive energy.

Eye for Observation

Many people have mentors or Gurus *outside the organisation, who influence their thinking. Vaman didn't have one.*

V: I am self-taught. A simple habit called *"observation"*, and the other, observance of *"80/20 rule"*, contributed significantly to my development. Let me put these two qualities in perspective. Right from my college days and early days in ICICI, I have been a very serious *observer* of *80/20 rule*. 80 per cent of the work can be done in 20 per cent of the time. You do that first and then see how much extra time is required to polish it up to 90 per cent. It not necessary to go to 100 per cent, i.e. I am talking of that endless pursuit of defining things, jotting ten times, really gets you no where. One has to be accurate in what one does. In 80 per cent one is still hitting quality.

S: *And the habit of observation?*

V: The habit of observation was ingrained in me when I returned to ICICI in 1996.

S: *Observation of what?*

V: One observes how other people manage, and lead; reads about that company or leader; tries to see if that practice is best adaptable in one's company; raises the bar and take it to the next step in one's own way. This has literally become my hobby. Today the habit of observation has gone to mundane levels like watching the way the tiles are laid in a hotel, or the boundary wall of a playground I am passing by, or the lights and fixtures that are there. It could be very mundane things like these that enables one to improve oneself.

S: Where did this habit of observation come from? Is it inherited?

V: I can't say, it has now become internalised. I tell people to pick up the same habit but I am not so successful. This habit of observation is not there even in some of my brightest people, though they are far brighter than I am. I must also admit that I did not always have a keen power for observation. In a way it got honed only in the last six or seven years. People don't do it. It doesn't come naturally. Probably they will acquire it when they head an organisation.

S: Is it learnable?

V: It is. One has to discipline oneself. Once you start seeing the advantages you will start going for it. The flip side is one is neither listening nor learning. One, you are not learning by listening; and two, you are not learning by observing. Three, one must have the ability to look at completely unrelated things in one's business and try the linkage in one's situation in one's own way.

A month back, I was in South Africa. At the airport, they were scanning the visa issued their embassy here, and feeding it in computer. It struck me that I could use it for my teller. Why does the teller have to write all those details, date, etc? The cheque is like a visa. There is a bar code as well as other uniquely distinguishing features. When it is presented, why don't we scan it? Everything will come out updated on the computer screen. I need to put down only the amount and the beneficiary. The rest is there. It can cut down the teller's time by half. It will speed up the process of payment, quick customer service! We are now working on it.

What it brings out, is the ability to look at things completely unrelated to one's job, understanding the underlying principles, and trying to see if one can fit them to one's operations. This ability to connect the unconnected, deriving generic conclusions from minute observation of unrelated phenomena, is high-level creativity.

S: Are you providing structured inputs on creativity to your top team, to develop leadership?

V: Managers are going through courses on creativity. I submit that one has to go beyond that. Such courses will provide only the tools. If one has the spirit of learning one can take in several things one observes and listens. There is somewhere a conviction in me that one doesn't have to reinvent the wheel each time. One has to understand which wheel is approximate to one's needs and then modify it. If one has the humility to learn from others it goes a long way. I think the obsession with observation contributed to several parts of my learning process and value creation.

This eye for observation is an especial attribute. In Sherlock Holmes, Arthur Conan Doyle says, "You see but do not observe". It is much more. It will be seen in leaders who are absorbed in large chunks of time in Reflexive Search Mode *(Pandit, S, 2001). In reflexive search, the executive is just curious to find out what works. He persists in playing with unrelated ideas, unconnected issues. His insatiable urge to grow leads him to reflect deeply on the reality of business problems and obstacles.*

In the metaphysical sense the thought leader is in an "ever-present awareness". It is the nodal point at which the immanent witness in him strikes the external object, event, person, which leads to connecting the unconnected. When Vaman says its just seeing things differently, he communicates this underlying profound significance. It means the eye that inspires you to a new meaning and resolution is the *eye for observation* a leader needs, to realise his full potential.

Building Brand Identity

S: Does your habit of observation take you to sounds, spaces, colours, architecture, texture, nature, water, etc.?

V: Yes it does. Then, I learn so many things I didn't know. Let me tell you about the brand identity work we did. I heard Tatas were working on it. I knew nothing about it. I laid my hands on some books on brand identity. I found all the books asked five or six main questions. Essentially, they sought consistency and continuity in image, communication, messaging, look, and feel of the brand.

Straightway I tried to respond to those questions in our situation, e.g. if we were to collect the publications we brought out in the last one to one and half years, did they tell one anything at all? They didn't.

First—page one was different from page two or three, the fonts were different. In the half dozen group companies of ours, each had a different logo. They represented ICICI differently. This was stupid. What was I doing here? Second—are you proud of the car your organisation uses? Are they in good condition? We are not talking of whether they were old or new cars. Are they in good condition? How are their maintenance, upkeep, and interiors? What does it tell you? Some of these things were not fundamental and did not need an identity change. I needed to fix it right there and I did.

Clearly ICICI needed an identity which everyone would celebrate. The logo, font, size, colours, image, all had to provide a group synergy. The creation of a common identity effectively positioned ICICI as a virtual universal bank, offering a wide range of products and services. The brand message conveyed that offerings from ICICI are safer, simpler, and smarter.

S: *How did you conduct this exercise?*

V: We got an identity consultant, not a brand advisor. We deliberated whether we should get someone from abroad or from home. Several people I met abroad were too expensive. Then I met someone in India who agreed to do it for a fraction of the cost, in a fraction of the time. We engaged him. We worked together and evolve our brand identity, which we have carefully nurtured since then.

Now when I look back, I find most of the companies don't do it. The tiny minority that do, get the visibility, standing, and brand image. The most important facet of brand image, is performance of the organisation in finance, services, products, and employee morale. The brand becomes lustrous.

In his latest Laws of Branding, *Al Ries says, "There's a seismic shift taking place in the world of business. The shift from selling to buying. This shift is caused by the rise of brands. A brand becomes stronger when you narrow the focus. Its launch and success depend on the concept of singularity". ICICI applied the law of contraction, glued all splintered identities together, and built a powerful bankable brand.*

Empowerment

Kamath exhibits the true traits of transformational leaders:

- a vision he was passionate about, which required an extremely high level of organisational preparedness and commitment towards achieving it
- a paradigm shift affected by espousing meritocracy
- a culture of merit—the meritorious were, and are highly rewarded; the non-meritorious found it difficult to continue—a seemingly harsh policy, but it was the cornerstone of the organisation's success.
- empowerment provided to employees to achieve their goals
- relentless appraisal of performance, and result orientation
- almost complete freedom to the teams in the way they want to achieve the goals
- created a highly energised atmosphere where teams quickly internalised vision and targets, and went after them as if they were running their own business rather than working for someone else

- failures are taken in the stride, and employees encouraged to learn from their mistakes

- allowed decision-makers to think and act very much like entrepreneurs, and are therefore achieved remarkable speed of execution, unheard of in very large organisations

Adopting the Effective System of Garage Start-Ups

S: While extolling the virtues of observation, one must not overlook that people learn more through their ears than through the eyes. The Indian ethos is embedded in katha, kirtans, vocal music, sabhas, and discourses. This habit gives credence to the theory that people learn more through the ears. Did you ever pick up any ideas from hearing a story?

V: I once attended a dotcom seminar. There were several participants. I picked up a phrase there called a *90-day rule of the garage start-up*. One may be a big organisation but must think like a garage start-up. One learns why they give one a run for money. It is because they think differently. They don't have to deal with layers of bureaucracy. At the end of the day, they execute the order in 90 days, from scratch to testing, to market. Probably one's organisation is asking for 180 days or even more. Can one not benchmark? Can one do it? We did.

S: Did what?

V: On the flight back from New York, I was deliberating with myself. We had 12 projects in hand in the dot.com area, falling into the trap that I described just now. From London, I called up my people. I told them that we were moving into 90-day schedule. We have one project already one month old, it will take 120 days; the rest 90 days; They did it.

They organised themselves like start-ups, very lean, no hierarchy, and an average age of 24. Every three weeks they would review and make corrections. They did away with seniority and bureaucracy. They organised themselves as project teams, just like in the IT sector. Actually, once it was set in motion, it gathered momentum on its own. I did not have to intervene. The team leader appraised whether they were on the 90-day course or not.

In The Alchemy of Growth, Meherdad Baghai and his co-authors noted:

> By mimicking the speed and responsiveness of start-ups, small units overcome some of the disadvantages of being connected to a mammoth enterprise. And working in small unit gives people a greater sense of purpose, ownership, and control.
>
> (Baghai, M, et al., 1999)

Vaman and his team successfully mimicked the start-ups' success formula.

This is a measure of Vaman and his team's commitment to making processes more effective. Efficiency is the ratio between input and output. By changing the cycle time of projects, and conceptually owning the philosophy of de-layered temporary set up of a sub-organisation, Vaman transformed the very nature of work. This is a good example of action-centred leadership.

Demolition of a Mindset

S: *Was lack of appropriate mindset any obstruction?*

V: I think by then, it was very clearly established that an obstruction anywhere on account of mindset would be demolished.

S: *How did you carry out the demolition exercise?*

V: Youngsters were willing to change. In the hierarchy, if there was any obstruction in the higher-ups I would take a stick to it.

> *His favourite phrase*—if I find such a thing I will take a stick to it. The bigger the problem bigger the stick. *Essentially it is a demolition exercise,* demolition of a mindset. *Neither the carrot nor the stick will work if applied to the wrong end of the horse, is the quote Vaman knows best. That is why he takes so much care to establish a consensus on criteria, to ensure that the outcome meets the objectives.*

S: Along with demolition, how did you build a new one?

V: Through meritocracy, customer focus, technology route and speedy execution ethics.

Going Global

S: Could you give an example of a project you undertook that had global implications?

V: We wanted to list on NYSE—New York Stock Exchange. It was a bold move. The proposal was submitted to the Board and we received it approval. Then I appointed a team leader. We assembled a team. We did a quick analysis of what was required. Others would have taken 180 days to get listed, I said we should do it in 90 days. This might require working in three shifts. You want beds to sleep three-shift kitchen, we will provide them. If anybody stops you, come to me. Anyone shows you a rule book, come to me. Now you guys go and build your teams. Believe me, ICICI became the first financial institution outside Japan to get listed (September, 1999) on NYSE, with the whole process taking just about four months.

S: While entering the global market what did your SWOT look like?

V: Seven years back we were not too strong in many of the areas we are talking about, like finance, technology, HR.

S: And now?

V: The core elements of our strategy now, are aggressive capital management, optimal size, technology-intensive multi-channel delivery architecture, world-class skill bases, and enduring customer relationships.

Our strong point was the core team of professionals, who had tremendous ability to forge ahead. We were poor at using technology and change management. We had a great deal of ethics—no questions! We had the ability to attract talent in areas where we didn't have competency, and create a talent pool. We had access to technology early on, and that was a strength, but its usage was poor. We had no product knowledge, no distribution knowledge, and no structure. We built all that.

All employees were compelled to undergo e-learning. A recruitment drive to man the branches was launched. We saw the opportunity in providing convenience banking to customers—convenience using technology, longer hours, different channels, and in being available to the customer everywhere. These were the same reasons that provided us an opportunity in the domestic market.

ICICI Bank has already taken strides in international foray. After opening representative offices in New York and London last year, it has recently opened an off-shore banking unit in Mumbai, an off-shore banking branch in Singapore, a banking subsidiary in London, and representative offices in Shanghai and Dubai. It will soon be launching a banking subsidiary in Toronto, Canada.

S: *In developed markets will this all be there?*

V: Yes, but our first customer is Indian. He wants to transact business with an Indian. Although dispersed, it is a huge market, as profitable as the domestic market. Value numbers are significantly higher. Our initial thrust revolves round home country linkages. Indian companies are thinking of acquisitions abroad, or setting up joint ventures. They are going international first and then global. We will grow with them as they are comfortable with the familiar.

Also an Indian abroad, who wants to transact with India, will have somebody who will provide that level of service at the western end. We are building the bridge. The moment he comes to us through this channel, we at the eastern end will provide the service levels he is used to.

The international department wanted to assess this potential. With us, it is the user department that dictates the strategy for its growth. To start with, it is NRI centric. Later, it will be ethnic population since a huge migration is taking place. We will take advantage of the global shifts.

Speed Capital

S: *The response time required for such service will be high. Our response time is slow compared to the international standards. Indians do not execute things speedily. Is it a strength or a weakness with ICICI?*

V: The observation is by and large correct, but it was a strength with ICICI Bank. Part of the issue is that every Indian starts thinking de-novo on every problem, re-inventing at each stage. We have to cut that. We cannot afford to be lethargic in response and execution.

We plan to capture the ensuing opportunities by continuing to leverage the four capitals, namely finance, technology, human resources, and speed. The adoption of new technology not only adds to the "speed capital" of the company but also increases the productivity of the human capital engaged in providing these services. In the digital competitive world, whether international or domestic, one can gain space only through speed.

A Branch with a Difference

V: The major challenge now, is the geometric explosion in the customer base. It requires us to maintain service levels on a high note. I am talking of a bank branch which cross-sells its products. We want to increase the proportion of cross-sell to our existing customers, and mop up the income. We are exiting from non-performing loans. We have undertaken a major drive to recover loans by sending notices to defaulters.

In India, we have sometimes 1,000 customers walking in and out of the bank every day. 65 per cent of them go to the teller for money despite ATM networking. In the west, one will probably find 65 to 70 customers visit the bank per day. We decided on moving ATMs closer to the customers so that they did not have to come to the branch to withdraw the cash. The result was *ATM on wheels*. Mumbai saw India's first mobile ATM.

While talking about innovation, Prof. C. K. Prahalad cited the example of ICICI kiosks, and added that when they spread across the country, it would be the most creative and innovative thing in all developing countries, because five years back India was a non-entity as far as ATMs were concerned. Prahalad, who sits on the board of NCR, was speaking from experience, that India and China were the fastest growing markets for ATMs and together will account for 40 per cent of all ATMs worldwide.

V: I conveyed this problem about customer behaviour and the need to improve efficiency and productivity per employee to a big name consultant. They brought a drawing of what an ideal branch should look like. The teller counter was towards the end of the branch to ensure that the customer could walk through the various other service counters on his way and become aware or even be tempted to buy another product or service.

My problem is that when a customer has to come to the branch to withdraw money, he shouldn't find that the place so crowded. 70 per cent of the people that come to the teller are not the customers themselves but third parties such as office assistants, etc. Such a person is not interested in other services at all. He is only interested in getting the cash quickly.

S: What are you proposing?

V: I am looking at a structure where the teller is in front so that the customer doesn't even have to enter the branch and walk through to the end of a hall. A canned solution doesn't work. One has to invent new services and facilities, taking into account the nature of transactions, the customer needs, and his behaviour. Our strategy is to build a huge distribution network and provide cross, multiple channel offerings. We are strengthening our recovery arm, sell of assets and mobilise money through deposits.

Learning from Adversity

S: Your experience from Asian Development Bank (ADB) must have been handy while re-engineering ICICI. What did you learn during your stint with the ADB?

V: I had a great opportunity to study the Asian landscape—business and industry. ADB is a classic bureaucracy. It provided tremendous scope to get a feel of how all that works.

S: What about the politics in management and bureaucracy, the interpersonal conflicts, and all that?

V: More than the politics, I had to manage the bureaucratic pace and hierarchy—there was no control. Even a two-line telex acknowledging something had to travel through three channels.

S: How was it at Bakrie?

V: It gave me a completely different perspective—how a private company works. It was a wonderful interaction with the real world. While planning in the real world, one has to face the real issues. You come to know how the other side works, how the real world functions.

S: You mean issues of ethics, non-ethics, is it?

V: No, I had no issues in that area. I could stay in the zone I was comfortable with. What I got, was tremendous experience in restructuring the business, merging, de-merging and creating value. I was advisor to the Chairman. I had complete authority in what I did. All the three companies in the group had to fall in line. I had to explain and carry people with me. I was dealing with diverse businesses. I had to learn how to deal with them.

S: *Were you required to face people with hidden agendas?*

V: No, I have been lucky in this regard. Even here, in ICICI, I haven't faced many of those people. I know they exist, and I wonder how CEOs handle them. At some point, I would like to know how they managed it. May be it is utopian over here, but...

S: *Did you face any adverse situations?*

V: Several. In ADB, there was a complete lack of attention to ground realities. That led to tremendous frustration. At best, one got quaint ideas of how the role of ADB in private sector should be played. I was using 5 per cent of my energies working on projects.

In Bakrie, we faced resistance from people down the line. It was an issue of mindset. There was a tremendous disbelief in new things that one could do and one wanted to do. I learnt how to influence people to favour change. ADB taught me how to manage day-to-day running of bureaucracy, and also how not to build one. Back home, here in ICICI, I have tried to implement the latter. In ICICI, I had no hesitation in applying ADB's wonderful administrative set up which looks after its employees very well.

While I was drafting this profile on my computer an incident of grave magnitude unfolded at ICICI Bank, Gujarat. Vaman's leadership and ICICI's core competencies were put to acid test. This is how it happened.

On April 11, 2003, the news of an unusually high number of withdrawals on ICICI branches in Valsad, South Gujarat, reached corporate office in Mumbai. It all started with a Surat based Gujarati newspaper reporting that the bank was facing a huge liquidity crunch. The journalist probably saw big lines of people outside the branch for withdrawals. It was a pay-day, and the bank has payroll accounts of some four or five companies. People must have queued in large numbers because the banks were going to remain closed for four days after 11th April.

Rumour mills churned out a story that the Bank had lost a fortune in the previous two days in stock market crash. In depositors' minds, the run on Madhavpura and Kapol

Cooperative banks, and their failure to meet depositors' demand, was still fresh. One must also remember that Gujarat had to face a series of calamities like:

- earthquake, drought, burning of a train compartment leading to death of over 100 people

- communal clashes, fiercely fought state election with the emergence of a new leader, and the murder of a heavy weight politician

All this had made it a very sensitive and emotionally charged state. This news therefore lit instant fire. The panic withdrawals spread to Ahemadabad, Surat, and parts of Mumbai.

It needs to be noted that this happened despite the fact that the bank has triple A ratings from three domestic rating agencies—ICRA, Crisil, and Care—and investment grade rating from international rating agency, Moody's. The situation evolved and what one saw was crisis management at its best. Vaman's team monitored to him every move it made to quell rumours that the ICICI bank was folding up, and stemmed the panic.

The Bank had a sound cash balance with Reserve Bank of India (RBI). There was no liquidity crisis of any kind. But abundant cash had to be reached to ATMs and branches all over in record time. Simultaneously, the entire management had to be geared into action, to counter the false rumours spreading through press and media. The RBI issued a statement on the financial soundness of the Bank. These and many other actions were initiated at a lightening speed. Within 48 hours, operations returned to normalcy.

Vaman refused to describe the incident as a crisis.

V: It was a challenge. We had no crisis in terms of liquidity or solvency. It was a logistics issue, and we tackled it swiftly and methodically.

S: What lessons did you learn?

V: First lesson, technology has changed the entire equation. We have to scale up technology in all our operations. If one was running the bank from 1000 to 1400 hours for transactions, then this sort of the situation would not arise, because then one could have demonstrated that the vault was full of money and there was no shortage of cash. When one has inanimate things like machines dispersing cash on a 24-hour basis, the whole equation changes. One has to find money from whichever safe, and run it to stuff those machines. If your normal stuffing cycle is three days, it has now to become may be once in three hours, and therefore I said, we had a logistics issue. Our basic health was sound, so I eliminated that as an issue; but I still can't say I did not have an issue. I did have one, and that was logistics.

S: *Exactly when did you realise that you had a logistics issue?*

V: On that Friday at 1800 hrs, we saw heavy usage of ATMs at a few places in Gujarat. Within two hours we knew that the news was spreading like wild fire through all communications channels, especially SMS, which I call the tipping point. As we were thinking on corrective action, we realised it was a logistics issue. The second lesson, information travels at the speed of thought, which creates situations, which have to be handled with equal dispatch. Quickly, we put together a plan to move Rs 3,000 crore cash from various currency chests to the branches.

S: *The thought and action merged seamlessly, requiring intuitive jumps in perception. Did you localise the issue to Gujarat and Mumbai, and rush cash accordingly?*

V: No. We couldn't have assumed like that. Next day was Saturday, the only working day. After that it was Sunday, followed by a holiday on Monday. We had to get enough money for three days. Our branches run for 12 hours; our 1,700 ATMs for 24 hours. We had to make broad assumptions on the likely withdrawals, make some quick calculations and estimate the requirements of cash: it came to Rs 3000 crore.

S: *Probably the next question was how to reach it.*

V: We needed the cash immediately. RBI issued a statement on our financial soundness, which was significantly helpful. Response from currency chest officers was positive. At some places other banks also helped. The next day, we had again to get it at 0700 hours, i.e. Saturday. Their work begins at 1000 hours, so a lot of coordination, and personal follow-up from our officers was required, to get currency chests of other banks to open very early in the morning and allow us to move the cash. Additional vehicles were deployed. Trucks moved all over the country covering almost 10,000 kms at the span of eight to ten hours. Massive operation it was, the second biggest challenge! Non-standard trucks were moving, and they did not know the exact locations of ATMs or branches.

S: It must have been a centralised operation conducted from here.

V: Our centralised control room here came handy. We can see online how much cash is available at each ATM. The third lesson led to the critical decision we made to keep the branches open on Sunday and both holidays. We had also told our people to keep the branch open until the last customer left. The fourth lesson, led to the launch of a parallel communication drive to inform about bank's financial soundness, arrangements being made to rush the cash, the decision that the bank branches would be open on Sunday and the two holidays, and also that every customer would be paid whatever cash he wanted. The media and press were very cooperative, and the situation returned to normalcy fast, in fact, by Saturday afternoon. On Sunday, there were hardly any customers. Monday was absolutely quiet.

S: Looks like you mobilised the whole bank!

V: Well, we allocated the task to each leader, and they in turn did the same thing to their colleagues and subordinates. I did not have to push it. They volunteered themselves. I had only to get their focus right. If someone was selling loans, he went to the nearest branch and helped out. It was a hot summer day, so water was served to the standing customers. Volunteers were moving along the queues and telling customers that each one could withdraw whatever cash he wanted. Extra counters were opened. So the entire bank came together, dropping all boundaries of roles and departments. They stayed late, as long as they were wanted.

S: *Were any panic buttons pushed, and did you receive any calls from ministers, senior government officials, etc?*

V: No, none. I carried on as usual. I called on the key persons and once we had taken the decisions and put the system in operation, I ensured that I did not dabble in execution. My top aides also did the same thing, they did not interfere in tasks once they were allocated. It is because we have developed a certain way of working and we have been accustomed to taking on challenges.

S: *These actions were reflexive as the situation evolved. Often managers on a job engage in reflective conversations with their situations, as must have happened at ICICI headquarters on that fateful day. In* The Reflexive Practitioner, *Donald A. Schon (1983) lucidly puts it:*

> *The reflection-in-action of managers is distinctive in that, they operate in an organisational context and deal with organisation phenomena. They draw on repertoires of cumulatively developed organisational knowledge, which they transform in the context of some unique situation.*

How does a reflexive executive spring into action on the spur of the moment in an evolving crisis? What steps did you take?

V: First, actions taken in handling the problem have been recorded. And second, a decision has been taken to set up in the next six months, ICICI's own currency chests, at key locations.

Remember Warren Bennis' observation: leaders learn by leading, and they learn best by leading in the face of obstacles. As weather shapes mountains, problems shape leaders. *In the critical situation Vaman displayed quintessential leadership in management of logistics when storm lashed at ICICI, Bravo! Adversity is a great learning lab.*

S: *What is your philosophy about learning?*

V: A *key differentiator* to winning in the electronic world, is the ability of an organisation to teach itself. I think many organisations miss this. ICICI invests 79 hours, or nine working days per staff per year, on training. A lot of it is in re-learning, which serves today's needs. I am no exception. I spend nine days learning myself—six days on technology, and three days on management practices.

I thought Peter Senge's Fifth Discipline, *had found disciples and a well-equipped gymnasium for practice in Mumbai's Bandra-Kurla hub. In any case management in all its facets is essentially enforcement of discipline.*

Managers crib about being unable to spare time (too busy running to "think on their feet") for learning. However, reflective executives do seem to find time for learning from incessant activities. Vaman did, because he is humble enough to see the need for it. He believes successful leaders today would need to be the leaders of that industry and not just a leader of only an organisation. Such a leader must have the skill to build a learning organisation with exceptionally talented people. The future belongs to learners, not knowers!

The Gut Feel in Decision Making

S: How did you take decisions on incomplete information under time pressures in mergers, technology ventures, and strategy formulation?

V: That's a very good question. First, information is never complete or fully accurate. Second, people around you will give 99 reasons why not to do a thing. If one is a successful leader one should find that one reason why one should do it. Third, One has to do a deep study of available information, talk to relevant people, and take a decision, usually under conditions of uncertainty. One might apply a scientific process, think of probabilities, alternatives, roll it back to get a broad idea. But what finally matters is the *gut feel*.

S: I concur gut feel *is needed. How does one develop it?*

V: Ultimately one has to have that entrepreneurial spirit. Data doesn't provide answers. You can't teach it. You can example it. It is not hunch. It actually means taking a step forward in one's business, where data is scanty and clear-cut analysis not available. Since there are no road maps, there is a risk element. If one plays by given rules one will grow incrementally. If one, wants a step change one has to change the rules of the game.

Many a brilliant leader wastes time on the endless pursuit of more and more information. And many times the situation itself finds a solution, the leader not being required to take a decision.

S: Can you illustrate?

V: We decided to take the technology route. Nobody else had taken that. It involved pushing ATMs, Internet connections, and phone banking. It involved huge investment. We knew the gains that would accrue. What was not known was the volume of customer response. At that point of time, 95 per cent of our customers came to the branch to transact. Now, we are populating the country with ATMs. We are populating people with Internet access. We expect people to phone us, and the branch traffic to go down by 50 per cent. But will it really? One has got to take the decision on investment today. One has a choice. One can say other banks have managed with 90 per cent traffic coming in bank, I will also manage it, or one can take the risk of investing in futuristic technology. At that time there wasn't enough data to prove our projections right. At that point of time, I had to take a gut call.

S: You mean to say no other bank had taken this step.

V: Even today, nobody has gone towards technology to the extent we have. The constraints in India were completely different then. Telecom connectivity was not what it is today. If one set up an ATM, one needed to put in three levels of redundancy—a VSAT, a leased line, and a normal phone line. Connectivity was not guaranteed. Forget phone banking, it was impossible to get even a single number which customers could call in from any city in the country. On top of all this was the fact that we were not sure how the Indian customer would respond to these services. Inspite of this, we decided to take the technology call. All we had was a deep analysis of the emerging trends and we felt it would be a step change in the organisation's interest. We took the technology decision.

S: Do RBI and financial circles accept that ICICI is a pioneer in the field?

V: There is no doubt about that. At one time, the regulatory authorities weren't very comfortable with this step. We had all sorts of issues coming up. On the other hand, we clearly saw the benefits.

S: What are the benefits?

V: First, we would not have grown the way we did if we had not brought in technology. Second, look at the figures—it costs us Rs 45 when a customer walks into the bank, less than Rs 15 when he transacts through ATM, Rs 13 when he talks on phone, and less than Rs 5 on Internet. Clearly the pay-off is tremendous.

S: What structural changes do you see coming?

V: The economy is going to be driven by retail business. Although we were only a project finance institution, we clearly identified this trend, though many were questioning it. Others had not grown or equipped themselves for this emerging market. We felt we could get a large share of this growing market if we planned well.

There are two parts here. The first part is fairly clear that there is growth which others do not see. There is no question of a decision. It is the ability to see differently. The second part, is a conscious decision to enter the market with a resolve to succeed. We had to earmark capital, hire people and do many things. It meant setting up a proper business, doing trial runs, puting up a pilot, scaling it up, advertising, replicating and then letting it grow. The retail diversification was a major step change. We were not equipped and there were risks. Will we stand up to the competition and grow? I got the Board's approval. The decision was taken.

S: So you must have also been required to grapple with dot.com turbulence?

V: Very much. To take decisions in the days of dot.coms was most difficult. We were constantly barraged with information—we could face competition from unexpected quarters. It could have been a telecom company, deciding to provide online banking, or an Amazon.com, or a company like that. We had to counter that threat by going the e-commerce way ourselves. We managed to e-enable all our businesses and they are holding us in good stead today. We also entered some competitive dot.com areas as a counter strategy to the dot.com threat. Once the threat blew over, a couple of these initiatives ceased to be relevant. We took some decisions during the dot.com phase. Some went wrong, some right.

There is a saying, business decisions based purely on instinct may be risky. The next time you have a gut feeling about something make sure it isn't just indigestion. *However a study of 60 Californian entrepreneurs revealed that while they took into account relevant information, they applied their gut feelings to sense whether the decision would be right. They treated gut feeling also as data. Napolean said, "Nothing is more difficult and therefore more precious, than be able to decide".*

S: How is the situation today?

V: Gut decisions are required about technology, not so much in business. Should I go to the mainframe or stay in the distributed processing paradigm? The former will immediately escalate our costs, the latter is low cost. I am comfortable with what there is, but I always think one year ahead. Therefore my issue is, will my business growth outpace the current technology? I may have to go beyond the current technology in use. These decisions about the future have to be taken now and therefore the involvement of the gut feel.

S: How do you pace yourself?

V: For the last two years we have been comfortable. However, from our matrix and algorithms we know change has taken place. We could build an assumption.

S: You seem to be at a strategic inflection point and there is a paradigm shift.

V: Yes. In technology change, there are equations and there are steps. My growth path is below the steps. What I mean, is that we like to keep in-sync with the technology developments, maybe just a step below the latest technology development so that we are never caught with obsolescence on our hands, nor do we bring in technology which is so futuristic that it will be difficult to implement it in a cost-effective and meaningful manner.

What one has to maintain then is that one cannot migrate. Very quickly it becomes one's legacy. It starts affecting all things. One gets into a silo. One is not able to talk between organisations on a technology platform. These minute issues start coming in the way. I would rather be in the free world with flexibility on my side. I can use Microsoft today, Sun tomorrow, or vice versa, or switch vendors if required. Where one gets locked into a legacy system, all options get closed. The way organisations function become completely different. And then one will be dictated by the technologies of supplier companies. The gut decision, do I close the options to commit to a legacy, or keep options open to maintain flexibility; and is the timing right? Take your call.

In The New Leaders, *Daniel Goleman says:*

> The brain applies the decision rules it has silently registered. The emotional brain activates circuitry that runs from the limbic centres into the gut, giving us the compelling sense that this feels right. The amygdala, then, lets us know its conclusions primary through circuitry extending into the gastrointestinal tract, literally, creates a gut feeling.

What Goleman is saying is that gut feelings offer a guide when facing a complex decision that goes beyond the data at hand, and for which the cultivation of emotional intelligence is essential.

The Crux of Governance

S: The boards approval and support is required in such crucial decisions. How did you convince the board?

V: Basically they took the decision on an evaluation of facts. The board factored three things:

(a) we could take on the technology bet

(b) we have good talent force with the ability to use technology

(c) ability to attract talent.

In Competing for the Future, *Hamel and Prahalad view the firm as a portfolio of competencies. They think it necessary to possess a disproportionate share of requisite competencies to gain a corresponding higher share of future profits, because such competencies represent the persistent accumulation of intellectual capital rather than God given endowment. One has to build strengths by acquisition.*

Nations, and particularly America, are in this race to acquire maximum intellectual capital from other countries. What is a "brain drain" for other nations is a "brain gain" for them. We understand better now why America manages its competency portfolio by resorting to selective and flexible immigration policies.

Good governance depends upon the quality of the board members. Any company in this situation would have said, we do not have the experience in this, but that goes against the principle of core competence. My question to proponents of core competence: before you built core competence, where were you? You must start at some point. And that is where we were in retail business. You don't get core competence on day one. You must have the ability to build it and we demonstrated that we had that. We could acquire it wherever we couldn't muster it from within. That was the Board's opinion too and they supported us.

The Board's decisions are mission critical. They provide direction to the organisation, and have a significant impact on employee morale. Therefore, the selection of right members for the board is always very important. It has become more so in the light of corporate frauds that have become the editorial chef's special menu in financial press and media. The boards are not only expected to carry out the fiduciary responsibility—demands for transparency, are really inchoate demands for evaluation of the Boards' contribution. Good Board members know this. They want to transform the coffee-cashewnuts chat sessions into value-adding dialogues and decisions.

S: *Will you please explain your selection process for the constitution of the Board?*

V: That process is actually driven by the governance committee of the board. People have a wrong notion that the CEO makes the decision. He evaluates the expected contributions, against the criteria we had set for ourselves. He contributes to the deliberations; the governance committee narrows it down. We are fortunate in having Vaghul to head this committee. The Board processes have improved tremendously in the last six years. It has taken us to the best practice levels in terms of what we do.

In Boards at Work *Ram Charan (1998) says:*

> In their quest for better governance, shareholders, directors, and CEOs have arrived at a common realisation: the true potential of the board lies in its ability to help management prevent problems, seize opportunities, and make the corporation perform better than it otherwise would.

Engineering a Paradigm Shift

As Vaman was speaking about Vaghul, my mind visited the portrait gallery that housed the illustrious men of this fine institution. The founder, the late H T Parekh was there. Parekh later built another superb institution HDFC. The late S. S. Nadkarni was next, who looked to horizons beyond the regulatory framework. He opened the gates to investment banking and leasing. Then followed Vaghul who set up the country's first rating agency, Crisil, the venture capital Company ICICI Venture, and an infrastructure outfit SCICI. To succeed such men of eminence is not easy.

V: Well ... I can be linked to transforming or revolutionising—for want of a more appropriate phrase—financial services with technology, and retail banking awareness in the market place. Technology can enable the offering of a complete range of products on multiple platforms, and provide a paradigm shift in the delivery of products to the individual.

Paradigms are basic assumptions about reality. They change. In Management Challenges for the 21st Century, *Drucker (2000) provides a new paradigm:*

> *Management's concern and responsibility, are everything that affect the performance of the institution and its results—whether inside or outside, whether under the institution's control or totally beyond it.*

S: Is it a paradigm shift, and if so which way?

V: Before we came in, a bank dealt with the customer on its own terms. We changed that paradigm. We deal with the customer the way he wants us to deal with him. To do that, we had to align ourselves with the entire paradigm shift in business caused by e-commerce. I would say electronic financial services are the key to the future. It is not as if no small foreign or Indian Bank may have tried it, but here I am talking of the scale, 5–10 million customers. Even banks in public sector now want to emulate it.

V: We get enough currency from results and what people say. We actually underplay it. Before merger for a year and half, I did not hold any media meetings. I consciously stayed out of picture. I said to myself, *let me be like grass, which bends down and blows, or oscillates with the flow of the wind.* I took that to heart. Otherwise, it was likely to create animosity. I ensured that the organisation did not suffer through my self-imposed exile.

Vaman has the backing of the Talmud, which states: Every blade of grass has its Angel that bends over it and whispers, "grow, grow".

Make Colleagues the Brand Ambassadors

S: *However your colleagues were all over the press.*

V: We employed a very sound strategy. I wanted my colleagues to be in front of the media. They had to get good coverage in the media. Images get built up. When people see ICICI has such a talent pool, it helps build the brand image.

S: *Right, and it appears to me that having five or six women at the top is a USP. Everybody says that ICICI is not only an equal opportunity employer at lower positions but also at the highest. It has so many women. It indicates that you actually promote equal opportunity. How did this happen?*

V: It is very simple. We run a meritocracy right from entry point. Those recruited at the campuses are on merit. The assignments are given on merit. The growth is on merit. The postings abroad are done on merit. So the question doesn't arise whether a lady, selected on merit, can do the job or not. Nobody ever doubted whether Lalita, Kalpana, or Chanda, could do the job. We have changed the mindset.

S: *You are giving your colleagues media and press space. In the process, you made them brand ambassadors of ICICI, provided them identity and meaning in their jobs, and built a team! In one stroke you hit multiple targets. Great job!*

V: My team is my greatest asset. Credit for my success goes primarily to them.

However, the technology people have not come up with innovations. Why is it that I have to see things somewhere and tell them? I am most happy when my guys run ahead of me. Several departments have now become self-starters.

S: It happenes because you made demands on them.

V: No, they now understand it is required for survival in changing contexts. It is a continuous process.

Vaman is identifying gaps and opportunities. In such a mindset, gap is an opportunity because in gap there is a space. This is creative thinking. He reiterates, one must not make the basic mistake of re-inventing the wheel. One must know what others have done and take it to the next best practice. Probably one to migrate to a conjoint field.

Change Masters Transform the Mission

V: We are now in branch banking and we are adding something like 250,000 customers a month. One can say that there is no other bank in the world getting such a response. I have to build skills for handling such phenomenal growth. I can take this model globally.

S: *Is the mission changing?*

V: We had to change from a company offering only project finance to a company offering a gamut of corporate banking products, and from there to bringing in the retail focus. Now we are adding to it the international piece. At each stage, there are underlying improvements in technology, processes, products, delivery, etc.

This is phenomenal change. Rosabeth Moss Kanter will be happy to incorporate ICICI story in the new edition of her classic Change Masters. *These change champions—Vaman Kamath, Lalita Gupte, Hoshang Sinor, Kalpana Morparia, Subrata Mukherji, Chanda Kochar, Nachiket Mor—transformed mission, mindsets, and ground realities in the damn difficult Indian market.*

S: *If the institutional support had not been there, would it have been possible for you to do it alone?*

V: I am an institutional entrepreneur where basic things are available. I build on them. I am not the type who can start a business from scratch.

S: *What are the differentiating skills between a manager-entrepreneur and an entrepreneur?*

V: The first is an opportunity taker who requires a platform. The second one, is a big risk taker. He starts on his own and builds his venture single-handed. He bets on all or none. The first one mixes several things and carefully calculates risks because he is using third party money. If one is using one's own money, the second option is fine.

Changing mindsets, re-engineering businesses, or starting new ones requires high levels of creativity. They entail connecting the unconnected, spotting gaps, searching for opportunities, adding value, and creating businesses. Where did you find the robust concepts, models, frameworks, stories, symbols that you could apply to the situation at hand. Where do you get such sparks?

V: The environment around. Life literally is the source. Seeing mundane things differently. This faculty grew in me. Frankly, it wasn't there until I took this position. It is a post 1996 phenomenon. I don't think I was as observant then as I am today, or that I had these many ideas earlier.

S: *It is a direct consequence of taking on responsibility. After assuming office one realises that one's ability to respond to situations must improve geometrically. There are no copy book solutions.*

Role Models: Dhirubhai Ambani and Narayana Murthy

V: As one starts pushing boundaries and stretching the envelope, one looks for every single edge. I do a fair amount of reading. Suddenly, one realises life itself provides so many avenues to opportunities. One looks at people around to see how they are doing. Take the example of the late Dhirubhai Ambani. He was a great role model. He thought unconventionally. Reliance executes things well. They employ simple concepts to get great things done. They execute, literally never taking "no" for an answer. I thought it was worth emulating.

We did that in ICICI, and things started moving. Essentially, it meant one started asserting for execution. Dhirubhai never thought anything was impossible. I started with administration, and then moved on to other departments. People responded with imagination. The ability to say we can achieve anything is what we developed. People started building these muscles.

S: *The inspiration came from Dhirubhai?*

V: Yes, also from Mr Narayana Murthy. When I first visited the Infosys campus at Bangalore, I was amazed not by the glamour of the place but by the order in the meeting room where we sat. Murthy said, "I do this by giving importance to the person who looks after the room. I take time to introduce him to the guests and what he does. He takes pride in his work because of the importance I give it in the presence of visitors".

S: *Worth emulating!*

V: On return to Mumbai I implemented it. For every floor I made one secretary responsible for ensuring upkeep, decor, uniform seating order and arrangement in rooms on that floor. To me this is important. It shows the discipline of the organisation and the creation of excellence.

Orbit Change leads to Friction

V: When we were going through the phase of getting listed on NYSE we faced lots of constraints, pitfalls, problem with shareholders, issues with regulators for approval, etc. I remember I had not met Dhirubhai for sometime. He sent me a message through his son Anil—tell Kamath *when you change orbits there is always friction.* You won't believe, I thought over it again and again.

That message charged me. I said to myself, what are we doing? By raising this sort of money, we are changing orbits. We are now trying to be different than the rest. If I know that there is going to be friction, I must be prepared to handle it rather than complain about constraints. That single message gave me sustenance. It provided me a fresh look on life. Instead of worrying about little odds, I started looking to the next step change, treating friction as a temporary phase.

S: *This might sound like a philosophical observation but you seem to have become a detached observer?*

V: No, I have not arrived to that level. If I say I have, then I become static. The environment is never static. I think there is one major problem with mission statements. People believe they can be cast in stone. As we said earlier, missions are changing. India is changing; the global banking scenario is rapidly changing; and ICICI is also changing to play a role in it.

The Indian diaspora across the world has built a brand for itself, for IT skills and entrepreneurship. To name just two, Infosys and Wipro, have amply demonstrated our capabilities to build global organisations of world class. The fastest growing business segment is retail services, showing almost 50 per cent growth. The auto sector including the two-wheelers is growing at compound rate of 30 per cent. The key drive, quadrangular road projects, have caused a spurt in construction equipment demand at 50 per cent. The river linking project will similarly provide a boost to a variety of demands in the next five years.

Banks like ICICI and HDFC, are setting new benchmarks in customer service. There are bottlenecks in government policies, union approaches, and in the execution ethics of bureaucracy. Despite this, the expectation levels are sky high. There is a growing national belief that India is destined for higher levels of growth.

Against this backdrop, Vaman feels we are growing faster than we think we are. This debate, whether there should be an aspiration target is an issue of mindset problem. Once we overcome that, we will achieve 8 per cent to 10 per cent growth. One has to look at the fundamentals. Serious entrepreneurs are thinking in terms of building up capacities for global competition. They ought to do many things, but Vaman is optimistic. With his global ambitions, the size, volume, and character of ICICI Bank will change. The atmosphere within seems to be echoing Napolean Hill's famous adage Think Big Grow Rich.

The 80/20 CEO

The 80/20 principle underlies meritocracy, the art and science of meritorious differentiation. The science of creativity has many examples of individuals feeling trapped, or suffocated in a problem, or reaching a dead end, when they come out of it with new insights provided they are looking for a breakthrough.

For example:

- Gandhi's journey from British rule to freedom
- Drucker's new insights into the art and science of management
- Kuhn's discovery of paradigm shifts, Pareto's discovery of patterns in distribution of wealth [later known as 80/20 rule]
- Juran's rule of the 'vital few' in spearheading the quality movement
- Kurien's white revolution
- Narayana Murthy's transformation from communism to compassionate capitalism through Infosys' globalism

These are all creative acts born out of a feeling of imprisonment. Creative business leaders or entrepreneurs go through the same process when they hit a roadblock. They fight it out. That's what happened with Vaman.

In addition to introduction of meritocracy, Vaman implemented the garage start-up system to manage projects, and most importantly transformed ICICI by internalising the concept of *speed capital*. What it brings out is that Vaman is on a constant look out for enhancing the effectivity of ICICI in thought and action.

What is helping Vaman? He has been a keen observer of the 80/20 principle throughout his life. That speaks volumes about the effectivity of both, *observation* and the *80/20 rule*. If one develops the combinatorial skills of observation and execution of the 80/20 principle in one's individual and organisation learning processes, both are positively placed on the trajectory of exponential growth. ICICI's performance demonstrates that *Vaman is the 80/20 CEO.*

★ ★ ★

7

The Nature of Qualitative Transformation

- ❖ A Peep Beyond Eternal Role Conflicts
- ❖ Self-Transformation Germinates Organisational Renewal
- ❖ The Mantle of a Mentor
- ❖ From Emotional to Spiritual Intelligence
- ❖ The Quintessence of Quality Culture

- ♦ Exemplar—The Embodiment of Quality Performance, Venu Srinivasan

> "By making a personal commitment to our own individual transformational process, we automatically begin to transform the world around us. As we discover and express more and more of the spiritual potential within us here in our human lives, our personal reality changes to reflect our shifts in consciousness.
>
> —Shakti Gawain
> The Path of Transformation

Introduction

This chapter examines the self-transformation process of leaders that lead organisations to renewal and qualitative growth. Their focussed voluntary efforts are based on seeking guidance about spiritual aspects of heightened self-awareness from gurus and emotional intelligence skills from mentors. How systematically the role conflicts are minimised and quality culture is institutionalised by using Japanese and western management techniques is described here, with contemporary examples.

A Peep beyond Eternal Role Conflicts

Role conflicts are the stuff of our daily existence, especially in the work environment. Internet, computerisation of office work and automation of manufacturing processes have dramatically altered the pace and nature of work. Its seamless nature cannot be measured with old work-study and job evaluation methods.

Prof. Henry Mintzberg's (McGill University) pioneering research on managerial roles is presented in his book *The Nature of Managerial Work* (1973). He describes ten observable roles for all types of managers:

- **Interpersonal Roles**—figurehead, liaison, and leader

- **Information Roles**—monitor, disseminator, and spokesman

- **Decisional Roles**—entrepreneur, disturbance handler, resource allocator, and negotiator they form a gestalt, an integrated whole.

Such a configuration can only be achieved through alchemist skills. Transmuting skills have acquired immense significance because the nature of managerial work has dramatically altered due to technological and Internet revolutions. In his fascinating book *The New Alchemists*, Charles Handy (1999), the world-renowned social philosopher offers new insights to beleaguered managers. Says Handy, *"The world needs new ideas, new products, new services, new institutions, new art, and new designs, which come from new individuals—the new alchemists"*. The passion to make a difference through sheer doggedness is the key alchemy.

The major transition, is that work input and efforts are not the most important factors of measurement; results and output are. There are however, quality checks within the work processes. So the means–end continuum is well monitored. In such a metamorphosis, jobs have become multi-skilled and interdependent. As a consequence, roles are transformed, demanding more coordination, cooperation and skills in teamwork.

These people related processes are organic in character. Competency in handling overlaps in the "Flow" of work, is an important measure of quality performance in leadership roles. A business is now managed through networks of organisations and individuals. Organisations small, medium, or large, are no more managed through boxes and histograms. "Out of box thinking" has landed them in overlapping circles of responsibilities, which has blurred job boundaries. This new reality is compelling managers and leaders to play multiple roles, which require constant updating of skills.

The multiple roles that the current business leaders have to play are so complex that friction is inevitable in the circles of responsibilities. It is the nature of circles to revolve and evolve. They are in constant motion. They expand or contract, like ripples in still water, when you throw stones in it. They are like *chakras* in the body. They are the influencing auras of individuals, groups, and organisations. The need to co-create in that conjoint space (overlapping area between circles) is paramount.

Jobs have become multi-skilled for assemblers in the factory, clerks in the office, and managers of all functions. The combination of different activities and roles alone saves costs and increases productivity. Cost cuts and self-reliance through multiple skills is the offspring of technology, and competition for survival. The minute splitting of job functions and roles are expensive, non-sustainable fractionations. Instead of divisions, addition provides better returns. Adding functions and combining roles add more value.

In *Making Organisation Roles Effective,* Prof. Udai Pareek (1993) gives a detailed account of how roles can be systematically made effective. He says:

> *We have to move from positions based on power and privileges assigned in hierarchical structures, to roles based on mutuality of obligations in loose, minimal hierarchical structures. Such flexible arrangement is based on cohesive functioning of teams, which are formed and dismantled depending on organisation needs.*

It is of paramount importance to remove the role ambiguity through dialogue and spelling out role expectations.

In *Corporate Success and Transformational Leadership,* Professors P. Singh and Asha Bhandarkar (1992) give exhaustive evidence of how systematically the leaders of the five organisations they studied applied theory and practice to corporate renewal. Minerals and Metals Trading Corporation's (MMTC) chairman S. V. S. Raghavan removed role ambiguities by establishing clarity through involvement and consensus. Afterwards, a joint divisional manager said, "Now we know where we are going". Even the directors were assigned specific roles. Raghavan played a supportive role. He used to say, "Use me extensively, tell me what I can do for you".

Venu Srinivasan redefined the roles of owner CEO, President, and COO, at TVS Motors using the Japanese TQC principle of sharing managing points. Looking after stakeholders' interests and a small portion of long-term vision and medium term plans himself, he delegated the other functions to the President and COO. Long back, Drucker had predicted the demise of the schizophrenic one-man chief executive and it's evolution to a small team job. This has happened.

Trust in business is low at present especially in post-Enron America. McKinsey Quarterly report (*ToI—Ascent*, March 22, 2004) says, "Reinforcing the independence of corporate boards, by separating the positions of Chairman and CEO could help. In UK, that has been the practice—95 per cent of all FTSE 350 companies adhere to the principle of separating the responsibilities between the Chairman and the CEO. The Chairman runs the board and CEO runs the company. One of the functions of the Chairman is to monitor the performance of the CEO. In US, only 25 per cent of the organisations have separate Chairmen and CEOs. This practice, to concentrate all powers in one person, is changing in US after recent spate of scandals.

The Cadbury committee report advocated the same reasoning for keeping the roles separate. We have largely followed the same principle, exceptions like ITC, Hindustan Lever, are there to prove the rule. Such a separation fits into the Indian companys' upbringing because we have been acculturated to the British way of management for over two centuries. Moreover it makes sense since it provides the needed "checks and balances".

In the volume *The Future of Leadership* (Bennis, W., et al., 2001), Cathy L. Greenberg-Walt and Alsrair G. Robertson have described what the evolving role of executive leadership means. They discuss three key topics:

- shared leadership and the devolving CEO
- leading across generations
- global leadership and the next generation

The authors say:

> *The Unilever structure exhibits both forms of dual leadership: split chairmanship, supported by an executive committee. The current example in which the role of chairman and chief executive is divided by Citigroup, formed out of an equal merger between the US bank Citigroup and the Travellers' Financial Services group.*

Chief executives of both corporations have become Co-Chief Executive Officers after the merger. The synergy expected from them must reflect in their balanced scorecards.

Leading across generations is a difficult task, both for professional and family run organisations. There is the proverbial generation gap, plus the knowledge driven self-aware, self-led identity gap. There is also a huge gap in expectations from leadership, needed to drive the business through change. It is the job of the CEO to communicate succinctly the values, so as to bridge the generation gap. Otherwise, misperceptions about values may lead to conflicts.

The undergraduates, interviewed by the Accenture Institute for Strategic Change, identified behaviour that successful leaders need to develop in the global workplace:

- communicate a global vision
- be technologically savvy
- embrace an open-minded leadership style
- champion diversity (style, culture, and leadership)
- display flexibility and respect toward employees
- foster a corporate culture of teamwork

Bennis' observation that CEOs see their central task as developing other leaders and actively helping followers reach their own leadership potential, supplements these expectations of the new generation.

If one treats family as the basic organisation unit then one observes that there also, the roles have changed beyond recognition. Role conflicts have extended to the family because career minded working spouses are striving to achieve work-life balance. Children with their changing demands make role conflicts more intense. Again, one requires management skills, and far more importantly, responsibly sharing multi-faceted collaborative competencies.

The conflicts are rendered more complex because of the asynchrony in time structures of our organisations, institutions, transport and domestic services, and what have you. The external factors are beyond control. One can imagine the kind of societal leadership and innovation required to make this century ours. Complexity challenges the creative! This peep beyond the eternal role conflicts is showing leaders how to rise above the fray, and share.

In a professional organisation, role conflicts deteriorate into worst kind of infighting, politics, and demoralisation of staff. In MNCs, wage costs skyrocketed in no small measure due to such fights in management, of which the unions took advantage, and why should they not? A very respected high profile professional once told me, "If you have politics, look at the CEO". I did, and found the answer.

In family managed organisations, such conflicts are the basic cause of feuds amongst members, resulting in splits, and eventual rot. The down side of our one-time stars provides some lessons for current family organisations, to amend their ways, and resolve conflicts.

In addition, the family members could learn from epics like *Mahabharat* and current Indian organisation research. The bulk of India's GNP is made of family organisations. It is critical that they learn from the experience of others to avoid unproductive battles, which drive out the Goddess *Lakshmi* from their precincts.

In *The Nature of Leadership* John W. Gardner (1986) says:

> *In this fast moving market environment filled with shrewd manipulators, a high value is placed on trust, keeping commitments, and returning favours punctiliously. Machiavellian principles defeat themselves; unscrupulous, unreliable, untrustworthy members end up isolated. Candour is valued because it usually means predictability.*

An added factor: we in information age are crying for good governance. Transparency is demanded in every transaction. The knowledge worker prefers to talk up-front. The sea change in legal requirements, and the needs of all stakeholders to have more and more information, leaves little scope for wheeler-dealers. No one likes surprises, unless they are ethically pleasant and add value. Leaders have to take role conflicts seriously because space for double talk, double deals, and behind the screen manipulations, are literally shrinking to nil.

Self-transformation Germinates Organisational Renewal

Clarity in roles is therefore necessary for organisational renewal processes to fructify. Renewal here means more than that management has to look at expenditure to better existing fixed assets; it has a comprehensive connotation in which the leader is expected to take a fresh look at organisation health, its vision, mission, goals, environment, results, competition, products, service—and something more vital, involved in its renewal.

It is the restoration of faith in the capability of the leader to take the organisation out of the morass, provide it new direction, and rejuvenate the human side of enterprise to recommit to new tasks and responsibilities. This is very important. The leader must seek revision in systems as demanded by the ever-changing reality. He re-dedicates himself to the original mission for which the founding fathers created the organisation. That purpose fades over the years. It requires renewed articulation, infusion of new ideas, and fresh blood.

Renewal is a blend of continuity and change but paradigm changes occur with disconcerting swiftness, as we witnessed at the beginning of the nineties. We cannot avoid the change brought in by globalisation and Internet. Leaders have the responsibility to see what kind of change will preserve the constituent core values, energise the system, and ensure a better future for their organisations.

Leaders make use of scenario building tools to formulate a vision, as Dr. Mashelkar did in Council of Scientific and Industrial Research (CSIR). It helps regain focus and commitment to vision, values, and goals. Leaders are mainly accountable for rekindling the spirit of organisations. They need tools to do so, and scenario building is one such.

This is precisely what Jack Welch did at GE. His six rules for transformations of organisations are:

- control your destiny, or someone else will
- face reality as it is, not as it was or as you wish it were
- be candid with everyone
- don't manage, lead
- change before you have to
- if you don't have a competitive advantage, don't compete

Based on his successful experiment in transforming the ailing company HMV, Pradip Chanda wrote *The Second Coming* (2000). Chanda argues with conviction, that the surgical solution of restructuring, cost cutting, closing factories, and reducing workforce, is not a healthy, sustainable way for the rejuvenation of a company in Indian ethos. It is possible to effect turnarounds by better utilising the existing assets of the firm.

Says Chanda:

> *If the company is to revive, a change in its personality is the starting point. The first obstacle is the mindset of the middle managers and the office staff. The CEO needs to be aware of these forces at work. He has to trigger a cultural metamorphosis that will reshape the mindset.*

Effective performance in such situations depends upon refinement, by combining methods, because innovation is blocked in a thicket of fixed attitudes, laws, precedents, practices, perceptions, assumptions, and traditions. The naysayers shout, "That's not the way we do things over here, we have weird souls here who think they know everything". These are the zealous defenders of status quo because change threatens their preferred ways of thinking and acting.

My experience corroborates that lack of role clarity is a non-starter in any change programme. However, one cannot wait to establish that, because nothing will then move forward. Change undermines established interests and the glib talkers benefit from non-clarity about roles. Confusion helps them perpetuate disorder. Let me illustrate. In a major initiative I took, I directed the industrial relations, policies, and practices between management and union from confrontation to collaboration.

I succeeded in realising the objectives I had set for myself. There was a lull for some years. I thought I had achieved durable peace and therefore lowered my guards. Some interested players got side-lined in the change process; deprived of a field for their old games. However, they re-grouped and lit the fire. I was caught unawares. The inflamed atmosphere forced me to retire, hurt. No one said anything on my face. My long-standing companion—the habit of laughing at myself—healed the wounds gradually.

None the less it was a period of fertile reflection. What was the lesson in it for me? I should not have sent my sensors on long leave; this is an afterthought. I lacked the political skills to make fast moves, regroup my forces, etc. My net asset came to be the art of digesting with equanimity, success and failure. It freed me from their bondage. For some time, I rested in the profundity of my realisation. That spell however, was short lived.

From the sixties to the eighties, many organisations saw role conflicts between the CEO, CFO, Works, and HR chiefs. Responsibility, accountability, and managing points about overlaps in HR and IR were rarely fixed, leaving immense scope for role and personality conflicts. Machiavellian thinking led to low trust levels, which in turn made the atmosphere smoggy.

Sharing information, responsibility, and understanding roles correctly, were not the order of the day. None were conscious of the escalating costs of such unproductive and demoralising conflicts. Since, in the controlled economy, such tangible and intangible costs could be recovered by hiking the product prices, it did not hurt the organisations!

John W. Gardner in the *Leadership Papers/3* termed such situations, systemic stagnation. In most systems which need renewal, people are satisfied with things as they are; the leaders are satisfied too. But disasters, competition, and cold realities make a breakthrough in that order. They upset the balance. A strategy for avoiding the trance of non-renewal, is to keep measure of the diversity and dissent in the system. That diversity is being strengthened in the new systems of governance, with overlapping circles of responsibility being shared.

Apart from the fact that the leader has to be technologically savvy, he must also possess charisma and a thorough understanding on what works in a particular culture. A charismatic leader plays more on his vision, articulation, the emotions of his subordinates, and has the ability to take risks. Such a description holds ground even if Kenneth Lay, Martha Stewart, and other such CEOs have used their charm for financially unethical objectives. Such things happen, and further validate the important role "charisma" plays in influencing a situation.

The role of charisma and art of influencing are situation neutral. They cannot evade deception. Employed for the right cause, charisma is a much valued catalytic agent in the transformational leadership, along with individualised consideration, intellectual stimulation, and inspirational behaviour. A transformational leader sets new goals, and restructures the organisation. He is pioneering and innovative. A transactional leader however, is the exact opposite of him. He gets work done in exchange of rewards and promises. His style is "management by exceptions". In the Indian ethos, charisma plays a prominent role.

The predominant Indian cultural values, which facilitate corporate success rather smoothly, as documented by Singh and Bhandarker, are: role of *Karta*, relationship orientation, proximity to power, security, simple living and high thinking, and survival. It is significant that Indians have more reverence for saints than for kings and emperors. The former command respect for their plain living and high thinking. Narayana Murthy, our current IT icon, is a classic exemplar of this style. The author of *The Cultural Context of Leadership and Power*, Prof. Jai B. P. Sinha (1995) believes, *"Leaders create the culture and this culture shapes the next generation of leadership"*.

Sinha describes the role of *Karta*:

> *The karta is a father figure who is nurturant, caring, dependable, sacrificing and yet demanding, authoritative, and a strict disciplinarian. He evokes feelings of security, trust, and dependability, in creating a familial culture. He empowers, guides, and protects.*

This corresponds to the profile of "nurturant task leader" developed by Sinha. Such a leader (*karta*) has to first change himself before dwelling upon organisation change.

The *karta* orientation is primarily satisfied through a person centred or people focused approach. This means empowering people, supporting them, providing a family atmosphere, a sense of purpose, and model behaviour. The team work emphasis builds trust. The CEOs come from different backgrounds, cultural settings, disciplines of study, and face peculiar problems in their respective organisations. It is easier for some to leverage the person centred thrust because they have better interpersonal relations and social skills. They thrive on working with people.

One quality is common to all CEOs: they are great learners. They try to transform their attitudes, skills, and behaviour. Often, their efforts at self-transformation are either undertaken first, or they run parallel to organisation change initiatives. Such personal transformation implies that the leader raises his consciousness to a higher level of synthesis, a kind of a vantage point, from which he is able to visualise solutions to conflicts and dualities within himself and in the outside world. Venu Srinivasan overcame his brashness, became patient. There was a content change in his nature (*swabhav*). It was *tamasik*; it became *sattvic*.

CEOs do not like to talk about such efforts, or the methods they employed in self-change. Most of them rely on parents, mentors, and gurus' words of wisdom, scriptures, and literature, with whoever they interact. Some do daily practice (*sadhana*) to achieve quiescence and objectivity in handling critical issues that confront them time and again.

They are unanimous that the CEO must renew himself continuously to successfully transform his organisation. Without that, change efforts would not build people assets.

The Mantle of a Mentor

Mentors, counsellors, guides, and coaches, help bring about beneficial changes in thinking, skills, and conduct of those they advise. Basically, they assist their wards in upgrading their overall competencies. They do it gently because they do not have the authority of the boss or school teacher.

The management guru Peter Drucker learnt five leadership lessons from his three mentors.

- Treat people differently based on their strengths
- Set high standards, but give people the freedom and responsibility to do their jobs
- Performance review must be honest, exacting, and an integral part of the job
- People learn the most while teaching others
- Effective leaders need to earn respect—but they don't need to be liked

The most important lesson Drucker learnt was that it was the manager's job to make human strengths productive and weaknesses irrelevant.

Mentors earn respect for their knowledge, experience, and persuasive personality. Their diagnostic and listening skills are of a superior quality. They provide the conceptual framework and share a perspective that helps counselees to look at their personal issues through a kind of a prism.

Anu Aga, Kiran Mazumdar, Humayun Dhanrajgir, Prakash Ratnaparkhi and such leaders profiled in my earlier book *Thought Leaders,* had mentors. Handy observes in *The New Alchemist* (1999) that mentoring is a continuing need. This is borne out by the recent examples of Narayana Murthy relinquishing the CEO position to become chief mentor at Infosys, the company he founded; and Tarun Das CEO of CII (Confederation of Indian Industries), who became its mentor on retirement.

Gurus are a separate category. They are spiritual mentors. They bring about spiritual transformation in their *shishyas* (disciples). The *Guru–shishya* relationship has a sacrosanct code of ethics and behaviour. The disciple is expected to completely surrender to the guru. It is believed that those disciples that break the code come to grief later.

There is no such strict code of conduct in the mentor–protege relationship. It is freewheeling. The objectives are different. The executive is not subjecting himself to a course in spiritual transformation. Interestingly, many executives practise meditation and yoga for stress relief, poise, focus, and attitude change.

You can see that the techniques and processes of upgrading thinking skills and functional competencies of executives are grounded in spiritual discipline. It is therefore more likely that such training may fundamentally transform the trainees' attitude towards life and living. It has the power to mature him through different passages of life.

According to mentoring consultant Mike Pegg, "Mentoring aims to balance creativity and commerce, soul work and salary work. It is about letting people explore options". People need time and space to reflect on what options are available. Unless they are taught to take a "helicopter view", their "seeing" doesn't change, and they do not become empowered. It helps eject them from the "victim" position, to take charge of their lives. At Microsoft, the management found that mentoring helped employees find fulfilment; it helped them stay put.

Two models of mentoring processes can be combined. One starts with a learning group of say five people and the mentor. In the first (group) phase, information regarding responsibilities, expectations, and benefits of participation are provided. This helps build a peer network where participants can share experiences. The critical element in these sessions is the development of dialogue in the Socratic manner, as J. Krishnamurti did in the recent years. It has had a great impact.

In the second phase, one goes the traditional way by building one-to-one relationships between mentor and protege. This personal–confidential phase, provides mentor and protege space for establishing trust. The protege is helped identify his specific needs. They also define the time commitment for actual work, reflective search, and the concluding date for the assignment. Mentors don't dictate, they suggest. They are available even after the stipulated period if the protege so wants, and the organisation keeps the channel open. Such an arrangement is helpful for both, the protege and organisation.

In *The Mentor's Spirit,* Marsha Sinetar (1998) points out that the true mentors' unseen, affirming influence and positive energy pervades the atmosphere around one. They are "artists of encouragement", who help one discover what is unique about one's calling in life, and support one in pursuing it. The mentor's spirit is the pervading healthy relationships between productive managers and subordinates, and resourceful leaders and their constituents.

Mentors do not give pep talks. They guide one to follow one's spirit and change the script of life whenever needed. They do not dish out high sounding metaphysical abstractions, and recite scriptural truisms. They are practical men and women who provide a mirror to reflect one's image, and true worth.

Mentors love people and life, they are non-judgmental. In their company, one feels unconditional acceptance. They show how to be authentic and true to oneself despite shifting circumstances. One grows in their aura. They share their experiences to sharpen one's internal compass. The tactics of the moment are not their responsibility. In their company one learns to turn to one's deepest, most intimate truths.

A mantle is regarded as a symbol of preeminence. For a mentor to advance to that stage requires sustained practice and the guidance of an adept guru. A productive mentor acquires a very stable orientation towards life's goals. He encourages others to love, live and learn.

In his best seller *Living, Loving & Learning,* Dr. Leo F. Buscaglia (1982) says:

- to love is to risk not being loved in return, to hope is to risk pain

- to try is to risk failure, to laugh is to risk appearing a fool

- to weep is to risk being called a sentimental, to reach out to another is to risk involvement

One cannot expose feelings because one risks showing one's true self; most people want to hide their true self. If one places one's ideas and dreams before the crowd one risks being called naïve. And as Buscaglia concludes, the person who risks nothing, does nothing, has nothing, and is nothing.

This is a tall order for the best of mentors to fulfil. Yet, that is the kind of soothing personality one develops to meet new challenge in business. The knowledge worker requires the company of mentors even if they are not perfect.

Sinetar warns, that we should not think our mentors blemish free, ministering angels. If we do so, we invite disappointment. No sooner do others fall short of our illusions than we cast aside their teachings, some of which could be valuable. We might perhaps feel hurt and depressed but that is okay in the bargain of learning. Mentors do not produce magical formulae of success because they have none.

Establishing trust is a mentor's job but proteges must be supportive. It's a two-way continuing process. For it to be successful, management must prepare the ground. The protege must however be aware that he is not there to assess the mentor's competencies. He must have the humility of a learner otherwise the exercise is a non-starter.

Mentors mature in their practice of productive, dialogue-based relationships. Mentors' efforts are focused on making their proteges:

- autonomous–prepared to accept the consequences of their choices, and ever ready to seek the company of healthy, positive people
- identify life and career goals
- grow organically
- affirm life and its potential
- stabilise the continuity of their efforts because they themselves are grounded
- study their lives in a framework of individual vision, values, ambitions, and criteria for fulfilment
- understand what leadership legacy they would like to leave behind
- elevate their performance in the context of organisational and individual needs

The ultimate benefits are to be seen in the mentor's spirit animating the top line.

From Emotional to Spiritual Intelligence

The mentor's spirit is grounded in spiritual intelligence. The time to move from emotional intelligence to spiritual intelligence therefore has arrived. In ten years, 1994–2004, we moved from narrow interpretation of intelligence (IQ) to emotional intelligence (EQ) since Daniel Goleman's brain and behavioural research brought to our notice why people with modest IQ do better than those with high IQ.

In *Emotional Intelligence*, Goleman (1995) says that EQ is a basic requirement for the effective use of IQ. It pervades the thinking of people with high EQ. Such people show more effectiveness in their jobs and interactions. These factors cause it:

- self-awareness, self-discipline, empathy, and the art of listening, resolving conflicts, and cooperation, which makes one look inwards
- a person grounded in his belief system—emotional intelligence hinges on the link between sentiment, character, and moral instincts; impulse is the medium of emotion, which calls for self-restraint and compassion, not impulsiveness

In ten years number of seminars on emotional intelligence, theory and practice have been conducted, to train executives in emotional, cognitive, and behavioural skills. Awareness about it has considerably enhanced. Says Sinetar, executives who sense a discrepancy between their potential and careers, are perfect candidates for spiritual work. I find that such candidates understand the concepts but shy away from putting themselves through some disciplined practice to develop the needed attributes. Spiritual intelligence (popularly titled, SQ), is our fingerprint as well as the individuated peek into the oneness of things.

Computers have taken over most of the functions of IQ, higher mammals possess EQ, and only humans have SQ. It is our quest to find meaning in work and life, which only spiritual awareness can enlighten. It is our longing for meaning, vision, and values. It enables us to dream, strive for excellence and shape our lives and careers, the way we want. SQ is that intelligence, which forms the backbone of our struggles to triumph over matters mundane; over the dualities of existence.

In *SQ*, Danah Zohar and Ian Marshall (2000) have described spiritual intelligence.

- The primary process could be called EQ (based on "associative neural wiring" in the brain), the second IQ (based on "serial neural wiring" in the brain); and SQ (based on is the brain's third neural system, the synchronous neural oscillations that unify data across the whole brain) offers us a viable tertiary process for the first time.
- We need SQ to dialogue between dualities. It facilitates such a discourse between reason and emotion, between

mind and body. It provides the fulcrum for growth and transformation of the self with an active, unifying, meaningful centre.

- Self-awareness is one of the highest criteria of spiritual intelligence but one of the lowest priorities of our spiritually dumb culture. Though we consider India a land of spiritual wisdom, current ethos calls us to question that assumption.

There is as yet no quantitative measurement tool developed for assessing SQ. No one has any clue when such an instrument will be available, or whether it is at all possible to develop one. Spiritual Intelligence is embedded in the spirit—the vital force—of humans. Its chemistry defies analysis. It is a subjective and qualitative phenomenon.

In the *Guru–shishya* tradition, the *Guru* with his extrasensory (atindriya) knowledge assesses the *shishya's* preparedness (sadhana).to enter the next step of development (siddhavasta).

The guru takes into account the disciple's:

1. relevant experience—how he has faced obstacles on the path

2. correctness of spiritual practices, and possible themes for future development

3. depth of discipline, faith, commitment, and potential for maturity

Spirituality is an experiential subjective reality not amenable to the establishment of mathematical formulae. But that does not mean such a virtual reality does not exist. As much as EQ is not in common use in management's evaluation process, SQ will also not be there.

However, the need to develop SQ is felt by leading thinkers on leadership and management. There are acclaimed spiritual paths, roadmaps, signs, guides, laws of success, and tons of experiential literature that provides direction. One needs to avail of that to become a true leader.

The Indian scriptures, mythology, culture, and literature have exhaustively investigated and established spirituality. Based on centuries of experience, the nature, process, and method of enquiry has been codified in various authoritative texts like *Upanishads, Vivekchudamani, Yogavashistha,* to name just a few.

Mahabharat and *Ramayan* are eternal classics. Similar texts are available in other religions as well. What is conveyed by the progress in brain science, is that there is now rational, scientific validation for the central metaphysical enquiries of life, living, and purpose.

It means we have to be responsive to the deep self to live in harmony with our true longings, and the ecology of Earth. Our hunger for fulfilment compels us to launch a reflexive search for meaning. We find it, when we learn to transcend pain while struggling to free our minds from the past, by making healing choices on the way. This is a context invariant universal need, which psychologists term "field independent". The spread of yoga all over the world appears propitious in this context.

The march of globalisation at the macro level, is leading man to deep, integral personal development at the micro level. This holistic transformation in the leadership movement promises a sane non-opulent life style, which will eventually temper the rampant consumerism of the west. The global cultures are undergoing a metamorphosis. It is a question of our perception.

The Quintessence of Quality Culture

Japan, once known for shoddy products, became the symbol of quality products in the 1970s, because it started "seeing" products qualitatively. Continuous quality improvement, total quality management involving personnel from all levels, quality manuals, and quality circles became the buzz words all over the world, as the Japanese skilfully marketed and exported their quality know-how.

It was the tough competition for better products and services that led the Japanese to invest step by step in zero-defect products, just-in-time manufacturing, and deliveries. From quality inspection, to planning, management, and total quality, the movement was an epic journey towards excellence. It is an example of non-linear thinking. They went past quality in production to quality in management. It was a backward and forward integration of quality consciousness, from supply chain management to deliverables. They achieved astonishing results.

Skilled tradesmen had already disappeared after the arrival of mass production factories during the industrial revolution. The Japanese hunger for innovative ideas, like vigorous follow through of suggestion schemes, and they quest for superior products through continuous improvement in knowledge, methods and techniques. This has provided them a magnificent edge in the capture of global markets. They meshed modern techniques with their cultural traits, national pride, discipline, and security of employment.

The quality gurus that guided Japanese thinkers and channelled the energies were Deming, Juran, Crosby, Shingo, Taguchi, Ishikawa, and Feigenbaum. We need not dwell on the frictions that were caused by the diversity in their philosophies, principles, and methods. On the whole, they had a positive impact on raising the country to higher quality standards.

The differences were in the focus on the technical needs of quality control and the human dimension of its management, the easily measurable quantifiable activities, and the difficult to measure human inputs. The main problem that the management faces is acceptability of all the employee constituencies to what is a fair and equitable method, and we know there is none. The gurus stumbled at this age-old battle of how to accurately measure people contribution in input and output, efforts and results, immediate and long-term needs, expediency and solidity, because the entire quality upgradation process is based on the principle of "flow".

We have to understand that it is the political and coercive dimension of management that led quality gurus to take their differences to the boardrooms. They were also concerned with fast results and recognition. They were involved only in the commercial organisation and not in the other activities of institutions. Therefore, they do not mention much about the quality of the society, which is a very important consideration for every other developing country.

In India we were, and still are, infested with unproductive, obstructive labour laws; with anti-government, anti-work ethics, protests driven culture, which substantially eroded our pride in work and nation. In addition, undisciplined mobocratic governance and the controlled economy ethos nurtured non-quality stunted growth.

Many years back, in a meeting on the introduction of quality exercise in our company I had raised the following issues.

- How are we going to achieve quality improvement—meaning "mindset change"—in people, in the midst of all the above stated ingredients, liberally present within the organisation and in the country?

- Who is supposed to pilot it, be responsible and accountable for it?

- How are the proponents going to make the interventions in the system?

The sellers of the package had no convincing answers. The works chief had a derisive smile. I was aware that the organisation dynamics, which also means "politics", played a pivotal role in changing the tracks. Who would be responsible for total quality improvement across the organisation becomes a major issue. Venu Srinivasan is of the firm belief that the issue of "quality" is fundamentally a question of change in the mindset of the people. He has therefore put HR and quality together under one head.

Quality improvement is not a cosmetic exercise. Its human dimension is far more important than techniques and methods. I was not opposed to the quality movement. In fact, it was and is always essential to have an in-built system for improving quality consciousness and standards.

I knew that the markets at that time were not competitive for our products and stature. There was no threat and therefore no overwhelming pressure to go all out to improve quality. Nonetheless, we went ahead with no visible discernible difference except scheduled mechanical presentations of the status-quo reports!

Later, the TQM package provided some answers to the above questions and standardised methods for interventions. Organisations now see the difference "socio-cultural systems thinking" makes to the total quality management. It comprehensively addresses the entire complex set of interacting issues involving everyone at all levels. The approach passes through three phases: creativity, choice, and implementation. It amounts to "thinking about thinking".

The quality of Indian products improved gradually because the adverse factors mentioned above, operated on a low key and did not obstruct or inflict noticeable damage in the last twelve years. Since 1991, the atmosphere in the country has been far more conducive to quality upgradation. Certainly, we gave Japan good business but our returns in the bargain have been encouraging too.

The proof of the pudding lies in the eating. If an organisation has adopted TQM in letter and spirit it will be seen in its zero-defect products, timely deliveries, and prompt service. The essence of quality culture is found in the creativity, innovation, and a high level of awareness of its people. One sees them engaged in continuous improvement.

However, the quintessence of quality culture is the leader's self-transformation. That is the kernel of truth. Without that condition precedent being honestly fulfilled, organisation renewal will not be genuine or durable. When a leader is transformed, he has a new found enthusiasm, which inspires others to follow him. His words carry weight and wisdom. In his person, one sees three strands merging: technology upgradation (IQ), quality enhancement (EQ), and spiritual intelligence (SQ).

What I saw at Apollo hospitals was proof of the difference Prathap Reddy's presence makes with the staff. The seven leaders profiled in this book (as well as Murthy, Mazumdar, Aga, Mashelkar, Parekh, Tirodkar, Dhanrajgir from *Thought Leaders*), gives me the confidence to say that their *a priori* transformation contributed significantly to the success of the organisations they lead.

Of course, none other than Venu Srinivasan is exemplar of the nature of qualitative transformation that I have described here. I draw your attention to Venu's profile, because it is replete with his candid observations on this topic.

The Embodiment of Quality Performance— Venu Srinivasan

TVS Group is the first Indian group with the distinction of its two flagship companies Sundaram-Clayton Ltd (Turnover Rs 300 crore) and TVS Motors (Turnover Rs 2700 crore) winning the Deming Application Prizes. The group, which comprises of twenty-nine companies, is the largest automotive component manufacture and distribution group in India. Venu Srinivasan is its self-effacing Managing Director.

Exemplary CEOs

"Customer is not the King He is God"

I used to visit Madras regularly from 1973 to 1991. Thereafter I did not visit it again in its new *avatar*, Chennai, until one humid October day in 2002. In the intervening decade (1991–2002) we had both changed somewhat, for the better.

Chennai airport looked new, the roads broadened, glassy skyscrapers dotted the skyline, famous hotel brands were visible, and shopping complexes had tall, wide fronts. My visit to Chennai is never complete without visiting The Theosophical Society at Adyar. It has maintained its dignified serenity but the rest of Chennai has changed. I like to get lost in that place.

I was to meet Venu at Chaitanya on Nawaz Khan road. His secretary Girirajan was as courteous in person as he was on phone. Tall and lean, Venu has a delicate frame. He is simple, and conveys humility in his smile. I start by sharing my thoughts on Madras of 1991 and Chennai of 2002.

Born with a Silver Spoon

Grandson of the famous T. V. Sundaram Iyengar, founder of TVS Group, Venu at 53, can be justly described as born with a silver spoon in his mouth. He grew up in a conservative Iyengar joint family, where the rich Tamil traditional provides a solid philosophical base for organic growth and values. Venu graduated in engineering from Madras University, and obtained an MS in management from Purdue University, USA.

His internship in his company began under a bus in an asbestos-roofed shed. By putting Venu through mill, his grandpa tried to blunt the abnormal growth of "ego" that permeates a rich aristocratic setting. However, it did not prevent Venu from becoming arrogant, brash, and impulsive to start with.

It would have been a surprise if all those trappings of wealth, education, power and position, bestowed over a prolonged adolescence (till 27), had not gone into his head. Said Jonathan Swift, *"The first springs of great events, like those of great rivers, are often mean and little"*. How Venu lost his egocentric garments is an eclectic story of personal transformation and concomitant organisational renewal.

Formed in 1925, the TVS group deals in two-wheelers, computer peripherals, automotive components, spares, etc through its 29 companies. The jewels in the crown are Sundaram-Clayton and TVS Motors, which acquired fame through the TVS-Suzuki. Venu's father T. S. Srinivasan's vision of developing and delivering an indigenous moped for every family led to the phenomenal growth of the company. In 1996, the two TVS brands, XL and Champ, became the largest selling vehicles in the country. Venu is currently the Chairman of the group, and Managing Director of both these brand leaders.

2002 has been a significant year in Venu's career and in his group's history as well. After ending its joint venture with Suzuki in May 2002, TVS launched its most popular product, the four-stroke 110 cc motorcycle, Victor. Sundaram-Clayton, which had already won the prestigious Deming prize for quality in 1998, also won the exclusive Japan Quality Medal in 2002. Only Deming winners qualify for this medal. In 2003, TVS Motors bagged the Deming prize for quality.

These wins arterialised the TVS conglomerate. Venu's leadership came of age in his forties, and began to lay down further milestones in his fifties. The New York based prestigious *Business Week* records Venu in the top 25 "Stars of Asia" in its June 2003 issue.

The Mobile CEO

S: The role of a CEO has changed. He has become technologically savvy, far more market driven, and networked in his approach. His time has become his scarcest resource. What is the practical impact?

V: Once the size of business and geographical spread reaches a particular mass, travel becomes a punishing schedule for a CEO. He is no longer managing only hands-on. Evolution of management in India has led him to perform the true role of a CEO, viz. provide broad direction of the policy, and allow people to take leadership.

S: *It is not still clear what the distinguishing feature of the new role is?*

V: One should be motivating, demonstrating, and providing visible leadership—and that requires travel. Dealers, suppliers, institutional investors, bankers, policy makers, environmentalists, regulatory authorities, all want to see one in person. They want to meet one to share information and hold meaningful dialogues to convey their points of view. Neither of us wants to catch the other by surprise. The need for constant exchange of information and ideas has increased manifold. If one cannot meet this expectation of theirs, they will not meet one's own, when time comes, and that time is already here. This change requires one to transport oneself throughout the world.

S: *This means you have become* a mobile CEO, *like the* Man on the Spot?

V: *A mobile CEO*, yes, not *Man on the Spot* though. He is not the branch manager of a bank. A CEO needs to meet people face to face because "seeing is believing". When one visits, one sees the place, the body language, facial expressions, symbols, signs, dress, and feels the ambience. One is better informed. That makes the difference for both, on the same criteria.

The important point Venu made was that the social mobility of a CEO is vitally important to business and people. Modern communications have improved one's movements. It has made one more available to one's stakeholders. Mobile phones help keep one connected for follow-up and urgent matters. Nothing then waits for one's arrival, except perhaps the better half and kids. If one honours their non-negotiable harmonic need to be with one, it will save expenses and time on attending seminars on "work-life balance"!

S: *How did you manage that balance?*

V: Obviously, building an organisation makes enormous demands on time. It takes a hell of a lot of energy. The priority of building the organisation is on one's mind all the while; therefore, my social engagements have become minimal.

S: *Would you not say that Mallika being a professional in her own right, is a kind of help?*

V: Well, it's mutual. Basically it is a symbiotic relationship. We both use each other as sounding boards, and that's a unique thing. Again, since socially both of us have stature, we can represent each other, and we often do. The house would not move, if we were not able to do that. Therefore, there is certainly a balance we are able to provide because of our professional background.

S: *What about children rearing?*

V: Well, she is a good teacher, I am not. I can give examples but cannot hold hands, and teach. I don't have that kind of patience. Teaching a child is an ultimate test of patience—it's really a big challenge.

S: *It comes naturally to a female, the mother instinct.*

V: Yes, but I am not willing to take it on a gender basis. I can say she has it to a great extent. It is a personal skill. Some inherit it. Some of my male relatives have it too.

The Roles of Owner CEO, President, and COO

S: *Does all this change demand a different role from an owner?*

V: In a family business, we had to redefine the role of the family CEO with the help of our mentor. We thought he was primarily an owner with a small portion of President functions, viz. in developing long-term vision, and medium term plan. Leave all the rest of the functions to the President.

In our organisation, he has more authority than CEOs of many other companies in similar situations. To look after family businesses, internationally, there are many models. They demand much more travel in the interests of stakeholders because that responsibility is cast on him by being a member of the family. One is their trustee and that function cannot be delegated.

S: The President has to play executive and operational roles.

V: The President has some operational responsibilities, but the COO is really fully responsible for operations. There is an interface between owner CEO, President, and COO. Nothing in life is crystalline because they are all people related processes, and therefore by definition organic. The critical factor for success is 100 per cent trust between the owner and the President. Trust includes self-trust, which can be cultivated if one is true to oneself.

Says Francis Fukuyama: *trust has a large measurable economic value.* The owner provides a continuity of commitment, representing the owner's interests and traditional cultural values. With involvement of the President at every stage, he shares and shapes the vision of the company. He is personally responsible for high-risk, long-term calls. The two roles in fact, must seamlessly merge while trying to achieve a delicate balance between the two in a mutual learning relationship. The CEO's role can be shared but not the owner's. This demarcation of roles is consistent with the TQC principle of sharing the managing points.

Way back in 1955, Drucker exposed the fallacy of "The One-Man Chief Executive" in his hugely popular book The Practice of Management. *He identified three distinctive characters in one role, the "thought man", the "man of action", and the "front man". At best he felt, two characters may be combined in one person but he asks, "Do you want a schizophrenic in the CEO's job?" The conclusion Drucker reached is that the CEO's job is a team job. That's what Venu has done. The functions of the CEO are performed by a triumvirate.*

S: *Can you tell me a little more about how the mission is shaped.*

V: When I say I shape it, I mean I take the lead. The Presidents can facilitate it as well and they do. It is shared by them. Before it goes further, they vet it for their respective companies. I have two excellent Presidents: Mr Narsimhan for Sundaram-Clayton and Mr Raman for TVS Motors. From the day both of them came, they have behaved as if they belonged here. That's a big advantage.

S: *What selection process did you go through?*

V: We kept an ongoing dialogue for almost 2 to 3 years—a fairly long courtship. It was a major decision for Narsimhan. His wife, who had been in Mumbai all her life, was working at Reserve Bank of India. It was a big decision for her as well. Finally both of them decided, that Narsimhan and I vibe well. This match over a period of time was again a kind of organic development.

S: *Were you simultaneously courting others?*

V: We looked at some others and finally honed in.

S: *What contributes to the three of you working together as well-knit team?*

V: All three of us have a consistency of approach towards TQM and sharing managing points. It gives us a clear definition of roles, and provides them enough space and flexibility to act. The interface is manageable because of complete trust between us. The seamless areas typically come when say, they want to introduce six sigma, or JIT, do we go over to three wheelers, i.e. the key major initiatives are taken jointly. Personally, I do not order them. I ask, "Don't you think we should do this, would you like to do this?", and so forth.

S: *How do you assess individual contribution?*

V: Very clear: what has he to deliver? Once that is agreed upon it is his call, e.g. if I say two new suppliers should be introduced and the share of one supplier should be reduced, I would not know who those suppliers are—that is his call. Take another example. Team building, organisation learning, management of mentors are his responsibilities. We have five major accountabilities: customer satisfaction, profits and profitability, geographical and product-based business growth, new product development, and people and systems. Each of these accountabilities has three deliverables, making in all, fifteen deliverables.

S: *Do you use a formal appraisal form?*

V: No, not for President. If there is an issue with him, the group HR comes in—RR (R. R. Nair, ex-Hindustan Lever employer) is called, and we discuss and sort it out across the table. We go into a huddle. And there we do face a problem occasionally.

S: *Since your mission is* wealth creation, *we need to judge whether the person has that commercial acumen, the entrepreneurial touch. How do you assess whether he has it, or if he does not, how do you develop it?*

V: You can see the way he takes an initiative. Say, I am increasing the sale in a particular region, I can observe how the RM acts. Is he going beyond the brief? What new initiatives has he taken? How much original new value has he brought in? Has he created a new unique business model, which has made a dramatic change? All such questions are raised and answered. In a learning organisation, one is always on a look out for people who bring in new knowledge, who possess those skills to create new learning.

S: *Some of our communities like Marwaris, Gujaratis, have these inborn skills.*

V: Prof. Tsuda and we have always discussed this—who is creating unique knowledge? We are not just looking at results, e.g. we had a programme of extending rural two-wheelers. The head of that project came up with a brilliant idea on new ways of promoting sales. The same happened with our scooty project; some brilliant ideas came up. These ideas produced skills, to create new business models. I do not have a perfect answer, but I know you can judge. At the end of the day, it is a judgement call. You cannot put it on a matrix or simulate it on a computer. That's what managers are paid for, to assess people, hone their skills, and get results.

The Process of Self-transformation

The creation of wealth, entrepreneurship, and commercial sense require assessment of the person's capacity to create new knowledge that adds value. This creative capability can be developed only if a person is willing to undergo a process of self-transformation. Venu voluntarily and successfully underwent this process.

To say that the process of self-transformation is extremely difficult is at best an understatement. Unless one is prepared to lose one's earlier identity, self-transformation is unachievable. In Managerial Transformation by Values, *Prof. S. K. Chakraborty tells us what* transformation *meant in the context of a corporate change programme that he conducted for Godrej & Boyce (Pvt) Ltd at Mumbai.*

> It implies a process whereby an individual attempts to elevate his or her consciousness (chetana) so that various commonplace conflicts and dualities begin to be resolved or reconciled at higher levels of synthesis.

Venu took this route. His candid confessions are a lesson in courageous self-disclosure, rarely seen in the corporate gallery of glossy masks.

S: *Is your vision today different from the original vision?*

V: In terms of company value system, culture, behaviour, efficiency, and effectiveness of operations, I am much more closer to the original. It has taken me twenty years, to do it. In the first ten years, I made my mistakes; the worst place to do the apprenticeship is at the top. It was quite a humbling experience to reflect on one's own follies. Fortunately, I had old, experienced people around me who would tell me the unvarnished truth. They would say these are the changes you have to make in yourself before you can carry your vision forward. That is when I came to realise that the change has to begin at the top.

S: Why?

V: Because if the leader changes, he can effect changes in the organisation. Never was there a greater need for integrity, consistency, and vision in leaders. If the leader does not have the ability to change, but stands alone and saying, I am perfect, I am superior and the organisation SWOT has to change, then what happens? One has to look at all one's defects, correct them, and then go to the organisation, and say these are the changes we need to do. *One can't change people; one can only change oneself*, and that too visibly, so that others can see and feel that one had the courage and humility to change first. In this process of self-change one realises how difficult it is to change and why others are not changing. One seeks inwardly for God's help all the time.

S: *I understand, one then has the moral authority to say that, but were the mistakes pointed out were in attitudes, skills, or both?*

V: At any time of life, it is both. Attitudes have a higher priority and require greater change, skills follow.

Venu meant, he changed his perspective about people, and the way the old organisation was functioning. To get across to people, he learnt the skills to get them to listen to him. That meant he had to be humble in approach, rather than throw his weight around feeling, "no one here is listening to what I have to say".

S: *I am not talking about the organisation. What skills did you personally learn?*

V: First skill: how to be a CEO? After that one starts getting a clear picture in mind of the kind of organisation one wants to build and then goes about building the same. I did not know these things at that time. I had to learn, brick by brick, to build my capabilities as a CEO. Second, how to plan, and deploy that plan, throughout the organisation. Third, how to set a control mechanism, motivate, and plan people development, which includes identifying behaviour and attributes that are beneficial and positive. Fourth, and the most difficult to learn to implement, how to remove people with negative attributes.

S: *You got these skills by talking to people? Did the veterans guide you?*

V: We have many mentors, like Prof. Tsuda from Japan, and Prof. Bhattacharya from Warwick. Prof. Tsuda helped me bring clarity and define the roles of owner CEO, President, and COO; how to prepare an inventory of people skills; how to build a team, etc. Prof. Bhattacharya coached me on how to network, become a leader, and all that. He is my mentor.

S: *Is it possible for you to explain the elements of skills in your learning, like more concentration on the correct use of language for improving the art of communications, or mathematical modelling, or the literature on creativity, etc?*

V: No, I don't think I can dissect it like that. I am a very intuitive person, organic in learning. You build a picture or a model, change that, proceed further, and evolve.

Habits die hard, *we know. Stephen Covey defined habit as the intersection of knowledge, skill, and desire. In his famous book on* 7 Habits of Highly Effective People, *Covey emphasises that habits are powerful factors in our lives because they are consistent, they express our character and effectiveness or ineffectiveness. Their gravity pull breaks deeply imbedded habitual tendencies such as, say, impatience.*

After certain habits are broken, it requires more than a little willpower to move over to the newly won freedom. This is because that freedom takes on a whole new dimension. It seems that people are afraid of freedom. They feel secure in given conditionalities. That is their concept of a happy life, would you not say cocooned life?

I have experienced that changing cultivated habits, which have run out their utility, is very difficult. To slavishly allow such habits to play with our lives makes us unproductive and also, unhappy. Substituting one such habit with a more desirable one, and devoting some regular time for its cultivation gives better results.

S: *Was any habit reformulation required to facilitate learning and absorption?*

V: Yes, particularly in terms of behaviour. You know, I was brash. I had to learn to be patient while operating under certain constraints. One cannot wish them away. One must not act like a monkey, pulling down the Banyan tree to see how far it has grown. Particularly when one realises that one is building the Banyan tree like organisation, one must have the patience to wait. It's a seed, a small sapling, a bit sized plant, and then a large sized tree. All good thoughts, ideas, require a gestation period to fructify into a design, plan, good product, or service. In 1980, I was new, inexperienced, straight at the top, and didn't have the patience. By 1990–91, I had lot more patience, I had developed confidence, put right people in the right jobs, had given them ideas and the freedom to act, and trusted them to deliver—and they did.

S: *So you were personally liberated in 1990–91, when India's economic liberation also came about. This is a good case study in conscious learning undertaken by a CEO. I am privileged to know it first hand.*

V: Patience was the key thing. One doesn't disturb people but allows them to do what they want to do. During that period I really learnt the skill of making an organisation tick, and grow; learnt the kind of environment that when created enables the leadership to function and a learning culture to thrive. My key achievement in the second phase, was the creation of a learning organisation. I would use the simile of "Agar" to explain what I did. Agar is a medium of growth. If one puts bacteria in it, the bacterial population grows. So, the first thing I learnt was about the medium of growth. The second thing I consciously learnt, was to give people the space and opportunity to learn.

S: *What about those who cannot grow, no matter what environment and facilities you provide?*

V: Remove them. The weeding out has to be an ongoing process, not a one-time affair. GE has system of eliminating 10 per cent. It's too high for us. We have taken many youngsters, we shall remove 4–5 per cent. While retaining people, we look for their attitudes and skills. There is a big difference between having an intellectual capacity and delivering results. What is potential energy and kinetic energy? One needs a balance. Many people have a high degree of intellectual ability and potential, but are weak on deliverables. They cannot understand the connection between having good ideas and converting them to action, i.e. getting things done through other people. One has to slow down on expectations. Patience I repeat, is the biggest virtue.

S: Patience is passion tamed, and to develop patience one has to spend time on keeping quiet, stilling the mind.

V: You are absolutely right, keeping quiet. That is the toughest thing. Time management is not applying one's energy to most things or different things. In fact, it means to learn to keep quiet within the time allotted for it, to begin with. In practical terms, I had to start spending time on networking with industry associations and other stakeholders, rather than following the people in the organisation. I left that to VPs, GMs, and others. That changed the focus in the right direction. And consciously, I started reserving time for keeping quiet.

S: Did meditation, or any particular exercise, or a cleansing discipline help develop patience and quiet?

V: Half way through the process, I started meditation. Without meditation, patience becomes difficult to cultivate. Meditation helps still the mind, and then patience become easier to practice.

S: Did you decide your KRAs for meditation, in order to come out of habitual reflexes? A certain regimen is certainly required, isn't it?

V: One has to find one's own solution. Let me give you an example. We started the "Art of Living" meditation programmes, and I wanted to know what the progress was. Most people had dropped out, about fifteen continued. I was sceptical at the beginning. One cannot programme these things. I know of people who don't meditate, and yet have the skills and patience. I also know those who meditate and do not have these qualities.

S: *But meditation helps, doesn't it?*

V: *Each human being is unique, and therefore one can't go to a doctor and ask for a universally applicable formula.*

The process of self-transformation that Venu undertook brought changes in him, which were essential in the context of problems of his organisation growth.

- *Realisation that unless the leader changes, the organisation will not change.*
- *Consciously undertaking a programme to change himself.*
- *Vision change—alignment with values.*
- *Perspective shift—attitudes and skill change.*
- *Habit reformulation, which develops patience.*
- *Allow others to grow.*
- *Genuine use of mentors' help in the process of transformation.*
- *The tool of meditation helps create space within for quiet reflection, which concomitantly leads to making space for others to grow.*

This is not small, incremental change. All together, it is tantamount to self-transformation. Venu attempted to elevate his consciousness (chetana) whereby the conflicts and dualities in his mind got dissolved, paving the way for resolution of issue on ground level. His values-as-means got aligned in his daily actions and choices. Prof. Chakraborty's description of the process of transformation stated earlier stands validated. A change in Venu led to changes in his TVS Group. A fundamental achievement indeed!

Rohit Mehta, author of The Secret of Self-Transformation, holds the view:

> only on a successful synthesis of the principle Indian traditions of Yoga and Tantra, depends the flowering of the individual, and only a transformed individual can become the nucleus for fundamental social change.

An organisation is a social entity. Venu went back to the basics. Here basics, mean learning by looking within oneself. He did it with the help of mentors, a sort of Guru–shishya *relationship, revered in the Indian culture. He achieved his aim of getting back to the heritage and tradition that TVS had always stood for.*

When, in 1998, the brakes division of Sundaram-Clayton got the Deming prize, Venu said, "The Deming prize only means that we have been given the ticket to get into the (TQC) train. It does not mean we have reached our destination". Similarly, the process of self-transformation for Venu may be just the beginning of such a voyage to self-realisation.

The Retrieval of TVS Culture

V: When I started my career, I had only one goal: how do I go about bringing that culture back? The essence of that culture lies in the name TVS where *T* stands for *Trust,* *V* for *Values,* and *S* for *Service.* The name epitomises the culture.

The group started as a small business, graduated into cycle parts, auto parts, General Motors (GM) dealers, bus and lorry transport, production of automobile components and then to moped business, electronics, etc. GM rated TVS as the best dealership network in the world.

Not only did its buses run on time, one could set the clock by TVS bus schedules. That was their reputation for punctuality all over southern India. They had 400 buses, each covering 40 stops a day, i.e. almost 1,6000 stops (trips) per day, and there were zero breakdowns and zero late arrivals. There were three elements to that excellence. First, every employee felt that he owned the company, e.g. if the parcel service lorry driver saw a breakdown of a TVS car on the road, he would stop his vehicle and help out. That was the kind of belonging felt by employees in different parts of the company. Second, they had 100 per cent customer satisfaction. Every customer of a TVS car had a post card sent by the company after 30 days, with reply pre-paid, to enquire how the car was working. If a car did not come for service, a salesman was sent exclusively to the customer, to pick up the car and bring it in for service. If the customer did not get back his car on time, he would be given a spare car to use. This happened in India and that too in 1940s! Lastly, they had a complete 7S system, i.e. TQM, as efficient as any in Japan today.

Once, an international customer had a problem. The company sent its service people with remedial parts to the customer's doorsteps, serviced them and returned. The customer was struck that an Indian company provided such service, from such a distance. Such quality service is driven by an all-pervasive value that the customer is not the king, he is God. This value is translated into practice: if a customer has a problem, TVS hastens to provide help.

Venu's father had a vision: like the American had his car, so the Indian should have his two-wheeler. He thought of a basic product, which could carry two people comfortably at low cost. Mopeds are light vehicles, not very tough but affordable. The concept was new then. They have not looked back since. They improvised the design as they began manufacturing, and did not use any imported components. They created a new market. It was a paradigm shift.

This rich heritage was built upon outstanding qualities of leadership, ownership at all levels, and discipline of the highest standards in adhering to operating norms and procedures. Everything was proudly carried out in the TVS way. Any deviant behaviour received reprimand. This attitude got diluted in the era of shortages and rations engineered by the socialist ethos. The "licence and control" philosophy of governance killed competition and therewith, the urge for excellence. That policy in collaboration with price control led to ten-year wait lists for the delivery of vehicles!

Old people retired and new ones did not know what competition and visiting customers meant. Unavoidably, the quality of vehicles dropped. The customer had no choice. He had to buy either Fiat or Ambassador. Both guaranteed poor vehicles and even poorer service.

V: The original TVS culture was lost. Since TVS started manufacturing rather late, people there were new and did not know the TVS quality culture. So it fell to me to retrieve the lost culture. I had to take that emergency call.

Gardner aptly describes the demands of such situation ethics in The Task of Leadership *(1986). He says, "One of the milder pleasures of maturity is bemoaning the decay of once strongly held values. Values always decay over time. Societies that keep their values alive do so not by escaping the processes of decay but by powerful processes of regeneration". That comes with constant communication about revaluation.*

Gardner recommends perpetual rebuilding. Each generation must rediscover the living elements in its tradition and adapt them to their realities. The task of leadership is to assist in that recovery.

Venu did just that. Sumantra Ghosal declared: you cannot manage third generation strategies through second generation organisations with first generation managers—satisfactory under-performance is a far greater problem than crisis. Ghosal is right, it is well nigh impossible to bridge the generation gaps in thinking and actions. The returns on time investment is at best passable.

Values are sacred for restoring the glory of TVS. It is the middle column of the pillar Trust, Value, Service, *which epitomises TVS. Said Albert Einstein, "Sometimes what counts can't be counted, and what can be counted doesn't count". However, in business, these do not remain ethical values only but become measurable assets. A customer measures performance of both, product and service. To create value for the customer one first builds those values in one's organisation.*

Honesty, integrity, customer care, time management, zero breakdown, after-sales service throughout the life of the product, were all value monopolies built by TVS, decades before Edward de Bono popularised the phrase in 1992 through his book, Sur/petition. *The retrieval of these values was an a priori necessity for the retrieval of the quality of service and product, with 0.15 per cent re-work. Preserving those values was sacrosanct, and Venu realised the route it was through*

TQM. Deming built the edifice of TQM by the application of simple statistical quality control methods. What looked mystical became do-able. Said Venu, "It's a methodical, structured, concrete, measurable approach, suited to the engineering mindset".

The mindset of people in pre and post independent India underwent change. The old concept of obeisance, loyalty, and obedience, changed. Pontificating old values did not inspire people to fall in line. Old, cherished principles were uninspiring. Against this backdrop, Venu's search for quality began in the mid-eighties, along with that of many other companies sailing the same boat.

On his first visit to Japan, Venu saw the functioning of the Suzuki factory, Honda Motor Company, the quality service in hotels, the trains running on time; and he felt that the factories were working the TVS way. There was respect for humanity, cleanliness, and discipline, as had been there in the old TVS working style.

That's when Venu decided to retrieve the TVS culture, through the TQM system. He felt, he could build different scenarios with the involvement of multifunctional teams to recapture the essence of TVS culture and glory, and in the process set new vision and direction for the organisation. Venu was able to achieve all this, through involvement and consultation.

Weeding out the negative elements, i.e. those low on attitudes even when they were highly skilled, had to be done gently. As against this, those high on attitudes but low on skills were retained, nurtured with compassion.

V: I came to the conclusion that skill cannot be a singular guiding factor. It's a multidimensional issue and not unidimensional. In the early days, I made that mistake, I was inhuman. When I joined, there was gross inefficiency and poor attitudes that I cut through like scissors. What I was doing was right but the way I was doing it was not, because I did not uphold the values of my forefathers—compassion and humanness. I had to change. Now I do it after taking into account the individual sensitivities.

S: *What about the politicians with vested interests in maintaining the status quo?*

V: The naysayers and obstructionists with their hidden agendas, hierarchical authorities, and who felt threatened by change, were sent away. It took us three years to change the managerial mindsets.

S: *Are you now building a consensus around your decision?*

V: I am. The old guards with basic value system had to be preserved. Many of them don't change, some do. It's a long-term process and I had to be patient to balance the needs of change and stability. In any organic body, at any given point of time, there are decease producing agents. If the body is strong, it ensures its balance. You must not allow the immune system to become weak. These agents or viruses do not necessarily come from outside. Mostly the decease is always resident. One must ensure that the health of the organisation is not endangered by the presence of such agents. One controls, by weeding some out and keeping others under control. I do that with equanimity and feel satisfied.

I feel that by using TQM, our people will internalise their implicit value systems so that even when the generation changes, the legacy will be passed on to new managers. Our standard procedures and training will help carry it forward without many hitches. In 1990, we engaged two Japanese professors, Washio and Tsuda. Under their guidance, we started building teams, right from QC Circles to suggestion schemes; cross functional task forces to "managing points" (KRAs) and "check points" (sub-result area).

This led to considerable improvement but nowhere near the world benchmarks, when, in 1998, we became the first company in India to receive the Deming prize. That's why our journey to total quality has just begun—the destination is far off. If in 1979, 15 per cent re-work was considered acceptable, it came down to 0.15 percent in 1998. It took us that long because we had to get out of our way, many bad practices and wrong attitudes.

It is not my claim that it couldn't have been done faster, but I had to balance between the old school of thought and new, plus my own learning in the process. The retrieval is nearly complete. Retrieval here, means restoring the old values and works practices. The customer focus is regained. If *customer is God*, then we have treat him as such. Order followed chaos. We have reinstalled the "God" customer, and provided TVS "good orderly direction" from chaos.

Now maintenance is the challenge, which is far greater than project retrieval. Indians are good project managers but poor maintenance managers. The journey has just begun.

The following steps are taken to maintain the momentum and deepening the process of TQM internalisation:

- *Make employees work to a common goal and align the department activities in furtherance of that goal*

- *Change the work culture to meet the changing needs through change seminars*

- *Provide customer feedback to all employees on products and services, plan targets, achievements, and gaps, successes and failures, and counter measures for improvements through regular monthly meetings (as Deming says, "The customer is the most important part of the production line. Without him there is no production line")*

- *Keep constant communication with employees through daily work management, sunrise meetings, etc*

- *Hold annual QCC conventions, where management announces the theme, based on policy objectives, and QC circles commit to the number of projects they will complete in the year.*

- *Hold monthly QC circle meetings, where completed projects are presented. A three-judge bench adjudges the best QC circle. A senior manager of that circle identifies three good points and two improvement points. Then, there is an audit check after six months, and the circle facilitator presents its report. After all the presentations are over, Venu gives his diagnosis. The best QC circle is rewarded.*

Every year on Dassera *day, employees worship tools and machines in the morning. Then it is celebration time!*

In trying to transform the company through this quality route, Venu empowered the managers and employees to make meaning out of their mundane jobs. In the book Why Leaders Can't Lead, Warren Bennis (1997), the authority on leadership says:

> Closely linked to the concept of quality is that of dedication to, even love of, our work. The dedication is evoked by quality and is the force that energises high-performing systems.

In adopting the TQM system, Venu restored that dedication to the details of quality work. It meant leading them to the specifics, where God is hidden, because Venu knows God is in details.

The Council of Mentors

For TQM, Venu used the services of three Japanese professors, Kurahara, Washio, and Tsuda. Prof. Bhattacharya of Warwick University, UK, was his mentor. Venu appears to have found consultants useful.

S: You seem to be one of those few who feel consultants are quite useful.

V: We do not use consultants, we use mentors. I come with a belief to you, pay obeisance to your knowledge, and say please teach us we want to become a "learning organisation". We want you, our teachers, to tell us how to learn, and not give us a solution to the problem.

Probably Venu knew that the shortest distance between "ignorance-information-knowledge" is a straight line to whoever has the knowledge. And he discovered it in a rich minefield of mentors. He did not engage coaches because he knew the difference between coaching and mentoring. Coaching is more role/job/project/task specific and is generally understood to upgrade skills, whereas mentoring is fundamental in scope and impact. It helps to build a life long career.

I was literally thrilled to hear why and how he approached mentors—it was a privilege to hear of it from the CEO of a prestigious business group. His personality was soaked in his craving for knowledge while giving expression to his sincere belief that mentors guide and mould, and one needs them badly. As he finished his sentence I could hear and feel inside me a whisper of benignity.

S: You have brought me to a central point. The fact that you have a sincere desire to learn is itself an indication that you have changed. Tell me what did you learn from your mentors?

V: In the early days of learning, when someone said to me you have to do this, I would immediately say, we are already doing it, or I know it, etc. That "I know" itself shows, you don't know. When one says one is already doing it, it is a sure sign that one is not doing it. Why is it that the other person is saying so, if one is already doing it? He is not dumb. The Indian mindset in the early seventies was rigid and closed. We were in a protected market, even maintaining status quo showed enormous profitability and there was no inducement for change.

When Venu shared this experience I felt he was voicing my experience. People use the word advice/counsel/mentor with a shared meaning, help. Concomitantly, there is a shared ignorance that there is no introspection or learning, or anything that would be expected of them. They do not know that help includes self-help. I would summarise my personal experience in the following sequence.

- *A person states his problems or issues in a long winded manner. He expects me to listen, quite understandable.*

- *In the diagnostic phase, or afterwards, one makes some suggestions to find out what the person has tried, what routes he has chosen. Whether the person is describing his own problem or that of his organisation, the response is: "We have done it"; "we know it"; "it hasn't succeeded"; "the others in the drama are unchangeable, difficult, the problem is not resolvable and you subscribe to our view". All modern clichés like, "I am okay, he is not okay, personality syndrome", are generously used in describing the situation.*

- *It takes a few sittings to arrive at an acceptable diagnosis.*

- *When one starts suggesting some approaches towards the solution, he reverts back to causes and personalities. He endlessly argues about the righteousness of his stand and wants acknowledgement for it. In fact, he is often fishing for compliments and sympathy for his hardships and non-acceptance of his position. Any suggestions for others are readily accepted with occasionally a derisive comment, "He will not look at himself"; "this might not work"; "I will give it a try but…".*

- *Even when empathy is shown, the unwillingness to come out of the sticky situation is rampant.*

- *In the first place, several dropout when they realise they are a part of the problem, or they have to take a hard look at themselves. Even when they come to appreciate that they have to do the hardwork to eject them out of the quandary, they leave the process when the actual time comes to implement what is agreed. The next dropout phase comes, when the person realises that he has to do many self-corrections to overcome his weaknesses.*

- *At this stage, the person stands face to face with the real self. It is a turning point when he makes a decision to courageously undertake the leap into the unknown. The only tool he has is self-confidence in learning, and a desire to improve. Those who cross this turning point with deep reflection, become genuine learners. I found leaders I interviewed had turned themselves into sincere learners.*

Counsellors and mentors are not defect free **Rishis.** *They falter occasionally. In fact, the skilled ones take a joint* *problem solving and co-learning approach. And if it's an organisation, the mentor prefers to work with all members of the team, in order to develop the need for group self-introspection and solution-mindedness. His objective is to provide a prism for developing new perspectives and synergy.*

The qualitative use of mentors as seen in TVS, is rarely found in Indian organisations. The reverence with which they are treated shows their sincere commitment to Indian values. They are looked up to for learning. Venu has shown other CEOs the path to walk on. For the business minded though, there lies an idea for a money-spinner. Start seminars on The Art of Learning *and market them shrewdly!*

Obstructionists, and naysayers are not amenable to change, as Terry Lunn, a former personnel director of Joshua Tetley once said, "Don't try to teach the pig to sing: it annoys the pig and wastes your time". The time scale in which leaders and managers must change has shrunk dramatically.

However, they need to be given a fair chance. The chances of changing such people, increase with group pressure. If this doesn't work, they will have enrolled themselves for VRS. They do not recognise that this is their voluntary act in having talked themselves out of the job. The organisation need not feel at all guilty.

We know that the majority of the people are interested only in debate and gossip. They do not advance to a "continuous learning mode" because learning involves unlearning and relearning. It is an arduous, time-consuming process, requiring infinite patience, self-forgiveness, and readiness to go through the hard drill of learning new skills, developing fresh perspectives, and above all an indefatigable urge to improve. Few therefore, undertake this steeplechase.

Here again the 80/20 rule applies. The learners are in minority. Competition, market pressures, dearth of jobs, need to build entrepreneurial skills hold out the hope that 80/20 may become 60/40 by 2040. The need for mentors has always been there. One gets very few CEOs like Venu who feel so deeply about the need to have them.

S: What are you doing to put your colleagues and employees into a "listening-learning" frame of mind?

V: Well, we use so many mentors: they do it, not I. The CEO/COO spearhead the change movement. They get the mentors in and work through the process. The current generations rebel more rationally than we used to. If you show them data, they look at it and listen. We had to put them through rapid action learning programmes. The outsider provides fresh views, with detachment. He is not attracted to our way of doing things. He can say, "Hey, I have seen the world, and what you are doing is not correct". We brought them in as mentors, so that they were not seen as threats.

S: You are almost a college!

V: We are not almost a college, we are a college. Our whole system is a collegiate system of learning. Prof. Bhattacharya is my mentor. Take R. R. Nair, Rama Bijapurkar, or the two professors from US—they all come in for specific mentoring needs. Some come in for design, some for JIT or competency development, or whatever. They all penetrate the organisation, interact directly, and provide new impulses.

Intellect to Introspection to Intuition

It is evident that Venu is an intellectual. His intellectual power was initially superior to his power of feeling: he had a strong IQ and weak EQ. We know it for a fact that many students with high IQs do not make it to the top, they fail to become leaders. Whereas many with average IQs become admirable leaders because they have a high EQ.

Managers with high EQ show more empathy, compassion, and motivation. Their ability to respond appropriately to pain and pleasure is considerable. They relate well with other people. Said Goleman: of the two, emotional intelligence adds far more of the qualities that make us more fully human.

S: *Can you dissect the skills that you have learnt?*

V: I am a very intuitive person. An intuitive person possesses direct knowledge without evident rational thought or cogent explanation for inferences. He just knows, period. However, in the early days when I did not rely on my intuition, I made blunders

---

Management is both a science and an art. Let us concentrate here on its art persona. Donald Schon (1983) believes art has a two-fold meaning. It may mean intuitive judgement and skill—the feeling for phenomena and for action—called knowing-in-action. This is how seasoned professionals think in action. The art content however, is reflected in action only if the manager is emotionally aware that action is not all logic and science. Vaman Kamath felt that a lack of understanding of art affects a manager's perspective and performance. It's the manager's reflection in the context of action. Michael Polanyi calls this, "reflections on tacit knowing". Venu had to concentrate on this art faculty—the science of management he knew.

One has to face the painful dilemma of rigour or relevance. It is the ability to retrieve material that has social acceptability and which satisfies the user. Where the manager is deeply involved in problem solving, he is engaged in reflective conversations with the situation. Some cue flickers, and he just knows: that is intuition.

What activated Venu's intuition? I think it was his intensive search coupled with deep self-introspection to find a solution to the sagging morale, and shrinking bottom-line. It brought him to the turning point, during his first visit to Japan. He saw the Japanese discipline, keenly observed their working practices, studied their culture, and intuitively came to the conclusion that, this was it! He realised that the TQM package would restore TVS culture. So the process of introspection catalysed intuition.

S: *Were you a part of that club in TVS, which gave those responses like, "I know, I have done it before, No sir, it doesn't work here", etc.*

V: Very much. I realised that my responses are abetting the maintenance of status quo. There was no enabling move. This guy in desperation would finally say, "This 'No Sir' of yours is my biggest problem. Am I criticising because I like to? I am telling you this because I am concerned. So why don't you listen? Go back and think on what I am saying. Come back and tell me what you think of it. Maybe I am wrong, but that is my view".

S: That's correct.

V: To get into the learning mode it was necessary to get into a listening mode. One must say, I need to examine certain things because my mentor says so. I must not question his competency, authority, role, or proficiency, etc". Not only should one listen, but when somebody suggests something, whether it is right or wrong, do not argue, just introspect. One might say, "Sir why do you say so? Let me go back and check". Then study, and report what is factual, right, wrong, or partially correct. Adduce your evidence the way it actually is. Then offer your solution.

This is the correct approach. I have also faced this dilemma. This "know all" attitude is inbuilt in many executives, including chief executives. They first open up and then close the shutters suddenly for reasons which are rarely honestly discussed.

The turning point during his visit to Japan was the result of his desire to make a breakthrough back home. He saw that the TQM process could restore TVS discipline. The process was methodical. He needed a process tool, and he got it. He felt what he wanted to learn was available in that comprehensive package. We see here, intellect deepening the process of introspection, which generally leads to context specific explicit learning.

Conscious or unconscious, introspection is a process. The word "process" derives its root from Latin processus *meaning a going forward. The goal here, was to restore TVS culture. When Sundaram-Clayton got the Japan Quality Medal Venu said, "Medals are not a goal. Awards don't improve your profits. It is the* processes, *which you put in place in the course of applying them, that improve your company's profitability, capability, and market share".*

The ability to re-orient, enables a leader to develop his intuitive faculties to understand the relation between unrelated concepts and abstract ideas. In this information age, the intuitive leader is able to traverse beyond the deluge of facts to deeper generative possibilities. For CEOs, developed intuition is a prime necessity. Many leaders whom I interviewed have vouched for this need.

However, what Virginia Burden says in The Process of Intuition (1975) needs to be kept in mind.

> *If we are to arrive at the intuition level, we must reach down and rediscover our forgotten instincts and draw them up through the intellect, to form the groundwork for intuition ripening. Instinct without intellect is not serviceable. Too often it is haphazard and immoderate, claiming too much for itself.*

Intuition is not knowledge; it is a key to pertinent knowledge. It is important to understand this. Intuition is certainly desirable but it is not knowledge in itself. Making choices is the job of the informed intellect.

S: *You are intuitive. Can you tell us how to design a format for others who want to develop their intuition?*

V: I use only rational models, because they function. But I am not sure if I can teach you that. Seriously, this is a personal issue. Those who are engaged in worldly affairs may not be interested in its development. It's a question of family traditions, upbringing, association with *vasanas* (desires), etc.

Stephen Covey however, has formatted the habit reformulation process and put it into a model in his popular, The 7 Habits of Highly Effective People. *It is easy to understand and follow. Rational western models are based not on newfound wisdom but on ancient wisdom. Such models are built by systematically collecting data, preparing flow charts, and providing meaning to it. They try to take out the mystical part to show that it is attainable through a spelt out process of self-efforts. Their neat presentations made in persuasive language induce readers to act. Venu admitted frankly that he had not got into the deeper aspects of systematising his knowledge.*

Many take recourse to meditation to develop intuition. There are thousands of meditation centres, books, tapes, videos, and gurus available to guide one. Let us look at the TVS example for practical guidance. To regain its strength in the quality of its products and service, TVS adopted TQM as a practical meditation method. It's discipline of dos and donts are clearly laid down. TVS executives practise them well, and get their results. One has an easily available model to learn from. If one follows the discipline of TQM in one's self-development, the chances of improving intuition are high. First, one has to team up with oneself, and second, one needs a mentor or a team of mentors to guide one through.

Leaders Build Trust

In their fundamental transformation, the group did major re-girding and reinforcement work on the three pillars, Trust, Value, and Service. Venu provided the leadership. Leaders build trust *is a known cliché, but exactly how?*

S: *How did you build trust?*

V: I am talking as an Owner-CEO, not a manager. To start with, one must be worthy of trust. One must be transparent. Non-leaders are non-transparent. They are opaque. People talk about loyalty, it has to be earned. Most people forget that salary doesn't beget loyalty. Everybody pays a salary. It is the feeling of loyalty given by the company to the employee that echoes obligation beyond the call of duty. Loyalty is a two-way journey. A small minority may be disloyal. It is very important that one first demonstrates humility, trust, patience, and loyalty to the people.

In explaining the chemistry between leader–constituent interaction, John W. Gardner, in The Heart Of The Matter, *says:*

> Leaders must not only forge bonds of trust between themselves and their constituents, they must create a climate of trust throughout the system over which they preside.

S: At times, trust is the glue that holds the human group together; when it dissolves, the capacity of that group to function effectively is seriously impaired. As a leader, you took the initiative and demonstrated in action that you were worthy of their trust. What happened next?

V: A new learning culture is emerging: new developments, new processes, new software, new material. Intelligence is now embedded in the products. The crux of management is in devoting time to people development. It's a continuing education process, which must enhance the capabilities of people to constantly discover new things. If somebody discovers new knowledge, we must disseminate it across the company. We have built structures for it, like, "Best Practices" sharing meetings, and other communication channels. And as you said, we need entrepreneurial business leaders, not leaders as they are in politics, army, or social work. We need unique CEOs, sharing vision, and enabling others to contribute.

S: What is the essence of this atmosphere? Could you give a recent example?

V: It is immediate feedback and encouragement. Koreans gave a wonderful demonstration of it at the recently held Asian games. They knew that teams from different countries would not have supporters from their respective countries to cheer them. So they created *cheering squads* for the other countries. They created an atmosphere of encouragement for the competing teams. This demonstrates a deep understanding of human need, a need for immediate feedback and encouragement. It shows tremendous creativity.

S: What an inspiring example! For such acts of creation one requires thought leaders with a personal capacity to create, or at least a capacity to enable creation.

V: Therefore, one must find ways of choosing leaders who know how to think. Those who led great movements were people who thought while travelling, walking, reading, eating: some led after serious thought, some intuitively, and some combined both.

S: *You find great thinkers can be poor doers. Execution is a serious problem.*

V: Well I mean, leaders who think, act, and allow execution. Such leaders with innate proclivity to build trust give more to the organisation, or to the society, than they take. Leaders sacrifice more. They may not appear to do so but they actually end up doing that. The one golden rule I have learnt: *sharing space, whether psychological, emotional, or intellectual, has a value in time.*

The Exemplar of Quality Culture

There is no doubt that Venu has candidly shared his personal space, and added tremendous value, not only to TVS but also to the leadership dynamics of corporate India. TVS has become known for its quality of products, especially after its first Deming prize in 1998. When I say its brand value has shot up, the following indicators formed my opinion:

- *the young owners of its two wheelers proudly speak about the all round performance of their vehicles*
- *the quality turnaround of the group is a topic of executive discussions*
- *good press coverage for the group's performance, and for Venu's leadership and contribution*
- *brand Sachin, which lent credence to brand TVS after it scaled the quality heights*

There would be other indicators as well, like the price of shares, expert analyses of bottom line results, ranking by business journals, and the tally of different awards.

The methodical rejuvenation of TVS that Venu engineered could go into the syllabi of management institutes as a case study, with multiple lessons on:

- *quality revolution*
- *McKinsey's seven Ss—strategy, structure, systems, skills, shared values, staff, and style*
- *creative leadership*
- *creating a learning organisation*
- *revival of organisation culture*
- *process of self-transformation*
- *value addition of mentors*

Venu brought clarity to various issues at every stage eg. in the roles of Owner-CEO, CEO-President, and COO, is one such.

V: We have reinvented this role of the CEO. He is the *exemplar of quality culture, continuity, and commitment*, because he acts as a trustee.

You asked me about change. Let me tell you this "exemplar" role is the most demanding. One does things one does not like doing at all because one is the exemplar. One had to learn to do it if one did not know how to go about it. I have no problem in rolling up my sleeves to participate in cleaning toilets. One does it twice, it becomes a practice.

S: *What are the most significant elements of the change process you have undergone?*

V: Change in one sense is that which one knows most intimately, is taking place. Sensitivity is a great source of learning about oneself and others. With the awareness one gets, one learns a lot about the difficulties and frustrations one faces. One starts empathising with other people who are also changing. That's one major change in me.

S: *I suppose the feeling that we are passengers in the same ship, brings satisfaction. Earlier you had the hard edge.*

V: Now I have a tough edge but not a harsh one. We smile. And this can be attributed to the ideas I got, which I explained.

S: *In addition to the mentors, have you any spiritual gurus outside the organisation?*

V: Yes, they are fortunately there. Our family traditions have gurus. They give one spiritual strength—which to me is fundamental. If one does not have spiritual strength, however strong one may be, like an *asura*, one will break. A man with spiritual strength outwardly bends but is tough inside. I always believe the grace of God is fundamental and in our thinking and tradition, one obtains it through one's guru.

S: *This is understood. Spiritual growth is very attractive. It makes one renounce the world inside one's mind with the belief, and a correct one too, that this whole world is* maya *(illusion). It drives one to renunciation. I know the* Gita *doesn't subscribe to that but it happens. People with performing capabilities and good potential become withdrawn from the productive fields, and I feel, that is a sad loss to the nation's economic growth.*

V: If many people go that way, it could be a cause of concern, I do not know. But that is not what the *Gita* says. Our family is alone in this respect. You are right, the imagined state beyond *maya* is extremely alluring but that is also *maya*. Therefore, one has to break away and decide: I am a warrior, this is war. My arms may be tired and my legs cribbing but I have to pick up the bow and go. I have seen *Arjunaj* in retirement also, my grandfather for instance, or someone in community work from our company.

What Venu said means, *if this world is maya, the imagined state beyond maya is also maya.* I agree. Nonetheless, it is accepted that those who follow the spiritual path and renounce the material world, eventually become evolved souls. They help humanity in more ways than we know.

That said, we also need balanced leaders whose performance inspires us. Therefore, however exalted self-introspection may be, I would not like executives to deepen that process so much that they switch tracks completely. Their personal advancement on the path of renunciation will deprive the country of astounding wealth creators, who have the competence to contribute to the gigantic task of poverty alleviation.

Not only have we to turnaround hundreds of organisations but also build several more institutions of excellence. Jean Monet said, *"Nothing is possible without men, nothing is lasting without institutions"*. We need for guidance for this mammoth task role models with a track record of integral performance, and Venu provides one. He is the quintessence of quality culture!

★ ★ ★

PART TWO

The Alchemy of Changing Leadership

8

Adversity, The Father of Mindset Change

- ❖ The Nature of Adversity
- ❖ Multidimensionality of Issues
- ❖ Strategic Deployment of Resources
- ❖ The University of Adversity–Opportunity

"If Necessity is the mother of invention, adversity is the father of mindset change."

—Shrinivas Pandit

Introduction

This chapter provides a sketch of the nature of business adversity. It unfolds the underlying multidimensionality of issues and strategic deployment of resources for achieving sustainable growth. Globalisation has incubated a conundrum, which appears to have, at the macro level, a "university of Adversity–Opportunity". It has only one aim: change the mindset of leaders and their teams to nurture aesthetic growth of organisations.

The Nature of Adversity

The evolution of Indian business in the last 300 years from moneylending and trade to industry has been through the combination of different aspects of adversity through ages.

- The traditional 18th Century communities of traders and moneylenders had entrepreneurial skills but no supportive environment in which to move forward to industrial capitalism. Buying power and restrictions on movement of goods, even within the country, limited the market size.

- The business ethic did not spread because of absence of social recognition, which left the field to traditional mercantile class. Coupled with this, was the non-availability of opportunities, which kept away new entrants belonging to other communities and castes. The inborn lack of entrepreneurial drive in other communities also prevented the growth of business class.

- The British rule made a significant difference. They built the infrastructure of roads, railways, ports, communication, and a system of disciplined governance, to manage a vast country. In the process, the business climate was transformed. It increased trade and commerce, and led to the expansion of the mercantile class. More non-traditional business groups emerged in that milieu.

- Increased interaction with societies of the world, particularly European societies, either for education or for trade and commerce, provided exposure to new ideas, different living styles, and systems of world business operations. This expanded the opportunity base and opened up large vistas for business growth.

- The laws and rules introduced by the British served their political and economic interests. Reforms we needed to make during the British rule, including fixing currency rates against the Rupee, had to be won through political and social pressures. Partnerships and sole proprietorship remained the dominant mode of conducting business.

- The abolition of managing agencies led to the establishment of a managerial system in joint stock companies. Production processes were imported from the west, and private enterprises did well under the British rule.

- After Independence, businesses faced a hostile environment under the control mechanisms of "licence and permit" raj. The socialist ideology led the government enact unproductive labour laws and anti-growth legislation like the Monopolies and Restrictive Trade Policies Act (MRTP). The highly regulatory regime corrupted the entire system to the very fabric of its governance.

- The public sector was instrumental in giving a boost to basic industries like oil, steel, coal, etc. It played a catalytic role in dispersing the industry to remote places, and spurring industrial growth in those regions. A certain geo-political equilibrium was achieved. However, politicians treated the public sector as ranches for providing employment without any consideration for business or enterprise economics. In the process, they made that sector as unprofitable as they possibly could.

- The restrictive policy and regulatory framework coupled with political, union, and bureaucratic control, killed many industries. The small-scale industries set up in different industrial estates became sick for various reasons—the menace of unions was an important factor.

- Certain large undertakings however, did well when they had good leaders who followed professional management practices. Some names come immediately to mind, Luthra of Damodar Valley corporation, Krishnamurthy of SAIL, S. V. S. Raghavan of Metals and Minerals Trading Corporation, S. N. Jain of National Fertilisers Ltd—there are many more.

- The mindset of the people was soaked in an ethos of living on "reduction of wants", "world is *maya*", and poverty and spiritual growth are compatible bedfellows. In addition, social and political reforms were indoctrinating "poverty" as virtue and "prosperity/affluence/material enjoyment" as vice. This was against growth. Material ambitions were based on simple living, and high thinking. Simple meant bare minimum, i.e. affordable by the lowest denominators of society. However, the business of business is to create "wants", and these wants face this socio-cultural mental block.

- The adversarial ethos enshrined in labour legislation gave birth to inter-union rivalries and protests of various denominations like, go-slow, pen-down strike, work-to-rule, general strikes, violence, etc. Labour cases, court delays, adjudication, and conciliation proceedings, further polluted the atmosphere. This culture was created and nurtured by muddled socialist ideology that gave a mortal blow to productivity and growth of business, even those belonging to the cooperative sector.

The common thread through the times is that Indian businessmen never had a friendly regime. They were not fortunate enough to experience a Japanese Meiji era. The preconditions for business growth were absent. The socio-cultural, economic, and political ideologies were decidedly anti-business. In such constant adversity, those who continued to do business despite being jeered as "monopolists", survived. G.D.Birla, in his speech to FCCI, on March 4, 1949, said:

> *Any fool can establish business when there is boom. But it is during a period of depression that's once ability to establish and run business is tested. I therefore appeal to businessmen not to be disheartened but to learn to take risks.*

Gita Piramal notes that this was not mere rhetoric. When small businessmen ran aground, four men (G. D. Birla, Walchand Hirachand Doshi, Kasturbhai Lalbhai, and J. R. D. Tata) did their best to help. I haven't heard of such magnanimity in recent times.

The ability to take risks, foresight, passion, commitment to society, and preparedness not only to withstand adversity but pull the organisation out from depression, and constantly look for opportunities, are touchstones of business acumen. Such businessmen show tremendous acumen in dealing with politicians, bureaucrats, foreigners, competitors, colleagues, and employees. This means their people skills are of a high order.

The Entrepreneurship Development Institute of India (EDII), Ahmedabad did a very interesting study of successful entrepreneurs in 1988. The study and findings are published in the book titled *Self-made Impact Making Entrepreneurs*.

Most of the leaders featured in the book are doing well today. Their practices have stood the test of time and proved to be sound. The EDII found that the majority of the impact making entrepreneurs had achieved their success mainly through their policies and practices, identified in the form of entrepreneurial heuristics, which appear applicable even today. Most of these entrepreneurs selected products or modified product lines which were relevant to their education or work experience. The IT graduates are doing the same now. They also took up challenges by competing with big business houses, including multinationals. They set their sights high.

Since the nineties, so have new generations. The leaders nurtured their enterprises in the initial stages by exercising tight control over operations. There is much more sharing now because the nature of businesses has undergone major shifts over the last two decades.

They developed indigenous technology for economic reasons, such as reducing the cost of the project, and for non-economic reasons, such as pride in doing things on one's own. This also, is happening now, on a larger scale. Quite a few, had long-term perspectives, and never resorted to business practices leading to short-term gains at the detriment of long-term interests. They established themselves in market by understanding users, by educating customers, and by emphasising quality products, low prices, timely deliveries, and efficient post-sale services. This is difficult to accept as representative. That consciousness is now seen in many. A select few concentrated on research and development activities, and spent substantially on R&D. Such focus was unique in those days, but is the norm today. Substantial responsibility was delegated to a professional team after having reached a certain level of operations, so that the leaders could devote their time to expansion and diversification. Most of them evolved effective strategies for motivating dealers, maintaining close contacts with customers, and responding expeditiously to customer complaints. They maintained industrial peace and high employee satisfaction, by offering welfare schemes, personalising relationships, and encouraging expression of labour concerns. MNCs, and most Indian organisations, did not have this culture.

More and more educated entrepreneurs are now venturing into new, technically advanced business fields. The demand for managers with entrepreneurial competencies is also on the increase. Whether embarking on diversification, expansion, creating new SBUs for domestic or international markets, CEOs are on a look out for entrepreneurial talent. All of them find the profiles of successful entrepreneurs useful. These entrepreneurs are strategists. They overcame initial hardships through foresight, vision, proper planning, and creativity.

However, the mortality rate in new ventures and corporate sector is extraordinarily high. 70 per cent of corporates, change every decade in major stock exchanges like Dow Jones, and BSE Sensex. They face hardships, which they understand are often self-made and avoidable. Entreprenurship is not just guts, ideas, risk-taking (thoughtless?), and luck. Realisation of business goals is a long and arduous journey. Proper study and thorough preparation are minimum prerequisites to success.

It is therefore essential for an aspiring entrepreneur or manager to develop entrepreneurship talent taking into account the mistakes that can be avoided. He would profit from reading S. J. Phansalkar's book, *How Not to Ruin Your Small Industry* (1996). The findings are based on research he did on the small-scale sector. He identified some important mistakes:

- excessive or exclusive dependence on one buyer and doing "informal" business

- unrealistic project planning and expanding fixed assets before making provisions for working capital

- borrowing in the cash market to stock up materials spawning too many firms

- marketing myopia, or the inability to look at the needs of customers

- hiring employees for reasons other than competence

The winds of liberalisation have blown hot and cold since 1991. The atmosphere has now become business friendly. The government is listening to employers' lobbies. Their suggestions are given serious consideration. The Government's disinvestment policy and programme are moving in the correct direction, though haltingly. The first generation entrepreneurs are making headway in local and international business. Dwijendra Tripathi in his excellent volume *Business History* (2004) says:

> There is no doubt that under the more liberalised economic regime, the Indian private sector has embarked upon the most progressive, creative, and competitive course in its entire history. And the sky will be the limit for its growth, if it continues on this course.

However, while sculpting an edifice one also needs to take into account the main characteristics of the changing nature of adversity.

External Changes

The ingredients of external adversarial convergences changed with the advent of liberalised policies.

Before liberalisation, socialist regimes known for their anti-business stance were in power. They remained there for nearly four decades. The governments were wedded to public sector controlled growth; bureaucracy was committed to red tape under "Licence and Permit" dispensation; and powerful unions set the agenda and direction for company governance.

Globalisation injected massive change leading to liberalisation, and fierce competition.

A paradigm change occurred when Government control over business was liberalised. Acceptance of the forces of market economy led to business growth, transparency, and accountability.

Though the constellation of adverse factors, made up of governments, unions, regulatory framework, and bureaucracy, have still to be reckoned with, its ferocity is on the decline. The new constellation, provides its own combination of opportunities and hardships:

(a) World Trade regulatory framework—unfavourable up till now

(b) more fierce competition—global as well as local

(c) technological advances and upgradation

(d) need to climb up the value chain

(e) Product–Service innovation and packaging

(f) 24 × 7, prompt deliverables

(g) environmental concerns, and poverty alleviation

Internal Changes

Organisations were static, inward looking with old mindsets, and outdated leadership styles.

The paradigm change occurred when organisation change programmes gave up unworkable command styles. Efforts at mindset change, forced leaders to introspect deeply. This process gathered momentum after liberalisation because fierce competition multiplied the need for change many times.

Organisation restructuring, governance, mindset change, and talent management: what are their lessons? There is a certain amount of historical baggage one carries from generation to generation, which contains a package of assets and liabilities which one controls only when one acts discriminatingly. The legacy of each event, relationship, and loss-gain calculations, have to be understood on an individual and organisation plane. The individual and organisational balance sheets reflect not only monetary gain and loss but that of reputation, brands, and assets as well.

The impact depends upon the gravity of the adversity. What one needs to think about is one's own contribution to the making of that adverse situation, and what circumstances have conspired to put one in a limbo, i.e. distinguish between adversity created by oneself, and by others. It is easy to escape this by blaming others. What one tends to forget is the old chicken and egg story: which came first?

The inherent character of adversity is changing. Earlier, it was bipolar and had boundary walls. Its fixate nature has now given way to the dynamics of seamless market evolution on a global scale. Therefore we need to look at its multi-dimensional character.

Multidimensionality of Issues

Take any issue—fixing agricultural prices, patent laws, restrictive labour legislation, trade, commerce—it acquires at once a global and local connectivity, and has simultaneous impact on both levels. Similarly, issues of immigration, religion, race, autonomy, supra-national and sub-national identities, have reverberations at global, regional, and local levels, within minutes.

Boundaries have become blurred. The sovereignty of national governments and the autonomy of regional governments is sacrosanct only on paper. Whether it is lowering tariffs, custom duties, or octroi, the principles of independence and interdependence are at loggerheads from macro to micro levels. Everything is becoming conjoint, from naval exercises to commercial alliances. MOUs, mergers, and acquisitions are only tools.

Business no longer is:

- bipolar, i.e. between governments of two countries; between a government and business house; etc.
- free from the influence of technology, markets, consumers, media, press, communications, and peoples' aspirational goals.

These factors are the major determinants of business. The governments are being driven back to the basics, i.e. good governance. That does not mean a free-for-all market supremacy. Roles are being redefined to allow more free 'flow' of ideas, products, services, and options, for cost effective different life styles. It's a movement from the restrictive ideologies of the past, to creativity and freedom.

The world of business has become multipolar and multidimensional. It does not matter whether the size of business is big or small, macro or micro level, general or niche market, or grey or black in complexity. All it asks of management is to develop multiprocessing competencies, period.

Whether it is the export or domestic market, customers expect:

(a) advanced high-value IT product–service package, or high yield crossbred seeds for agriculture, and so forth

(b) cost effective quality product and service

(c) reliable deliveries

To fulfil these customer expectations, management has to have:

(a) the latest process technology

(b) brand building and new marketing drives

(c) off the shelf deliverables

Look at automobiles, banking, insurance, two wheelers, automotive components, hospitals, or hospitality businesses: one notices their bandwidths have increased their reach factor manifold. This has been achieved through induction of new technology, collaborations, mergers, acquisitions, improved capacity utilisation, better yields, systematic upgradation of employee competencies, and above all, through the improvement in the morale of employees. This is the formula used by businessmen across the country for better growth and a solid base. Let us now look at the deployment of resources, which led to this revival.

Strategic Deployment of Resources

Each organisation has to deploy its available resources to achieve targets and results. The leaders I interviewed, revamped their organisations using certain tools.

1. **Change management:**

    They conducted programmes which focused on customers, quality products, timely deliveries, prompt service, cost cutting, speedy execution, and mindset change.

2. **Organisation restructuring:**

    Flat hierarchies and autonomous divisions were created on network architecture. Reporting to more than one person became the rule rather than an exception.

3. **Manager and employee participation:**

    Active participation was achieved through the formation of task forces, which led to a cross pollination of ideas and thinning of departmental boundaries.

4. **Voluntary Retirement:**

   Voluntary separations were carried out by giving personal attention to loyal old timers, with regard for their sensitivities and age.

5. **Assortment:**

   Accomplished through TQM, SWOT analysis, Six Sigma, benchmarking, Balanced Scorecard, competency mapping, outsourcing, 80/20 rule, cannibalisation and planned obsolescence.

One of the challenges Drucker talks about is the need to develop new concepts of "performance", and new measurements of it. At the same time, performance had to be defined non-financially so as to be meaningful to knowledge workers, and to generate commitment from them as a value return. It is easier said than done in a mercenary world, built and nourished on mammonic industrial culture. However, to restore them is the job of new leaders.

In such a system, there are no means of measuring loss in profit incurred through the inadequacy of managers, or of their performance with regard to their potential. So the cost to the company is not only their salary and perquisites but also such non-estimable losses. In the past, such candidates were carried forward on the value of their loyalty, or service guaranty. Management does not want legally enforced service guarantees but treats loyalty with compassion in the interest of keeping organisation morale intact.

When one finances a particular project that has been prioritised for action, one's commitment to its execution becomes visible: it is strategic deployment of financial resources into building a future. That alone does not ensure execution. The execution culture gets a boost if rewards are linked to it. People have to be trained into following certain norms of behaviour and practice, with regard to execution.

The essentials of strategic deployment of resources are:

(a) right people in right jobs

(b) debate over assumptions so that the varoius departments of the organisation can move forward with mutual understanding about external environment—political, economic, and market competition

(c) company-based SWOT

(d) customer service

(e) investment in areas of thrust

The most damaging mistake management can make is to put unsuitable people in key jobs. I have seen top management preoccupied with maintaining seniority balance and accommodating plateaued executives in important positions. The need to maintain balance supersedes strategic deployment considerations.

Top colleagues of CEO jockeying for the promotion of their favourites is a sustained pastime, which pushes companies to the lowest common denominator in meritocracy, team management, and performance.

Expatriate CEOs of MNCs who come for a fixed tenure of 3 to 5 years, easily fall in this trap because their eyes are set on showing results over their short tenures. This enables them to earn early promotions and sugarplum positions in the corporate hierarchy back home.

Such power play empowers competitors, and affects executive morale. It generates cynicism about management's integrity. CEOs and top executives who indulge in such practices in the name of *realpolitik* don't care for management discipline. This gives a lethal blow to the idealism of young graduates looking forward to building bright careers. Sad but true.

Be that as it may, there are examples of successful CEOs, who gave deep thought to strategic deployment:

(a) Venu Srinivasan, who spent over a year scouting and hiring executives at the corporate presidential level.

(b) Vaman Kamath, who spelt out his policy for promoting competent executives without gender bias.

(c) Mallika Srinivasan, whose logic made a non-technical executive leader of a technical task force.

There are many more like these. In the long run, *right solutions add value, expedient ones, damage*. A leader may be a good strategist and may yet fail if he has no strategic insight in the deployment of key human resources. There is no secret formula to success. Graduating from a business school is not necessary but studying at the university of adversity–opportunity seems absolutely essential.

The University of Adversity–Opportunity

This institution for practical learning could be nicknamed AOU, "Adversity–Opportunity University". One can observe from the leaders' profiles that they have gone through different kinds of adversities, to tap opportunities:

Amrita Patel	Faced MNCs on a spree to capture markets, cooperatives in a disarray, and major disagreements with mentor Verghese Kurien on policies, direction, and marketing strategies
Jamshed Irani	Turnaround of TISCO, massive reduction in workforce, resolve problems left over by his predecessor, and shift self-limiting boundaries to improve his abilities to face challenges and improve his performance
Mallika Srinivasan	Rejuvenated the organisation caught in prolonged market depression.
Prathap Reddy	Getting into hospital business without any entrepreneurial background
Simone Tata	Exiting cosmetics to start business in retailing
Vaman Kamath	Transformed a project finance institution into a big bank
Venu Srinivasan	Ushered quality revolution in the company with conscious and serious attempts at self-transformation

Difficulties appear to work like tonics: they spurred these leaders to greater exertion and better achievements.

If we aspire towards a free market economy with minimum government control, then the responsibility of good governance will automatically pass on to organisations. Every organisation will have to share the responsibility of governance over neighbourhood and community. The stakeholders will demand transparency and accountability. Unions will be replaced by social activists, environmentalists, the unemployed, and a host of such groups. They will form the nucleus of external adversaries.

Under such circumstances, mindset change will be a constantly evolving phenomenon where the basics of civilised, enlightened behaviour will remain somewhat unchanged but the skill–competency sets will require constant update. Daily rigorous routine will be followed to cultivate and maintain vibrant, positive attitudes. Management will innovate in these spheres to keep up the tempo.

If one tries to take a holistic perspective in the midst of overwhelming turbulence one realises that the adversary is located within one. We therefore need to take a fresh look at our mindsets. *There are times in everyone's life when something constructive is born out of adversity.* If one believes this, one must garner the courage to first introspect and see what changes are required in one. Said Samuel Johnson, *"Adversity is the state in which a man most easily becomes acquainted with himself, being especially free from admirers then"*.

While identifying the common threads in adversities faced by different leaders, it becomes evident that business organisations are becoming colleges, or continuous learning centres, attached to the conceptual AOU. I am not talking about corporate universities. The concept of AOU germinated from:

(a) Managers' queries about leaders' experiences in handling difficulties, facing hardships, and failures. Were there any common pitfalls which could be avoided, and what could be practised to surmount similar situations?

(b) Leaders themselves saying that in top leadership positions they look for such qualities and competencies, which can ably navigate the organisation through adverse situations.

(c) The psycho-philosophical dimensions that come up for discussions in various forums.

The first Jewish Prime Minister of England, Benjamin Disraeli said, *"There is no education like adversity"*. That, I discovered, was the foundation of grit in these leaders. If "continuing education" is a need of the 21st Century leadership training, then it is incumbent upon business leaders to put their fast trackers on hardship postings and the most difficult assignments. This practice existed in the Foreign Service, Armed Forces and Civil Service.

Such complex assignments and classroom training, provides participants an integrated view of ground realities. Management development and training has become a specialised craft. Trainers use modern techniques of simulated games, case studies, group discussions, and outdoor physical exercises (rafting, rock climbing, etc). The package inputs help in changing mindset, leadership styles, and team work functioning. It enhances awareness about oneself, others, and the organisation.

Leaders who face adversity and failures during their voyage of business growth, feel that the attributes they possessed gave them the grit, resilience, and fortitude to survive and grow, and a passion to excel. These leaders think such attributes can be instilled in their managers.

Dharni Sinha's research on *Leadership in Unpredictable Times* showed that resilient leaders had a definite personal profile, which integrated seven characteristics and was reflected in their behavioural pattern. The characteristics he found matched many earlier studies carried out here and abroad. What is pertinent is that he identified them whilst organisations were passing through the unpredictable times.

It seems the nature of change also changes but the characteristic of leadership remain constant. They provide guidance in future turbulence as well:

1. clarity of purpose embedded in values
2. strong personal identity
3. self-driven; self-motivated
4. commitment to life long, continuous learning
5. active personal and professional networks
6. well articulated internal standards
7. action orientation

The in-company training and development is basically on the job, where one learns to face adversity, supplemented by experiential inputs though a variety of need-based programmes. In addition to all the behavioural training, there are urgent needs to focus on Sinha's recommended actions. I would add the following:

- developing resilience, grit, and patience in facing adversity
- intellect to intuition
- biographical studies
- story telling
- philosophy of integral development
- *Upasana*, the vital discipline for achieving success and significance

To gain acceptance to behaviour oriented training, it is imperative that the CEO's faith and commitment are visible. It would do a world of good if he is seen relieving executives for training, and making special efforts to put them through hardship module on the job.

Also, those who failed or succumbed to adverse circumstances, candidly confess that they failed to develop a comprehensive perspective, and skills to find a way out of the quagmire. That is my experience too; failure is never fatal. Quite a few failures are due to lack of self-introspection or correction, a lack of nerve in handling complex interpersonal relationship and political issues.

In my experience of major organisational restructuring, the factory heads of departments did not become the heads of a division, especially where marketing and factory responsibilities was grouped together. However, the marketing heads attained those positions rather easily.

Barring certain exceptions, marketing executives did not succeed in handling factories or gaining aaceptance among their manufacturing colleagues. Those who succeeded, were sensitive to the emotion choked atmosphere of the factories. They were prepared to understand and learn the ropes of a different ball game.

The reason for many not succeeding is simple. Managing factories is a hardship assignment because of the high interconnectedness of issues, groups, people, unions, and different leadership styles, functioning in a closed environment. It requires a high level of emotional intelligence to handle ambiguous, seamless, and fluid situations with patience and foresight. Marketing chiefs did not possess that skill set or did not show a desire to learn it. The learning curve had dipped even before they reached 50.

In the new regrouping, functional silos have been broken. Transparency in operations, sharing information, and communication across functions, has improved considerably. Companies now operate in the knowledge economy. This paradigmatic change compels them to think that they cannot provide value added product–service package on the high end of technology unless they acquire cutting edge proficiency in action.

Success is not measured in IIT or B school degrees, and jobs at Infosys or Wipro. Nor is it measured in Citibank-like postings in US for a couple of years, before hopping over to another company. To manage change, one needs to become stable in a job, and not jump as soon as the ship faces rough weather. Success is never final; it does not give durable prosperity. Says Edward de Bono:

> *Any style of success must also include a style of failure. Failure takes different people different ways. It can utterly destroy or build a person's confidence; it can activate a spiral of depression or be a stimulus.*

Sydney Finklestein, professor of Management, Dartmouth's School of Business, did a study of 51 companies in UK, US, Germany, Japan, Singapore, Australia, and South Korea, and wrote an interesting book titled *Why Smart Executives Fail*. Companies like Satchi & Satchi, Motorola's Iridium project, and Wang Labs appear in the book.

These companies had records of success. The leaders were not rogues or foolish. They did not lack perspective or intelligence. They were knowledgeable. Six factors contributed to failures:

1. not coping with innovation or change
2. brilliantly fulfilling the wrong vision
3. ignoring vital information
4. misreading the competition
5. clinging to an inaccurate view of reality
6. identifying too closely with the company

Human beings try to avoid the repetition of their mistakes and failures. The latter have therefore, cultivated an uncanny art of sneaking through when we become complacent, lower our guards, or are even temporarily possessed by the persuasive spell of our egos.

In the explosive growth of *positive thinking* literature in the last three decades, many people became somewhat blind to the ground realities. Hope and optimism are necessary for sound health and growth. One cannot ideate a positive future without them. But one must ensure that they do not make one impractical. Everything is not rosy once one joins a good company. That's why there is the need to carry both success and failure styles in one's style book.

The fundamental message of cataclysmic change is, be ready to face and learn from unpredictable, severe hardships. The cry for mindset change is heard all over. However voluntary change is 5 per cent, enforced one is 95 per cent. Initiating change in oneself is difficult because it requires the confrontation of one's ghosts, one's SWOT. Hence, one prefers to shelter behind a mask, until one's employability and survival are threatened. If one is ambitious, one might take cognisance of change because one's chances of promotion and growth may be in jeopardy.

Enforced change comes from socio-economic pressures, legal compulsions, threats to reputation and public image, and inimical forces released by God. When such circumstances entrap one without any alternatives in sight, one perforce begins to change.

However, those who are self-conscious (and their numbers are growing), equip themselves to face change proactively. There is also a realisation among some people that freedom is difficult to handle unless we change responsibly. The constellation of new adverse forces holds out hope and alternatives for self-aware knowledge workers to change themselves. This book presents role models. And there are many others around one, whom one would find, if one sees and observes differently!

The paradigm change in my thinking is stimulated by the daunting process of transmutation underway in almost all organisations. Adversity, I see, is constant. It recurs frequently. When one starts handling adversity adroitly one learns to spot opportunities. A reassuring Welsh proverb, *adversity brings knowledge, and knowledge wisdom,* puts one on the path of hope if one enrols in this unconventionally conceived abstract university for continuing education!

9

Spiritual Perspectives within the New Leadership:
Globalisation, Organisational Renewal and Devotional Path of Significance

- ❖ Is there anything spiritual about Globalisation?
- ❖ Spiritual Development leads to Integral Development
- ❖ Upasana: A Path to Significance

*"Yadeva Viddyaya Karoti Shraddhayopanishada
Tadeva Viryavattaram Bhavati"*
(Whatever is done with knowledge, faith, and attitude
of Upasana becomes most vigorous and fruitful.)

—Chandogya Upanishad (1.1.10)

Introduction

Globalisation through market mechanism has not rectified the global disequilibrium. Some would argue that it has further eroded the global balance. The economic life has become inane. However, no country will be able to help restore its own balance or the world equilibrium by remaining isolated from the forces of globalisation.

It is only through gainful participation in global change that we can strengthen our economic growth. To achieve this objective, we need more transformational leaders who can rejuvenate organisations and institutions. Never before was this need so acute and urgent.

Against this background, the chapter explores the spiritual perspectives of globalisation. It describes how a path treaded with discipline and devotion (*Upasana marg*) can lead a person to live individually a life of significance, and collectively to revitalise organisations and institutions.

Is There Anything Spiritual about Globalisation?

We could not ride the boat of industrialisation due to the exploitative goals and policies of British. Later we missed it by engaging in Marxist-Socialist ideology. Nor did we have the protestant Calvinist work ethic, nor the Zen tradition of perfectionism found in Japan.

Perfectionism comes naturally to the Japanese. They have a terrific concentration over their work—whether in carpentry, wire wielding, painting, silk weaving, archery, or swordsmanship. That kind of focus has religious roots rather than economic ones. The success of its quality movement is due to these ingrained habits, and the spirit of nationalism.

We had neither of the above preconditions available as launching pads for our industrial growth. *Bhagwad Gita's central message on Karma Yoga was shamelessly consigned to the dustbin by promoting labour aristocracy, anti-work ethic, and deadly labour laws, all patronised by undisciplined socialist governance.*

It compounded our tragedy in that our government could not establish command or control, of either the Russian or the Chinese variety. Our professional protestors, with government connivance, promoted indiscipline and landed us into man made chaos.

For industrial progress, a nation requires a very high level of discipline either imposed by dictatorial regimes or built into the cultural fabric of society. Rational utilitarian economic models alone do not guaranty economic prosperity. A senior social scientist at the Rand Corporation, Francis Fukuyama, confirms this when he says that human beings frequently do not act like rational utility beings in any narrow sense of the term utility, but they invest economic activity with many of the moral values of their broader social lives.

Fukuyama also found that the degree to which people value work over leisure, their respect for education, attitudes towards family, and the degree of trust they show towards their fellows, all have a direct impact on economic life, and yet cannot be adequately explained in terms of the economist's basic model of man. The correlation is difficult to establish.

In India, we do respect education and family responsibilities, but we stopped valuing work under the negative influence of unproductive labour laws, and politicisation of the entire industrial and commercial working class. Our trust levels deteriorated rapidly. As against this, the migrant Sindhi, Jain, Sikh, and Gujrati communities have done extremely well abroad with exactly the same value set, identified by Fukuyama in *TRUST*, and Kotkin in *TRIBES*. *Tribals have trust amongst them, whereas tribes of professionals have it in the least!*

For business to prosper, or for political organisations to become stable, spontaneous sociability is required. In this respect, we suffered from the centuries old baggage of religion-language-casts configuration, which has been inflamed by politicians rather than contained. As a consequence, we do not have high secular trust levels.

Our upbringing, habits, norms, and traditions determine our preparedness to mix socially, lend money to each other not in times of difficulty alone but also for business. It widens the social network, and builds social capital and trust. This has not happened.

However, our community based trust levels have always been fairly high. This is the reason Gujratis, Parsis, Marwaris, Sindhis, and Jains are able to do business. Their spontaneous sociability and social capital is solid. Kotkin gives many examples of the spread of these trading communities over the continents across the globe.

Sindhis uprooted from their homeland Sindh, in Pakistan, have dispersed globally and captured business. Theirs is a remarkable story of values inculcated by the Hindu religion—values like thrift, belief in education, strong family ties, self-help, entrepreneurship, and communal living. It is quite inspiring to say the least.

The system of money transfers across the global tribes of Chinese, Koreans, Jews, Gujaratis, Sindhis, etc, happens out of such family-community considerations rather than merely economic ones. The volume of money transactions through private channels must have been in trillions of dollars a few decades back. Now that they have become established and naturalised citizens of their respective countries, transactions may occur through official banking channels.

The progress of the business world was powered not only by channelling the destructive energies of the warrior class into commercially adventurous tribes. Adds Fukuyama in TRUST—The Social Virtues and the Creation of Prosperity:

> It seems that what has happened in the modern world is spiritualisation of economic life and the endowment of the latter with the same competitive energies that formerly fuelled political life.

The first step at globalisation was taken at Brettonwoods in 1944. World bodies like the United Nations, World Bank, IMF, ILO, WTO, GATT, etc, came into being one after another. However, there was little, if any, market globalisation between the fifties and eighties. The dissolution of USSR in the early nineties, coupled with advances in IT, particularly Internet technology, gave a boost to economic globalisation.

It was a paradigm shift for socialist countries, who opened up their markets to the forces unleashed by western technological advances. The socialist governments of Asia, eastern Europe, China, and other parts of the world had to give in because of near bankrupt economies, and public demands for market reforms. However, there is a strong feeling that the utilitarian philosophy of marketing every facet of life, is promoting consumer values and homogenisation of cultures, thus inviting human and environmental disaster. There are two telling observations, in this context, which need reproduction:

The World Bank chief economist Joaseph E. Stigliz:

> The West has driven the globalisation agenda, ensuring that it garners a disproportionate share of the benefits at the expense of the developing world. The result was that some of the poorest countries of the world were actually made worse off.

The leading authority on international money management, George Soros:

> Many people, particularly in less developed countries, have been hurt by globalisation without being supported by a safety net; many others have been marginalised by markets. The heedless pursuit of profit can hurt the environment, and conflict with social values.

Since the labour movement is on the retreat and socialism on a stretcher, there is no counter effective force to unbridled free-market capitalism. The World Social Forum and the resurgence of religions have just started gathering some momentum. However, the spectre of job famine, dependence on governments, and the sheer incapacity of a large mass of people to do something on their own, are daunting problems for which these movements have no solutions.

The pathologically anti-government militant leaders, who organise protests at the drop of a hat, do not have alternative manifestos either. When they come to power, they realise that the management of the economy is embedded in the international geopolitical and financial network. It functions on its own socio-politico-business agenda. It compels them to abandon their idealistic promises, or do something half-hearted, face saving gimmickry.

Very few militants turn mystics to carry the masses with them like Vaclav Havel, who said:

> *We cannot devise, within the traditional modern attitude to reality, a system that will eliminate all disastrous consequences of previous system. In a world of global civilisation, only those who are looking for a technical trick to save that civilisation need feel despair.*

However, those who in all modesty believe in the mysterious power of their own human being, which mediates between them and the mysterious power of the world's Being, have no reason to despair at all. This reassurance from a sensitive poet, an experienced militant thinker, and a ruler of Havel's stature, should give us the confidence that our mysterious capabilities will shape human destiny towards more order than chaos.

The fact of the matter is that businessmen do thrive in unstable conditions, paradigm changes, technology jumps, and demographic shifts, even without reading Tom Peters' *Thriving on Chaos*. The inequities in wealth, consumption patterns, epidemics like AIDS, malnutrition, environmental degradation, and stark poverty in parts of the world, are all issues which governments on their own are unable to handle, let alone solve. They are therefore coming to the doorsteps of the corporate world, which is struggling to add value and create wealth in market marathons. They must flourish. Unless they create wealth, none of these problems can be tackled.

My curiosity drove me to find out if there was any spiritual base to this upheaval. What is functional behind the conspiracy of these events? We start seeing the spiritual profundity in mind-boggling happenings when we go beyond logical thinking and scientific reasoning.

By criticising the west's intentions and despairing at technological advances, one is not able fathom what is implied behind this change, this illusion (*Maya*), this reality. One has to move beyond one's perspectives, assumptions, and pet theories to implore the "third eye" or "sixth sense" to throw light on it. Gradually the path gets lit. The dilemma had been badgering me for seven to eight years. I allowed the structural tension to raise its own questions, collect data, and search for meaning and solutions. It took me three years to present these findings to you.

The resurgence of religions and spread of yoga in the last forty years, the flurry in temple building activities, and the reams of new age literature, are pointing to some silent convergence in thinking, taking place on a global level and lifting us from the abyss of extreme bipolarities.

My memory lane took me down to the late sixties at Marks & Spencers, Oxford Street, London. While seeing the *Hare Krishna*, head shaven, dhoti clad devotees of western origins singing *bhajans*, I wondered about the meaning behind the movement. The upsurge in the west for studying eastern religious practices was on the increase, making me think, is there any order unfolding right in front of us?

There were other movements belonging to Buddhism, Judaism, Christianity, Bahai's, and other religions, that were also spreading. The spread of *yoga* was providing practice in stable postures (*Aasana*) to the roving minds of the westerners. Bookshelves carrying catchy titles on humanism, self-help, leadership, meditation, and such other topics were multiplying in Europe and US. All these developments lead me now to conclude, that global spiritual awakening underwent a paradigm shift.

Parallel to these developments, a conviction was gaining ground in the east that material perspective had to be adapted in addition to the spiritual one. We could not have fed our people on the philosophy of fasts. Aspirational goals of the society embraced creation of wealth and prosperity, as primary requirements for the alleviation of poverty.

These metamorphoses in the east and west about the exact relationship between material and spiritual orders is leading towards the spiritualisation of economic globalisation. It has led to the rejuvenation of religious institutions and a competition between religionists to interpret and communicate the values in new jargon using the most modern devices and media. It is not revivalism of the religions as is commonly understood. It is a reinterpretation movement with much broader frames of reference.

One difference is noticeable: there is no dogmatic assertion. It is resulting in the acceptance of other points of view. The world is being seen through different lenses, and that's a great leap forward when we know that something deep within us tells that the traditional view is the truer vision.

While searching for a set of assumptions and values that are shaping the destiny of four interdependent variables like globalisation, governments, organisations, and individuals, Ira Rifkin's *Spiritual Perspectives on Globalisation* (2003) came in handy. Rifkin tries to make some sense of this economic and cultural upheaval in this book. He says:

> *...humans are programmed to search the inner cosmos for meaning, and recent world events underscore how important their religious conclusions are to actions taken. Understanding how these beliefs motivate individuals is crucial if we are to cope successfully with the stresses...*

As many executives are experiencing, these stresses threaten to blow the world apart. It seems that the stresses are only aggravated by globalisation and are unlikely to reduce their pace and intensity in the near future.

My interaction with leaders gives me the toehold to say that they have a strong foundation in spiritual belief systems. I did not specifically discuss spiritual issues with each leader.

However, in the course of the conversation it came up naturally with Venu Srinivasan, Prathap Reddy, and some others. They have abiding conviction in that spiritual forces are guiding world events like globalisation, progress in technology, the future of their organisations, and their own leadership function. Their faith does not go anywhere near fatalism. It is firmly rooted in *Karma Yoga*.

Prathap feels that we have built walls between our inner strengths, i.e. potential, and what we have performed so far. We are unaware of God's bounty. If we knew only how to tap it, we would get much more. Prathap's faith in God, gurus, and the coincidences in his life, look to me as a function of his heart. Said William Wordsworth *"Faith is a passionate intuition. It is a spiritualised imagination"*.

In any case, Prathap is a heart surgeon passionately putting his *mantra* "Tender Loving Care" into action at his Apollo Hospitals, to make India a global healthcare destination. His faith deepened as he started practising meditation. Now it has become a part of life. As soon as he sits in his car, he takes off his shoes and starts meditating. I once observed this practice when we drove together to the Chennai airport. With his permission I interrupted it for a while to finish my list of questions.

I had discussed the spiritual aspects with some thought leaders: Ravi Khanna of Controls and Switchgears, and Dhananjay Bakhle, now of Aventis Pharma, come to mind. They have gurus who guide, and their spiritual leanings are a great source of strength to them.

Meditation is central to all processes that enable transpersonal development. Easterners always believed in the benefits of meditation, westerners did not until the sixties. Their interests widened and deepened once they were able to get scientific proof of its positive effects on blood pressure, heartbeats, and most of the other aspects of physical and mental health. Since then, there has been a veritable explosion of professional, popular, and research interests. It was reported that over six million Americans had taken to serious meditation by 1980. Current guess, fifteen million!

Those who did not talk directly about spiritualism, also gave me the impression that their belief system is not too different. Spiritual forces are operating at inflection points and have invisible links that cohere to take individuals, organisations, and globalisation, towards a new unfolding world order.

This new world order is ushering in a new global civilisation. That's why the boundaries between different nations, sciences, and cultures are becoming porous and blurred. We have moved through agricultural to industrial, to technological, and now to knowledge revolution. This knowledge revolution is taking us away from land based traditional cultures.

Culture forms, whereas civilisation transforms. Both are developmental processes with no fixed life spans. In fact, they are overlapping cycles in constant interaction between two opposite and complimentary forces, whether you call them *Yin-Yang, Male-Female,* or whatever.

As with every other civilisation, this one has its own characteristics. It is taking us beyond dualities now that we have enough experience of them. Dualities gave us the experience of relationship and mutuality, which made us realise that interdependence is inevitable. By teaming up, we have to move beyond; although the future will polarise the past. According to the composer, philosopher, and poet, Dane Rudhyar, no culture is omniscient, omnipotent, or permanent. In *Culture, Crisis, Creativity* (1977), he says:

> *There comes a time when for the sake of our spiritual heritage, we should consider breaking away from established patterns and values that have been imposed upon us through culture. "Spirit creates, culture reproduces". Crisis appears to be necessary to the creative process.*

We must allow space for our creative spirits to guide us safely through this unprecedented crisis. The process of civilisation is one of transcendence, and transcendence implies crisis. The act of walking implies a fall from a position of equilibrium. It is only through the medium of meditation that we regain our equilibrium. Rudhyar thinks that dissatisfaction, fall, and recovery is inherent in the process of civilisation, and Man, archetypically, is the civiliser.

We can now imagine where Mahesh Yogi's movement of Transcendental Meditation came from; and why the Beatles, artists, composers, and professionals got hooked on to that wave of the future. Such transcendental developments, I would argue, indicate that the fusion of economic and spiritual globalisation is in sight. Quite a few of the leaders I studied appear functional on the transformational plane, consciously and unconsciously. The call for acquiring spiritual intelligence is coming from these changed ground realities, not from any crystal gazing.

A superficial understanding that spiritual intelligence means some higher form of intelligence is not sufficient for gaining mastery over it. It does not come by following traditional rituals, the daily *pooja*, standard prayers, and all that. They have their own important place in our belief system, which is not belittled; yet we must know more about spiritual intelligence and the method to acquire it.

Spiritual Intelligence Leads to Integral Development

A spiritual approach bridges the gap between your inner and outer self. Thomas A. Stewart, editor Harvard Business Review noted: a leader gets into trouble when there's dissonance between the inside and outside—what today we'd call a disconnect.

In Chapter 7, The Nature of Qualitative Transformation, we dealt exhaustively with the need to move from emotional to spiritual intelligence to develop keener insight into one's being, to bridge the gap between one's potential and performance.

In *SQ—Spiritual Intelligence, The Ultimate Intelligence,* Danah Zohar and Ian Marshall conclude from the experimental research:

> *The 40 Hz oscillations are the neural basis of SQ, a third intelligence that places our actions in a larger*

context of meaning and value, thus rendering them more effective. Here I am assuming that the 40 Hz oscillations are required proto-conscious bits into consciousness. Our spiritual intelligence is rooted in life itself...

It grounds us in the wider cosmos. We know very well that life has a purpose and meaning within the larger context of cosmic evolutionary processes. This belief makes us human. Our business icons have to ready themselves to play a far more significant role in the current global crisis, at the micro Indian level as well as the macro world level.

Therefore, the need to have spiritual intelligence for integrated development is not a new find. The new development is the increase in our awareness about the nature of evolutionary processes. Technological advances and the Internet revolution are a part of that evolutionary process, which has awakened us to its profound impact on our lives.

We cannot remain aloof from the consequences of our inputs of intelligence, which have ushered in this technological civilisation. The key differentiate of this phase of evolution is the speed, and the threat that if human intelligence does not take a leap with the same speed to garner benefits, then the economic and environmental losses will be disastrous.

The progress in brain research, behavioural and leadership styles, performance criteria for measuring results, and eastern spiritual practices has reached a plateau. What is measurable is not worth measuring any further, and what is worth practising is immeasurable because it emanates from the realm of spirituality. People are stuck at Peter Drucker's observation *"What is measurable gets done"*. However, research on intelligence brought us from IQ to EQ. We are knocking at the doors of SQ but afraid to enter because it's correlation to success, results, growth, and contribution, cannot be directly established and demonstrated.

When I asked Venu and Mallika Srinivasan about correlating EQ/SQ competencies to results, they were very clear that it is not possible to do so. Venu is convinced that these capabilities are vital for individual and company progress but that they are not chemical components, which can be assigned weights and taken into account for action in rational world.

Both said that flashes of brilliance, intuitive prompting, gut feeling, convergence of ideas, or synchronicity are describable phenomena, but not measurable for the designing of a scheme on performance payments. Other leaders have voiced identical opinions.

We need more creativity to progress through our current predicaments. It means we have to enter the unconscious mind. The approach is through the development of SQ. It is therefore essential for one to know:

- where one is now
- where one wants to change
- ones deepest desires, i.e. life motivations
- which path to select among those available
- reflection which leads to understanding and wisdom
- which daily discipline to undertake; monitor its progress also daily
- one's obstacles—guilt, laziness, fear, jealousy, anger, ignorance, obsessions, self-indulgence, whatever

When Drucker coined this phrase "knowledge worker", he had a far deeper meaning in mind. He was not thinking only of technology, computer savvy graduates working in IT, Life Sciences, Biotechnology, Banking, and other sectors at the high end of the value chain. His emphasis was on making the knowledge worker responsible for continuous innovation, learning, and teaching.

Although we are passing through a kind of knowledge explosion, following *Dnyna yoga* (yoga of knowledge) alone won't help unless we intersperse it with *bhakti* (devotion). By knowledge, we mean split logical thinking, more analytical than synthetical, more grammar than substance and meaning. At the high end of knowledge-value chain, we will not achieve breakthroughs unless we become creative, and for that we need SQ. And that will come through the practice of integral *yoga* with emphasis on devotion.

The reason is simple. People make one successful. One has to approach them, influence them. It cannot be done through rational approach alone, nor with an additional flavour of emotional intelligence (after attending a seminar on it), because it is susceptible to being labelled as emotional blackmail. One has to be more creative in reaching colleagues' hearts. The ability to discover what one can do well, and enjoy doing it, is the hallmark of creative people. SQ helps develop that ability. One becomes a more authentic person.

Inspiring leadership means spirited and educative leadership. The spirit provides heightened energy, to connect people to a common cause beyond materialistic aspiration. It embraces the future as if it were the present and give impetus to bouts of creativity.

If one has spiritual disposition, the change in the pattern of one's energy use and consumption will have a positive impact on others. Whatever transformative disciplines (integral practices) one undertakes to study must be suitable to one's make-up. A few important traits commonly possessed by creative people are:

- a strong desire to develop intuition and find pattern and meaning
- tolerance for ambiguity
- attraction to complexity, adventure, unknown territory, and asymmetry
- flexibility of perception
- ability to spot similarities in dissimilarities, and create order from chaos
- willingness to float in uncertain situations by temporarily setting aside reality testing
- readiness to explore latent capacities

Artists, scientists, and initiates are generally supposed to have these traits. They weave a new tapestry of awareness which enhances our aesthetic sense and capacity for experiencing new meaning in our relationships. They select problems from their domain expertise and operate in the field they enjoy most. They have a childlike curiosity and tremendous interest in finding a solution to the problem they have chosen to solve. It's the same temperament which children display in solving crosswords and puzzles.

The motivation for a creative artist is neither money nor position, but a burning desire to find new expression. He tries to establish a new understanding by going beyond what is already known. His insight then presents a reformulation which bears the stamp of his personality. This comes to him not from his intellect but more from deep feelings embedded in the assortment of his memorable experiences.

It is not necessary to control knowledge. This is one unlimited area, welcome because it procreates knowledge and therefore wealth. It also procreates wisdom when immersed in the spirit of devotion.

As against this, the CEO is required to find solutions, or to get someone, or a team, to find them. This is where his talent management, insight into capabilities, potential, and learnability of people come into play. In one's exploratory journey one has no signposts for developing new value-added products and services if one is at the high end of the value chain. One is venturing to make a breakthrough in grey areas, new territories, interdisciplinary and interdependent domains, which requires a very high level of creativity. All our psychological and somatic (relating to body) processes are interdependent. It is well nigh impossible to separate proactive outcomes and methods into precise categories. Integral yoga combines both.

Desired capacities however, can be cultivated directly or indirectly, by reciting a *mantra, pranayam,* concentration on a single point, *upasana,* surrendering to a difficult regime of a seminary, or quiet meditation, whatever is suitable to the individual.

One cannot afford to lose one's grey cells. Only integral learning practices can keep them nourished. In *The Future of the Human Body,* the co-founder of Esalen Institute Michael Murphy says:

> *Integral practices reorder elements of the body and mind, as if they were artistic materials, into new forms of power and beauty, and for that reason require those personality traits that promote creativity in general.*

Here also one identifies and adopts "best practices" from various fields like sports, music, art, science, athletics, aikido, karate and other marital arts, religions, craft skills, meditation, somatic disciplines, yoga, mathematics, philosophy, psychotherapy, etc. Such an interdispciplinary approach is more reliable. These practices are used in the development of attributes, traits, and values, e.g. movement abilities like speed, flexibility, coordination, vitality, self-regulation, perception of external events, communication, cognition, volition, empathy, desire that others strive, independence, courage, resilience, mathematical abilities, language proficiency, etc.

The exact combination of what training is needed can be decided by going through the literature on the subjects, and consulting experts and relevant institutions in the field. There are tools available to monitor progress. One should be able to endure long learning curves, and love practice for its own sake. Sharpening the skills to achieve mastery whether in archery or empathy is likely to be overturned by one's weak will and feeble self-discipline. If one expects instant results from transformative practices one is on an ego trip!

Murphy feels we can anaesthetise ourselves and remain addicted to external activities through our outbound habits, or re-channel our energies into integral practices that offer creative alternatives to the social and ecological problems we confront at home and work.

Management is doable but leadership is increasingly requiring more knowledge to handle equally knowledgeable colleagues and technically qualified managers. Transformational leadership transforms one's very being, and in doing what one wants, it takes one through the trial by fire (adversity). Chapter 7 on The Nature of Qualitative Transformation and the profile of exemplar Venu Srinivasan covers this ground exhaustively.

In my endeavour to find out what I thought or did wrong in the failures I faced, I was brutally honest with myself. I always found some error here or there. I tried to share these occasionally but there was no interest in providing a fresh viewpoint. In fact, in counselling sessions also, I found counselees were not prepared to dig deep. They wanted to hide themselves from their true selves.

I was happy to note that Danah Zohar also thought that one must have the honesty to admit that these are failures of one's own making. It is not that I have not met the right person or that I was not there at the right time. The kernel of truth is that I must want to be different, must long to broaden myself to a larger and more diverse group. Zohar acknowledges that these are the reasons the path of knowledge requires discipline in reflection, prayer, meditation, and study.

Upasana: A Path to Significance

Patience was Venu's KRA for development. Without meditation, patience becomes difficult to cultivate. In any craft, practice is the only means to success because the underlying principle of all development is practice intelligently, practice regularly, and practice hard. The practice in following the process of quality circles led to quality enhancement. The theory does not matter as much as the practice itself does.

Manuals are available for all functions whether it is quality, safety, personnel management, audit, manufacturing, internet, or whatever else, but what matters is practice. Therefore, companies benchmark best practices of best companies against their own to find out where they can improve performance.

In *The Benchmarking Book*, Michael Spendolini defines benchmarking as a "continuous systematic process for evaluating the products, services, or work processes of organisations that are recognised as representing the best practices for the purposes of organisational improvement". Regardless of industry, location, and ethnic background it is a search for excellent practices across the world, with which to compare ones own level of achievements.

For companies that want to become global organisations, benchmarking serves a good tool for improving performance. As much as managers need a framework for strategic thinking, CEOs need framework for plotting competitive advantage. Benchmarking provides that. After studying hundreds of organisations world wide, Aurther Anderson formed a six-stage scheme for incorporating customer-oriented processes.

In *Best Practices*, Anderson state:

> *In our practice, we have found that this habit of mind, this ability to seize the core insight of a best practice and then use it as a performance catalyst, is transferable.*

Anderson recognised that there was indeed a pattern of three common, lasting messages to be found in these thousands of best practices. In the study of best practices, the intention is to establish a pattern in the meaning underlying the repeated messages conveyed by participants.

In this study, Anderson found that the companies constantly searched for better ways, developed serious, positive, ongoing relationships with key stakeholders, and adapted a strong process view of business.

What Anderson has done is to identify transferable and adaptable practices for improving performance. Global search helped him change the lens. Breakthrough thinking came from focussing on universal processes—the key enablers. He found out the context invariant, culture-free variables that are transplantable everywhere.

However, certain leaders are exceptional because of their sustained performance, predictability in achieving success, durable influencing capacity, and use of source code. They have high credibility, use vivid language with compelling evidence, and they connect emotionally. They are not paragons of virtues. They do not lay claim to great wisdom. They readily acknowledge their shortcomings and deeply revere their humble beginnings.

These findings apply to the leaders covered in this study as well. However, I went ahead to unravel the **one constant practice** that was catalysing their intuitive capabilities, emotional and spiritual intelligence, strategic insight, creativity, aesthetics, flexibility, and discipline to become functional and show better performance year after year. Said Lao-tzu,"*Knowing the constant gives an impartial perspective*". It does. That "constant", I discovered, is the discipline of *Upasana*—devotional practice.

Take music, orchestra, sports, acting, or any other field of art, and one will find it has its own disciplines of practice. The legendary coach of Green Bay Packers, Vince Lombardi said, *"Nobody ever attained greatness in anything who was not willing to continuously practice, drill, and rehearse"*. We know, great athletes spend a lot of time practising and comparatively less time in performing. When our cricketers increased their practice sessions, they showed a marked improvement in their performance. Our executives however, have no time for any practice. Executives spend no time practising and all of their time performing. No wonder they recycle their problems. It is understandable that they are pressed for time, but the desire to learn and make time for it, is low. In order to reach their targets and complete their tasks, they starve themselves of learning to lead better.

The key lies in mastery over old habits. Musicians rehearse so much that finally their fingers move on instruments as automatically as rhythmic breathing. Practice develops fluency.

To lead one through the prescribed practice lessons with discipline, one requires direction from teachers, counsellors, coaches, mentors and gurus. Although the common vocation of all these professionals is teaching, and their specialties overlap, they play different roles.

No matter how expert one is, or what celebrity status one may have achieved, one needs to constantly follow the discipline of practice. For example, to learn new skills, and keep mind, body, and crucial centres of performance in a well-groomed state, one needs daily practice. One needs to do specific practice, which has its own strict code of conduct and demands. In fact, practice means to perform repeatedly with discipline.

The importance of disciplined thought and action was stressed by all leaders without exception. The reason is simple. *Opportunities are in chaos but the business lies in solutions*. And solution implies bringing order through systems discipline. If we apply that principle to ourselves, we find that the chaos is in our minds—stress is a symptom of chaos—and therefore, we have to first find order in the mind.

To bring order in the mind we process thoughts, sequence them, see patterns, segregate emotions, see through different lenses, understand the big picture, arrange the pieces differently, and see the emergent whole. But to establish such clarity we require a certain disciplined mental training.

Unfortunately, few leaders are good at inquiry, most are excellent at advocacy. Inspiring leaders move from habit to discipline. Drucker is right when he says, "Innovation is discipline". Says Peter Senge, "Many have talent, but real learning requires discipline, the process through which we draw out our potential through commitment, practice, passion, patience, and perseverance".

In *Celebration of Discipline*, Richard J Foster (1998) divides discipline into three movements of spirit, which contribute to a balanced spiritual life. The inward disciplines of meditation, prayer, fasting, and study, which offer avenues for personal examination and change, and the outward disciplines of simplicity, solitude, submission, and service, which help us make the world a better place. The corporate disciplines of confession worship, guidance, and celebration bring us nearer to one another and to God.

And I like the definition of God given by Julia Cameron in her classic *The Artists Way*: *God Means Good Orderly Direction* (1992). When we open ourselves to exploring our creativity, we open ourselves to God. Here again, we are back to basics: *God is order, demon is disorder.*

One cannot invoke God unless one dissolves ego, because ego propels one to edge God out. Whichever way the essence is understood, it takes us to ancient wisdom. All gurus affirm that devotional discipline for developing SQ is a must.

If one's emotional intelligence is high, one will empathise well with the feeling of the other. However, changing feelings affect one's perception of things. One must be able to understand them in a larger context. That one can do if one meditates on improving one's perception. To perceive better one must focus ones attention properly.

It is important to pay attention to *how* one pays attention. The habits of placing your attention will determine what one knows. Dr. Paul Brunton said, "*The faculty of fixing attention at will and retaining it ultimately helps burn a way through the hardest of intellectual problems*". Where attention goes, energy flows.

Leaders emphasise heavily on practice that produces excellent results but they have not spelt out the details of their methods. I term it "devotional practice" because I feel that they must have carried out their tasks with unwavering commitment, faith, intensity, regularity, vigour, and a focus on results. They must have vibrated some feelings, though not necessarily from religious texts.

Devotional practices in Indian culture are described as *tapasya, sadhana, abhyas, upasana*. They convey, that practice permeated with *bhakti* (devotion) stills the mind. It awakens faculties of inner knowing. In *Meditation and Life*, Swami Chinmayananda says:

> *To cultivate the faculty of contemplation and to brighten it up in us is the content of all spiritual practices, Yoga-Sadhana. Meditation is a process by which the seeker develops in himself this faculty of contemplation, which is already in him.*

Thomas Merton provides guidance in *Contemplation in Action* (1998):

> *The contemplative prays for particular intentions when he is strongly and spontaneously inspired to do so but does not make it his formal purpose to keep asking for this and that all day long.*

Upasana, means devotional practice. The devotee chants prayers (*bhajans*) in a sitting posture in front of God. It has a different import. When one sits in front of God, follows certain rituals, prays, recites mantras, meditates, and performs all this with total faith, it is pure devotional practice. When one sits studying *Upanishads* with one's guru in total faith, it is devotional practice. The important point is the sitting posture, faith, and prescribed prayers for invoking God's blessing.

There is no need to go into the details of *upasana* here. It is sufficient to understand its significance for our purpose. The practice is performed with feelings. One has to understand the deeper meaning of love, compassion, and blessing. They are communicated through those sentimental renderings. A devotee becomes so involved in those moments that he forgets his own existence.

The central concept is that when one is dealing with the mind one cannot make it receptive to intellectual appeal only. It is aroused to act only when one entreats it with feelings imbued with affection, faith, commitment, compassion, and love. Such sincere imploring emanates from the heart.

It is true that life must become prayerful. Every moment must be soaked in the knowledge that power is the creator and I am that. For one to become so subsumed in His grace one needs to devotionally practice invocation. The difference between ordinary practice and devotional practice is that the latter is filled with feelings. It requires emotional imploring. In effect one prays to one's mind to respond, to provide insight.

Based on her work at the Foundation for Mind Research and Human Capacities Training Programmes, Jean Houston wrote *The Possible Human* (1997). Jean describes the new breed of heroes—people who have a healthy and spirited appreciation of the complexities and capacities of their own being:

> *They regularly spend time in discovering, refining, and applying the latent potentials of their own body-minds. They take time to prepare themselves so that they can listen to the rhythms of awakening that may be 'pulsing' from a deeper, more coherent Order of Reality.*

I now recall what former managing director of Glaxo and Kodak, Humayun Dhanrajgir, said to those who wanted to launch an idea: *create an opinion and pulsate with enthusiasm*. After this comes sincerity and determination which should shine through presentation and body language. Humayun's gesture radiated a vitality which electrified me into carrying on our animated discussion with added zeal (Pandit, S., 2001).

I would draw your attention to the phrase Humayun uses: *pulsate enthusiasm*. And Jean Houston uses "*pulsing from a deeper, more coherent order of reality"*. The connection I see in use of these phrases suggests that Humayun, although suffering from prostrate cancer (or because of it, i.e. suffering from a fatal affliction), must be unconsciously sensing some unknown order of reality, which was vibrating to enthuse others.

Take the example of yoga practice. It is not merely physical training or bodybuilding. It is yoga *sadhana*. It aims to train the mind and body. One does yoga postures *(asanas)* to improve mental and physical faculties. Along with meditational practices, prayers and chanting of mantras form a main part of the spiritual discipline of yoga.

In the context of the importance of devotional practice, Lin Yutang's observations in the introduction to his book *Wisdom of India* (2000) is quite relevant:

> *India is a land of people intoxicated with God. It is my belief that it is entirely unimportant which God one worships, monotheistic or polytheistic; what is important is that belief should produce the true spirit of devotion in the life of the worshipper.*

The western materialist assumption—fixation?—based on perceived wisdom seen only in "bottomline financial results" monotheism is being seriously challenged. This is where the paradigm change in thinking businessmen comes from. There is life here on earth beyond such financial goals, which needs attention and investment.

Lin Yutang believes that in modern terms, it is important that religion be efficient, i.e., it should produce results, and that modern monotheism is less efficient than when men believed in the spirituality of trees and rocks, and mountains and rivers. Indians believed in the spirituality of the ecology of earth.

The current drive towards gaining SQ is leading the most powerful block of leadership in the direction of enlightenment. This may sound idealistic but the undercurrents—spread of yoga, inter-faith dialogues, spiritual literature, paradigmatic shifts, etc—bear testimony to the transitions various societies around the world are going through.

We are concerned here with the intermediate step of renewing organisations and ourselves to meet the change we face in our work life. We need integral development of attitudes and competencies to become better leaders. One cannot correlate each input to a specific outcome. It is not possible to separate methods and practice outcomes with great exactitude since our psychological and somatic processes are interdependent.

Integral yoga means the scientific study, and practice, of the body and mind. Although both are important, mental training is given precedence over physical training. The postures do not give desired results unless the dos and don'ts of mental training back them. The practices apply to the body and mind simultaneously.

The integral conscious engagement of the body and mind sharpens one's overall faculties. In *The Eye of Spirit—An Integral Vision for a World Gone Slightly Mad*, Ken Wilber (1997) says:

> *It soon became obvious that to engage in genuine transformation required time, work, and sustained intentionality—in word and practice.*

In support of this, Wilber says Michael Murphy came to the same unmistakable conclusion in his book, *What Really Matters: Searching for Wisdom in America*, that integral practice is now the only viable mode for human transformation. In his work Murphy drew on the pioneering insights of Aurobindo.

To prove the point further I will cite the example of Nandan Nilekani, CEO of Infosys. He also heads the Bangalore task force for improving that metropolis. It shows high social awareness, commitment to a specific improvement cause, finding time for work, self-discipline, and such other qualities that a professional of his stature shows in taking his company to the high end of the business value chain. He has, in modern parlance, achieved work-life balance! To me, it means Nandan has taken a path of significance.

He learnt this from his mentor Narayana Murthy. This is *upasana* in practice, which means one learns by devotionally following ones guru. The word "devotion" and the concept behind it, has little value, if any, in the lexicon of western professional management. I dare to introduce it as USP of Indian management. It connotes affectionate loyalty (applied emotional intelligence) to ones mentor, the cause he stands for, and the values he cherishes. It is not religious devotion.

Even when one is learning to wield, programme, or design skills, one shouldn't do it mechanically. One should pour ones emotions in the practice; be devoted to one's teacher, mentor, coach, whoever it is. Such practice takes one beyond intellect to intuition and insight. It is not rote learning, memorising, or cerebral understanding. It is digesting, and self mutating.

The hypothesis I tested:

> *Vocationally integrated leaders are disciplined practitioners of certain integral daily practices. Such practices are not merely a mechanical drill of skills and routine remembrance of some eloquent proverbs. They're emotionally involved exercises for internalising values, visions, and refining competencies that become the drivers and raise the bar of their performance higher and higher.*

My discussions with the leaders featured in this book has given me the confidence to say that the hypothesis has been validated. It has stood the scrutiny, as organisational results speak for themselves. My intuitive assumption that such leaders must be leading a fairly ordered life founded on daily disciplined integral practices, carried out with deep emotional feelings and commitment, was confirmed by the manner in which they responded to these issues. Their disposition unquestionably corroborated that they were speaking on the actual experience of their daily regimen.

More importantly, I trust my assessment that they were speaking and relating from the bottom of their hearts. Their responses reflected sincerity, integrity, and the mileage they accumulated from their daily walk on the path. That context invariant "disciplined practice" is therefore the key differentiate between ordinary leaders and CEOs who produce sustained results.

The pagoda of excellence of any eminent CEO is founded on orderly thought processes, which he has cultivated painstakingly. Excellence is closely linked to order. I was interested in understanding the meaning behind such processes, rather than the ritual each one followed. From the elements of that "order" I have formatted a model easy enough for anyone to adapt.

Now that we have understood the spiritual perspective behind globalisation at the macro level and how leaders internalise the concept at micro level through daily *upasana*, we have a deeper insight into the source code presented in my previous book, *Thought Leaders*.

Such daily, disciplined, ardent practice of thoughts and action leads to the creation of value and wealth. We shall know more about its process and roadmap in the next chapter.

10

Creating Value, Wealth, and a Better Future

- ❖ Creating Value and Wealth
- ❖ Creating a Better Future

"The value you add comes from the values you hold, and wealth provides the power to do what you want, our task however is to fix the course of the future by creating both".

—Anon

Introduction

This chapter looks at the process of creating values and wealth that pathfinders have followed so far. It then lays down a road map that individuals and teams can follow to a better future.

Creating Value and Wealth

Creating value and wealth is the fundamental purpose of business organisations and the principal responsibility of CEOs that head them. It is the business of business to create value-based wealth. However, when moneymaking becomes the objective, as distinct from wealth creation, we procreate corruption.

In such a corrupt ethos, the society becomes bereft of value maps to guide. Values are maps, not territories. Honesty and truthfulness are principles, which form territories. They are guidelines, which have permanent values. As we go through, we shall see how leaders have created values and wealth; and along with it built tangible, and intangible but priceless, Indian assets.

Amrita Patel has been facing a conflict of values and vision with her mentor Verghese Kurien, the architect of "white revolution". The differences are about the direction NDDB should take in further development of milk cooperatives and the marketing of products through tie-ups, to meet the challenge posed by MNCs.

Circumstances and contexts determine the values. It is pertinent to note that Deepak Parekh said:

> *Visions can be wrong, hopelessly off the mark, if they are not born from strong values, strengthened, and nurtured by an analytical ability to constantly assess emerging alternatives.*
>
> (Pandit, S., 2001)

The differences between Kurien and Amrita appear to be in their perceptions about the role NDDB should play in shaping its future, and the mechanisms it requires to realise the vision. It is essential to build the social capital on certain value commitments in the face of changed ground realities. Whenever there is a conflict of values at the top, growth suffers.

There are two urgent needs in India:

- create wealth and social capital
- reduce corruption to negligible levels, if not totally eliminate it.

Both are interdependent variables of the value set. If we create more value-based wealth, corruption will automatically go down. Victor Frankl (1963) identified a set of three central values: attitudinal, experiential, and creative. How we respond (attitudes) to difficult periods (experiences) in life, together with what we create, determine the values we practice in life. Adverse circumstances show one's true metal, one's new reference frames, and shifts in perspectives. This is what we are seeing at Anand.

Jamshed Irani wrote thirteen action guidelines for himself. The one about values is worth recapitulating: *Preserve the core values of Tatas (and my own)*. In adding "and my own" Jamshed showed the significance of coherence in values required in a top executive to steer the organisation through a mammoth disequilibrium.

Covey (1989) thinks it amounts to being responsible for one's own first creation, to rescript oneself so that the paradigms from which one's behaviour and attitude flow are congruent with one's deepest values and in harmony with correct principles. When Jamshed drafted his own charter, Covey had not written his book. Even if he had, in all probability, Jamshed would not have read it because there is no love lost between him and management books!

Creating wealth is an age old vocation. The world has passed through periods: Stone age, Iron age, Agricultural age, Industrial age, and Technology age. It is currently in Knowledge and information age. These periods have been linked to the technologies of their time. The development from steam engine to turbo jets, booster rockets to robotics and Internet, procreated needs for advanced technical skills at each stage.

The investment patterns of merchants and entrepreneurs in factories, machinery, huge organisations, technology, and scientific discoveries, underwent radical changes in these periods. Thinking on the management of enterprises, assets, manufacturing, logistics, strategies, and marketing, saw concomitant shifts. We have now transited from hierarchical to networked organisations and from the "strategy-structure-systems" to the "purpose-people-process" model.

These periods also mark certain disequilibriums in local and global economies. In such transitions, merchant-entrepreneurs make money by taking risks in forging a new combination of assets, which create new values.

As markets developed, a new class of business leaders emerged. They and their organisations perfected the art of exploiting the opportunities presented by chaos, and scientific inventions.

Technological, sociological, and developmental disequilibriums, paradigm changes, natural calamities, technological complexities, conflicts, and chaos, all present opportunities for creating wealth. If it was Andrew Carnegie and Bill Gates in U.S.A., in India it was Jamshetji Tata, Ghanshyamdas Birla, Dhirubhai Ambani, L. N. Mittal, Azim Premji, Brij Mohanlal Munjal, Rahul Bajaj, and Narayana Murthy, to name a few. *Business is embedded in difficulties and complexities; and opportunities are in providing simple solutions.* Such leaders:

- creatively built physical, financial, employee, customer, and organisation assets
- made combinatorial and purposeful use of assets, which they traded to build social capital
- had the foresight, risk-taking ability, and capacity for creative hard work
- designed sturdy, realistic business models
- assessement of life cycles of assets, and trends in market, which enabled them to strategically move across the paradigmatic economic phases of growth
- built companies, which are not just profitable, but create value.

In *Cracking the Value Code,* Richard E. S. Boulton (2000) provides the example of Chicago Bulls:

The long answer: it was the management of assets-although mostly intangible assets-that made the difference. It was the players and coaches, systems, and processes, leadership and values, customers and suppliers. The Bulls' management built a portfolio of assets that created extraordinary wealth.

The recognised intangible assets which produce superior market value are: leadership, speed, talent, efficiency, innovation, learning, accountability, collaboration, shared mindset, and customer connectivity (contact network). Attempts to assess the value of these assets on a 0 to 10 scale are made in some companies abroad. However, is it still not considered a very reliable measure and therefore has not found general acceptance. One can imagine how difficult is it to measure the portfolio of personal assets described in this book.

The management of the Chicago Bulls experiment is applicable to our national obsession—cricket! In fact, in the major paradigm shift to the "purpose-people-process" model over the last decade, these factors have acquired special significance. After having built assets by subjugating people assets, organisations have come to realise that only people assets multiply other assets.

What doesn't get commoditised easily are the intangibles, like leadership, integrity, risk-taking ability, enterpreneurship, faith, courage, and professionalism. Our minds think linearly, although the reality is non-linear. Of late however, there is a realisation that such intangibles alone can create lasting value.

This awakening is a divine gift of the knowledge era. At last, in the land recognised as the seat of eastern wisdom, knowledge (*Dnyan*) is regaining its lost status. Coincidentally, the Indian spiritual diaspora is getting official recognition and social acceptance in many foreign countries.

The spine of this spiritual expansion is *yoga*. The sitting posture, *Swastikasan* (the Lotus pose) has become a symbol of peace, tranquility, and balance world wide. Our presence abroad has acquired a new respectability.

Narayana Murthy, Rajesh Hukku, Kiran Mazumdar, Prathap Reddy, Arun Jain, Anji Reddy, B. Ramalinga Raju, and many such people did not hold any land, gold, oil, or other natural resources; not any industrial processes either. How have they created such enormous wealth right in front of us in the last fifteen years?

1. Six breakthrough technologies—microelectronics, telecommunications, computers, new man-made materials, robotics, and biotechnology—have interacted to create a new knowledge-based economic world. These wealth creators have built knowledge assets to create wealth.

2. We are a "service society" like U.S.A. and Italy, not a "product society" like Germany, Japan, China, and Korea. The differentiating characteristic between the two are:

    (i) service society—democratic, individualistic, heterogeneous population lacking collective discipline

    (ii) product society—periodic dictatorships, homogeneous, non-individualistic, and capable of high level of collective discipline

3. What gets commoditised gets done, viz. tangible goods and skills, and short cuts. When we commoditised knowledge into IT skills and 24 × 7 service package, we established our brand as excellent IT service providers, the world over. We will therefore do much better in the entire service sector like hospitals, hospitality, tourism, etc, provided our labour laws become more work-ethical and performance cultured.

4. Consumerism has crept into our society and the leftist factions of the media and press have started criticising this. Unless the "saving" to "spending" journey begins, how are we going to become prosperous? We must realise saving money does not make one rich.

5. Successful businessmen are good at cannibalisation. Eliminating one unit, product, service, or part, to save another is a necessity. Similarly giving VRS to some, to recruit the skills one requires is a need imposed by the massive change.

6. Radical technological change and developmental disequilibriums leads to high growth. It jerks the society to change paradigms and action.

7. There are no institutional substitutes for entrepreneurial change agents. One can provide capital structure to cooperatives, but they cannot create wealth unless the management is entrepreneurial. The reason for the dismal failure of our cooperatives becomes clear from this perspective.

8. A successful knowledge-based economy requires large public investments in education, infrastructure, data collection and storage, research, and development. The corollary is that a knowledge worker should invest his private time in self-education, improving his infratitude, and research into his personal competencies.

9. This new economy, with its flat structured organisations does not provide careers. How to build one, is the dilemma a professional has to face and resolve, if he loves to call himself a knowledge worker!

Lester Thurow's observations in *Creating Wealth* (1999) are relevant:

> *Knowledge creation requires highly educated skills at the very top of the skill distribution. Superior deployment skills in the middle and lower skill ranges allowed America to generate higher levels of wealth than Germany. In modern times, mathematically trained workers make just-in-time inventories.*

His three words of advice for individuals are skills, skills, and skills. *Brawn earns little and brains much.* We would add, *attitudes, attitudes, and attitudes*. Said William James, "The greatest discovery of my generation is that man can alter his life simply by altering his attitude of mind".

In *The Creation of Wealth*, R. M. Lala (1991) makes the following profound observation:

> *If words and slogans could create wealth, the streets of India would be paved with gold. It takes more than that…the wealth created by an industrial house is to be measured not only on the basis of its balance sheet but also in terms of the skilled manpower, its advanced technology and in terms of its ripple effect on a nation's life.*

Way back in 1963, my mentor, the late S. R. Bhise of Bank of India, in the course of a conversation on abilities and capacities asked me, "What is the age of your uncle?" I said, "He has three grownup children". A usually serious Bhise gave me a quizzical look and said, "That does not tell me his age". It suddenly dawned on me that at 30, a person married at 18 could have three children in the age group 10 to 13. We both shared a smile and I left.

While returning to my seat it occurred to me: merely having the capacity to be a parent does not make one a parent. To become a parent, one needs to procreate. To create something out of nothing one needs to be original. One may or may not need the stimulus to create. M. F. Hussain creates on a blank canvass. Creating wealth is something like that. One brings that result into existence, which was not there before.

There was no steel city, named Jamshedpur, in 1907. But it was taking shape in the creative mind of Jamshetji Tata. Lala writes:

> *In 1902, five years before the site of the steel plant was finally located, he (Jamshetji) wrote from abroad to his son, Dorab, of what his dream city of steel should look like,*
>
> *"Be sure to lay wide streets planted with shady trees, every other of a quick-growing variety. Be sure that there is plenty of space for lawns and gardens. Reserve large areas for football, hockey, and parks. Earmark areas for Hindu temples, Mohammedan mosques, and Christian churches".*
>
> *Jamshetji had seen it all in the mind's eye.*

It is noteworthy that Jamshetji, although a Parsi himself, did not propose to build an Agiary (Parsi temple). In due course, at a village called Sakchi near the meeting point of two rivers Kharkai and Sabernarekha, a couple of miles away from the railway station Kalimati in Bihar, Jamshedpur came into being.

This is creating. The creator had a clear picture of his creation in mind. He loved something before it came into being. This is proactive behaviour, not responsive. The focus is on creation and the creator is able to negotiate the structural tension between the result he wants and the reality he faces. It was unfortunate that Jamshetji did not live to see his steel plant come up.

A creator like Jamshetji stretches himself to pursue what he wants, step by step. His creative visualisation of what he wants, concentration and capacity to send positive inputs to his mind in the entire creative process, is far more important for his desired objective to come into being. Such legends operate from third-person orientation, which helps them focus on the actual creation rather than their own identity.

One example is sufficient to prove the point. There are many others like Kasturbhai Lalbhai, G. D. Birla, J. R. D. Tata, Walchand Hirachand, K. M. Mammen Mapillai, Raunaq Singh,

Anji Reddy, Dhirubhai Ambani, Shiv Nadar, T. P. G. Nambiar, Rahul Bajaj, T. V. Sundaram Iyengar, Brij Mohanlal Munjal, Azim Premji who created wealth in a big way. They did it by exploiting the opportunities presented by techno-sociological and developmental disequilibriums.

The important point to note is that whatever the background, these people mastered wealth-creating skills with a blend of rational and intuitive thinking. They trusted their abilities to secure results through sheer hardwork and infinite patience. More importantly they had implicit faith in the higher powers of God and a firm belief that they were born to create wealth.

Said Narayana Murthy:

> *There are only a few people who can lead the task of wealth creation, just as there are only a few surgeons, professors, and lawyers...for heaven's sake there is absolutely nothing wrong in creating wealth by legal and ethical means.*

Leaders with ambition and values drive successful companies. Dwijendra Tripathi, a business historian and author of *Indian Business* (2004) says about Kasturbhai Lalbhai:

> *Kasturbhai's reputation was disproportionate to his business power but he earned it because of his values and ethics.*

Business legends have not taken easy road to prosperity. Gita Piramal observed that Birla, Walchand, Lalbhai, and Tata hacked through jungles, built factories in villages, and transformed barren tracts of land into profitable assets. The contribution of such businessmen, who have placed industrial ethos in the mindset of peasants, is very significant and invaluable.

That apart, their patriotic entrepreneurship, their pioneering spirit and their promotion of education, is unequalled. These men are legends because of their rare sense of economic nationalism. Our current business leaders need to carry forward this legacy.

Many businessmen create ethical wealth and imperishable values to shape society. There are black sheep in all flocks. One has to discern the *satvic* (pure) from *tamasik* (impure) by bearing in mind the 80/20 rule. Those who cannot create anything are cynical and envious about others' creations. Envy never enriched anybody. The problem with socialist ideologues is that they never chose between inequality and poverty. Creation of wealth is a difficult vocation. Few have the ability to venture into it. We must encourage such people to do their jobs.

Creating a Better Future

Having said that, a dispassionate view of the current reality based on certain changes suggests that we have a better future.

- The government is business friendly. It is disinvesting from its huge loss-making portfolios. It is creating space by deregulating a number of unwarranted controls imposed on business.

- Phenomenal opportunities for growth are opening up, and more people are taking the entrepreneural route. Small is beautiful has become a reality. In software industry also, 90 per cent of the firms are small.

- Young India is gradually taking interest in governance, politics, social, and environmental matters. They are demanding transparency. It is moving from "saving" to "spending" habits. Fortunately, it is not carrying much of the old baggage of communal and casteist thinking.

- The emergence of knowledge workers is a forerunner to the period of Indian renaissance.

- Unions and socialism are on retreat.

- The Week has recently published *Prophets Of New India*, a compilation of their "Man of the Year" series. They have profiled twenty social workers, who transformed the lives of thousands of people. They are relatively unknown but their vision has endured in the form of institutions and people to carry on the work. Prophets like Baba Amte, of Anandwan, Maharashtra; Dr. B. V. Parmeshwara Rao of Dimri village, Andhra Pradesh, Abhay and Rani Bang, both MDs of Gadchiroli District, Maharashtra, and 17 others profiled in the book are real torchbearers of Gandhian legacy. Society learns from them, loves them, and contributes its humble might. They are admirable role models.

The most important point is that these social workers do not go on protest marches disrupting normal social life, and causing public inconvenience. They do not force the government to spend enormous amounts of money in policing their *morchas*, fasts, and other sterile fads claiming to represent the deprived.

It must also be noted that many young qualified graduates are devoting their lives to such noble causes. To opt for such peaceful transformational careers surrendered to the noble causes is one of the most significant factors in our renaissance. It has many lessons for the NGOs which have brought disrepute to a promising movement in our developmental efforts.

As I said earlier, a total free market system of the American variety, mindless consumerism, lavish styles of the rich and famous, is not the cherished future of business. Even Americans have woken up to this fact. In *Good Business*, Mihaly Csikszentmihalyi (2003) shows concern that if business continues to be oblivious to the responsibilities attached to the power it has acquired, sooner or later the immune system of the society is going to reject the free market paradigm. The greens and world social forums have begun to flex their muscles.

A very small beginning is noticeable in American organisations' philosophies, GE Plastics, Amex Life Insurance, The Body Shop, and Des Moines Water Works, Semco in Brazil, who have undertaken social work, involving employees in decision making, etc.

However, the infrattitude, history, civilisational values, and culture of Americans are eminently different from ours, except for faith in democracy and individual freedom. They will take quite some time to come out of their free market OCD.

We have many examples:

- Wipro's involvement in education
- Narayana Murthy's wife Sudha is engaged in social work initiatives
- Tatas have decades worth of contributions to public life, from science and education, to community work
- Lupin's Gupta has adopted a village
- Excel Industries' Shroffs have discharged their social responsibilities excellently

Our record in this respect is much more admirable than that of other countries. What the Americans or the west do is not a role model for us.

The impetus to growth is borne out by the general boost in stock and other markets. The upbeat mood is here to stay, as many learned commentators confirm. The growth has its own momentum, and the youth of India will not allow it to halt. Even farmers' second and third generations are looking forward to a paradigm change in their life styles.

The connectivity of young India is more humane. It has crossed income and status barriers. The mixing of graduates from elite institutions, partially educated from *jhopadpattis* of the metros, and new generation farmers living in villages, is taking place. There are no income barriers to understanding each other. Bollywood has played a significant role in building acceptance between classes and segments of society. So also Internet, cell phones, and media images of modern India. All this change is visible to the naked eye, and the movies reflect it.

Arun Maira has shared his experience of a recent scenario planning exercise, involving people from different fields, viz. Jharkhand state, Keggfarms in Bangalore, Bharat Petroleum, and Confederation of Indian Industries (CII). These are pathfinders in business and communities, who are working to make change happen. The Generative Scenario Thinking approach was used to understand and align the "know-wants" of diverse people. It also provided insights into complex systems by combining many perspectives.

The driving forces were to facilitate local initiatives in strengthening infrastructure, new models and skills of leadership, and enable children and women to access relevant knowledge through new technology. What made an impact on me was the effort to propagate successful stories and build confidence. This is the most important gap in our training methods. We use case studies, but not group story building and story telling techniques for effective participation and motivation in training sessions.

Bennis identifies one requirement which enables a future leader to develop new models and skills in leadership. He should have the ability to identify, woo, and win the mentors, who will change his or her life. The real test of character for a leader is to nurture those people whose stars may shine as brightly as—or even brighter than—their own. One has to be so self-effacing and self-sacrificing to become such a leader that it dissuades most. Amrita is finding it extremely difficult to nurture such a breed at NDDB, and also at the cooperatives.

In *Evolution and Business*, Gary Zukav makes telling observations on licentiousness, male-female principles, and authentic empowerment:

> *The economics of abundance is a direct reflection of the profligacy of life that is at the heart of the female principle. It will produce businesses in which the equality of the male and female principles is fundamental, as more and more individuals begin the journey toward authentic empowerment.*

We are experiencing this difficult journey. The antagonisms between men and women and between business and environment have been there for centuries. But Zukov thinks they will reduce and be replaced with new, harmonious and mutually reinforcing relationships between men and women, and between business and the environment. The progress though might be at a snail's pace in traditional societies all over the world.

The "environmental health" of the planet Earth is being damaged beyond recuperation. The movement to preserve the environment—forests, croplands, water resources, topsoil, ozone layer, etc—started some forty years back. That process of awareness building has taken firmer roots in the last decade, and businesses have woken up to their responsibility to preserve the national resources for common weal. The old paradigm of the west, based on science, mechanical systems, advances in technology, and total belief in unlimited material progress, has driven them to demolish the walls of ecology and destroy its natural harmonic balance. The new paradigm is holistic, deeply ecological, and recognise the interconnectedness and interdependence of all animate and inanimate systems.

In *A Systems Approach to the Emerging Paragdigm*, Dr. Fritjof Capra, observes:

> *Ultimately deep ecological awareness is spiritual or religious awarenes. As far as thinking is concerned, we are talking about a shift from the rational to the intuitive, from analysis to synthesis, from reductionism to holism, from linear to non-linear thinking.*

There is a corresponding value shift from competition to cooperation, expansion to conservation, quantity to quality, and domination to partnership. We had a demonstration of this value shift and the resultant friction in Amrita Patel's story. While facing stiff competition from MNCs she is trying to regain her competitive position in marketing battles on one side, and trying to expand the vision of the NDDB and milk cooperatives to include concerns for ecology on the other.

Amrita is trying hard to make them own responsibility for that. This is a fight for values. Thinking based on Cartesian philosophy leads to fragmentation. Amrita with her integrative thinking is trying to put into practice a systemic approach to management of all resources in order to secure a balance.

The prime responsibility of business organisations is to create wealth and recreate time-tested values. In a discontinuous world, strategy innovation is the key to wealth creation.

Strategy innovation is the capacity to reconceive the existing industry model in ways that create new values for customers and produce new wealth for all stakeholders.

Business leaders have tremendous power, and society will not allow them to misuse it for voluptuous use. That means, the western obsession of mindless consumerism and unlimited material progress, which is a cultural anathema for Indians, will find no great takers over here. It is the job and responsibility of CEOs and their teams to demonstrate holistic life styles, while sculpting a better future through their organisations. And I dare say, quite a few are showing in action that maturity and common wisdom shown by Indians for centuries.

The reason for confidence, is our frame of reference in living a balanced life, and our inborn proclivity towards spirituality. Our leaders will not easily give up this precious legacy. Or shall we say that the inherited conditioning of our great civilisation will not permit them to do otherwise.

The current ethos of successful business progress has been shaped in the last twelve years by Indian leaders. It is quite motivating. Many inspiring role models have emerged. The future now being carved out looks promising in the hands of current generation of young leaders. But the demand outstrips supply. We need more, and someone to show us the path. The roadmap shown here will be fully lit by the source code in next chapter.

11

Source Code Leads to Seven Assets

- ❖ Cracking the Source Code
- ❖ The Holistic Tri-circle of Influence
- ❖ Revealing Interviews
- ❖ Discovery of Seven Assets

"It is the complex interaction of mixed assets — its economic DNA—that creates or destroys value".

—Richard E S Boulton
Cracking The Value Code

Introduction

This chapter cracks the source code given in my previous book, *Thought Leaders,* and puts together the context invariant practices discovered in earlier chapters. These practices are the real assets of a leader. They create value and wealth during the recurrence of disjointed periods of change.

Cracking the Source Code

In *Thought Leaders,* I have provided the source code of exceptional managers and entrepreneurs. The code was derived from my observation of the combinatorial use of traits, tools, methods, preparation, and practice that the twenty-two leaders made to give expression to their talents and convictions. For easy reference the findings are reproduced here:

- There are three clusters in the source code. All three interact and cohere to produce exceptional results. I call these clusters: Reflexive Search, Leveraging through Domain, and Value-Added Branding. Figure 11.1 shows the components of each cluster.

- At the heart of the reflexive search is the desire to make a difference; leveraging through domain involves thorough preparation to optimise ones skills; and value-added

Reflexive Search	Leveraging through Domain	Value-Added Branding
Conceptualisation	Focus	Stand for something
Commitment	Learning	Self-expression
Persistence	Methodology	Persuasion
Difference	Quality	Branding
Curiosity	Innovation	Positioning
Meaning	Preparation	Packaging
Reflection	Tools	Bonding

Fig. 11.1 Clusters of the Source Code

branding demonstrates that one stands for excellence in ones field

- It is the purposeful use of these clusters, which accelerates the thinking process and velocity of action in thought leaders.

The Holistic Tri-circle of Influence

- The manager's search to make a difference is the starting point, which encompasses a mode, a circle called reflexive search, which includes characteristics like commitment, curiosity, etc. These are not mutually exclusive traits. In fact, these traits collectively cohere to provide reflection.

- The second circle, leveraging through domain, consists similarly, of characteristics like focus and learning, which allow the executive to leverage his strengths in his domain, the primary field of engagement.

- The third circle, value-added branding, has characteristics like packaging, and positioning, which stamp the executive's value-addition with a brand name. The scheme of the interacting circles is given in Figure 11.2.

- The three circles should be seen as interacting wholes. They overlap. They are organic in character, therefore

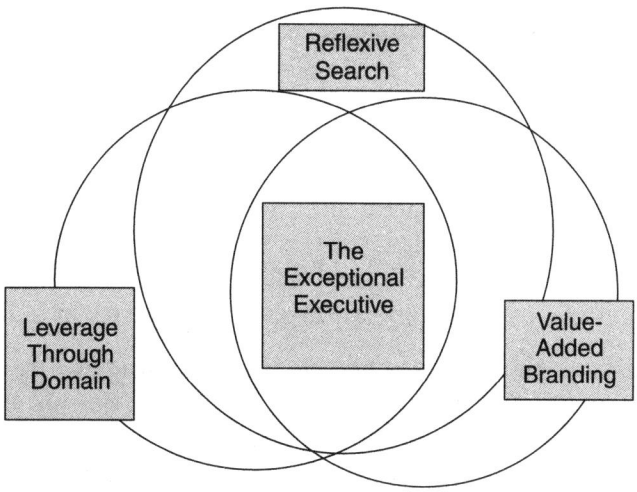

Fig. 11.2 The Tri-circle of Influence

holistic. The more they mingle, the more likely they are to produce an exceptional executive. Such confluence (*sangam*) of the tri-circles creates the individual's catchment of influence. The larger the width of confluence of design, architecture, and performance, the greater the influence. It determines whether the individual becomes a local, regional, national, or global brand.

- Each one of our exceptional managers is a brand by himself—a role model of sorts. His influence zone depends upon what he has decided to carve out for himself. There are no zonal restrictions. All of them have accessed the source code to be where they have reached. The reach factor depends upon the vision, creativity, and the degree to which each one fine-tunes the component clusters.

These very practices, viz. reflexive search, leveraging through domain, and value-added branding, figure in the make-up of the seven CEOs featured in this book. My reflexive search helped me crack the source code only to discover that there are four additional context invariant practices, hereafter called *assets*.

Revealing Interviews

The search was conducted though in-depth interviews, which helped me understand the persons behind the personas. I relied on my interpretative skill, which came to light when I had an interesting assignment at London School of Economics (LSE) in 1970. The school had completed a communications project at an organisation in port industry at UK.

Prof. Desmond Graves, who was then teaching us Organising Development (OD) at LSE, had worked on the project. He asked me to listen to the transcripts of interviews, study them, and state why their assignment was not successful. The researchers were not able to evoke the necessary degree of commitment from the Board of Management. Desmond wanted to know why?

I adopted the following method of study:

- read over the transcripts a couple of times
- did a content and non-numerical analysis
- recorded the salient points under heads like technological change, industrial relations, personnel policy, business strategy, and opinions/observations of some fourteen board members against each topic
- Recorded recurrent responses using criteria such as DIF (Difficulty, Importance, and Frequency: in other words, what the interviewee found DIFFICULTY in explaining, or a DIFFICULT subject to comment upon, and/or mentioned it as IMPORTANT for some reasons, and/or occurred FREQUENTLY in the interview.)

While I was intently listening to the tapes, a clearer picture of the characters began to emerge in my mind from the words used, tone, and emphasis on pet themes. The profiles penned by me coincided with the assessment of the researchers who had actually taken the interviews. Desmond found it remarkable.

I could even figure out as to what disciplines they had graduated from, and their mental make-up, from the gist of what they said. I presented a model showing which character must have fought with whom and why, e.g. the operations director must have had a fight with the personnel guy, or the strategy chap with marketing director.

My main observation was that if a guy has graduated in statistics, and another in arts, and both worked only in their respective domains, they fight. In other words, core subjects lead to fights or collaboration. The personality types vectored in to make conflict worse or less damaging.

The opinions were horizontally lumped together on separate sheets of paper to find out, on which issues there was consensus or lack of consensus. I introspected deeply on all subjects and people, individually and holistically on the group. The model showed that the organisation was schizoid. There were major irreconcilable differences of opinion under the façade of consensus. Although some members of the board knew that there were conflicting undercurrents, they didn't know the origins. I found that each one singly, and at times jointly, was greater than the team.

This study made a great impact on my mind. I realised that deep understanding of a person's thoughts culled from in-depth interviews would help to sketch reasonably reliable personality constructs, helpful in assessing the potential and correct fit for top jobs.

I thought I would use the same technique gainfully in book projects. The leaders' thoughts would take me to the core of their personalities, and they did. I was able to peep in their inner thought worlds and search for the foundation of their mental make-ups. The approach was integrative. It became clear to me that the seven integrative practices enabled them to create value, and become real assets and brands in their own domains.

To understand the meaning behind feelings, I had to keep the subjectivity of such exercise to the bare minimum. The intention was to understand the feelings (use of emotional intelligence) behind the rational answers. Therefore, the phrases used for explaining important points, the body language (because the body manifests what the mind harbours), the facial expressions, the voice, and the simple tone were all important to me.

There was not even a trace of arrogance in their demeanour. They all were transparent and affable. Their humility stood out gently and gracefully. Their sense of humour lightened the tone of discussions occasionally. They had thoughts with profound meaning to convey. I felt refreshed in their company.

I went beyond the hype and public image of these leaders to learn their drivers. I am not an aura reader but I could feel the texture of their integrity, simplicity, and creativity. Each one had a distinctive presence that symbolised his or her strength; the ability to use a particular asset more gainfully, e.g. Prathap Reddy is effective in instituting a culture of *Tender Loving Care* at Apollo hospitals with his spiritual perspective. Likewise, Simone Tata adds to the reputation of Tata Brand through her aesthetic taste in creating the value-added products, Lakme and Westside.

Discovery of Seven Assets

The four new practices together with the earlier three create a set of seven valuable assets. These seven assets have transformed organisations with conviction. That makes the people who use them inspiring leaders.

The four new assets are:

1. adversity, the driver of mindset change

2. the new leadership: spiritual perspectives

3. *Upasana*: globalisation organisational renewal, and devotional path of significance

4. creating value, wealth, and future

The CEOs use these personal resources, i.e. assets to add to their strengths and make them durable. Their unique contributions make the difference, which multiply their assets.

The whole purpose of my search was to demystify the overemphasis on charisma and the "born leader" belief. I wanted to first analyse the elements of the alchemy, understand how it functions, and then assemble a model for adoption. This, as you will see, has been done.

All CEOs have used the seven assets volitionally or when compelled, e.g. under adversity. They made virtue out of necessity by mastering adversity. They skilfully blended the assets to enhance their combinatorial use and value. The seven assets shown in Figure 11.3, alchemise leaders into inspiring CEOs.

The organic nature of these assets makes them holistic. When seen as overlapping circles or interacting wholes (Figure 11.4), the model looks like a flower. An enlightened CEO is like a lotus flower.

This circuit of seven revolving wholes renews itself constantly. It releases energy, enthusiasm, and confidence. The presence of the CEO is felt. Those working with him are inspired. When the person is stressed, tired, or sick, only rest and *upasana* help him recuperate. Leadership is difficult and taxing. That's why there is a dearth of inspiring leaders. We need more of them to create better future.

The three-year study, search, and reflection have brought me to the simple elements of a leader's chemistry. It is a rediscovery of the principal assets possessed by all leaders. It is the holistic, integrative approach to body-mind complex that becomes the knob.

Americans first took to *Hata Yoga*. The attraction was to improve the body through physical exercise. However, they realised that the science of body, mind, soul cannot be mastered by a fragmentary approach. For balanced growth, the practice of integral yoga is essential. The objective is to keep balance but stretching is required for expansion and results. Each leader produces exemplary results through the combinatorial use of the assets. Situationally, everyone stretched one ingredient of the assets to get the desired result.

- Amrita Patel has taken a missionary approach to meet the demands of a new paradigm at NDDB.

- Jamshed Irani became the change agent to pilot the change movement at TISCO through reflexive search.

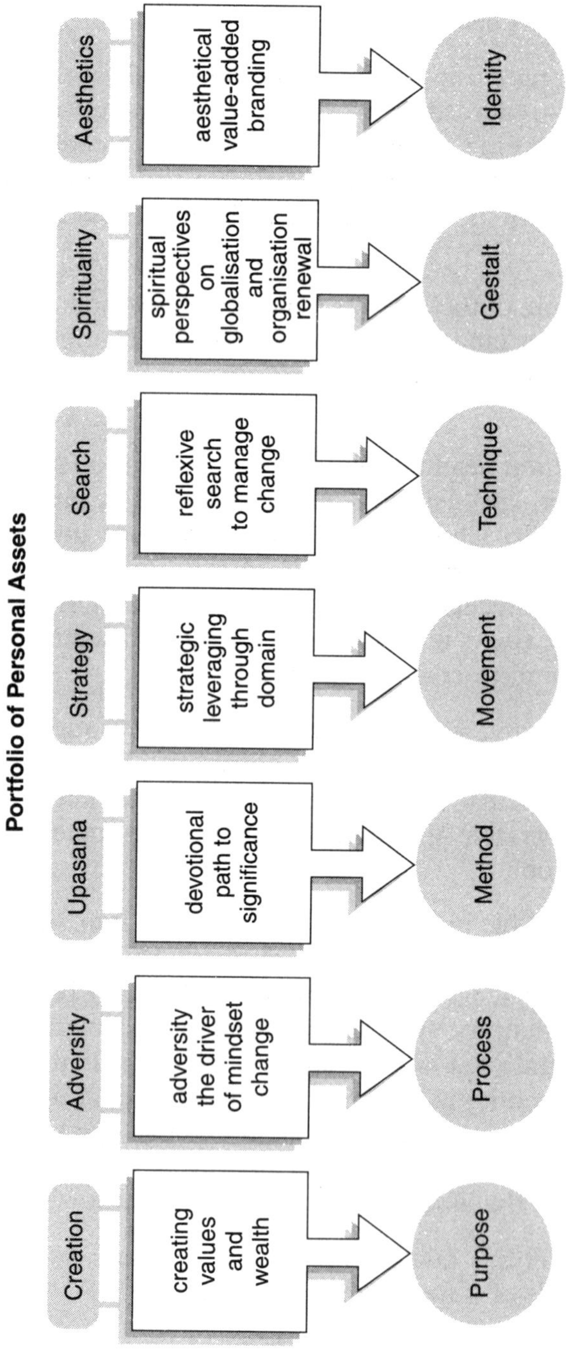

428 Exemplary CEOs

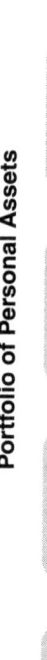

Fig. 11.3 The Seven Assets

Source Code Leads to Seven Assets   429

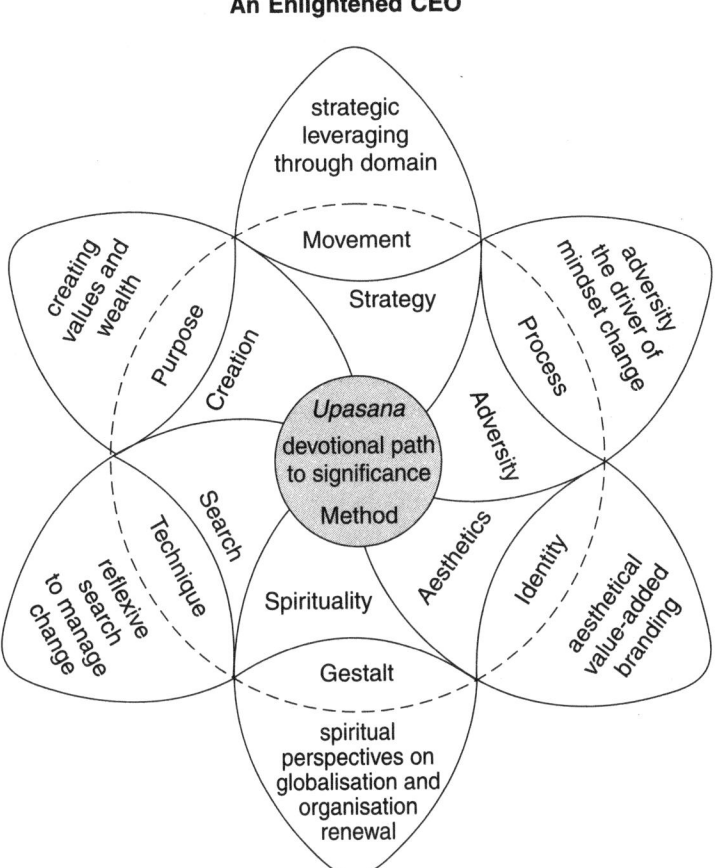

Figure 11.4 The Holistic Circuitry of Seven Assets

- Mallika Srinivasan leveraged her strength in strategy formation to lead TAFE through droughts.

- Prathap Reddy's spiritual perspective is guiding him to institutionalising a new "Tender, Loving, Care" approach towards patients at Apollo.

- Simone Tata's creativity opened up vast business space for Tata in aesthetics, through classy value-added brands.

- Vaman Kamath ensures that at the end of the day ICICI creates value-based wealth.

- Venu Srinivasan undertook the task of self-transformation through *upasana*, which qualitatively transformed TVS Motors.

In future, the contribution of people assets will be measured more strictly. Issues of governance and transparency are at the centre stage of corporate debate. The time is not far off, when specifics of contributions made by the CEO and his entire cabinet will be mandatorily required to be furnished in the balance sheet. The stakeholders will exercise their right to know.

What is important for individual managers from this unfolding scenario is to become effective through a process of self-renewal by the smart use of one's assets. Each asset is not measurable and even if some are, the whole is more than the mere sum of its parts. In any case, exact correlation of all assets to results cannot be established.

When management expects better results year after year, the standards and expectations rise simultaneously. One is compelled to raise the bar higher because of the competition. The way to improve one's performance and tap potential is to first understand what successful leaders have done, and are doing. This book tells you precisely that. Following the role models, is a reliable age old practice.

The message of this book is:

> *Build a strong portfolio of personal assets, improve your performance through self-transformation, and organisational renewal, and in your own right become an exceptional leader, an inspiring CEO.*

It is both simple and doable. These assets have universally yielded dividends. It is the self-culture of eminent leaders that stands out in the autobiographies, biographies, and other literature on them. Measurable and demonstrable achievements come from what is not measurable, the transmutation of assets. Mental chemistry defies measurement.

However, the discovery of assets and their transformation process are reliable guides for a leader's development. The best way to validate a model is to apply it first to oneself. In the last chapter I propose to do exactly the same, valuation of assets and validation of the model.

12

Valuation of Personal Assets to Validation of Model

- ❖ Introduction
- ❖ Background
- ❖ Creating Value and Wealth
- ❖ Adversity, the Driver of Mindset Change
- ❖ Upasana for Self-Renewal
- ❖ Reflections on the Whole Portfolio
- ❖ Experiencing Creativity
- ❖ The Basic Tool—Diary Writing
- ❖ Validation of Model
- ❖ Delivery

"It is the integration of a CEO's spiritualised personal assets, that create permanent values for the organisation."

—Shrinivas Pandit

Introduction

In this concluding chapter, I propose to do a candid valuation of the portfolio of my personal assets. The purpose of this valuation is to assess self-worth, and the applicability of the model. The model provides the criteria, and the self-evaluative process will test its validity. The model will then become usable to you.

Although organisations are becoming learning centres, in strict theory, an individual for them is the instrument, not the purpose. In the new paradigm he might become one, but as of today it is not so. There is a view that all work should be a calling or vocation; that the wealth creation of business is as worth doing and as valuable as the health creation of a hospital. Charles Handy supports this in *The Empty Raincoat* (1995). He says:

> ...If I adopted a portfolio approach to life, a part of that portfolio would be the "core", providing the essential wherewithal for life, but it would be balanced by work done purely for interest or for a cause. For "going portfolio or going plural", you have to keep on growing your assets.

To build assets one has to keep one's skills up to date. Ultimately, the discovery of oneself is far more important than the discovery of the world. It is from this angle that I proceed to assess my core worth. The objective in making ME a test case is to provide a measure of authenticity to the model. It enhances my self-confidence in recommending the model to you. Also, I make no claims that I have succeeded in fully putting into practice all that is emphasised or recommended in this book. It is important to note that this is not my autobiography. The contribution of teams to my success is recognised fully. The exercise is sincerely carried out, and shared with humility.

Here I treat myself as the property, the product to be evaluated. This is not a valuation of my estate, ornaments, securities, cash, etc. This is a valuation of my core ingredients in the portfolio of assets discussed so far. The portfolio, i.e. "ME Inc." is portable and tradable if I want. Even otherwise, knowledge of true self-worth helps further enrich the quality of life. A portfolio means a loose binder or a flexible case carrying loose papers, pictures, and pamphlets.

"Me Inc." means one treats the body-mind complex as a corporation and oneself as its CEO. The following assets matter:

- resources in terms of integrity, attitudes, competencies, domain and transferable skills, contacts, getting things done, leadership, solution finding, and experience

- vision, values, goals, temperament, recognising patterns, and strategies for execution

- one's worth on which people will be able to bet their money, i.e. one's performance, but more so, one's potential

In other words, what investment does one expect friends, or a venture capitalist to make on oneself? Such a look at oneself will tell ones real worth. It is necessary to appreciate that the investor is not going to invest on ones past performance. It may be acceptable as a guide. But what he is going to look at, is the potential of ones assets. For him to make the decision that his investments are not only safe but will yield him sumptuous dividends, potential is important. He is investing on future, not on ones medals and accolades.

Having said this, the job now is to go down the memory lane, and reflect on assets built up over the years. The idea is not to give any weights and ranking, or to arrive at a final numerical score to compare against benchmarks, because there are none.

From the study of role models we have discovered that their context invariant practices are their real quality assets. It is the alchemy of assets that produces durable results. There is no mathematical formulae or statistical standard measure for evaluation. It is essentially a qualitative assessment.

Assets get built over a period of time. Visions get formed early in ones career. A reflective glance at the life provides insights on why one did what, when, and how. One is able to scoop meaning from outer and inner journeys, and the connection between the two. Also the dimensions—rational-intuitive, luck-effort, and cerebral-mystical, become clear. Therefore, I am beginning from the start of my career. I shall be as brief as possible.

Background

My father and grandfather were renowned lawyers in Ratnagiri, Maharashtra. Naturally they wanted me to complete graduation there and go to London to become a barrister. But I wanted to be on my own. I came to Bombay in 1954. To continue education, I enrolled in college for Intermediate Arts.

Getting a job in those days was not very difficult. I got one at the prestigious Burmah-Shell Oil Company. Attending morning and evening classes, and working at a reputed company was the in-thing then. "Earning while Learning" boosted sky high the feeling of independence. Living in the Dream City, with no concept of what a company or career meant, the mind was a fertile ground for images to make an impact. And they did.

Interests in college and company extra curricular activities kept me joyously engaged in studies and work. My eye for beauty used to keep me glued to the décor of managers' offices, their impressively dressed personalities, and their deportment.

In about three months, I became a little acquainted with the functioning of the company, its hierarchy, what managers do, and how they are directly recruited to those exalted positions! Exalted not because I understood fully what they did, but because of the aura surrounding some officers, their styles, power, and all their attributes, as I gleaned from the active grapevine.

One thought riveted the mind continuously, viz. the power a personnel manager had in giving jobs, transferring people, giving promotions, and negotiating with unions. This position was called Staff & IR Manager. The PM (personnel manager) and other officers in the department were always at the centre of our discussions. What made an indelible impact, was the authority vested in his position to do things for people, especially giving jobs. My dream to become a PM originated in that milieu. All my thoughts were bent towards the achievement of my goals to become a PM. My visualisation about occupying the PM's chair became more deeply grounded as days passed by.

In those bizarre days, I explored constantly the qualifications I needed to become a PM. I found out which institutes held such specialised courses in India and abroad. And without hesitation, I zeroed in on the London School of Economics.

The beauty of the process was that although the vision took root in 1957–58, it took almost twelve years before I could realise it. In that period I had completed my B.A, LL.B. I was then working at the Bank of India. I proactively canvassed for a posting to London so that I could study at the institute of my choice. I was posted to the London office in 1967. Taking advantage of it, I took the study leave after finishing my three-year tenure. I completed the postgraduate course in Personnel Management and Industrial Relations from LSE in 1970 and did some research work on projects of organisational change. On my return to India in 1972, I became personnel manager at Blue Star Ltd.

The purpose emanates from the vision. Behind the obsession to become a personnel manager was the desire to give jobs to people. The intention in pursuing that goal was not personal aggrandisement. It was neither completely altruistic nor totally unselfish. It was a mix. The power orientation sought was more for "giving" than "taking".

In the twenty years that followed, I became the chief of personnel division at different companies. I was able to realise my dream of giving jobs and promotions to many. I negotiated many settlements with unions and interacted at various levels of management freely and effectively. The portfolio, 'Me Inc.', is assessed against the following ingredients of assets shown in the model.

Creating Value and Wealth

The settlements with unions were mutually satisfactory and management was happy for the costs saved in the hey-days of aggressive unionism. This value-added achievement was recognised when the rate busters were on rampage. The most reputed union leaders and shop floor representatives remained good friends. Tremendous change in the culture of organisations was seen during most phases of my tenures.

I created value through collaboration in the most turbulent adversarial ethos of the seventies and eighties. I saved some money for the company, as I won the wars without going on actual wars. I did not take confrontation and crutches of strikes, lockouts, and court battles to manage industrial relations.

Adversity, the Driver of Mindset Change

Passing through such adversity in IR and management politics I was able to make a significant breakthrough in the thinking of unions and workers, but not much in management approach or concepts.

I learnt that it was necessary to pamper the egos of some powerful managers to get them on my side. My policy of keeping distance from them was not diplomatic. They also needed a listening post, a feeling that they were not being ignored, and that their views mattered.

Reflexive Search to Manage 'ME Inc.'

Searching reflectively was my obsession. It gave me good dividends in terms of successful turnarounds in IR history, with all companies that I worked. On the OD front, the creative initiatives yielded good dividends. When an outside event was unfolded at the organisation, I used to watch if there was any reflection of it inside me. My diagnosis was mostly correct but corrective measures in self-improvement were rather half-hearted at times.

Strategic Leveraging through Domain

The strategic leveraging of my assets namely, excellent drafting skills, oratory, negotiating skills, and making space by accommodating people with their differing viewpoints were very good. I was able to create space, to go out of the way to provide deserving people jobs and promotions. The HR domain is interpersonal relationship. I was largely successful in it. The movement in resolving tricky personnel issues was very good.

Aesthetical Value-added Branding

I provided an aesthetic angle in my professional presentations to management and unions, at seminars and conferences. I made an impact at workers and union meetings, training sessions, and conferences. The products were the presentations, but the process was communication. Examples of beauty, neatness, grace, art, i.e. what is a pleasure to the eyes and ears, were sumptuously given at training seminars, team, and communication meetings. This aesthetic approach always received high praise.

Spiritual Perspectives and Upasana: *Globalisation, Organisational Renewal, and Devotional Path of Significance*

The interventions I proposed and carried out were successful in renewing the organisations. I know that I made significant contributions, and received recognition in the feedback. The spiritual thinking base and emotional appeal helped take organisations and unions towards a path of collaboration.

The spiritual perspective deepened after I retired, especially when I took to studying the lives of leaders and writing about them. That there is a spiritual meaning behind the process of globalisation, is a thought that has occupied my mind, since Gorbachev's new thinking embodied in *glassnot* and *perestroika* announcements, the dissolution of USSR, and American push to the concept in 1990.

Upasana (Devotional Practice) for Self-Renewal

My energy levels and motivation were always very high. *Upasana* for self-renewal was patchy. I did not fully internalise the messages from the spiritual and biographical literature that I read. However, constant reading of spiritual literature and the practice of *upasana*, inconstant though it was, did keep the ship on course.

Reflections on the Whole Portfolio

The Japanese inputs on raising quality consciousness had by then started showing results. The process of organisational transformations had gained some momentum. The practice of integral *yoga* as a reliable method for relieving stress and for self-rejuvenation, had gained world wide acceptance. Organisational and leadership gestalts had started working in bits and pieces.

All these environmental factors, and self-assessment, led me back to the vision I had formulated in the fifties, of becoming a personnel manager. It was realised. The purpose (giving jobs and the rest) was served. But that limited vision did not allow me to tap my full potential to create wealth. I was unaware of my potential and despite offers of positive help, I ignored them.

The CEO of Herdillia Chemicals, late Suresh Agarwala had on a couple of occasions said, "Pandit you are CEO material. The potential is there. You have an excellent network of contacts. If you are interested we can work out something, I would like to help". A similar offer came from a friend of mine who was running a company.

In addition, my mother was constantly prodding me, "You know so much Shrinivas, why don't you start a small unit and build a company of your own. I don't understand anything about companies but I think instead of working for others you could create something of your own".

My son gave me some excellent ideas on manufacturing bar codes and other products after he went to US in 1978, but I threw cold water on his bubbling enthusiasm! It took me a long time to forgive myself for this disheartening response and lack of initiative.

It looks as though "non-listening" took its toll. But why did I not listen? Deep reflection led me to identify the following mental blocks:

1. the vision was not expansive or inclusive enough
2. obsession with HR did not permit me to look beyond

3. the importance to creation of values was higher than to wealth creation—my hereditary DNA may have been a limiting factor

4. I disliked arithmetic, or shall I say calculations, accounts, and financial matters, and I believed that for CEO, grip on finance was essential

5. my desire to learn such subjects, which I did not like, was below average

6. it appears that somewhere along the way, I had concluded that business entrepreneurship was not my cup of tea

Said Lin Yutang, "Sometimes it is more important to discover what one cannot do, than what one can do." I do not regret for a moment that I did not become a CEO. I had surrendered to the vocation of HR. I am completely fulfilled in having realised my ambition. The driving force was the desire to provide opportunities for others. The early conditioning was not malleable enough to cross boundaries. The vision for wealth creation was not powerful enough.

If I had ventured beyond my domain, the business world might have found an unsuitable CEO, and lost a good HR chief. This became a win-win game. The business world won because it was not saddled with an ineffective CEO. I won because I did not court failure but succeeded in what I had set my heart on. The decision to remain within my integral domain and perform the role I had originally wished for, was a rational and thoughtful choice.

My forty-plus son and daughter were reading the first draft when they came across this self-evaluation. They giggled like ten year olds, and said, "Dada, how could you have been so wise then?" I felt elated because I thought they meant, "wise at that age" to take such a thoughtful decision. But when I heard their mischievous whispers and looked back, I understood the subtle pun. They meant, so wise *then*, but not now? We burst into uncontrolled fits of laughter.

The product was good in its function, and there was scope for further development, as there always is in any vocation. Working on the battlefield is riskier than giving advice. That's probably why we have more people like *Shrikrishnaj* than *Arjunaj*. It appears that the central message of *Bhagavad Gita* has been lost. We do not have enough warriors, but we have more than enough advisors, author included!

The need for CEOs with a militant grit is great. The best exposition on this topic came from Venu Srinivasan:

> *Beyond maya, the imagined state is extremely alluring but that also is maya. Therefore, one has to break away and decide I am a warrior, this is war. My arms may be tired, and legs cribbing but I have to pick up the bow and go. I have seen Arjunaj in retirement also: my grandfather, or someone in community work from our company.*

The coaches are in the practice nets and pavilions. We require a team, and the likes of Tendulkar and Sehwag on the battleground, to demolish the opposition. The same is applicable to CEOs and their teams in business management. One can imagine the scope there is for leadership development.

In the on-going study of my life, certain events raised my "satisfaction index" higher; they still do.

- 1950–51, when I was studying and preparing for the secondary school certificate examination.
- Preparing project reports in teams at LSE.
- Formulating strategies to handle complex problems.
- Collecting information and preparing for wage negotiations, or management meetings on critical issues.
- Interviews of *Thought Leaders* and writing the book.
- Organisational assignments on leadership development.

To my great surprise, I found common feelings enveloped me during these events.

- I was making a creative contribution to the projects at hand by using my skills.
- Ecstasy, because I was finding new meaning.

- Growth through learning.
- Building models and testing their validity by first applying the criteria to myself.
- Guiding and inspiring managers to undertake systematic personal development.

In short, collection of data, actual study, preparation, writing, focused development sessions, and "single-minded immersion" are what I enjoy most. It is a pleasant surprise because I was never a serious student. I cannot believe that I like studying, *Eureka! !Eureka!* It provided me the much needed space for quiet contemplation.

Experiencing Creativity

When I remembered all those events I felt I was sitting on the bank of a very quiet river with my feet in the water, which was silently flowing in its own given direction. The flow of water was a reflection of the smooth "flow" of thoughts. That was for me the optimal experience of the creative self.

In *Emotional Intelligence*, Goleman reports that the moods of students at a Chicago high school for sciences were analysed, when both the high and low achievers spent a great deal of time during the week being bored by activities, such as watching TV. A telling discovery emerged:

> *The key difference was in their experience of studying. For the high achievers, studying gave them the pleasing, absorbing challenge of flow 40 percent of the hours spent at it...the low achievers found pleasure and flow in socialising, not in studying.*

While reading this, my self-esteem skyrocketed. However, I wasn't allowed to remain airborne for long. In a few minutes, my ten year old granddaughter came running in with a completed puzzle, we had tried solving earlier, and said, "Dada, you don't understand simple things!" I touched ground zero instantly.

Studying is absorbing. This concept is probably not new to scholars and academicians. But for me, indeed it was a great revelation. One has to spend a lifetime to understand simple things!

The Basic Tool—Diary Writing

Goleman's observations correlate with my personal experience and findings, that disciplined practice and deep reflection are anchors of superior performance. Such study is not merely an exercise in intellectual dexterity but a form of devotional engagement (*Upasana*) with the inner self and domain skills use.

The dos and don'ts of devotional practices, e.g. the fixed daily time, fixed place in the corner of a room, *aasana*, silence, etc, are too well known for recapitulation over here. However, such practice did not become a habit with me.

Great men like, Gandhi, Churchill, Disraeli, and numerous others, have extolled the virtues of writing a diary daily. The diary of Anne Frank is world famous. Many spiritual men have written their autobiographies and diaries. Swami Rama's *Living with Himalayan Masters* is based on his diaries kept faithfully while he was growing up.

That the diary writing is an excellent tool for reflecting on past life and carving out a better future is stuck in mind from reading such autobiographies, biographies, memoirs, and connected literature, for a long time.

However, like the New Year resolution, this practice did not find favour with me beyond the first fortnight of January each year until I chanced upon Julia Cameron's classic, *The Artist Way*, some seven years back. Says Cameron, "The way to tap the spiritual resource is through use of two basic tools, *The Morning Pages* and *The Artist Date*". I found them refined tools, made attractive by the structured approach. Her simple, confident, and persuasive style charmed me into writing morning pages regularly.

I did not ask CEOs whether they wrote diaries, but I do. I record both the mundane and the surprising. It's amazing how refreshing it is. It habituates one to look for the kink. It is a sure-fire anti-depressant, which neutralises unpleasant memories of regrets that flash into one's awareness.

These days I observe, "one constant" works wonders. And that is the daily practice of refining attitudes and skills with devotion. When it continues without a break I am able to make significant contribution to organisational and writing assignments that are simultaneously underway. The feedback from organisations, participants, readers, reviewers, friends, and family is quite inspiring.

Cameron senses the presence of something transcendent—a spiritual electricity in herself while writing the daily morning pages. This morning exercise catalyses her spiritual connections. She thinks it unfolds creativity in the blocked artist, shows that everyone has a spiritual base, and that one is not able to reach one's potential because of early conditioning.

The morning pages are three pages of longhand writing, strict stream-of-consciousness recording of the free flow of thoughts at that time. These daily morning meanderings are not meant to be art. None, repeat, none, should be allowed to read these pages. This is daily emptying of the mind, discharging its contents—the thoughts. Whatever crosses one's mind, at that time, in that hour, one should write. It is not thoughtful writing. It has no logic, no order, and no plan. It is not censored. It's a free flow from the child in one.

There were times when I found the writing colourful, hopeful, sexy, eventful, and flooded with bright happenings. Whereas at other times it was negative, degrading, belittling, self-pitying, silly, funny, and fragmented. In the course of that one-hour one swings back and forth between negative, positive, neutral, and outrageous thoughts. Often I got the feeling that the diary measures one's fresh thoughts, like a one-touch meter, which measures one's fasting blood sugar. Both are indicators of the state of one's health. Wonderful!

One sees peaks, valleys, deserts, water, jungles, and plateaus. One sees shades of different colours and at times a rainbow. One hears the sounds of birds, trees, animals, and children.

One smells different scents and odours. One smiles, laughs, cribs, and cries. Occasionally, one is just stuck, the pen doesn't move, one faces a drought of thoughts. At other times, one cannot stop their gushing flow. After some months, or years, one gets more order than chaos in one's thoughts. Then the chaos-order-chaos-order cycle begins and achieves its rhythm. One gets glimpses of one's true being, in bits and pieces. One starts savouring its transience, the me and not me!

Writing morning pages is a form of meditating. It is a sort of *aksharsadhana* where one cultivates unknowingly the habit of using appropriate words for one's thoughts, one's core being. One is freeing oneself of the burden of thoughts through the medium of writing. It is tantamount to a devotional study of words.

The Artist Date is a block of time, especially set aside every week to nurture one's creative inner artist. One:

- spends that time in solitude, in a garden, on a beach, in a mall with one's artist "child"

- takes the child for a stroll, gives him chocolate, buys a balloon, or whatever

- makes an effort to show love and affection to the child and treats him as one would treat one's little daughter (literally cuddle yourself; poke fun at your idiosyncrasies, misunderstanding, and the way you may be completely fooled)

- thinks of magic, a circus of animals, delight, fun, no serious reflections, and no mastery

This time-off is quite self-nurturing. One then records the thoughts.

If morning pages are prayer, then the weekly artist date brings solutions. In *Uncommon Wisdom*, Fritjof Capra (1988) says *"During these periods of relaxation after concentrated intellectual activity, the intuitive mind seems to take over and can produce the sudden clarifying insights which give so much joy and delight"*.

Cameron skilfully and artistically opens up the spiritual path for us through the ancient practice of maintaining diaries. It is generally understood that a diary is meant for keeping appointments. It is not. Cameron takes us to the deeper purpose of the practice of diary writing, possibly to the very intention with which great men penned their thoughts every day.

Cameron explains the rationality and philosophy behind the practice of writing morning pages. It's a step-by-step guide to reclaiming the imprisoned child spirit in one, one's creative self. In three months one might become addicted to the practice, as I did.

The benefits are:

- it quietens the mind

- circuitous thoughts give way to a more sequential arrangement

- precision replaces circumlocution

- some chapters (events, history, relationships, etc) are closed in mind; and new ones open. (Said Ann-Wilson Schaef "You need to claim events of your life to make yourself yours")

- clarity of thoughts trains the mind to look for alternatives—opportunities to make a breakthrough, and move on from stuck positions—one gains momentum in life.

- access to deeper layers of one's personality which takes one beyond the thought waves created by outside forces— one becomes more autonomous, equipped to deal one's real self

- provides the most authentic feedback about oneself, and the four dimensions of life, viz. Life/Time, Depth, Dialogue with your true self, and Meaning light one's life

- sudden insights into tricky issues and the confidence to tackle them

- one becomes forgiving towards others, but also towards oneself

- establish some invisible spiritual link to forces that guide one's destiny; to a GOD defined as "Good Orderly

Direction"—the universe is helping one with what one is doing.

- gradually to more order, less chaos—feel relaxed that so many complex nagging issues of life have been sorted
- refine domain skills
- acquire a balanced view of one's tendency to over react to adversities and periods of elation
- put life in perspective, which deepens the level of experience
- sharpens discernment capability
- daily action, i.e. writing morning pages, and keeping the appointment with one's child—artist date—leads to measuring weekly movement, monthly progress, and quarterly results. It fits into the professional framework of measuring "organisation annual results". In effect, it becomes an online assessment of personal growth through creativity.

I feel like Cameron, that:

- once one accepts it is natural to create, one begins to accept a second voice, a higher harmonic, an uncensored flow of clear thoughts adding to and augmenting one's inner creative voice.
- exercise is often the movement that moves us from stagnation to inspiration: action has magic, grace, and power in it—action energises
- success occurs in clusters and is born in generosity and forgiveness

The important point to note is that through disciplined use of a reliable ancient tool—now completely refined—one gets habituated to the daily practice of updating ones skills and rejuvenating oneself.

Similarly, in his book *At a Journal Workshop*, Ira Progoff (1997) has explained the "Intensive Journal Process". This process teaches one to access the power of the unconscious and evoke one's creative abilities. The process of regular journal entries in the prescribed formats, given in the book, empowers one to get to deeper layers of the inner self and gain a fuller perspective of life.

Covey also notes that writing is a powerful way to sharpen the mental saw. Keeping a journal of thoughts, experiences, insights, leanings, and learnings, promotes mental clarity and exactness in the particular context.

A diary is like a prism. One is able to look at the direction of one's life from different angles. Cameron's and Progoff's are slightly different methods. The objective of both methods is the same: to make one aware of one's variegated inner thought world, and induce one to change the course of one's life. Progoff's process is much more detailed, while Cameron's is simple. I recommend, begin with Cameron.

Although I am personally good at working on computer, I prefer to write the diary by hand. It's an old habit. I like to see my handwriting. The pattern of flow of thoughts through fingers and wrist movement impact the actions in a powerful way. However, if one prefers to maintain the diary on a PC, it is one's own choice. Technically it may not be inaccurate. One has to assess the results of the exercise for oneself.

Our model shows the portfolio of assets and emphasises the need to undertake *upasana*. Dairy, is a basic tool for the practice of *upasana*. Writing it empowers one to inculcate the necessary discipline and commitment to a structured process of multiplying one's assets. If one feels the need to, say, improve one's numerical or communication skills, or speed, or bodybuilding, one goes to a gym avails the services of a coach, and uses recommended instruments and methods for practice. Similarly, the diary writing process opens up the gateway to self-renewal.

If one feels the need to improve one's thinking competency, or build positive attitudes, one would go deeper into the inner self, read relevant books, see videos, seek mentoring. One would do whatever is relevant in the field of psychology, philosophy, and spirituality, since an integral view of these subjects initiates the process of mindset change.

In both cases, i.e. improvement in skills and attitudes, the important point to note is that one must get emotionally involved in learning. It is the devotional engagement in learning that brings results; mere cerebral understanding is of little help, if any.

In an era suffocated with stress, this time-tested tool—diary writing—has potential to work wonders; try it, its culture free!

Validation of Model

This candid valuation of my assets, experience of flow, disciplined use of the basic tool diary writing, supporting conceptual evidence, and practical experience of others validates that the portfolio approach to management of personal assets makes CEOs resourceful, exceptional, and inspiring. Obviously, CEOs do not know this, but it is what my muse has collaged from the invigorating life stories narrated by them.

Delivery

I am handing over to you this compendium of seven brilliant CEOs. I hope you will find it instructive and use it as the model. It provides you with the nutrients for creative growth and fulfilment, as it did me while I studied and wrote it. The exemplars in the book will continue to be my health packs in periods of relaxation, reflection and *upasana*. Trust me, so will they be yours.

Bibliography

1. Aurther Anderson, *Best Practices*, Simon & Schuster, London, 1998.

2. Baghai, Meherdad, *In The Alchemy of Growth*, Perseus Publishing, Cambridge, Massachusetts, 1999.

3. Barron, Frank, Montuori, Alfonso and Barron, Anthea, *Creators on Creating*, Penguin Putnam Inc. New York, 1997.

4. Bennis, Warren, Spreitzer, Gretchen M, and Cummings, Thomas G, *The Future of Leadership*, Jossey-Bass, A Wiley Company, San Francisco, 2001.

5. Bennis, Warren, *Why Leaders Can't Lead*, Jossey-Bass Publishers, San Francisco, 1997.

6. Bossidy, Larry and Charan, Ram with Burck, Charles, *Execution*, Random House Business Books, 2002.

7. Boulton, Richard E S, Libert, Barry D and Samek, Steve M, *Cracking the Value Code*, Harper Business, 2000.

8. Burden, Virginia, *The Process of Intuition*, A Quest Book, The Theosophical Publishing House, 1975.

9. Buscaglia, Leo F, *Living, Loving & Learning*, Balantine Books—A Division of Random House, New York, 1982.

10. Cameron, Julia, *The Artist's Way*, Jeremy P. Tarcher/Putnam Book published by G P Putnam's Sons, New York, 1992.

11. Capra, Fritjof, *A Systems Approach to The Emerging Paradigm*, (Ray, Michael and Rinzler, Alan, *The New Paradigm in Business*, Penguin Putnam Inc., New York, 1993.)

12. Capra, Fritjof, *The Uncommon Wisdom*, Flamingo, Fontana Paperbacks, London, 1988.

13. Chakraborty, S K, *Managerial Transformation by Values*, SAGE Publications, 1993.

14. Chanda, Pradip, *The Second Coming*, Tata McGraw-Hill Publishing Company Limited, New Delhi, 2000.

15. Charan, Ram, *Boards at Work*, Jossey-Bass Publication, 1998.

16. Collins, Jim (James) C and Porras, Jerry I, *Build to Last*, Century Business, 1996.

17. Conger, Jay A, *Learning to Lead*, Jossey-Bass Publishers, 1992.

18. Cook, John, *The Book on Positive Quotations*, Fairview Press, Minneapolis, 1993.

19. Cousins, Norman, *The Healing Heart*, Avon Books, The Hearst Corporation, New York, U.S.A., 1983.

20. Covey, Stephen R, *The 7 Habits of Highly Effective People*, A Fireside Book, Published by Simone & Schuster, New York, 1989.

21. Csikszentmihalyi, Mihaly, *Creativity*, Harper Collins Publishers, 1996.

22. Csikszentmihalyi, Mihaly, *Good Business*, Hodder & Stoughton, 2003.

23. Das, Monica & others, *Health Care Expenditure in India*, 'Health, Poverty and Development in India', Oxford University Press, Delhi 1996, Chapter 14.

24. De Bono, Edward, *New Thinking for the New Millennium*, Penguin Books, 2000.

25. De Bono, Edward, *Serious Creativity*, Harper Business and APTT.

26. De Bono, Edward, *Sur/Petition*, Harper Collins Publishers, 1993.

27. De Pree, Max, *Leadership Is an Art*, Bantam Doubleday Dell Publishing Group, Inc., 1987.

28. Drucker, Peter F, *Management Challenges for the 21st Century*, Butterworth-Heinemann, Oxford, U.K., 2000.

29. Drucker, Peter F, *The Practice of Management*, Mercury Books, 1962.

30. Eccles, Robert G and Nohria, Nitin with James D Berkley, *Beyond the Hype*, Tata McGraw-Hill, 1992.

31. Fisher, Donna and Vilas, Sandy, *Power Networking*. Mountain Harbour Publication, A Bard & Stephen Book, 1991, 1992.

32. Flach, Frederic F, *Choices*, A Bantam Book, 1979.

33. Foster, Richard J, *Celebration of Discipline*, Harper, San Francisco, U.S.A., 1998.

34. Frankl, Viktor E, *Man's Search for Meaning*, Pocket Books, New York, 1963.

35. Frawley, David, *A Vedic Consecration to the Spiritual Heart*, The Mountain Path, Tiruvannamalai, Tamil Nadu, India, Deepam, 2003.

36. Fritz, Robert, *Creating*, Fawcett Columbine, New York, 1991.

37. Fukuyama, Francis, *Trust—The Social Virtues and the Creation of Prosperity*, Free Press Paperbacks Book, 1996.

38. Gardner, John W, *The Heart of the Matter*, Leadership Paper/3, June 1986, Leadership Studies Program Independent Sector, Washington.

39. Gardner, John W, *The Task of Leadership*, Leadership Paper/3, June 1986, Leadership Studies Program Independent Sector, Washington.

40. Gardner, John W, *The Nature of Leadership*, Leadership Paper/1, January 1986. Leadership Studies Program Independent Sector, Washington.

41. Gawain, Shakti, *The Path of Transformation*, Nataraj Publishing, Mill Valley, California, 1993.

42. Ghosal, Sumantra, Gita Piramal, and Bartlett, *Managing Radical Change*, VIKING, Penguin Books, New Delhi, India, 2000.

43. Ghoshal, Sumantra and Bartlett, Christopher A, *The Individualized Corporation*, A Harper Business Book, 1997.

44. Goleman, Daniel, *Emotional Intelligence*, Bantam Books, 1995.

45. Goleman, Daniel, *The New Leaders*, Little, Brown, 2002.

46. Gopalkrishnan, R, *The Changing Fabric*, Business Standard, 20 March 2004 special supplements on Bombay Management Association's golden jubilee.

47. Gourard, Sidney M, *The Transparent Self*, Van Nostrand Reinhold Company, 1971.

48. Hamel, Gary & Prahlad C K, *Competing for the Future*, Harvard Business School Press Boston, Massachusetts, 1996.

49. Handy, Charles, *The Empty Raincoat*, Arrow Books Limited, 1995.

50. Handy, Charles, *The New Alchemists*, Hutchinson, London, U.K., 1999.

51. Hindle, Tim, *Guide to Management Ideas*, Profile Books Ltd., London, 2000.

52. Houston, Jean, *The Possible Human*, Jeremy P Tarcher/Putnam Book published by G P Putnam's Sons, New York, 1997.

53. Jain, Gautam Raj and Ansari, Akbar M, *Self-Made Impact Making Entrepreneurs*, Entrepreneurship Development Institute of India, November 1998.

54. Juran, Joseph Moses, *The Quality Control Handbook*, McGraw-Hill, New York, U.S.A., 1988.

55. Kakri, Satish, *Management Goals Through Poetry*, English Edition Publisher & Distributors (India) Pvt. Ltd, 2003.

56. Kalam, A P J Abdul with Pillai, Sivathanu A, *Envisioning an Empowered Nation*, Tata McGraw-Hill Publishing Company Limited, New Delhi, 2004.

57. Kanter, Rosabeth Moss, *The Change Masters*, A Touchstone Book, 1983.

58. Kaplan, R S and Norton, D P, *The Balanced Scorecard—Measures that Drive Performance*, Harvard Business Review, January-February 1992.

59. Katzenbach, Jon R, *The Wisdom of Teams, (Leader to Leader)*, Jossey-Bass Publishers, San Francisco, U.S.A., 1999.

60. Khandwalla, Pradip N, *Corporate Creativity—The Winning Edge*, Tata McGraw-Hill Publishing Company Limited, New Delhi, 2003.

61. Koch, Richard, *The 80/20 Revolution*, Nicholas Brealey Publishing, London, 2002.

62. Kotkin, Joel, *Tribes*, Random House, New York, 1992.

63. Kotter, John P, *Making Change Happen*, Leader to Leader, The Drucker Foundation, New York, U.S.A., 1999.

64. Kotter, John P, *What Leaders Really Do*. Harvard Business Review Book, 1999.

65. Lala, R M, *The Creation of Wealth*, IBH Publishers Pvt. Ltd, Bombay, 1991.

66. Maira, Arun, *Shaping the Future*, John Wiley & Sons (Asia) Pte Ltd, 2002.

67. Mehta, Rohit, *The Secret of Self-Transformation*, Motilal Banarsidass, 1991.

68. Merton, Thomas, *Contemplation in Action*, University of Notre Dame, Notre Dame Press, 1998.

69. Mintzberg, Henry, *The Nature of Managerial Work*, Harper & Row, Publishers, 1973.

70. Moser-Wellman, Annette, *The Five Faces of Genius*, Viking, 2001.

71. Murphy, Michael, *The Future of the Human Body*, Jeremy P Tarcher/Putnam Book published by G P Putnam's Sons, New York, 1992.

72. Naisbitt, John and Aburdene, Patricia, *Megatrends 2000*, Avon Books, 1991.

73. Ogilvy, James A, *Creating Better Futures*, Oxford Universal Press, 2002.

74. Ohmae, Kenichi, The *Mind of the Strategist*, McGraw-Hill, Inc., 1982.

75. Pandit, Shrinivas, *Design Your Career*, Tata McGraw-Hill Publishing Company Limited, New Delhi, 2001.

76. Pandit, Shrinivas, *Thought Leaders*, Tata McGraw-Hill Publishing Company Limited, New Delhi, 2001.

77. Pareek, Udai, *Making Organisational Roles Effective*, Tata McGraw-Hill Publishing Company Limited, New Delhi, 1993.

78. Peters, Tom, *Thriving on Chaos*, Tata McGraw-Hill, 1990.

79. Phansalkar, S J, *How not to Ruin Your Small Industry*, Response Books, 1996.

80. Piramal, Gita, *Business Legends*, Penguin Books, 1998.

81. Prather, Hugh, *Notes to Myself*, Banton Books, New York, U.S.A., 1970.

82. Progoff, Ira, *At A Journal Workshop*, Penguin Putman Inc., New York, 1997.

83. Rama, Swami, *Living with Himalayan Masters*, Himalayan International Institute of Yog.

84. Ray, Michael and Rinzler, Alan, *The New Paradigm in Business*, Penguin Putnam Inc., New York, 1993.

85. Redfield, James, *The Celestine Prophecy*, Warner Books, New York, U.S.A., 1995.

86. Whittington, Richard, Andrew Pettigrew, and Winifred Ruigrok, *New Notion of Organisational Fit*, Financial Times special insert on "Mastering Strategy" page 8-10, November 29, 1999.

87. Ries, Al and Ries, Laura, *The 22 Immutable Laws of Branding*, Harper Collins Business, 2000.

88. Rifkin, Ira, *Spiritual Perspective on Globalization*, Skylight Paths Publishing, Woodstock, Vermont, 2003.

89. Rudhyar, Dane, *Culture Crisis, and Creativity*, A Quest Book, 1977.

90. Schon, Donald A, *The Reflective Practitioner*, Basic Books, 1983.

91. Schulman, Michael, *The Passionate Mind*, The Free Press, 1991.

92. Senge, Peter M, *The Fifth Discipline*, Doubleday/Currency, 1990.

93. Sheehy, Gail, *Passages*, Random House, New York, U.S.A., 1995.

94. Sher, Barbara, with Gottlieb, Annie, *Wishcraft*, Ballantine Books Trade Edition: May 1983.

95. Sinetar, Marsha, *Do What You Love, The Money Will Follow*, A Dell Trade Paperback, 1987.

96. Sinetar, Marsha, *Elegant Choices, Healing Choices*, Paulist Press, Mahwah, New Jersey, 1988.

97. Sinetar, Marsha, *The Mentor's Spirit*, St. Martin's Griffin, New York, 1998.

98. Sinetar, Marsha, *To Build the Life You Want, Create the Work You Love*, St. Martin's Griffin, 1996.

99. Singh, Pritam and Bhandarkar, Asha, *Corporate Success and Transformational Leadership*, Wiley Eastern Limited, New Delhi, 1992.

100. Sinha, Dharni, *Leadership in Unpredictable Times (From: Transformational Leadership)*, Response Books, 2003.

101. Sinha, Jai B P, *The Cultural Context of Leadership and Power*, Sage Publication, New Delhi, 1995.

102. Srinivasan A V, *Managing A Modern Hospital*, Response Books, 2000.

103. Sowell, Thomas, *A Conflict of Visions*, Ideological origins of political struggles, Quill, William Morrow, New York, 1987.

104. Swami Chinmayananda, *Meditation and Life*, Chinmaya Publication Trust, Madras, 1966.

105. Tead, Ordway, *The Art of Leadership*, McGraw-Hill Book Company, Inc., 1935.

106. The Drucker foundation, *Leader to Leader*, Jossey-Bass Publishers, 1999.

107. The Week, *Prophets of New India*, Penguin Enterprises, 1983.

108. Thurow, Lester C, *Creating Wealth*, Nicholas Breakey, London, 1999.

109. Tichy, Noel M and Sherman, Startford, *Control Your Destiny or Someone Else Will*, Harper Collins Publication Inc., 1994.

110. Tripathi, Dwijendra, *The Oxford History of Indian Business*, Oxford University Press, 2004.

111. Trout, Jack with Rivkin, Steve, *The New Positioning*, McGraw-Hill, Inc., 1995.

112. Trout, Jack, *The 22 Immutable Laws of Branding*, Harper Collins Business, London, U.K., 2000.

113. Trout, Jack, *The Power of Simplicity*, McGraw-Hill, New York, U.S.A., 1999.

114. Ward, Milton, *The Brilliant Function of Pain*, Optimus Books Plaza Hotel, N.Y. & CSA Press Lakemony, Ga., 1977.

115. Wilber, Ken, *The Eye of Sprit—An Integral Vision for a World Gone Slightly Mad*, Shambhala, Bostom & London, 1997.

116. Bridges, William, *Transitions*, Nicholas Brealey, London, U.K., 1996.

117. Yutang, Lin, *The Importance of Living*, Jaico Publishing House, 1961.

118. Yutang, Lin, *The Wisdom of India*, Jaico Publishing House, 2000.

119. Zohar, Danah, and Marshall, Ian, *SQ-Spiritual Intelligence The Ultimate Intelligence*, Bloomsbury, London, 2000.

120. Zukav, Gary, *Evolution and Business* (Ray, Michael and Rinzler, Alan), *The New Paradigm in Business*, Penguin Putnam Inc., New York, 1993.

Index

A

Action-centred leadership 265
Adopting the Effective System of Garage Start-Ups 264
Adversity, the Driver of Mindset Change 437
Aesthetical Value-Added Branding 438
Aestheticisation of Everyday Life 199
Aksharsadhana 446
Alice in Wonderland 214
Alternative Systems 148
Ambani, Dhirubhai 287
Art of influencing 302
Art of Recognising Gratitude 160, 161
Artist Date 446, 448
Assimilation of Cultures 206
Assortment 363
Assumptions Make the Difference 5
ATM on wheels 269
Atrophy of mind 252, 253, 257
Aurther Anderson 391
Autocracy 255

B

Baghai, Meherdad 265
Balanced Scorecard 75, 235, 245, 246, 297, 363
Barron, Frank 244
Bartlett 237
Basic Tool—Diary Writing 444
Belief System 182
Bell Curve 93, 253, 254
Benchmarking 6, 107, 390
Bennis, Warren 275, 296, 297, 335, 415
Berman 147
Best Practices 6, 344, 389–391
Better Future 412
Bhagawad Gita 237
Bhakti 386, 394
Birla, G D 356
Bonaparte, Napoleon 243, 279
Born with a silver spoon 316
Bossidy, Larry and Charan, Ram 79, 138
Boulton, Richard E S 406, 421
Brain gain 281
Branch with a Difference 268
Brand Ambassadors 284
Brand Identity 246, 261, 262
Brand 175, 176
Branding 181, 206, 423
Breakthrough technologies 407
Bridges, William 230
Brown, Joseph 164
Brunnet, Leo 240
Brunton, Paul 394
Build Robust Systems and Processes 127
Burden, Virginia 342
Bureaucracy 255, 264, 265, 270, 271, 288, 359
Buscaglia, Leo F 307
Business Designing 201
Business process re-engineering 128
Business Today 63, 209
Business Week 317
Business World 108, 182
Butler, Brett 25

C

Calling from Space 226
Cameron, Julia 393, 444–447, 449
Camus, Albert 25
Cannibalisation 408

Capra, Fritjof 416, 446
Cataclysmic change 6, 145
Celine 57
CEO 317, 318
Certain Things Just Happen 132
Chakraborty, S K 323, 328
Champy, James and Hammer, Michel 128
Chanda, Pradip 65, 300
Chandogya Upanishad 375
Change Agents 62
Change Management 86, 93, 94, 246, 252, 267, 362
Change Masters Transform the Mission 285
Change the Furniture in Mind 228
Change Trajectory 65
Change 359, 360
Charan, Ram 282
Charisma 302, 426
Check points 333
Checks and balances 296
Chesterton, G K 175
Chetana 323, 328
Chinmayananda, Swami 394
Churchill, Winston 11, 238
Circumstantial 182
Clinical Trials 148
Coalitions 59
Co-creation 11
Cogner, Jay A 137
Collins, Jim (James) 153, 156
Communication Skills 257
Competence opens up Opportunities 226
Comprehensive Strategy 105
Conflict of Values and Vision 37
Consumerism 408
Continuous learning 74, 236, 238, 338, 366, 368
Cooperatives, Cooperation, and Competitiveness 29
Council of Mentors 335
Cousins, Norman 145, 180
Covey, Stephen R 235, 325, 342, 405, 449
Craftsman 221
Creative Businesswoman 230
Creative people 205
Creative thinking 242, 285

Creativity leads to Competence 225
Creativity 443
Credo for Patient Care 152
Crux of Governance 281
Csikzentmihalyi, Mihaly 157, 208, 245, 413
Culture 246, 326

D
Dabewallas 8
Damocles Sword 119
Davos Diary 204
De Bono, Edward 8, 13, 202, 331, 369
Death of a Patient and Birth of a Hospital 162
Decisional Roles 294
Deming, Edwards W 334
Democracy 39, 48, 255, 413
Demolition of a Mindset 265, 266
Demolition of Myths 168
Deshpande, P L 200
Devotional practice 391
Dhanrajgir, Humayun 87, 395
Dhanvantari in Global Health Space 194
Diary Writing 444
Differentiator 275
Disciplined Practice 309, 398, 444
Discovery of Seven Assets 426
Disease Burden 148
Dismembering 37
Disney, Walt 240
Disraeli, Benjamin 367
Dnyna yoga 386
Domain 422, 423, 438
Doyle, Conan 261
Draught Ends, Eagles Fly 124
Drucker, Peter 12, 13, 62, 89, 178, 238, 245, 283, 289, 296, 304, 320, 363, 385, 386, 393
Duggal and Amin' study 147
Dwindling Tribe of Missionaries 41

E
Eccles, Robert G and Nohria, Nitin 86
Echaupal 60

Ecological Dimension 47
Economic Times 250, 251
Edison, Thomas 155
Einstein, Albert 111, 331
Emerson, Ralph Waldo 210
Emotional Intelligence 113, 188, 239, 280, 293, 308, 309, 339, 369, 387, 393, 398, 425
Emotional to Spiritual Intelligence 308
Empowerment 263
Enlightened CEO 429
Entrepreneurship 150
Evaluation of Experience 78
Evolution of Lakme 216
Evolutions and Transitions 208
Executive leadership 296
Exemplar of Quality Culture 345
Exemplar Shows the Way 14
Expectations 10, 241
Experience the Apollo 178
Eye for Observation 259

F
Faith in Gurus 169
Fallen Icon 39
Father shapes character 248
Field independent 311
Fisher, Donna and Vilas, Sandy 223
Flach, Frederic F 164
Flow 245
Forbes, B C, III
Ford, Henry 155
Foster, Richard J 393
Frames of reference 381
Frankl, Victor 404
Fritz, Robert 13, 205
Fukuyama, Francis 320, 376, 378

G
Galbraith, J K 200, 202
Gandhian model 15
Gardner, John W 298, 302, 331, 343
Gates, Bill 121, 238
Gauntlett, Suzanne 5
Generative Scenario Thinking approach 414
Getty, J Paul 124

Ghoshal, Sumantra and Bartlett, Christopher 237
Ghoshal, Sumantra, Piramal, Gita, and Bartlett, Christopher 87
Gita 347, 376, 442
Globalisation Leads to Co-creation 11
Globalisation Opens up World Health Space 145
Goleman, Daniel 66, 110, 113, 280, 308, 339, 443, 444
Good Orderly Direction 447
Gopalkrishnan, R 111
Governance 246, 281, 299, 302, 313, 330, 354, 447
Graham, Katherine, 12
Griswold, Daniel 209
Grit Enables to Realise Vision 120
Grove, Andy 238
Gurus 112, 117, 135, 169, 259, 293, 304, 305, 312, 343, 347, 382, 392, 393
Guru-shishya 305, 310
Gut feel 104, 276, 279, 280, 386

H
Haas, Robert D 72
Habits die hard 236, 325
Habits of Effectivity 235
Hallmark of Thought Leaders' is 'Giving' 10
Hamel, Gary 108
Handy, Charles 294, 305, 433
Harvard Business Review 384
Hata Yoga 427
Havel, Vaclav 379
Health Space 150, 151
Hill, Napolean 289
Holistic Circuitry of Seven Assets 429
Holistic Tri-Circle of Influence 422
Houston, Jean 395
How to Develop Leaders 89
Huxley, Aldous 244

I
Icon 39
Ignorance-information-knowledge 335

Image: Going Beyond Brands 33
Imaging Equipment 148
Import of Teclmology 149
Indigenous Systems 148
Infectious Diseases 148
Information Roles 294
Innovation 246, 422
Innovative Jamshed 81
Insight 108
Intellect to Introspection to Intuition 339
Interpersonal Roles 294
Intuition Nurtures Strategic Insight 111
ISO 9000 75

J
Jain Group 6, 7
Jain, Bhavarlal 6, 7
James, William 166, 236, 242, 409
Jamshed's solid foundation 68
Jamshetji Tata 72, 154
Johnson, Robert W 155
Johnson, Samuel 366
Jones, Quincy 204
Journal Process 448
Jung, Carl 208, 230
Juran, Joseph Moses 237, 289
Just-in-time 206, 312, 409

K
Kakri, Satish 7
Kalam, A P J Abdul and Pillai, A Sivathanu 149
Kamath, Vaman 9
Kane, Don 65
Kanter, Rosabeth Moss 57, 107, 127, 285
Kaplan, Robert 245
Karma Yoga 376, 382
Karta 103, 302, 303
Katzenbach, Jon R 71
Kearney, A T 128, 129
Kerr, Steven 94
Key result areas (KRA) 77
Khandwalla, Pradip 77, 204
Knowing-in-action 340
Knowledge workers 207, 237, 299, 307, 371, 382, 386, 408, 412

Koch, Richard 237
Kotkin, Joel 377
Kotter, John P 59, 60, 106
Krishi Ratna 139
Kurien, Verghese 25, 27, 29–32, 35, 46, 54, 65

L
Lakme means Lakshmi 218
Lakme to Westside 219
Lala, R M 154, 409, 410
Lao-tzu 108, 391
Law of Contributory Care 190
Laws of branding 34
Lead by Example 136
Leader 303
Leadership Development 90, 246, 442
Leadership through Personal hardship 110
Learning Culture 246, 326
Learning from Adversity 270
Learning from the Father 118
Learning organisations 276, 322, 326, 335, 346
Less is more 239
Lessons from Difficult Time 222
Leveraging Through Domain 421-423, 438
Listening-learning 339
Listening leadership 135
Listening Leads to Insight 108
Listening Organisation 110
Lombardi, Vince 392
Lunn, Terry 338

M
Machiavellian thinking 301
Mahabharat 298, 311
Maira, Arun 103
Make Colleagues the Brand Ambassadors 284
Making of a Tough Woman 19
Management by expectation 302
Management by Objectives 206
Manager and employee participation 362
Managing expectations 241
Managing points 296, 301, 320, 321, 333

Mantle of a Mentor   304
Mashelkar, Raghunath   28, 101, 102
Maslow, Abraham   180
Maya   355, 380, 442
McGregor, Douglas, 29
McKinsey Quarterly report   296
McKinsey   127
Me Inc   434, 437
Mehta, Rohit   328
Mentor-protégé relationship   305
Mentor's Spirit   258
Merck II, George   155
Meritocracy leads to Mindset Change   253
Meritocracy   255, 256, 266, 284, 289, 364
Merton, Thomas   394
Metallurgy of Leadership   83
Metamorphosis   76, 294, 300, 311, 381
Milk revolution   18, 41
MindsetChange   34, 102, 150, 246, 257, 313, 360, 362, 366, 370, 426, 437, 449
Mintzberg, Henry   253, 294
Missionaries   41
Missionary   52
Mobile CEO   317
Mobocracy   255
Model Change Agent   93
Monet, Jean   348
Morita, Akio   156
Morning pages   444–446
Moser-Wellman, Annette   242
Multidimensionality of issues   360
Munjal, Brijmohan Lall   76
Murphy, Michael   388, 389, 397
Murthy, Narayana   287, 411

N
Naisbitt, John and Aburdene, Patricia   64
Nature of Adversity   353
Naval encourages Simone to fly   214
Navratilova, Martina   244
Nehru, Pandit   218, 219

Neutral zone-confusion/distress   222
New beginning, 326
New Paradigms Leads to New Thinking   9
Noel M. Tichy and Startford Sherman   65
Non-communicable Diseases   148
Non-Performing Assets   96
Norton, David   245
Nurse Centred Brand   175
Nurturant task leader   303
Nurturing the Winners   116

O
Observation   239, 259
Obsessive-compulsive behaviour (OCB)   235
Ogilvy, James A   101
Ohame, Kenechi   99
One-Man Chief Executive   320
One constant practice   391
Operation Flood   26, 46, 50
Orbit Change leads to Friction   287
Organisation Change   110
Organisation cycle   448
Organisation restructuring   360, 362
Organisations   322, 326, 335, 346
Organised Abandonment   62
Out of Box thinking   65, 89, 105, 136, 229, 294
Outline of Health Care Market   146
Overview of Contributions   182

P
Pan Brand and Local Brands   31
Pandit, Srinivas   353
Paradigm Change   106, 299, 359, 371, 379, 396, 405, 414
Paradigm Shifts   6, 12, 29, 47, 89, 100, 146, 244, 263, 279, 282, 283, 289, 330, 378, 380, 406
Paradigms   5, 9-11, 62, 251, 283, 405, 408
Pareek, Udai   295
Parekh, Deepak   38, 404
Pareto, Vilfredo   236, 237, 289

Pasteur, Louis 82
Pathshala 249
Patient Care 152
Pattern of Growth 148
Peep Beyond Eternal Role Conflicts 293
Pegg, Mike 305
Performance 88
Performing Assets 96
Personal Background 435
Peter Principle 139
Peters, Tom 256, 379
Phansalkar, S J 358
Pioneering-Innovative 77
Piramal, Geeta 204
Piramal, Swati 204
Pitroda, Sam 81
Polanyi, Michael 340
Political football 30
Ponting, Ricky 14
Portfolio 440
Positive Thinking 236, 370
Powerful Women Alchemists 63
Prhalad, C K 100, 269, 281
Prather, Hugh 229
Pree, Max De 15
Premji, Azim 62
Proactive mode 106
Process of Self-transformation 323
Process the Efforts Continuously 191
Process-oriented 12
Product Life Management 136
Product society 407
Professional Model 165
Progoff, Ira 448
Project Management to Sector Management, 46
Pulsate Enthusiasm 395
Purpose-People-Process 405

Q
QC tools 129
Quality culture 206, 293, 311, 314, 331, 345, 346, 348
Quality Culture 311
Quality Improvement 75, 93, 204, 246, 311, 313
Quality Revolution 346, 365

Quality Value Award 75
Quality Value Process 75
Quantitative methods 100
Quintessence of Quality Culture 311

R
Rama, Swami 444
Ramayan 311
Ray, Michael and Rinzler, Alan 14
Reactive mode 106
Reality Bite 123
Realpolitik 364
Redfield, James 230
Reflections on the Whole Portfolio 440
Reflexive Search Mode 261
Reflexive Search to Manage 'ME' Inc. 438
Reflexive Search 261, 311, 422, 423, 427
Restructuring 207, 208, 256, 270, 300, 360, 362, 369
Result Producing Teams 246
Retention of Talent 246
Retrieval of TVS Culture 329
Revealing Interviews 424
Revitalising the Cooperatives 46
Ries, Al 34, 223, 263
Rishis 337
Rogers, Will 41
Role Conflicts 293
Role Models Dhirubhai Ambani and Narayana Murthy 286
Role of charisma 302
Roles of an Owner, CEO, and COO 319
Rudhyar, Dane 383
Rule of the Vital Few 237, 289

S
Sadhana 304, 310, 394, 396
Santayana, George 224
Sattvic 303
Scenario planning 101, 414
Scenario 149
Schaef, Ann-Wilson 447
Schon, Donald A 275
Schulman, Michael 252, 257
Sector Management 34

Self-transformation 293, 323, 328, 329, 346, 365, 429, 430
Self-Transformation Germinates Organisational Renewal 299
Self-Transformation 323
Senge, Peter 393
Service society 407
Setzer, Claudia 164
Seven Assets 426, 428, 429
Seven Ss 127, 128, 346
Shafer, Paul D 78, 166
Shakti Gawain 293
Sharing Experience 60
Shastri, Vamadeva 110
Sheehy, Gail, 308
Sher, Barbara 118
Shishyas 305
Sidney M Gourard 81
Sinetar, Marsha 180, 199, 259, 306, 307, 309
Singh, Pritam and Bhandarkar, Asha 295, 302
Sinha, Dharni 367
Sinha, Jai B P 303
Six-sigma 8, 76, 182
Six breakthrough technologies 407
Sixth Sense 380
Socialist ideology 354, 355, 376
Soros, George 378
Source Code 421
Sowell, Thomas 38
Speed and creativity, 243
Speed Capital 243, 268
Spendolini, Michael 390
Spiritual Development leads to Integral Development 384
Spiritual Globalisation 376
Spiritual Intelligence 308-310, 314, 384, 391
Spiritual Perspective on Globalisation and Self-Transformation 439
Spiritual Practices 174, 310, 385
Spiritual quotients 238
Srinivasan, A V 150, 195
Sriniwas pathshala 249
Star of Asia 317
Sternberg, Ernest 201
Stewart, Thomas A 384
Stigliz, Joaseph E 378

Story of Change 57
Strategic Deployment of Resources 362
Strategic grit 98, 99, 102-104
Strategic Grit 99
Strategic Insight 111
Strategic Leveraging through Domain 438
Strategic Thinker 139
Strategy-Structure-Systems 405
Swabhav 303
Swastikasan 407
Swift, Jonathan 317
SWOT 34, 41, 64, 79, 106, 183, 186, 189, 246, 266, 324, 363, 364, 370

T
Talent Management 110
Talmud 284
Tamasik 303, 411
Tata, JRD 73, 212
Tata, Ratan 102
Taylor 8
Tead, Ordway, 284
Team Working at the Top 70
Transformation of Tata Steel 73
Techno Vision 73
Technocrat in Lipstick 215
Technology Status 148
The Week 412
Theocracy 255
Third Eye 380
Thought and action 244, 399
Thurow, Lester 409
Tilloo, Sudheer 240
Time management 239, 327
Times of India 296
Tirodkar, Manoj 108
TQC 296, 320, 329
TQM 12, 62, 131, 313, 314, 321, 330, 332–335, 340, 341, 343, 363
Tracklayers of the Change Trajectory 65
Tractor Queen 116
Transcendental Meditation 384
Transformation 293, 323, 328, 329, 346, 365, 429, 430

Transformational leaders 61, 263, 302, 375, 389
Transformational-situational-nurturant 90
Transitions of a Craftsman, 326
Tribes 377
Tripathi, Dwijendra 358, 411
Trivial Many 237
Trout, Jack 122, 141
Trust 343

U
University of Adversity-Opportunity 353, 365
Upasana (Devotional Practice) for Self-Renewal 439
Upasana 368, 388, 390, 391, 394, 397, 399, 426, 427, 429, 439, 444, 449, 450
Upasana, A Path to Significance 390
Upsurge in Entrepreneurship 150
USP 146, 183, 200, 398
Ustinov, Peter 229

V
Validation of Model 450
Value Addition through Connectivity 149
Value creation 13, 238, 261
Value engineering 75
Value monopolies 13, 331
Value of money 221
Value-Added Branding 422, 423, 438
Values and Wealth 403, 437
Vasanas 342
Venture capitalist 96, 140, 187, 434
Vision 120
Visionary leaders 154, 157
Visuals are Persuasive 51

Vivekchudamani 311
Voluntary retirement 363

W
Ward, Milton 112
Wealth Creation 322, 403, 411, 433, 441
Webster 29
Weick, Karl 86
Welch, Jack 300
Welsh proverb 371
White revolution 403
Whittington, Richard, Pettigrew, Andrew and Ruigrok, Winifred 77
Whole Portfolio 440
Whole System 77, 168, 181, 182, 339
Wilber, Ken 397
Wilde, Oscar 179, 243
Wishcraft 117
Women Alchemists, 89
Wordsworth, William 236, 382
World Steel Dynamics 73

Y
Yoga 311, 376, 380, 382, 386, 388, 394, 407, 427, 440
Yogavashistha 311
Yogi, Mahesh 384
Yutang, Lin 396

Z
Zohar, Danah and Marshall, Ian 309, 384
Zukav, Gary 415

Others
7 QC tools 130
80/20 CEO 289
80/20 thinking 235, 338
90-day rule 264